FACTS ABOUT ALASKA

ALASKA

THE ALASKA ALMANAC® — 14TH EDITION

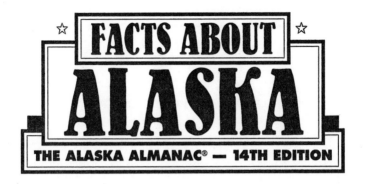

FACTS ABOUT ALASKA

THE ALASKA ALMANAC® — 14TH EDITION

Alaska Northwest Books™

Anchorage • Seattle

Fourteenth edition
Previously published as The ALASKA ALMANAC®: Facts About Alaska

ISBN 0-88240-247-1
ISSN 1051-5623
Key title: Facts About Alaska

From the publisher of The MILEPOST®, THE ALASKA WILDERNESS MILEPOST®
and NORTHWEST MILEPOSTS®

Compiled by Laurie K. Thompson
Edited by Carolyn Smith
Editorial Assistance by Fay L. Bartels
Designed by Cameron Mason
Illustrated by Val Paul Taylor and David Berger
Cover illustration by Mark Zingarelli

Alaska Northwest Books™
A division of GTE Discovery Publications, Inc.
22026 20th Avenue S.E.
Bothell, Washington 98021

Printed in U.S.A.

Contents

Agriculture

Agricultural production in Alaska is still confined to a relatively small percentage of the state's total acreage. In 1988, approximately 1.4 million acres in Alaska — less than one-half of 1 percent of the state — were considered land in farms. In 1988, crops covered 25,683 acres; the balance was idle in pasture or uncleared land. Since 1978, state land sales have placed more than 165,000 acres of potential agricultural land into private ownership. Most of this acreage is in the Delta Junction area, where tracts of land ranging up to 3,200 acres were sold by lottery for grain farming.

In 1988, the total value of Alaska's agricultural products was $30,000,000 ($527,000 higher than in 1987); crops accounted for $20.1 million of the total, livestock and poultry for $9.8 million. Broken down by region, the Matanuska Valley contributed 70 percent of the total value; the Tanana Valley, 22 percent; the Kenai Peninsula, 6 percent; and southwestern Alaska, 2 percent.

According to the state Division of Agriculture, the value and volume of principal agricultural products in 1988 were:

Products*	Sales Value (in thousands)
Milk (34,800 lbs.)	$7,044
Potatoes (204 cwt.)	3,305
Hay (24.7 tons)	3,458
Barley (228 bu.) (for grain)	775
Vegetables (49.7 cwt.) (except potatoes)	817
Pork (159 lbs.)	223
Silage (12.8 tons)	576
Beef and Veal (1,498 lbs.)	1,825
Oats (36.6 bu.)	90

*Volume in thousands

About 33,000 reindeer roam freely across much of western Alaska, with most of the state's reindeer population located on the Seward Peninsula and Nunivak Island. Sales of reindeer meat and by-products in 1988 were valued at $1,474,000.

The number of small farms has grown through state sales of smaller tracts and the use of farming as a supplement to other income.

In 1988, there were 650 farms with annual sales of $1,000 or more.

The Matanuska Valley, a farming region 45 miles north of Anchorage, sells primarily to Anchorage and military markets. Dairy farming, including feed crops for cows, is the dominant income source. The valley has a 120-day growing season, with up to 19 hours of sunlight daily (occasionally producing giant-sized vegetables), warm temperatures and moderate rainfall. During some years, supplemental irrigation is required. Residential development in the Matanuska Valley has contributed to a decline in the amount of agricultural land.

In September 1982, 13,780 acres of state land in the Point MacKenzie Agricultural Project, across Knik Arm from Anchorage, were sold by lottery. Of the 29 parcels sold, 19 were designed for development as dairy farms. Officials anticipate that the nondairy parcels will be used to raise crops for livestock feed.

In the Tanana Valley, near Fairbanks, the growing season is shorter than in the Matanuska Valley, with 90 frost-free days and low precipitation levels making irrigation necessary for some crops. However, the area has the greatest agricultural potential, with warmer temperatures during the growing season. Barley, oats and wheat are raised for grain and hay. (Most Alaska-grown grain is used for domestic livestock feed.) Almost all are spring varieties, since few winter varieties survive the cold and produce lower yields when they do.

The promotion of grain farming in the Tanana Valley has been a major effort by the state. In 1978, the Delta Agricultural Project sold 65,000 acres of land in the Delta Junction area by lottery, with 22 buyers getting roughly 3,000 acres each. By early 1983, one-third of the land had been cleared and planted. The primary crop is barley, which has proven to be the grain most adaptable to the valley's growing conditions. The Delta II land auction in March 1982 sold an additional 24,000 acres in 15 parcels for agricultural development. The Tanana Valley produces 83 percent of all grain grown in Alaska.

The Kenai Peninsula produces beef, hay, eggs and potatoes. Umnak and Unalaska islands provide grazing area for 2,000 sheep, the smallest number in many years — down from 3,900 in 1980 and 27,000 in 1970.

Based on Soil Conservation Service information, there are at least 15 million acres of potential farmland in Alaska suitable for raising crops, plus 118 million acres of range for livestock grazing and 100 million acres suitable only for reindeer and musk-oxen. State policy currently emphasizes farm development on agricultural parcels sold by the state in past years. Possible sales of additional land for agricultural development, such as in the Nenana area, will be re-evaluated in the coming years.

More information is available from the Alaska Department of Natural Resources, Division of Agriculture, P.O. Box 949, Palmer 99645.

Air Travel

Alaska is the "flyingest" state in the Union; the only practical way to reach many areas of rural Alaska is by airplane. According to the Federal Aviation Administration, Alaska Region, by April 1989, there were close to 9,682 registered pilots, 1 out of every 55 Alaskans, and 9,414 registered aircraft, 1 for every 56 Alaskans. Alaska has approximately 8 times as many pilots per capita and 15 times as many airplanes per capita as the rest of the United States.

According to the FAA, Alaska has more than 600 airports, including seaplane landing sites and heliports. That puts Alaska seventh, behind Texas, Illinois, California, Pennsylvania, Ohio and Florida, in the number of airports in the state. Of the seaplane bases, Lake Hood in Anchorage is the largest and busiest in the world. On a yearly basis, an average of 233 takeoffs and landings occur daily, and more than 800 on a peak summer day. Merrill Field in Anchorage records more than 250,000 takeoffs and landings each year, making it one of the nation's busiest general aviation airports. Anchorage International Airport saw 4,501,045 passengers pass through in 1988.

Flying in Alaska, as elsewhere, is not without its hazards. In 1989, there were 187 airplane accidents in which 30 persons lost their lives.

In security, the Anchorage International Airport ranked first in tests conducted by the FAA in late 1987. Pilots who wish to fly their own planes to Alaska may obtain a booklet titled *Flight Tips for Pilots in Alaska* from the Federal Aviation Administration, 222 W. Seventh Ave., #14, Anchorage 99513-7587.

According to the Alaska Transportation Commission, certified air carriers with operating rights within Alaska as of January 1988 included: 183 air taxi operators, 12 contract air carriers, 7 postal contract carriers, 12 subcontract carriers, and 41 scheduled air carriers. Scheduled passenger service is available to dozens of Alaskan communities (see Intrastate Service, this section). Contact the airlines for current schedules and fares.

Air taxi operators are found in most Alaskan communities, and aircraft can be chartered to fly you to a wilderness spot and pick you up later at a prearranged time and location. (Many charter services charge an hourly standby fee if the customer is not on time at the pickup point.) Most charter operators charge an hourly rate either per plane load or per passenger (sometimes with a minimum passenger requirement); others may charge on a per-mile basis. Flightseeing trips to area attractions are often available at a fixed price per passenger. Charter fares range from $140 to $175 per person (four-person and up minimum) for a short flightseeing trip, to $350 an hour for an eight-passenger Cessna 404 (multi-engine planes are generally more expensive to charter than single-engine planes).

A wide range of aircraft is used for charter and scheduled passenger service in Alaska. The larger interstate airlines — Alaska, Continental, Northwest, United and Delta — use jets (Douglas DC-8, DC-10, Boeing 727, 737, 757, 767); Reeve Aleutian flies Electra, YS-11, DC-4 and DC-6. MarkAir uses 737 and de Havilland Dash-7. Prop jets and

2

single- or twin-engine prop planes on wheels, skis and floats are used for most intrastate travel. Here are a few of the types of aircraft flown in Alaska: DC-3, 19-passenger de Havilland Twin Otter, 10-passenger Britten-Norman Islander, 7-passenger Grumman Goose (amphibious), 5-passenger Cessna 185, 9-passenger twin-engine Piper Navajo Chieftain, 5- to 8-passenger de Havilland Beaver, 3- to 4-passenger Cessna 180, 5- to 6-passenger Cessna 206 and single-passenger Piper Super Cub.

INTERSTATE SERVICE

U.S. carriers providing interstate passenger service: Alaska Airlines, Continental Airlines, Delta Air Lines, Morris Air, Northwest Airlines, United Airlines and Reeve Aleutian Airways. These carriers also provide freight service between Anchorage and Seattle. Reeve Aleutian Airways provides freight and passenger service between Cold Bay and Seattle.

International carriers servicing Alaska through the Anchorage gateway: Air France, British Airways, China Airlines, KLM Royal Dutch Airlines, Korean Airlines, Japan Air Lines, Sabena-Belgian World Airlines, SAS Scandinavian Airlines and Swiss Air.

INTRASTATE SERVICE
From Anchorage

Alaska Airlines, 4750 International Road, Anchorage 99502. Serves Cordova, Fairbanks, Gustavus/Glacier Bay, Juneau, Ketchikan, Kotzebue, Nome, Petersburg, Prudhoe Bay, Sitka, Wrangell and Yakutat. Additional routes served on a contract basis by local carriers.

Delta Air Lines. Serves Fairbanks.
Era Aviation, 6160 S. Airpark Drive, Anchorage 99502. Serves Homer, Kenai and Valdez.
MarkAir, P.O. Box 196769, Anchorage 99519. Serves Aniak, Barrow, Bethel, Dillingham, Dutch Harbor, Fairbanks, King Salmon, Kodiak, St. Marys and Unalakleet, with connections into 17 other cities.
Peninsula Airways, 4851 Aircraft Drive, Anchorage 99502. Serves Cold Bay, Dillingham, King Salmon and Kodiak.
Reeve Aleutian Airways, 4700 W. International Airport Road, Anchorage 99502. Serves the Alaska Peninsula, Aleutian Islands and Pribilof Islands.
Ryan Air, 1205 E. International Airport Road, Suite 201, Anchorage 99518. Serves Bethel, Kotzebue, McGrath, Nome and many other bush communities in Alaska.
Southcentral Air, 125 N. Willow St., Kenai 99611. Serves Homer, Kenai and Soldotna.
United Airlines. Serves Fairbanks.
Wilbur's Inc., 1740 E. Fifth Ave., Anchorage 99501. Serves Anchorage, Aniak, Cordova, Holy Cross, McGrath, Nikolai, Red Devil and Valdez.
From Barrow
Barrow Air, P.O. Box 184, Barrow 99723. Serves Atkasuk, Nuiqsut and Wainwright.
Cape Smythe Air, P.O. Box 549-VP, Barrow 99723. Serves Brevig Mission, Elim, Golovin, Shishmaref, Teller, Wales and White Mountain.
From Fairbanks
Frontier Flying Service, 3820 Univer-

sity Ave., Fairbanks 99701. Serves Allakaket, Anaktuvuk Pass and Bettles.

Larry's Flying Service, P.O. Box 2348, Fairbanks 99707. Serves Denali National Park and Preserve (McKinley Park airstrip).

From Galena

Galena Air Service, P.O. Box 188, Galena 99741. Serves Anchorage.

From Glennallen

Gulkana Air Service, P.O. Box 31,Glennallen 99588. Serves Anchorage.

From Gustavus

Glacier Bay Airways, P.O. Box 1, Gustavus 99826. Serves Excursion Inlet, Hoonah and Juneau.

From Haines

L.A.B. Flying Service, P.O. Box 272, Haines 99827. Serves Hoonah, Juneau and Skagway.

From Juneau

Wings of Alaska, 1873 Shell Simmons Drive, Suite 119, Juneau 99801. Serves Angoon, Elfin Cove, Gustavus/Glacier Bay, Haines, Hoonah, Kake, Pelican, Skagway and Tenakee.

From Kenai

Southcentral Air, 125 N. Willow St., Kenai 99611. Serves Anchorage, Homer, Seward and Soldotna.

From Ketchikan

Ketchikan Air Service, P.O. Box 6900, Ketchikan 99901. Serves Stewart, British Columbia, and Hyder.

Temsco Airlines, 1249 Tongass Ave., Ketchikan 99901. Serves Craig, Hydaburg, Klawock, Metlakatla and other Southeast points.

From McGrath

Hub Air Service, P.O. Box 2-TD, McGrath 99827. Serves Lime Village, Nikolai, Telida, Flat, Talalina Air Force Station and Takotna.

From Nome

Bering Air Inc., P.O. Box 1650, Nome 99762. Serves Kotzebue and points in western Alaska.

From Petersburg

Alaska Island Air, P.O. Box 508, Petersburg 99833. Serves Kake.

From Tanana

Tanana Air Service, P.O. Box 36, Tanana 99777. Serves Eagle, Fairbanks, Huslia, Manley Hot Springs, Nenana, New Minto and Rampart.

From Tok

40-Mile Air Ltd., P.O. Box 539, Tok

99780. Serves Boundary, Chicken, Delta Junction, Eagle, Fairbanks and Tetlin.

Related reading: *Winging It!,* by Jack Jefford. A pioneer Alaskan bush pilot's portrait of early Alaska aviation. *Skystruck: True Tales of an Alaska Bush Pilot,* by Herman Lerdahl with Cliff Cernick. A daring aviator's stories of the excitement, danger and rewards of flying in Alaska in the 1930s and 1940s. See ALASKA NORTHWEST LIBRARY in the back of the book.

Alaska Highway

(*See also* Highways)

This highway runs 1,520 miles through Canada and Alaska from Milepost 0 at Dawson Creek, British Columbia, through Yukon Territory to Fairbanks, Alaska. This well-traveled link between Alaska and the Lower 48 will celebrate its 50th anniversary in 1992. Throughout the year, special activities planned by Alaska and Canada will mark this great event.

History

The highway was built to relieve Alaska from the wartime hazards of shipping and to supply a land route for wartime equipment.

By agreement between the governments of Canada and the United States, the highway was built in eight months by the U.S. Army Corps of Engineers and was dedicated in November 1942. Crews worked south from Delta Junction, Alaska, north and south from Whitehorse, Yukon Territory, and north from Dawson Creek, British Columbia.

Two major sections of the highway were connected on Sept. 23, 1942, at Contact Creek, Milepost 588.1, where the 35th Engineer Combat Regiment working west from Fort Nelson met the 340th Engineer General Service Regiment working east from Whitehorse. The last link in the highway was completed November 20, when the 97th Engineer General Service Regiment, heading east from Tanacross, met the 18th Engineer Combat Regiment, coming northwest from Kluane Lake, at Milepost 1200.9. A ceremony commemorating the event was held at Soldiers Summit on Kluane Lake, and the first truck to negotiate the entire highway left that day from Soldiers Summit and arrived in Fairbanks the next day.

After WWII, the Alaska Highway was turned over to civilian contractors for widening and graveling, replacing log bridges with steel and rerouting at many points. Construction continues on the Alaska Highway today.

Road Conditions

The Alaska Highway is a two-lane road that winds and rolls across the wilderness. Some sections of road have no centerline, and some stretches of narrow road have little or no shoulder. The best driving advice on these sections is to take your time, drive with your headlights on at all times, keep to the right on hills and corners and drive defensively.

There are relatively few steep grades on the Alaska Highway. The most mountainous section of highway is between Fort Nelson and Watson Lake, where the highway crosses the Rocky Mountains.

Almost the entire length of the Alaska Highway is asphalt-surfaced, ranging from poor to excellent condition. Some rugged stretches exist with many chuckholes, gravel breaks, hardtop with loose gravel, deteriorated shoulders and bumps.

On the Alaska portion of the highway, watch for frost heaves. This rippling effect in the pavement is caused by the alternate freezing and thawing of the ground. Drive slowly in sections of frost heaves to avoid breaking an axle or trailer hitch.

Travelers should keep in mind that road conditions are subject to change. Be alert for bumps and holes in the road; some are signed or flagged, but many are not.

Watch for construction crews along the Alaska Highway. Extensive road construction may require a detour, or travelers may be delayed while waiting for a pilot car to guide them through the construction. Motorists may also encounter some muddy roadways at construction areas if there were heavy rains while the roadbed was torn up.

Dust and mud are generally not a problem anymore, except in construction areas and on a few stretches of the highway.

Don't drive too fast on gravel. Gravel acts just like many little ball bearings, and you could lose control of your vehicle. Driving fast on gravel is also hard on your tires, raises dust and throws rocks at oncoming cars. Heavy rain on a gravel road generally means mud. Considerable clay in the road surface means it is very slippery when wet.

Gas, food and lodging are found along the Alaska Highway on an average of every 20 to 50 miles. The longest stretch without services is about 100 miles. Not all businesses are open year-round, nor are most services available 24 hours a day. Regular, unleaded and diesel gasoline, and propane fuel are available along the highway. Both government campgrounds and commercial campgrounds are located along the Alaska Highway.

Preparation for Driving the Alaska Highway

Make sure your vehicle and tires are in good condition before starting out. An inexpensive and widely available item to include is clear plastic headlight covers to protect your headlights from flying rocks and gravel.

You might also consider a wire-mesh screen across the front of your vehicle to protect paint, grill and radiator from flying rocks. These may be purchased ready-made, or you may manufacture your own.

For those hauling trailers, a piece of $1/4$-inch plywood fitted over the front of your trailer offers protection from rocks and gravel.

You'll find well-stocked auto shops in the North, but may wish to carry the following for emergencies: flares; first-aid kit; trailer bearings; good bumper jack with lug wrench; a simple set of tools, such as crescent wrenches, socket and/or open-end wrenches, hammer, screwdrivers, pliers, wire, pry bar; electrician's tape; small assortment of nuts and bolts; fan belt; one or two spare tires (two spares for traveling any remote road); and any parts for your vehicle that might not be available along the way. Include an extra few gallons of gas and also water, especially for remote roads. You may also wish to carry a can of fluid for brakes, power steering and automatic transmissions. You do not, however, want to overload your vehicle with too many spare parts.

Along the Alaska Highway dust is at its worst during dry spells, following heavy rain (which disturbs the road surface) and in construction areas. If you encounter much dust, check your air filter frequently. To help keep dust out of your vehicle, try to keep air pressure in the car by closing all windows and turning on the fan. Filtered heating and air-conditioning ducts in a vehicle bring in much less dust than open windows or vents. Mosquito netting placed over the heater/fresh air intake and flow-through ventilation will also help eliminate dust.

Related reading: The MILEPOST® All-the-North Travel Guide®. All travel routes in western Canada and Alaska with photos and detailed maps. See ALASKA NORTHWEST LIBRARY in the back of the book.

Alcoholic Beverages

At this writing, legal age for possession, purchase and consumption of alcoholic beverages is 21 in Alaska.

Any business that serves or distributes alcoholic beverages must be licensed by the state. The numbers of all types of licenses issued are limited to the population in a geographic area. Generally one license of each type may be issued for each 3,000 persons or fraction thereof. Licensed premises include bars, some restaurants and clubs. Packaged liquor, beer and wine are sold by licensed retailers. Recreational site licenses, caterer's permits and special events permits allow the holder of a permit or license to sell at special events, and allow nonprofit fraternal, civic or patriotic organizations to serve beer and wine at certain activities.

State law allows liquor outlets to operate from 8 A.M. to 5 A.M., but provides that local governments can impose tighter restrictions. Juneau, Seward, Fairbanks, Ketchikan and Anchorage have cut back on the number of hours liquor outlets may operate.

In fiscal year 1989, approximately $11.6 million were generated through taxes on alcoholic beverages.

Local governments may also ban the sale of or otherwise restrict alcoholic beverages. Barrow, Bethel and Kotzebue have banned the sale of alcoholic beverages. Communities that have banned possession, and the sale and/or importation of alcoholic beverages (knowingly bringing, sending or transporting alcoholic beverages into the community) are:

Alakanuk	Marshall
Ambler	Mekoryuk
Anaktuvuk Pass	Minto
Angoon	Mountain Village
Atka	Napakiak
Atmautluak	Napaskiak
Atqasuk	Newtok
Barrow	Noatak
Bethel	Nondalton
Birch Creek	Noorvik
Brevig Mission	Nuiqsut
Buckland	Nunapitchuk
Chalkyitsik	Old Harbor
Chefornak	Pilot Station
Deering	Platinum
Diomede	Point Hope
Eek	Point Lay
Ekwok	Quinhagak
Elim	Russian Mission
Emmonak	St. Marys
Gambell	St. Michael
Golovin	Savoonga
Goodnews Bay	Scammon Bay
Grayling	Selawik
Holy Cross	Shageluk
Hooper Bay	Shaktoolik
Huslia	Sheldon Point
Iliamna	Shishmaref
Kaktovik	Shungnak
Kasigluk	Stebbins
Kiana	Stevens Village
Kipnuk	Tanacross
Kivalina	Tatitlek
Kobuk	Teller
Kokhanok	Tetlin
Kongiganak	Togiak
Kotlik	Toksook Bay
Kotzebue	Tuluksak
Koyuk	Tuntutuliak
Kwethluk	Tununak
Kwigillingok	Wainwright
Manokotak	Wales

On July 20, 1983, Governor Sheffield signed into law a tougher driving-while-intoxicated law. Under the new law first offenders face a mandatory 72-hour jail sentence, a minimum fine of $250 and loss of driving privileges for 30 days. A second offense receives a minimum sentence of 20 days, a minimum fine of $500 and loss of license for 1 year. The third offense brings a 30-day sentence, a minimum $1,000 fine and loss of license for 10 years.

Alyeska

Pronounced Alyes-ka, this Aleut word means "the great land" and was one of the original names of Alaska. Mount Alyeska, a 3,939-foot peak in the Chugach Mountains, is the site of the state's largest ski resort.

Amphibians

In Alaska, there are three species of salamander, two species of frog and one species of toad. In the salamander order there are the rough-skinned newt, long-toed salamander and northwestern salamander. In the frog and toad order there are the boreal toad, wood frog and spotted frog. The northern limit of each species may be the latitude at which the larvae fail to complete their development in one summer. While some species of salamander can overwinter as larvae in temperate southeastern Alaska, the shallow ponds of central Alaska freeze solid during the winter. All but the wood frog, *Rana sylvatica*, which with its shortened larval period is found widespread throughout the state and north of the Brooks Range, are found primarily in southeastern Alaska.

Arctic Circle

The Arctic Circle is the latitude at which the sun does not set for one day at summer solstice and does not rise for one day at winter solstice. The latitude, which varies slightly from year to year, is approximately 66°34´ north from the equator and circumscribes the northern frigid zone.

A solstice occurs when the sun is at its greatest distance from the celestial equator. On the day of summer solstice, June 20 or 21, the sun does not set at the Arctic Circle and because of refraction of sunlight, it appears not to set for four days. Farther north, at Barrow (the northernmost community in the United States), the sun does not set

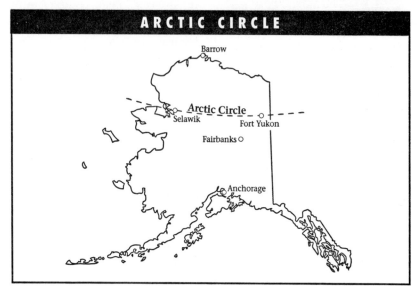

ARCTIC CIRCLE

Barrow

Arctic Circle
Selawik   Fort Yukon

Fairbanks ○

Anchorage

from May 10 to August 2.

At winter solstice, December 21 or 22, the sun does not rise for one day at the Arctic Circle. At Barrow, it does not rise for 67 days.

Arctic Winter Games

The Arctic Winter Games are a biennial event held in mid-March for northern athletes from Alaska, northern Alberta, Yukon Territory and Northwest Territories. The first games were held in 1970 in Yellowknife, NWT, and have since been held in Fairbanks and Whitehorse, YT.

Judo and table tennis were dropped from the 1984 games because the AWG board felt they didn't fit the northern spirit of the games and because Canada was unable to field competitive teams.

In 1984, speed skating and a speed skating-skiing-snowshoeing triathlon were added to the games. Other arctic sports, such as ice hockey, indoor soccer and the snowshoe biathlon, were expanded by adding more athletes and splitting the competition into junior and open divisions. Other competition includes badminton, cross-country skiing, curling, figure skating, basketball, broomball, gymnastics, silhouette shooting, ski biathlon, snowshoeing and volleyball. Participation by people of all ages is encouraged.

Aurora Borealis

The Phenomenon

The aurora borealis is produced by charged electrons and protons striking gas particles in the earth's upper atmosphere. The electrons and protons are released through sunspot activity on the sun and emanate into space. A few drift the one- to two-day course to Earth, where they are pulled to the most northern and southern latitudes by the planet's magnetic forces.

The color of the aurora borealis varies, depending on how hard the gas particles are being struck. Auroras can range from simple arcs to draperylike forms in green, red, blue and purple. The lights occur in a pattern rather than as a solid glow, because electric current sheets flowing through gases create V-shaped potential double layers. Electrons near the center of the current sheet move faster, hit the atmosphere harder and cause the different intensities of light observed in the aurora.

Displays take place as low as 40 miles above the Earth's surface, but usually begin about 68 miles above and extend hundreds of miles into space. They concentrate in two bands roughly centered above the Arctic Circle and Antarctic Circle (the latter known as aurora australis) that are about 2,500 miles in diameter. In northern latitudes the greatest occurrence of auroral displays is in the spring and fall months, owing to the tilt of the planet in relationship to the sun's plane, but displays may occur on dark nights throughout the winter. If sunspot activity is particularly intense and the denser-than-usual solar wind heads to Earth, the resulting auroras can be so great that they cover all but the tropical latitudes. However, the cycle of sunspot activity is such that it will be many years before the numerous, brilliant displays of the late 1950s are regularly seen again.

Some observers claim that the northern lights make a noise similar to the rustle of taffeta, but scientists say the displays cannot be heard in the audible frequency range.

Photographing the Aurora Borealis

To capture the northern lights on film, you will need a sturdy tripod, a locking-type cable release (some 35mm cameras have both *time* and *bulb* settings, but most have *bulb* only, which calls for use of the locking-type cable release) and a camera with an f/3.5 lens (or faster).

It is best to photograph the lights on a night when they are not moving too rapidly. And, as a general rule, photos improve if you manage to include recognizable subjects in the foreground — trees and lighted cabins being favorites of many photographers. Set your camera up at least 75 feet back from the foreground objects to make sure that both the foreground and aurora are in sharp focus.

Normal and wide-angle lenses are best. Try to keep your exposures under a minute — a 10- to 30-second exposure is generally best. The following lens openings and exposure times are only a starting point, since the amount of light generated by the aurora is inconsistent. (For best results, bracket widely.)

f-stop	ASA 200	ASA 400
f1.2	3 sec.	2 sec.
f1.4	5	3
f1.8	7	4
f2	20	10
f2.8	40	20
f3.5	60	30

Ektachrome 200 and 400 color film can be push-processed in the home darkroom or by some custom-color labs, allowing use of higher ASA ratings (800, 1200 or even 1600 on the 400 ASA film, for example). Kodak will push-process film if you include an ESP-1 envelope with your standard film-processing mailer. (Consult your local camera store for details.)

A few notes of caution: Protect the camera from low temperatures until you are ready to make your exposures. Some newer cameras, in particular, have electrically controlled shutters that will not function properly at low temperatures. Wind the film slowly to reduce the possibility of static electricity, which can lead to streaks on the film. Grounding the camera when rewinding can help prevent the static-electricity problem. (To ground the camera, hold it against a water pipe, drain pipe, metal fence post or other grounded object.) Follow the basic rules and experiment with exposures.

The first photographs to show the aurora borealis in its entirety were published in early 1982. These historic photographs were taken from satellite-mounted cameras specially adapted to filter unwanted light from the sunlit portion of the earth, which is a million times brighter than the aurora. From space, the aurora has the appearance of a nearly perfect circle.

Baleen

(*See also* Baskets)

Baleen lines the mouths of baleen whales in long, fringed, bonelike strips. It strains out small fish and plankton, and the tiny, shrimplike creatures called krill from the water. Humpback whales are the largest of the baleen whales, having a coarse baleen similar in thickness to human fingernails. The inside edges of the baleen plates end in coarse bristles that are similar in appearance to matted goat hair. The color of the plates varies from gray to almost black and the bristles from white to grayish white. The number of plates in an adult humpback mouth varies from 600 to 800 (300 to 400 per side); the roof of the mouth is empty of plates. The bowhead whale has 600 plates, the longest of any whale species — some reach 12 feet or more in length. The sei whale has finely textured baleen, and the minkes are the smallest of the baleen whales. Other baleen whales are the right, blue, fin and gray. Baleen was used for corset stays and buggy whips. It is no longer of significant commercial use, although Alaska Natives use brownish black bowhead baleen to make fine baskets and model ships to sell.

Barabara

Pronounced *buh-rah-buh-ruh*, this traditional Aleut or Eskimo shelter is built of sod supported by driftwood or whalebone.

Baseball

The Alaska Baseball League consists of eight All-Alaska amateur league teams: Anchorage Glacier Pilots (club started in 1969), Fairbanks Goldpanners (1966), Kenai Peninsula Oilers (1974), Mat-Su Miners (1980), North Pole Nicks (1980), Cook Inlet Bucs (1980), Hawaiian Rainbows (1986) and the Palouse Cougars (1986).

The baseball season opens in June and runs through the end of July. Each team plays a round-robin schedule with the other seven teams, as well as scheduling games with visiting Lower 48 teams, such as Athletes in Action. In 1988, however, for the first time, only the Oilers played because of insufficient funding for the other teams. The Oilers made it to the National Baseball Congress (NBC) tournament. The league has a championship series the first of August, followed by a state NBC tournament leading up to the NBC nationals at Wichita.

The caliber of play in Alaska is some of the best nationwide at the amateur level. Since 1968, Alaska teams have won nine NBC championships. (The Glacier Pilots in 1969, 1971 and 1986; the Goldpanners in 1972–74, 1976 and 1980; and the Oilers in 1981.) Major league scouts rate Alaska baseball at A to AA.

The Alaska league teams are composed of walk-on and recruited players alike, but primarily of college players, many of whom go on to professional baseball. (Any college senior drafted by a major league team cannot play in the Alaska league.) Since its inception in 1969, the Alaska league has sent more than 150 players on to careers in major league baseball. The list is an impressive one, including such current stars as Tom Seaver, Chris Chambliss, Bruce Bochte and Dave Winfield.

Baskets

Native basketry varies greatly according to materials locally available. Athabascan Indians of the Interior, for example, weave baskets from willow root gathered in late spring. The roots are steamed and roasted over a fire to loosen the outer bark. Weavers then separate the bark into fine strips by pulling the roots through their teeth.

Eskimo grass baskets are made in river delta areas of southwestern Alaska from Bristol Bay north to Norton Sound and from Nunivak Island east to interior Eskimo river villages. The weavers use very fine grass harvested in fall. A coil basketry technique is followed, using coils from one-eighth to three-fourths inch wide. Seal gut, traditionally dyed with berries (today with commercial dyes), is often interwoven into the baskets.

Baleen, a glossy, hard material that hangs in slats from the upper jaw of some types of whales, is also used for baskets. Baleen basketry originated about 1905 when Charles D. Brower, trader for a whaling company at Point Barrow, suggested, after the decline of the whalebone (baleen) industry for women's corsets, that local Eskimos

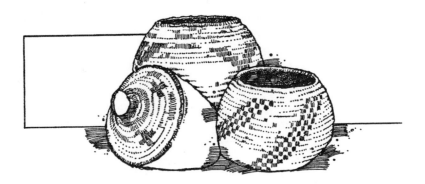

make the baskets as a source of income. The baskets were not produced in any number until 1916. The weave and shape of the baskets were copied from the split-willow Athabascan baskets acquired in trade. Men, rather than women, became the basket makers. Later, baleen baskets were also made in Point Hope and Wainwright.

Most birch-bark baskets are made by Athabascan Indians, although a few Eskimos also produce them. Commonly, they are shaped as simple cylinders and are held together with root bindings. Sometimes the birch bark is cut into thin strips and woven into diamond or checkerboard patterns. Birch bark is usually collected in spring and early summer; large pieces free of knots are preferred. Birch-bark baskets traditionally were used as cooking vessels; food was placed in them and hot stones added. Birch-bark baby carriers also are still made.

Among the finest of Alaskan baskets are the tiny, intricately woven Aleut baskets made of rye grass, which in the Aleutians is abundant, pliable and very tough. The three main styles of Aleut baskets — Attu, Atka and Unalaska — are named after the islands where the styles originated. Although the small baskets are the best known, Aleuts also traditionally made large, coarsely woven baskets for utilitarian purposes.

Tlingit, Haida and Tsimshian Indians make baskets of spruce roots and cedar bark. South of Frederick Sound, basket material usually consists of strands split from the inner bark of red cedar. To the north of the sound, spruce roots are used. Maidenhair ferns are sometimes interwoven into spruce root baskets in a technique that looks like embroidery. A large spruce root basket may take months to complete.

Examples of Alaska Native basketry may be viewed in many museums within the state, including the University of Alaska Museum, Fairbanks; the Anchorage Museum of History and Art, Anchorage; the Sheldon Jackson Museum, Sitka; and the Alaska State Museum, Juneau.

Prices for Native baskets vary greatly. A fine-weave, coiled beach grass basket may cost from $60 to $450; birch-bark baskets, which look like trays, may range from $30 to $100; willow root trays may cost $800; finely woven Aleut baskets may cost $200 to $600; cedar-bark baskets may range from $30 to $80; and baleen baskets range in price from $450 to more than $1,100 for medium-sized baskets. These prices are approximate and are based on the weave, material used, size, and decoration added, such as beadwork or ivory.

Beadwork

Eskimo and Indian women create a variety of handsomely beaded items. Before contact with Europeans, Indian women sometimes carved beads of willow wood or made them from seeds of certain shrubs and trees. Glass seed beads became available to Alaskan Athabascan Indians in the mid-nineteenth century, although some types of larger trade beads were in use earlier. Beads quickly became a coveted trade item. The *Cornaline d'aleppo*, an opaque red bead with a white center, and the faceted Russian blue beads were among the most popular types.

The introduction of small glass beads sparked changes in beadwork style and design. More colors were available, and the smaller, more easily maneuvered beads made it possible to work out delicate floral patterns impossible with larger trade beads.

Historically, beads were sewn directly onto leather garments or other items with the overlay stitch. Contemporary beadwork is often done on a separate piece of felt that is not visible once the beads are stitched in place.

Alaskan Athabascan beadworkers sometimes use paper patterns, often combining several motifs and tracing their outline on the surface to be worked. The most common designs include flowers, leaves and berries, some in very stylized form. Many patterns are drawn simply from the sewer's environment. Recently, magazines, graphic art, advertising, and patriotic motifs have inspired Athabascan beadworkers, although stylized floral designs are still the most popular.

Designs vary regionally, as do the ways in which they are applied to garments or footgear. Women from

some areas do beadwork so distinctive it can be recognized at a glance.

Related reading: *Secrets of Eskimo Skin Sewing,* by Edna Wilder. See ALASKA NORTHWEST LIBRARY in the back of the book.

Bears

(*See also* Mammals)

Three species of bear inhabit Alaska: the black, brown/grizzly and polar bear. Among the three of them, almost all of Alaska can be considered bear country, and for those wishing to spend time in Alaska's great outdoors, bear country becomes "beware" country. It's good to remember that sows are extremely aggressive if their young are around and bear behavior should always be considered unpredictable.

Black Bears. Black bears are usually jet black or brown with a brown-yellow muzzle, and weigh from 100 to 200 pounds as adults. The brown color phase can sometimes be confused with grizzlies, but black bears are generally smaller and lack the grizzly's distinct shoulder hump. Black bear habitat covers three-fourths of Alaska, with high concentrations found in Southeast, Prince William Sound, and in the coastal mountains and lowlands of southcentral Alaska. Low to moderate densities are found in interior and western Alaska. Their range coincides with that of semi-open forests, and though carnivorous, their diet consists mainly of vegetation due to the difficulty of getting meat or fish. Black bears often spend their lives within five miles of their birthplace and will frequently return to their home range if transplanted. They easily climb trees, with both cubs and adults using trees as a place of escape. Cubs are generally born in late January or February weighing 8 to 10 ounces, and while average litter size is two cubs, three or four is not unusual. Black bears den up in winter for up to six months, but are not true hibernators. Their body temperature remains high, and they awaken easily — even in midwinter.

Brown/Grizzly Bears. Brown/grizzly bear fur color varies from blond to black with shades of brown and gray in between. As adults, they can weigh over 1,000 pounds, but are usually smaller; size depends on sex, age, time of year and geographic location. Coastal bears, referred to as "browns" or "brownies," are the largest living carnivorous land mammals in the world and grow larger than Interior "grizzlies." Habitat for browns or grizzlies is most of Alaska, with the exception of islands in the extreme southeastern part of the state. The lowest populations are found in the northern Interior and the Arctic. Their range is wherever food is abundant, but they prefer open tundra and grasslands. Diet consists of a wide variety of plants and animals, including their own kind, and humans under some circumstances. In their realm, grizzlies are king and fear no other animal except man with a firearm. While attacks on humans are the exception, when they occur the results are tragic. These bears are also tremendously strong and have been seen carrying — off the ground — an 800-pound moose. One to two hairless cubs are usually born in late January or February weighing 8 to 10 ounces, and sows have been known to adopt orphaned cubs. Time of year and duration of denning varies with the location and physical condition of the bear, and can be up to six months of the year. Dens are frequently on hillsides or on mountain slopes.

Polar Bears. The only areas on a polar bear not covered with heavy, white fur are its eyes and large, black nose. The bears, seemingly aware that their noses give them away to prey, will hold a paw up to hide it when hunting. An adult polar bear weighs 1,500 pounds or more and has a long neck with a proportionately small head. Their habitat is the Canadian–eastern Alaska Arctic and the western Alaska–eastern Soviet Union, the latter being home to the world's largest polar bears. Their range is wherever the arctic ice cap flows, and they are more numerous toward the southern edge of the ice pack. Occasionally they will come ashore, but generally stay near the coast. While ashore they eat some vegetation, but their diet consists primarily of ringed seal, walrus, stranded whales, birds and fish. Cannibalism of cubs and young bears by older males is not unusual. Polar bears are natural swimmers, and reports exist of swimming bears seen 50 miles from the nearest land or ice. When swimming, they use their front paws for propulsion and trail their rear paws. Mother bears have been seen with a cub hanging onto their tail getting a tow through the water. Cubs are born in December with two being the common litter size. They weigh about a pound at birth and remain with their mother for about 28 months. Usually only pregnant sows den up, for an average of six months in the winter. Polar bears need stable, cold areas for denning, and dens in Alaska have been found 30 miles inland, along the coast, on offshore islands, on shorefast ice and on drifting sea ice.

Related reading: *More Alaska Bear Tales,* by Larry Kaniut. *Grizzly Cub: Five Years in the Life of a Bear,* by Rick McIntyre. See ALASKA NORTHWEST LIBRARY in the back of the book.

Berries

Wild berries abound in Alaska with the circumboreal lingonberry/lowbush cranberry (*Vaccinium vitis-idaea*) being the most widespread. Blueberries of one species or another grow in most of the state. Some 50 other species of wild fruit are found in Alaska, including strawberries, raspberries, cloudberries, salmonberries, crowberries, na-

Lingonberry/ Lowbush Cranberry, *Vaccinium vitis-idaea* (Reprinted from *Alaska Wild Berry Guide and*

goonberries and crabapples. Highbush cranberries (which are not really cranberries) can be found on bushes even in the dead of winter, and the frozen berries provide a refreshing treat to the hiker.

The fruit of the wild rose, or rose hip, is not strictly a berry but is an ideal source of vitamin C for bush dweller and city resident alike. A few hips will provide as much of the vitamin as a medium-sized orange. The farther north the hips are found, the richer they are in vitamin C.

Related reading: *Discovering Wild Plants: Alaska, Western Canada, the Northwest,* by Janice Schofield. More than 130 plants are profiled, with complete descriptions, habitat and harvest information, recipes, illustrations and photos included. *Plant Lore of an Alaskan Island,* by Frances Kelso Graham and the Ouzinkie Botanical Society. See ALASKA NORTHWEST LIBRARY in the back of the book.

Billiken

This smiling ivory figure with a pointed head, though long a popular Northland souvenir, is not an Eskimo invention. The billiken was patented in 1908 by Florence Pretz of Kansas City. A small, seated, Buddhalike figure, the original billiken was manufactured

by the Billiken Company of Chicago and sold as a good luck charm. Thousands of these figurines were sold during the 1909 Alaska-Yukon-Pacific Exposition in Seattle. Billikens vanished soon afterward from most Lower 48 shops, however, someone had brought them to Nome, and the Eskimos of King Island, Little Diomede and Wales began carving ivory replicas of the billikins.

Billikens are still being made elsewhere in the world in such materials as wood, concrete and glass.

A popular notion contends that rubbing a billiken's tummy brings good fortune.

Birds

Authorities at the Anchorage Audubon Society acknowledge 437 bird species in Alaska. If unsubstantiated sightings are included, the species total increases.

Thousands of ducks, geese and swans come north to breeding grounds each spring. Millions of seabirds congregate in nesting colonies on exposed cliffs along Alaska's coastline, particularly on the Aleutian Islands, and on islands in the Bering Sea.

Migratory birds reach Alaska from many corners of the world. Arctic terns travel up to 22,000 miles on their round trip each year from Antarctica. Others come from South America, the South Pacific islands and Asia.

Each May one of the world's largest concentrations of shorebirds funnels through the Copper River Delta near Cordova. Waterfowl such as trumpeter swans and the world's entire flock of dusky Canada geese breed there.

Other key waterfowl habitats include the Yukon-Kuskokwim delta, Yukon Flats, Innoko Flats and Minto Lakes. During migration, huge flocks gather at Egegik, Port Heiden, Port Moller, Izembek Bay, Chickaloon Flats, Susitna Flats and Stikine Flats.

Raptors, led by the bald eagle, range throughout the state. Alaska has three subspecies of peregrine falcon: Arctic, American and Peale's. Arctic and American peregrine falcons join the Eskimo curlew, Aleutian Canada goose and short-tailed albatross on the endangered or threatened species list for the state.

Following is a list of some geographically restricted birds whose origins are in Siberia or Asia, as well as a few of the state's more well-known species:

Aleutian Tern — Breeds in coastal areas, marshes, islands, lagoons, rivers and inshore marine waters. Nests only in Alaska on ground in matted, dry grass. Casual sightings in southeastern Alaska in spring and summer, and in northern Alaska in summer.

Arctic Tern — Breeds in tidal flats, beaches, glacial moraines, rivers, lakes and marshes. Nests in colonies or scattered pairs on sand, gravel, moss or in rocks. The arctic tern winters in Antarctica, bypassing the Lower 48 in its 20,000-mile round-trip migration. Common sightings in southeastern, southcoastal and western Alaska in spring, summer and fall, and in southwestern Alaska in spring and fall.

Arctic Warbler — Found in willow thickets. Nests on the ground in grass or moss in willow thickets. Common sightings in central, western and northern Alaska in spring, summer and fall.

Bald Eagle — Found in coniferous forests, deciduous woodlands, rivers and streams, beaches and tidal flats, rocky shores and reefs. Nests in old-growth timber along the coast and larger mainland rivers. In treeless areas, nests on cliffs or on the ground. There are more bald eagles in Alaska than in all the other states combined, and common sightings occur in southeastern, southcoastal and southwestern Alaska year-round.

Bluethroat — Nests on the ground in shrub thickets in the uplands and the foothills of western and northern Alaska. Casual sightings in southwestern Alaska in spring and fall.

Emperor Goose — Nests near water in grassy marsh habitat on islands, banks or in large tussocks. The bulk of the world's population nests in the Yukon-Kuskokwim delta, with a few others nesting farther north to Kotzebue Sound and a few more in eastern Siberia. Rarely is an Emperor Goose seen east or south of Kodiak. Common sightings in southwestern Alaska in spring, fall and winter, and in western Alaska in spring, summer and fall.

Horned Puffin — Nests on sea islands in rock crevices or in burrows among boulders, on sea cliffs and on grassy slopes. Breeds inshore, in marine waters and on islands. Common sightings in southwestern and western Alaska in spring, summer and fall.

Pacific Loon — Breeds in coniferous forests or in lakes on tundra, and nests on projecting points or small islands. Folklore credits the loon with magical powers, and several legends abound. Common sightings in southeastern and southcentral Alaska in spring, fall and winter, and in southwestern, central, western and northern Alaska in spring, summer and fall.

Red-faced Cormorant — Habitat includes inshore marine waters. Nests in colonies on ledges of sea cliffs, small piles of rocks and shelves on volcanic cinder cones. In North America this bird appears only in Alaska. Common sightings in southcoastal and southwestern Alaska year-round.

Red-legged Kittiwake — Breeds in the Pribilof Islands, and on Buldir and Bogoslof islands in the Aleutians. Nests on cliff ledges and cliff points. Common sightings in southwestern Alaska in summer.

White Wagtail — Found in open areas with short vegetation usually along the coast. Nests near or on the ground in crevices or niches in old buildings. Casual sightings in central Alaska in spring, and in southwestern Alaska in spring and summer.

Yellow Wagtail — Habitat is willow thickets on the tundra. Nests on open tundra under grass or overhanging banks. Common sightings in western Alaska in spring, summer and fall.

About 10 million swans, geese and ducks also nest in Alaska each year, making the state "critical" habitat for North America's waterfowl. In North America some species and subspecies use Alaska as their exclusive nesting grounds, while over half the North American population of other species nests in the state.

Five chapters of the National Audubon Society are based in Alaska: the Anchorage Audubon Society, Inc. (P.O. Box 101161, Anchorage 99510), the Juneau Audubon Society (P.O. Box 021725, Juneau 99802), the Arctic Audubon Society (P.O. Box 82098, Fairbanks 99708), the Kenai Audubon Society (P.O. Box 3371, Soldotna 99669) and the Kodiak Audubon Society (Box 1756, Kodiak 99615). In addition to trying to help people increase their knowledge of birds, the groups (except for Fairbanks) coordinate over 20 annual Christmas bird counts around the state. The Fairbanks Bird Club (P.O. Box 81791, Fairbanks 99708) conducts the annual Christmas count for that area.

Related reading: *Guide to the Birds of Alaska.* Revised Edition, by Robert H. Armstrong. Detailed information on all 437 species of birds found in Alaska. Fully illustrated with color photos, and drawings by wildlife artist John C. Pitcher. See ALASKA NORTHWEST LIBRARY in the back of the book.

Blanket Toss

As effective as a trampoline, the blanket toss (or *nalukataq*) features a walrus hide blanket grasped by a number of people in a circle. They toss a person on the blanket as high as possible for as long as that person can remain upright. Every true Eskimo festival and many non-Native occasions include the blanket toss, which was originally used to allow Eskimo hunters to spot game, such as walrus and seal, in the distance. Depending on the skill of the person being tossed and the number of tossers, a medium-weight person might typically go 20 feet in the air.

Boating

Travel by boat is an important means of transportation in Alaska, where highways cover only about one-third of the state. Until the advent of the airplane, boats were often the only way to reach many parts of Alaska. Most of Alaska's supplies still arrive by water and in Southeast — where precipitous terrain and numerous islands make road building impossible — water travel is essential. (*See also* Ferries)

According to the U.S. Coast Guard, there are 44,488 vessels registered in Alaska. Of these, approximately 3,258 are longer than 30 feet (many are commercial fishing vessels) and 16,219 are longer than 20 feet.

To accommodate the needs of this fleet, there are approximately 8,000 slips available at public small-boat harbors in Alaska. According to the state, actual service capacity is somewhat greater because of the transient nature of many boats and certain management practices allowing "double parking." There are also harbors at various remote locations; no services other than moorage are provided at these harbors.

The Alaska Department of Transportation and Public Facilities (P.O. Box Z, Juneau 99811), through its regional offices, has the major responsibility for providing public floats, grids, docks, launching ramps and associated small-boat harbor facilities throughout the coastal areas of the state. Often these facilities are leased to local governments at no cost. Moorage facilities constructed by the state are intended for boats up to a maximum of 100 feet, with a limited number of facilities for larger vessels where large boats are common. With the exception of Ketchikan, Sitka and Juneau, there are no private marine facilities.

Recreational boating opportunities in Alaska are too numerous and varied to list here; Alaska has thousands of miles of lakes, rivers and sheltered seaways. For information about boating within national forests, parks, monuments, preserves and wildlife refuges, contact the appropriate federal agency. For travel by boat in southeastern Alaska's sheltered seaways — or elsewhere in Alaska's coastal waters — NOAA nautical charts are available. (*See also* Information Sources)

Canoe routes have been established on the Kenai Peninsula (contact Kenai National Wildlife Refuge, 2139 Ski Hill Road, Soldotna 99669); in Nancy Lake State Recreation Area (contact Superintendent, Mat-Su District, HC32, Box 6706, Wasilla 99687); and on rivers in the Fairbanks and Anchorage areas (contact Bureau of Land Management, 1150 University Ave., Fairbanks 99709 and 222 W. Seventh Ave., #13, Anchorage 99513).

Travel by water in Alaska requires extra caution. Weather changes rapidly

and is often unpredictable; it's important to be prepared for the worst. Alaska waters, even in midsummer, are cold. A person falling overboard may become immobilized by the cold water in only a few minutes. And since many of Alaska's water routes are far from civilization, help may be a long way off.

Persons inexperienced in traveling Alaska's waterways might consider hiring a charter boat operator or outfitter. Guides offer local knowledge and provide all necessary equipment. The Division of Tourism (Pouch E, Juneau 99811) maintains current lists of such services. Recreation information on both state and federal lands is available at the three Alaska Public Lands Information Centers: 605 W. Fourth Ave., Suite 105, Anchorage 99501; 250 Cushman St., Suite 1A, Fairbanks 99701; and P.O. Box 359, Tok 99780.

Related reading: *A Guide to the Queen Charlotte Islands* by Neil G. Carey. Valuable information, photos, separate large map with services listing. *An Expedition to the Copper, Tanana and Koyukuk Rivers in 1885.* Adventures along waterways of interior Alaska. *Baidarka,* by George Dyson. The history and rediscovery of the Aleut kayak. See ALASKA NORTHWEST LIBRARY in the back of the book.

Bore Tide

(*See also* Tides)

A bore tide is a steep, foaming wall of water formed by a flood tide surging into a constricted inlet. In Cook Inlet, where maximum tidal range approaches 40 feet, incoming tides are further compressed in Knik and Turnagain arms and tidal bores may sometimes be seen. Though one- to two-foot-high bores are more common, spring tides in Turnagain Arm may produce bore tides up to six feet high, running at speeds of up to 10 knots, and even higher bores have been reported when unusually high tides come in against a strong southeast wind. Good spots to view bore tides in Turnagain Arm are along the Seward Highway, between 26 and 37 miles south of Anchorage; they can be expected to arrive there approximately 2 hours and 15 minutes later than the tide book prediction for low tide at Anchorage.

Breakup

(*See also* Nenana Ice Classic)

Breakup occurs when melting snows raise the level of ice-covered streams and rivers sufficiently to cause the ice to break apart and float downstream. Breakup is one of two factors determining the open-water season for river navigation, the second being the depth of the river. Peak water conditions occur just after breakup.

The navigable season for the Kuskokwim and Yukon rivers is June 1 through September 30; the Nushagak River, June 1 through August 31; and the Noatak River, late May through mid-June.

Breakup is a spectacular sight-and-sound show. Massive pieces of ice crunch and pound against each other as they push their way downriver racing for the sea, creating noises not unlike many huge engines straining and grating. The spine-tingling sound can be heard for miles. It marks the finale of winter and the arrival of spring in Alaska.

Sometimes great ice jams occur, causing the water to back up and flood inhabited areas. This natural phenomenon occurred at Fort Yukon in spring 1982 and at McGrath in 1990.

Bunny Boots

Bunny boots, also called vapor barrier boots, are large, insulated rubber boots to protect feet from frostbite. Black bunny boots are generally rated to –20°F, while the more common white bunny boots are even warmer and used in the most extreme conditions, including the heights of Mount McKinley. (The cumbersome boots are adequate for easy climbing but unsuitable for technical mountain climbing.) Prices for bunny boots range from about $50 for used boots to about $175 for new ones.

Bus Lines

Scheduled bus service is available in summer to and within Alaska, although buses don't run as frequently as in the Lower 48. (Local transit service is also available in some major communities.) Services may be infrequent; consult current schedules.

Alaska Sightseeing Tours, 543 W. Fourth Ave., Anchorage 99501. Provides service between Anchorage, Denali National Park, Columbia Glacier, Fairbanks, Golden Circle, Haines and Valdez.

Alaska-Yukon Motorcoaches, 543 W. Fourth Ave., Anchorage 99501. Provides service between Anchorage, Haines/Skagway, Valdez, Denali National Park and Preserve, and Fairbanks.

Alaskon Express, 547 W. Fourth Ave., Anchorage 99501. Provides service between Anchorage, Tok, Haines, Whitehorse and Skagway.

Atlas Tours Ltd., P.O. Box 4340, Whitehorse, YT, Canada Y1A 3T5. Provides service between Whitehorse and Skagway.

Denali Express, 405 L St., Anchorage 99501. Provides service between Anchorage, Denali and Fairbanks.

Eagle Custom Tours, 614 W. Fourth Ave., Anchorage 99501. Provides service between Anchorage, Portage Glacier and the Matanuska Valley.

Norline Coaches (Yukon) Ltd., 3211-A Third Ave., Whitehorse, YT, Canada Y1A 4T8. Provides service between Whitehorse and Tok via Dawson City and Fairbanks.

Royal Hyway Tours, 2815 Second Ave., Suite 410, Seattle, WA 98121. Provides city tours and tour packages in many parts of Alaska.

Seward Bus Lines, P.O. Box 1338, Seward 99664. Provides service between Anchorage and Seward.

Valdez/Anchorage Bus Lines, P.O. Box 101388, Anchorage 99510. Provides service between Valdez and Anchorage via Glennallen.

Westours Motorcoaches, 547 W. Fourth Ave., Anchorage 99501. Provides service throughout Alaska and the Yukon.

White Pass and Yukon Motorcoaches, 300 Elliott Ave. W., Seattle, WA 98119. Provides service between Skagway, Haines, Valdez, Glennallen, Whitehorse and Anchorage.

Bush

Originally used to describe large expanses of wilderness beyond the fringes of civilization, inhabited only by trappers and miners, "bush" has come to stand for any part of Alaska not accessible by road. A community accessible only by air, water, sled or snow machine is considered a bush village, and anyone living there is someone from the bush.

The term "bush" has been adapted to the small planes and their pilots who service areas lacking roads. Bush planes are commonly equipped with floats and skis to match terrain and season.

Related reading: *The ALASKA WILDERNESS MILEPOST®*. A complete guide to 250 remote towns and villages. *Winging It!*, by Jack Jefford. A pioneer bush pilot's portrait of early Alaska aviation. *Skystruck: True Tales of an Alaskan Bush Pilot*, by Herman Lerdahl with Cliff Cernick. A daring aviator's stories of the excitement, danger and rewards of flying in Alaska in the 1930s and 1940s. *We Live in the Alaskan Bush*, by Tom Walker. The life of the Walker family in their log cabin at Loon Lake near Mount McKinley. See ALASKA NORTHWEST LIBRARY at back of book.

Cabin Fever

Cabin fever is a state of mind blamed on cold, dark winter weather when people are often housebound. It is characterized by depression, preoccupation, discontent and occasionally violence and has been described as "a 12-foot stare in a 10-foot room."

Cabin fever is commonly thought to afflict miners and trappers spending a lonely winter in the wilderness, but, in truth, these people are active and outdoors enough to remain content. It is more likely to strike the snowbound or disabled. The arrival of spring or a change of scene usually relieves the symptoms.

Related reading: *Winter Watch*, by James Ramsey. For 266 days, the author tested himself against an Arctic winter in a remote cabin in the Brooks Range. See ALASKA NORTHWEST LIBRARY in the back of the book.

Cabins

Rustic cabins in remote Alaskan places can be rented from the Forest Service and the Bureau of Land Management (BLM). The modest price, $20 per night per cabin, makes this one of the best vacation bargains in Alaska. It offers visitors a chance to try living "in the bush."

Almost 200 Forest Service cabins are scattered through the Tongass and Chugach national forests in southeast and southcentral Alaska. Seven BLM cabins are in the White Mountains National Recreation area east of Fairbanks and are used primarily by winter recreationists. Some are located on salt water; others on freshwater rivers, streams or lakes. Aluminum skiffs and

oars are provided at most of the lake cabins.

Reservations may be made in person or by mail. Permits for use are issued on a first-come, first-served basis, up to 179 days in advance. Length of stay is limited to three consecutive days. The fee is due at the time the reservation is made.

The average cabin is 12 by 14 feet and is usually equipped with a table, an oil or wood stove, and wooden bunks without mattresses. Most will accommodate a group of four to six. There is no electricity. Outhouses are down the trail a little way. Visitors need to bring their own food, bedding, cooking utensils, and (usually) stove fuel. In addition, it's advisable to have a gas or propane stove for cooking, a lantern and insect repellent.

Some of the cabins can be reached by boat or trail, but because of the remote locations, visitors frequently come by chartered aircraft.

Information on cabins and their locations may be obtained from the National Forest offices listed below. The Forest Service recommends that visitors contact the office nearest the area they wish to visit, asking for a copy of the Recreation Facility booklet, and it's a good idea to do this at least six months before the date of desired occupancy. The booklet contains applications for cabin use plus tips on planning a stay.

Fairbanks Area
BLM Steese/White Mountains District Office, 1150 University Ave., Fairbanks 99709
Juneau Area and Admiralty Island
USDA Forest Service, Juneau Ranger District, 8465 Old Dairy Road, Juneau 99801
Ketchikan Area
USDA Forest Service, Tongass National Forest, Ketchikan and Misty Fiords Ranger District, 3031 Tongass, Ketchikan 99901
Petersburg Area
USDA Forest Service, Petersburg Ranger District, P.O. Box 1328, Petersburg 99833
Sitka Area
USDA Forest Service, Tongass National Forest, Sitka Ranger District, 204 Siginaka Way, Sitka 99835
Wrangell Area
USDA Forest Service, Wrangell Ranger District, P.O. Box 51, Wrangell 99929

Anchorage, Cordova, Seward Areas
Cabin reservations may be made *in person* at the following locations:
Glacier Ranger District, Chugach National Forest, Monarch Mine Road, Girdwood 99587
Cordova Ranger District, 612 Second St., Cordova 99574
Seward Ranger District, 334 Fourth Ave., Seward 99664

Cabin reservations may be made *by mail or in person* at:
Chugach National Forest, 201 E. Ninth Ave., Suite 206, Anchorage 99501

Cache

Pronounced *cash,* this small storage unit is built to be inaccessible to marauding animals. A cache resembles a miniature log cabin mounted on stilts. It is reached by a ladder that bears, dogs, foxes and other hungry or curious animals can't climb. Extra precautions include wrapping tin around the poles to prevent climbing by clawed animals and extending the floor a few feet in all directions from the top of the poles to discourage those clever enough to get that high.

Squirrels are the most notorious of Alaska's cache-marauding critters. To be truly animal-proof, a cache should be built in a clearing well beyond the 30-foot leaping distance a squirrel can manage from a treetop.

Bush residents use the cache as a primitive food freezer in winter. A cache may also contain extra fuel and bedding. Size is determined by need. Sometimes a cache will be built between three or four straight trees growing close together.

Calendar of Events

JANUARY

Anchorage — Nastar Ski Races, Alyeska Ski Resort; Sled Dog Races; Hatcher Cup Series, Hatcher Pass Lodge. **Bethel** — Sled Dog Races. **Fairbanks** — Sled Dog Races. **Haines** — Snow Machine Rally. **Homer** — Snow Machine Races. **Juneau** — Rainier Downhill Challenge Cup; Alascom Ski Challenge; State legislature convenes. **Ketchikan** — Winter Festival. **Kodiak** — Russian Orthodox Starring Ceremony; Russian Orthodox Masquerade Ball. **Seward** — Polar Bear Jump-off. **Sitka** — Russian Christmas and Starring; Alaska Airlines Basketball Tournament. **Soldotna** — Winter Games; Sled Dog Races. **Tok** — Sled Dog Races. **Unalakleet** — January Jamboree. **Willow** — Winter Carnival.

FEBRUARY

Anchorage — Fur Rendezvous; Iron Dog Iditarod; Sled Dog Races; Northern Lights Women's Invitational. **Big Lake** — Winter Carnival. **Cordova** — Ice Worm Festival. **Fairbanks** — Sled Dog Races; Festival of Native Arts; Yukon Quest Sled Dog Race. **Homer** — Winter Carnival. **Juneau** — Taku Rendezvous; Alascom Divisional Championships. **Ketchikan** — Festival of the North. **Knik** — Iditabike; Iditashoe; Iditaski

Nordic Ski Race. **Nenana** — Ice Classic Tripod Raising Festival. **Nome** — Dexter Creek Sled Dog Race; Heart Throb Bi-Athlon. **Palmer** — Sled Dog Races. **Sitka** — Basketball Tournament. **Soldotna** — Alaska State Championship Sled Dog Races. **Valdez** — Winter Carnival; Ice Climbing Festival. **Wasilla** — Iditarod Days. **Whitehorse** — Sourdough Rendezvous; Yukon Quest Sled Dog Race. **Wrangell** — Tent City Days.

MARCH

Anchorage — Iditarod Sled Dog Race begins; Native Youth Olympics. **Chatanika** — Chatanika Days. **Dillingham** — Beaver Roundup. **Fairbanks** — Arctic Winter Games; Curling Bonspiel; Ice Festival; Sled Dog Races; Athabascan Old-Time Fiddling Festival. **Homer** — Jubilee!; Snow Machine Poker Run. **Juneau** — Sourdough Pro/Am Ski Race; Southeast Championships; Rainier Downhill Challenge Cup. **Ketchikan** — Folk Fest. **Kodiak** — Survival Suit Races; Mountain Golf Classic; Comfish Alaska. **Nome** — Ice Golf Classic on the Bering Sea; Month of Iditarod; Sled Dog Races; Snow Machine Race; Dog Weight Pull; Basketball Tournament. **North Pole** — Winter Carnival. **Sitka** — Bazaar and Totem Trot; Herring Festival. **Skagway** — Windfest Winter Festival; Buckwheat Ski Classic. **Sutton** — Coal Miner's Festival. **Talkeetna** — St. Patrick's Day Bash. **Tok** — Race of Champions Sled Dog Race. **Trapper Creek** — Cabin Fever Reliever Days. **Valdez** — Winter Carnival. **Wasilla** — Iditarod Days. **Whitehorse** — Curling Bonspiel.

APRIL

Anchorage — Spring Carnival, Alyeska Ski Resort; Native Youth Olympics. **Barrow** — Spring Festival. **Cordova** — Copper Day Celebrations. **Haines**— ARTFEST Drama Festival. **Homer** — Spring Arts Festival. **Juneau** — Folk Festival; Ski to Sea Race. **Kotzebue** — Arctic Circle Sunshine Festival. **Nome** — Sled Dog Race. **Skagway** — Buckwheat Ski Classic. **Whittier** — Crab Festival.

MAY

Anchor Point — King Salmon Derby. **Delta Junction** — Buffalo Wallow Square Dance Jamboree. **Haines** — King

Salmon Derby. **Homer** — Halibut Derby. **Juneau** — Jazz and Classics Festival; May Day Mud Race. **Ketchikan** — Ocean Race; Rainbreak; Salmon Derby. **Kodiak** — Crab Festival and Fishing Derby; Chad Ogden Ultramarathon. **Nenana** — River Daze. **Nome** — Annual Polar Bear Swim in the Bering Sea; Firemen's Ball; Stroak and Cloak Tri-Athlon. **Petersburg** — Little Norway Festival; Salmon Derby. **Savoonga** — Walrus Festival, St. Lawrence Island. **Seldovia** — Fishing Derby. **Seward** — Exit Glacier Run. **Sitka** — Salmon Derby. **Skagway** — Gold Rush Stampede. **Talkeetna** — Miner's Day Festival. **Valdez** — Salmon Derby. **Wrangell** — Halibut Derby; King Salmon Derby.

JUNE

Anchorage — Renaissance Faire; Kite Day; Mayor's Midnight Sun Marathon; Basically Bach Festival; Midnight Sun Hot Air Balloon Classic; Semi-Pro Baseball. **Delta Junction** — Softball Tournament. **Fairbanks** — Tanana River Raft Classic; Yukon 800 Marathon River Boat Race; Midnight Sun Run; Sunfest '91; Midnight Sun Baseball Game; Air Show. **Kenai** — Kenai Kapers. **Ketchikan** — Salmon Derby. **Knik** — Museum Pot Luck. **Kodiak** — Freedom Days. **Nenana** — River Daze. **Nome** — Midnight Sun Softball Tournament, Festival and Raft Race; ARCO–Jesse Owens Games. **Palmer** — Colony Days; Mat-Su Miners baseball season opens; Bluegrass Festival. **Sitka** — Salmon Derby; All Alaska Logging Championships; Writer's Symposium; Summer Music Festival. **Soldotna** — Salmon Derby. **Tanana** — Nuchalawoya Festival. **Valdez** — Halibut Derby; Whitewater Weekend. **Wasilla** —

Museum Garden Party; Water Festival. **Whitehorse** — Dog Show.

JULY

Fourth of July celebrations take place in most towns and villages. **Anchorage** — Freedom Days Festival; Bluegrass and Folk Festival. **Big Lake** — Regatta Water Festival; Fishing Derby. **Dawson City** — Yukon Gold Panning Championship. **Delta Junction** — Softball Tournament. **Fairbanks** — World Eskimo-Indian Olympics; Renaissance Faire; Golden Days; Summer Arts Festival. **Girdwood** — Girdwood Forest Faire. **Hatcher Pass** — Rock Climbing Festival. **Homer** — Halibut Derby. **Ketchikan** — Logging Carnival; Salmon Derby. **Kodiak** — Freedom Days. **Kotzebue** — Northwest Native Trade Fair. **North Pole** — Summer Festival. **Palmer** — KSKA Bluegrass Festival. **Seward** — Mount Marathon Race; Softball Tournaments; Halibut Tournament; Silver Salmon Derby. **Sitka** — Fourth of July Celebration (four days). **Skagway** — Soapy Smith's Wake. **Soldotna** — Progress Days. **Sterling** — Moose River Log Raft Race. **Talkeetna** — Salmon Derby; Moose Dropping Festival; Mountain Bike Rush. **Valdez** — Pink Salmon Derby; Gold Rush Days. **Wrangell** — Logging Show.

AUGUST

Anchorage — Air Show. **Cordova** — Silver Salmon Derby. **Craig** — Prince of Wales Island Fair and Logging Show. **Dawson City** — Discovery Days. **Delta Junction** — Deltana Fair. **Eagle River** — Alaskan Scottish Highland Games. **Fairbanks** — Tanana Valley Fair; Iditafoot Race; Summer Arts Festival. **Haines** — Southeast Alaska State Fair; Horse Show. **Juneau** — Golden North Salmon Derby. **Ketchikan** — Alaska Seafest; Silver Salmon Derby; Blueberry Festival. **Kodiak** — *Cry of the Wild Ram* (outdoor historical pageant); Rodeo and State Fair; Pilgrimage to St. Herman's Monks Lagoon. **Ninilchik** — Kenai Peninsula State Fair. **Palmer** — Alaska State Fair. **Seward** — Silver Salmon Derby; Tok Run; Softball Tournament. **Sheep Creek** — Bluegrass Festival. **Sitka** — Labor Day Classic Softball Tournament. **Skagway** — Fun Run. **Talkeetna** — Bluegrass Festival. **Tanana** — Valley Fair. **Valdez** — Gold Rush Days; Silver Salmon

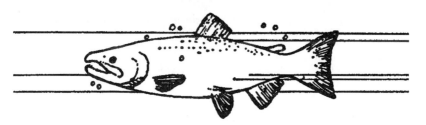

Derby. **Wasilla** — Museum Antique Show. **Wrangell** — Coho Derby. **Yukon** — Fireweed Festival.

SEPTEMBER

Anchorage — Oktoberfest; UAA Crafts Fair. **Cordova** — Salmon Derby. **Dawson City** — Klondike International Outhouse Race. **Dillingham** — Fall Fair. **Fairbanks** — Tanana-Rampart Labor Day Race; Equinox Marathon. **Kenai** — Silver Salmon Derby. **Ketchikan** — Salmon Derby. **Knik** — Museum Open House. **Kodiak** — Silver Salmon Derby. **Nome** — Worm-Burning Golf Tournament; Great Bathtub Race. **Petersburg** — Salmon Derby. **Sitka** — Softball Tournament. **Skagway** — Klondike Trail of '98 Road Relay; Antique Auto Show. **Valdez** — Silver Salmon Derby. **Whittier** — Silver Salmon Derby. **Wrangell** — Silver Salmon Derby.

OCTOBER

Anchorage — Quiana Alaska. **Fairbanks** — Oktoberfest. **Petersburg** — October Arts Festival. **Sitka** — Alaska Day Festival. **Wrangell** — Winter Fishing Derby.

NOVEMBER

Anchorage — Great Alaska Shootout; Symphony of Trees. **Delta Junction** — Winter Carnival. **Fairbanks** — Northern Invitational Curling Spiel; Athabascan Old-Time Fiddling Festival. **Juneau** — Veterans 10K Run. **Kenai** — Christmas Comes to Kenai Celebration. **Ketchikan** — Christmas Festival of Lights; Singing in the Rain Festival. **Wrangell** — Winter Derby.

DECEMBER

Anchorage — Seawolf Hockey Classic; Christmas Tree Lighting Ceremony. **Barrow** — Christmas Festival. **Cordova** — North Country Faire. **Delta Junction** — Winter Carnival. **Homer** — Renais-

sance Fair. **Ketchikan** — Festival of Lights. **Nome** — Firemen's Carnival. **North Pole** — Candle Lighting Ceremony. **Palmer** — Colony Christmas. **Seward** — Christmas Parade. **Sitka** — Christmas Boat Parade. **Talkeetna** — Christmas Lighting; Bachelor Society Ball and Wilderness Women Contest. **Wrangell** — Midnight Madness and Christmas Tree Lighting.

Camping

(*See also* Cabins; Hiking; National Forests; National Parks, Preserves and Monuments; National Wildlife Refuges; *and* State Park System)

Numerous public and privately operated campgrounds are found along Alaska's highways. Electrical hookups and dump stations are scarce. The dump station at Russian River campground is available for Chugach National Forest visitors. Alaska's backcountry offers virtually limitless possibilities for wilderness camping. Get permission before camping on private land. If the land is publicly owned, it's worthwhile to contact the agency that manages the land regarding regulations and hiking/camping conditions.

Additional details about camping are found in *The MILEPOST®* and *The ALASKA WILDERNESS MILEPOST®*. See ALASKA NORTHWEST LIBRARY at the back of the book.

The USDA Forest Service (Alaska Regional Office, USDA Forest Service, P.O. Box 21628-RN, Juneau 99802) maintains 25 campgrounds in the Tongass and Chugach national forests, most with tent and trailer sites and minimum facilities. All campgrounds are available on a first-come, first-served basis, and stays are limited to 14 days. Campground fees vary, from $4 to $8 per night depending upon facilities, which in the Chugach can include fire-grates, pit toilets, garbage pickup, picnic tables and water. Chugach campgrounds are open from Memorial Day through Labor Day, or until snow conditions cause closing.

The National Park Service (Alaska Regional Office, 2525 Gambell St., Anchorage 99503) at Denali National Park offers one walk-in campground and six campgrounds accessible by road; all are available on a first-come, first-served basis. Four of them require a $10 fee. Situated near the park entrance and open year-round are Riley Creek, for tents and trailers, and Morino, for walk-in tent campers. The others are open between May and September, depending on weather. Brochures may be obtained from Denali National Park, P.O. Box 9, Denali Park 99755.

Glacier Bay and Katmai national parks each offer one campground for walk-in campers, and Katmai now requires reservations. Backcountry camping is permitted in Denali, Glacier Bay, Katmai and Klondike Gold Rush parks, as well as other national parks and monuments.

Alaska Division of Parks (P.O. Box 107001, Anchorage 99510) maintains the most extensive system of roadside campgrounds and waysides in Alaska. Fees are charged and a yearly pass is offered.

U.S. Fish and Wildlife Service (State Office, 1011 E. Tudor, Anchorage 99503) has several wildlife refuges open to campers, although most are not accessible by highway. The Kenai National Wildlife Refuge, P.O. Box 2139, Soldotna 99669, however, has several campgrounds accessible from the Sterling Highway linking Homer and Anchorage.

The Bureau of Land Management (221 W. Seventh Ave., #13, Anchorage 99513) maintains about 12 campgrounds in interior Alaska; these campgrounds are free. The BLM has seven public-use cabins in the White Mountains National Recreation Area. A user fee of $20 per party per night (maximum of three nights) is required for permits, which may be obtained at the BLM Fairbanks District Office, 1150 University Ave., Fairbanks 99709.

Brochures describing BLM campgrounds are also available.

Canada-Alaska Boundary

In 1825, Russia, in possession of Alaska, and Great Britain, in possession of Canada, established the original boundary between Alaska and Canada. The demarcation was to begin at 54°40′ north latitude, just north of the mouth of Portland Canal, follow the canal to 56° north latitude, then traverse the mountain summits parallel to the coast as far as 141° west longitude. From there it would conform with that meridian north to the Arctic Ocean. The boundary line along the mountain summits in southeastern Alaska was never to be farther inland than 10 leagues — about 30 miles.

After purchasing Alaska, the United States found that the wording about the boundary line was interpreted differently by the Canadians. They felt the measurements should be made inland from the mouths of bays, while Americans argued the measurements should be made from the heads of the bays. In 1903, however, an international tribunal upheld the American interpretation of the treaty, providing Alaska the 1,538-mile-long border it enjoys with Canada today. If the Canadians had won their argument they would have had access to the sea, and Haines, Dyea and Skagway now would be in Canada.

The 20-foot-wide vista — a swath of land cleared 10 feet on each side of the boundary between southeastern Alaska, British Columbia and Yukon Territory — was surveyed and cleared between 1904 and 1914. Portions of the 710-mile-long boundary were again cleared in 1925, 1948, 1978 and 1982 by the International Boundary Commission. Monument and vista maintenance of 1978 and 1982 was conducted by the Canadian section of the commission and by the U.S. section in 1983, 1984 and 1985.

The Alaska-Canada border along the 141st meridian was surveyed and cleared between 1904 and 1920. Astronomical observations were made to find the meridian's intersection with the Yukon River, then, under the direction of the International Boundary Commission, engineers and surveyors of the U.S. Coast and Geodetic Survey and the Canadian Department of the Interior worked together north and south from the Yukon. The vista extends from Demarcation Point on the Arctic Ocean south to Mount St. Elias in the Wrangell Mountains (from there the border cuts east to encompass southeastern Alaska). This 647-mile stretch is one of the longest straight lines on record, varying less than 50 feet along its entire length.

Monuments are the actual markers of the boundary and are located so they tie in with survey networks of both the United States and Canada. Along the Alaska boundary most monuments are two-and-a-half-foot-high cones of aluminum-bronze set in concrete bases or occasionally cemented into rock. A large pair of concrete monuments with a pebbled finish mark major boundary road crossings. Because the boundary is not just a line but in fact a vertical plane dividing land and sky between the two nations, bronze plates mark tunnel and bridge crossings. Along the meridian, 191 monuments are placed, beginning 200 feet from the Arctic Ocean and ending at the south side of Logan Glacier.

Chambers of Commerce

(*See also* Convention and Visitors Bureaus)

Alaska State Chamber, 217 Second St., Suite 201, Juneau 99801; phone (907) 586-2323; 801 B St., Suite 406, Anchorage 99501; phone (907) 278-3741.

Anchorage Chamber, 437 E St., Anchorage 99501; phone (907) 272-2401.

Chugiak-Eagle River Chamber, P.O. Box 353, Eagle River 99599; phone (907) 694-4702.

Greater Copper Valley Chamber, P.O. Box 469, Glennallen 99588.

Cordova Chamber, P.O. Box 99, Cordova 99574; phone (907) 424-7260.

Delta Chamber, P.O. Box 987, Delta Junction 99737; phone (907) 895-5068.

Dillingham Chamber, P.O. Box 348, Dillingham 99576; phone (907) 842-2588.

Greater Fairbanks Chamber, P.O. Box 74446, Fairbanks 99707; phone (907) 452-1105.

Haines Chamber, P.O. Box 518, Haines 99827; phone (907) 766-2202.

Homer Chamber, P.O. Box 541, Homer 99603; phone (907) 235-7740.

Greater Juneau Chamber, 1107 W. Eighth, Suite 1, Juneau 99801; phone (907) 586-6420.

Kenai Chamber, P.O. Box 497, Kenai 99611; phone (907) 283-7989.

Greater Ketchikan Chamber, P.O. Box 5957, Ketchikan 99901; phone (907) 225-3184.

Kodiak Area Chamber, P.O. Box 1485, Kodiak 99615; phone (907) 486-5557.

Mid Valley Chamber, P.O. Box 86, Houston 99694; phone (907) 376-7533.

City of Nenana, P.O. Box 00070, Nenana 99760; phone (907) 832-5441.

Nome Chamber, P.O. Box 251, Nome 99762; phone (907) 443-5535.

North Pole Community Center, P.O. Box 55071, North Pole 99705; phone (907) 488-2242.

Greater Palmer Chamber, P.O. Box 45, Palmer 99645; phone (907) 745-2880.

Petersburg Chamber, P.O. Box 649, Petersburg 99833; phone (907) 772-3646.

Seldovia Chamber, Drawer F, Seldovia 99663; phone (907) 234-7816.

Seward Chamber, P.O. Box 749, Seward 99664; phone (907) 224-8051.

Greater Sitka Chamber, P.O. Box 638, Sitka 99835; phone (907) 747-8604.

Skagway Chamber, P.O. Box 194, Skagway 99840; phone (907) 983-2472.

Soldotna Chamber, P.O. Box 236, Soldotna 99669; phone (907) 262-9814.

Talkeetna Chamber, P.O. Box 334, Talkeetna 99676; phone (907) 733-2330.

Tok Chamber, P.O. Box 389, Tok

99780; phone (907) 883-2318.

Valdez Chamber, P.O. Box 512, Valdez 99686; phone (907) 835-2330.

Greater Wasilla Chamber, P.O. Box 871826, Wasilla 99687; phone (907) 376-1299.

Wrangell Chamber, P.O. Box 49, Wrangell 99929; phone (907) 874-3901.

Cheechako

Pronounced *chee-chak-ko,* or *chee-chak-er* by some old-time Alaskans, the word means tenderfoot or greenhorn. According to *The Chinook Jargon,* a 1909 dictionary of the old trading language used by traders from the Hudson's Bay Company in the early 1800s, the word cheechako comes from combining the Chinook Indian word *chee,* meaning new, fresh, or "just now," with the Nootka Indian word *chako,* which means to come, to approach, or to become.

Chilkat Blankets

Dramatic, bilaterally symmetrical patterns, usually in black, white, yellow and blue, adorn these heavily fringed ceremonial blankets.

The origin of the Chilkat dancing blanket is Tsimshian. Knowledge of the weaving techniques apparently diffused north to the Tlingit, where blanket-making reached its highest form among the Chilkat group. Visiting traders coined the blanket's name during the late nineteenth century.

Time, technical skill and inherited privileges were required to weave Chilkat blankets and other ceremonial garments. Both men and women wore the blankets and heavily decorated aprons and tunics.

Yarn for Chilkat dancing blankets was spun primarily from the wool of the mountain goat. The designs woven into Chilkat blankets consist of geometric totemic shapes that can be reproduced by the method known as twining. (Early blankets are unadorned or display geometric patterns lacking curvilinear elements.) Often, totemic crests on painted house posts and the designs woven into garments were quite similar. Weavers reused pattern boards of wood painted with a design.

A few weavers are producing the blankets today.

Chilkoot Trail

The Chilkoot Trail, from Skagway over Chilkoot Pass to Lake Bennett, British Columbia, was one of the established routes to Yukon Territory gold fields during the Klondike gold rush of 1897–98. Thousands of gold stampeders climbed the tortuous trail over Chilkoot Pass that winter. Those who reached Lake Bennett built boats to float down the Yukon River to Dawson City.

Today, the 33-mile Chilkoot Trail is part of Klondike Gold Rush National Historical Park and is climbed each year by hundreds of backpackers. The Chilkoot Trail begins about 8 miles from Skagway on Dyea Road. There are a dozen campgrounds along the trail and ranger stations on both the Alaska and British Columbia portions of the trail (the trail crosses the international border at 3,739-foot Chilkoot Pass, 16.5 miles from the trailhead). The trail ends at Bennett, site of a White Pass and Yukon Route railway station. For more information, contact Klondike Gold Rush National Historical Park, Box 517, Skagway 99840.

Related reading: *Chilkoot Pass: The Most Famous Trail in the North,* by Archie Satterfield. This revised and expanded edition is a historical guide to the hiking trail and includes photos. See ALASKA NORTHWEST LIBRARY in the back of the book.

Chill Factor

The wind's chill factor can lower the effective temperature many degrees. While Alaska's regions of lowest temperatures also generally have little wind, activities such as riding a snowmobile or even walking can produce the same effect on exposed skin.

Tempera- ture (Fahr- enheit)	Wind Chill Temperature at Selected mph			
	10	20	30	45
40	28	18	13	10
30	16	4	-2	-6
20	4	-10	-18	-22
10	-9	-25	-33	-38
0	-21	-39	-48	-54
-10	-33	-53	-63	-70
-20	-46	-67	-79	-85
-30	-58	-82	-94	-102
-40	-70	-96	-109	-117

The wind's chill factor, when severe, can lead to frostnip (the body's early-warning signal of potential damage from cold — a "nipping" feeling in the extremities), frostbite (formation of small ice crystals in the body tissues) or hypothermia (dangerous lowering of the body's general temperature). Other factors that combine with wind chill and bring on these potentially damaging or fatal effects are exposure to wetness, exhaustion and lack of adequate clothing.

Chitons

Chitons are oval creatures with shells made up of eight overlapping plates. The gumboot and the Chinese slipper chiton are favorite Alaskan edible delicacies. The gumboot, named for the tough, leathery, reddish-brown covering that hides its plates, is the largest chiton in the world. It has long been traditional food for southeastern Alaska Natives.

Related reading: *Cooking Alaskan.* Over 1,500 recipes explain everything about the art of cooking the Alaska way. See ALASKA NORTHWEST LIBRARY in the back of the book.

Climate

(*See also* Winds)
Alaska's climate zones are maritime, transition, continental and arctic. With the exception of the transition zone along western Alaska, the zones are divided by mountain ranges that form barriers to shallow air masses and modify those deep enough to cross the ranges. The Brooks Range inhibits the southward movement of air from the Arctic Ocean, thus separating the arctic climate zone from the Interior. The Chugach, Wrangell, Aleutian and Alaska mountain ranges often limit northward air movement and dry the air before it reaches the Interior's continental zone.

Other meteorologic/oceanographic factors affecting Alaska's climate zones are air temperature, water temperature, cloud coverage, and wind and air pressure. The amount of moisture that air can hold in a gaseous state is highly dependent on its temperature. Warm air can contain more water vapor than cold air. Therefore, precipitation, as rain or snow or in other forms, is likely to be heavier from warm than from cold air. Water temperatures change more slowly and much less than land temperatures. For this reason, coastal area temperatures vary less than those farther inland.

Climate Zones

The maritime climate zone includes Southeast, the Northern Gulf Coast and the Aleutian Chain. Temperatures are mild — relatively warm in the winter and cool in summer. Precipitation is heavy, 50 to 200 inches annually along the coast and up to 400 inches on mountain slopes. Storms are frequently from the west and southwest, resulting in strong winds along the Aleutian Islands and the Alaska Peninsula. Amchitka Island's weather station has recorded the windiest weather in the state, followed by Cold Bay. Frequent storms with accompanying high winds account for rough seas with occasional waves to 50 feet in the Gulf of Alaska, particularly in fall and winter.

The transition zone is, in effect, two separate zones. One is the area between the coastal mountains and the Alaska Range, which includes Anchorage and the Matanuska Valley. Summer temperatures are higher than those of the maritime climate zone, with colder winter temperatures and less precipitation. Temperatures, however, are not as extreme as in the continental zone.

(*Continued on page 30*)

AVERAGE TEMPERATURES (FAHRENHEIT) AND PRECIPITATION (INCHES)

	ANCHORAGE	BARROW	BETHEL	COLD BAY	FAIRBANKS	HOMER	JUNEAU
January							
Temperature	14.8	−13.7	6.6	28.4	−10.3	22.7	23.1
Precipitation	0.80	0.20	0.81	2.71	0.55	2.23	3.98
February							
Temperature	18.5	−19.2	7.3	27.5	−4.1	25.3	28.2
Precipitation	0.86	0.18	0.71	2.30	0.41	1.78	3.66
March							
Temperature	24.7	−15.4	12.3	29.5	10.0	28.3	32.0
Precipitation	0.65	0.15	0.80	2.19	0.37	1.57	3.24
April							
Temperature	35.2	−2.2	24.7	33.0	30.0	35.3	39.2
Precipitation	0.63	0.20	0.65	1.90	0.28	1.27	2.83
May							
Temperature	46.5	18.9	40.2	39.5	48.3	42.6	46.7
Precipitation	0.63	0.16	0.83	2.40	0.57	1.07	3.46
June							
Temperature	54.4	33.7	51.5	45.5	59.5	49.1	53.0
Precipitation	1.02	0.36	1.29	2.13	1.29	1.00	3.02
July							
Temperature	58.1	39.0	54.7	50.3	61.7	53.0	55.9
Precipitation	1.96	0.87	2.18	2.50	1.84	1.63	4.09
August							
Temperature	56.1	37.9	52.7	51.4	56.3	52.8	54.8
Precipitation	2.31	0.97	3.65	3.71	1.82	2.56	5.10
September							
Temperature	48.0	30.6	45.1	47.5	45.0	47.2	49.3
Precipitation	2.51	0.64	2.58	4.06	1.02	2.96	6.25
October							
Temperature	34.7	14.5	30.5	39.7	25.2	37.8	41.9
Precipitation	1.86	0.51	1.48	4.45	0.81	3.41	7.64
November							
Temperature	21.8	−0.7	17.4	34.4	3.8	28.8	32.8
Precipitation	1.08	0.27	0.98	4.33	0.67	2.74	5.13
December							
Temperature	15.2	−11.8	6.9	30.1	−8.1	23.3	27.2
Precipitation	1.06	0.17	0.95	3.16	0.73	2.71	4.48
Snowfall (mean)	14.0	7.1	9.0	9.7	12.5	11.7	23.2
Annual							
Temperature	35.7	9.3	29.1	38.1	26.5	37.2	40.3
Precipitation	15.37	4.67	16.90	35.84	10.37	24.93	53.15

KETCHIKAN	KING SALMON	KODIAK	McGRATH	NOME	PETERSBURG	VALDEZ	
							January
34.2	15.0	32.3	–8.3	6.5	27.6	22.6	Temperature
14.01	1.11	9.52	0.81	0.88	9.31	5.63	Precipitation
							February
36.4	15.1	30.5	–1.7	3.5	31.1	24.3	Temperature
12.36	0.82	5.67	0.74	0.56	7.85	5.08	Precipitation
							March
38.6	21.7	34.4	9.1	8.3	34.7	30.3	Temperature
12.22	1.06	5.16	0.75	0.63	7.19	4.06	Precipitation
							April
43.0	30.8	37.6	26.0	17.3	40.4	37.0	Temperature
11.93	1.07	4.47	0.73	0.67	6.94	2.89	Precipitation
							May
49.2	42.3	43.6	44.3	35.5	47.2	45.3	Temperature
9.06	1.25	6.65	0.84	0.58	5.92	2.74	Precipitation
							June
54.7	50.0	49.6	55.4	45.7	53.0	52.0	Temperature
7.36	1.54	5.72	1.56	1.14	5.00	2.64	Precipitation
							July
58.0	54.5	54.5	58.4	50.8	55.8	55.0	Temperature
7.80	2.10	3.80	2.16	2.18	5.36	3.77	Precipitation
							August
58.7	53.8	55.2	53.9	49.8	55.0	53.6	Temperature
10.60	2.96	4.03	2.87	3.20	7.57	5.73	Precipitation
							September
54.0	47.0	50.2	43.9	42.3	50.3	47.3	Temperature
13.61	2.75	7.18	2.19	2.59	11.15	7.99	Precipitation
							October
47.0	32.6	41.2	25.4	28.3	43.5	38.1	Temperature
22.55	1.98	7.85	1.24	1.38	16.83	8.23	Precipitation
							November
40.4	22.9	35.0	5.0	16.6	35.6	27.8	Temperature
17.90	1.45	6.89	1.18	1.02	11.99	6.09	Precipitation
							December
36.0	14.7	32.1	–7.6	6.2	30.5	22.5	Temperature
15.82	1.19	7.39	1.12	0.82	10.66	6.65	Precipitation
							Snowfall
9.2	7.8	9.9	17.1	8.7	23.9	62.9	(mean)
							Annual
45.9	33.4	41.3	25.3	25.6	42.1	38.0	Temperature
155.22	19.28	74.33	16.18	15.64	105.77	61.50	Precipitation

(Continued from page 27)
Another transition zone includes the west coast from Bristol Bay to Point Hope. This area has cool summer temperatures that are somewhat colder than those of the maritime zone, and cold winter temperatures similar to the continental zone. Cold winter temperatures are partly due to the sea ice in the Chukchi and Bering seas.

The continental climate zone covers the majority of Alaska except the coastal fringes and the Arctic Slope. It has extreme temperatures and low precipitation. There are fewer clouds in the continental zone than elsewhere, so there is more warming by the sun during the long days of summer and more cooling during the long nights of winter. Precipitation is light because air masses affecting the area lose most of their moisture crossing the mountains to the south.

The Arctic, north of the Brooks Range, has cold winters, cool summers and desertlike precipitation. Prevailing winds are from the northeast off the arctic ice pack, which never moves far offshore. Summers are generally cloudy and winters are clear and cold. The cold air allows little precipitation and inhibits evaporation. Because continuous permafrost prevents the percolation of water into the soil, the area is generally marshy with numerous lakes. (*See also* Permafrost)

The chart on pages 28–29 shows normal monthly temperatures and precipitation for 14 communities in Alaska. Included are mean monthly snowfall for December and annual average temperatures and precipitation. The chart is based on data from NOAA and the Alaska state climatologist.

Climate Records

Highest temperature: 100°F, at Fort Yukon, June 27, 1915.

Lowest temperature: –80°F, at Prospect Creek Camp, Jan. 23, 1971.

Most precipitation in one year: 332.29 inches, at MacLeod Harbor (Montague Island), 1976.

Most precipitation in 24 hours: 15.2 inches, in Angoon, Oct. 12, 1982.

Most monthly precipitation: 70.99 inches, at MacLeod Harbor, November 1976.

Least precipitation in a year: 1.61 inches, at Barrow, 1935.

Most snowfall in a season: 974.5 inches, at Thompson Pass, 1952–53.

Most snowfall in 24 hours: 62 inches, at Thompson Pass, December 1955.

Most monthly snowfall: 297.9 inches, at Thompson Pass, February 1953.

Least snowfall in a season: 3 inches, at Barrow, 1935–36.

Highest recorded snow pack (also highest ever recorded in North America): 356 inches on Wolverine Glacier, Kenai Peninsula, after the winter of 1976–77.

Highest recorded wind speed: 139 mph, at Shemya Island, December 1959.

Coal

(*See also* Minerals and Mining)

About half of the coal resource of the United States is believed to be in Alaska. The demonstrated coal reserve base of the state is over 6 billion short tons, identified coal resources are about 160 billion short tons, and hypothetical and speculative resource estimates range upward to 6 trillion short tons. The provinces containing the most coal are northwestern Alaska, Cook Inlet–Susitna Lowland and the Nenana Trend. Geologists estimate that perhaps 80 percent of Alaska's coal underlies the 23-million-acre National Petroleum Reserve on the North Slope. Although the majority of the coals are of bituminous and subbituminous ranks, anthracite coal does occur in the Bering River and Matanuska fields. In addition to the vast resource base and wide distribution, the important selling points for Alaska coal are its extremely low sulfur content and access to the coast for shipping.

Exploration, technology and economics will ultimately determine the marketability of Alaska's coal resources. Large-scale exploration programs have been conducted in most of Alaska's coal fields by private industry and state and federal governments. Maxus Energy, Inc., and Placer U.S. are developing the Beluga coal field west of Anchorage on Cook Inlet. Wishbone Hill Mine is in the permit phase and is scheduled to produce 1 million metric tons of clean coal per year. Small coal mines have begun producing: one at Cape Beaufort in northwest Alaska and one at Castle Mountain in the Matanuska Valley. Exporation continues in the Nenana coal field.

Alaska's production of coal in 1989 was estimated to be 1.45 million metric tons and came exclusively from the Usibelli Coal Mine near Healy. Of that estimate, 747,095 short tons were burned in interior Alaska power plants; and 705,258 short tons were shipped to Korea.

Coal production in Alaska was over $41.4 million in 1989, down from $44 million in 1988.

Conk

Alaskans apply this term to a type of bracket fungus. The platelike conks grow on dead trees. When dry and hard, conks are snapped off and used to paint on.

Constitution of Alaska

One of the most remarkable achievements in the long battle for Alaskan statehood was the creation of the constitution of the state of Alaska in the mid-1950s. Statehood supporters believed that creation of a constitution would demonstrate Alaska's maturity and readiness for statehood, so in 1955 the territorial legislature appropriated $300,000 for the cost of holding a Constitutional Convention in Fairbanks.

For 73 days in 1955–1956, a total of 55 elected delegates from all across the territory of Alaska met in the new Student Union Building (now called Constitution Hall) on the University of Alaska campus. William A. Egan, a territorial legislator and former mayor of Valdez, who later became the first governor of the state of Alaska, was president of the convention. Under his leadership, the disparate group of Alaskans hammered out a document that is considered a model for a state constitution.

The National Municipal League said that the brief 14,000-word document drafted by the convention delegates was "one of the best, if not the best, state constitutions ever written." By an overwhelming margin the people of Alaska approved the new constitution at the polls in 1956, paving the way for the creation of the 49th state in 1959.

(The complete text of the Alaska constitution can be found in THE ALASKA ALMANAC®, 1978 through 1990 editions.)

Continental Divide

(See also Mountains)

The Continental Divide extends into Alaska. Unlike its portions in the Lower 48, which divide the country into east-west watersheds, the Continental Divide in Alaska trends through the Brooks Range, separating watersheds that drain north into the Arctic Ocean and west and south into the Bering Sea.

According to Alaska Science Nuggets, geologists used to regard the Brooks Range as a structural extension of the Rocky Mountains. Recent thinking, however, assumes the range to be 35 million to 200 million years older than the Rockies. The Alaska Range is comparatively young, only about 5 million years old.

Convention and Visitors Bureaus

Anchorage Convention and Visitors Bureau, 1600 A St., Suite 200, Anchorage 99501; phone (907) 276-4118.

Barrow Convention and Visitors Bureau, P.O. Box 1060, Barrow 99723; phone (907) 852-5211.

Delta Convention and Visitors Bureau, P.O. Box 987, Delta Junction 99737; phone (907) 895-4355.

Fairbanks Convention and Visitors Bureau, 550 First Ave., Fairbanks 99701; phone (907) 456-5774.

Haines Visitors Bureau, City of Haines, P.O. Box 1049, Haines 99827; phone (907) 766-2234.

Juneau Convention and Visitors Bureau, 76 Egan Drive, Suite 140, Juneau 99801; phone (907) 586-1737.

Kenai Bicentennial Visitors and Convention Bureau, P.O. Box 1991, Kenai 99611; phone (907) 283-1991.

Ketchikan Convention and Visitors Bureau, 131 Front St., Ketchikan 99901; phone (907) 225-6166.

Kodiak Island Convention and Visitors Bureau, 100 Marine Way, Kodiak 99615; phone (907) 486-4782.

Mat-Su Convention and Visitors Bureau, 191 E. Swanson Ave., #201, Wasilla 99687; phone (907) 376-8000.

Nome Convention and Visitors Bureau, P.O. Box 251, Nome 99762; phone (907) 443-5535.

Sitka Convention and Visitors Bureau, P.O. Box 1226, Sitka 99835; phone (907) 747-5940.

Skagway Convention and Visitors Bureau, P.O. Box 415, Skagway 99840; phone (907) 983-2854.

Valdez Convention and Visitors Bureau, P. O. Box 1603, Valdez 99686; phone (907) 835-2984.

Wrangell Convention and Visitors Bureau, P.O. Box 1078, Wrangell 99929; phone (907) 874-3800.

Coppers

(*See also* Potlatch)

Coppers (*tinnehs*) are beaten copper plaques that were important symbols of wealth among the Pacific Northwest Coast Natives. Coppers are shaped something like a keyhole or a shield, are usually two or three feet long and weigh approximately 40 pounds. Coppers varied in value from tribe to tribe.

Early coppers were made of ore from the Copper River area, although western traders quickly made sheet copper available. Some scholars believe that Tlingit craftsmen shaped placer copper into the desired form themselves, while others maintain that coppers were formed by Athabascans. The impressive plaques were engraved or carved in relief with totemic crests.

The value of coppers increased as they were traded or sold, and their transfer implied that a potlatch would be given by the new owner. Coppers were given names such as "Cloud," "Point of Island" or "Killer Whale," and were spoken of in respectful terms. They were thought of as powerful, and their histories were as well-known as those of the noblest families.

Coppers were often broken and destroyed during public displays and distribution of wealth. Some parts of the coppers were valued nearly as much as the whole.

To this day, certain coppers that have been part of museum collections for years are still valued highly by some tribes, and are used as symbols of wealth and prestige during marriage ceremonies and potlatches.

Cost of Living

The cost of living in Alaska is high, and so is personal income. The main methods of travel in the state are by sea and by air. Alaska's size and its remoteness from the Lower 48 make personal and business travel expensive. Similarly, providing goods and services, such as medical care, to remote areas of the state is costly.

Agriculture and manufacturing in Alaska are limited, and so most consumption items are shipped in from Outside, adding to their cost. Lack of competition, particularly in the rural areas and in locations with small population bases, also keeps prices of goods and services high. Nevertheless, in recent years the increase in Anchorage consumer prices has been lower than the national average. Medical care is an exception to this trend of moderating prices: It rose at a higher rate than other prices and kept pace with the nationwide trend.

A housing market analysis done at the beginning of 1989 in more than 200 cities across the nation found that the price of a standard-quality Anchorage house, in what was judged to be an above-average to prime neighborhood, was above the median price. The $116,800 Anchorage price compared to $127,963 in Seattle, Washington; $238,800 in San Jose,

California; and $102,500 in Syracuse, New York.

Food — average cost for one week at home for a family of four with elementary schoolchildren (compiled March 1989; U.S. average $94.00): Juneau, $94.49; Anchorage, $91.08; Fairbanks, $94.84; Nome, $152.54; Dillingham, $150.40.

Housing — average cost of single-family residence with three bedrooms, including land (compiled March 1989): Juneau, $112,250; Anchorage, $117,000; Fairbanks, $102,480; Ketchikan, $152,667; Kodiak, $161,023.

Gasoline — average cost for one gallon (compiled March 1989): Juneau, $1.30; Anchorage, 97¢; Fairbanks, $1.12; Ketchikan, $1.30; Kodiak, $1.26.

Heating Oil — average cost for 55-gallon drum (compiled September 1988): Juneau, $67.19; Anchorage, $49.98; Fairbanks, $49.20; Nome, $76.18; Dillingham, $84.54.

Taxes — city and borough (Alaska has no state income tax), as of September 1988: Juneau, 4 percent sales; Anchorage, none; Fairbanks, none; Nome, 4 percent sales; Dillingham, 3 percent sales.

Annual per capita personal income: At $19,079, Alaska was 16 percent higher than the national average in 1989, and eighth highest in the nation in income standings.

Courts

The Alaska court system operates at four levels: the supreme court, court of appeals, superior court and district court. The Alaska judiciary is funded by the state and administered by the supreme court.

The five-member supreme court, established by the Alaska Constitution in 1959, has final appellate jurisdiction of all actions and proceedings in lower courts. It sits monthly in Anchorage and Fairbanks, quarterly in Juneau and occasionally in other court locations.

The three-member court of appeals was established in 1980 to relieve the supreme court of some of its ever-increasing caseload. The supreme court retained its ultimate authority in all cases, but concentrated its attention on civil appellate matters, giving authority in criminal and quasi-criminal matters to the court of appeals. The court of appeals has appellate jurisdiction in certain superior court proceedings and jurisdiction to review district court decisions. It meets regularly in Anchorage and travels occasionally to other locations.

The superior court is the trial court, with original jurisdiction in all civil and criminal matters and appellate jurisdiction over all matters appealed by the district court. The superior court has exclusive jurisdiction in probate and in cases concerning minors. There are 29 superior court judges.

The district court has jurisdiction over misdemeanor violations and violations of ordinances of political subdivisions. In civil matters, the district court may hear cases for recovery of money, damages or specific personal property if the amount does not exceed $35,000. The district court may also establish death and issue marriage licenses, summons, writs of habeas corpus, and search and arrest warrants. District court criminal decisions may be appealed directly to the court of appeals, bypassing the superior court. There are 17 district court judges.

Administration of the superior and district courts is divided by region into four judicial districts: First Judicial District, Southeast; Second Judicial District, Nome-Kotzebue; Third Judicial District, Anchorage-Kodiak-Kenai; and Fourth Judicial District, Fairbanks.

District magistrates serve rural areas and help ease the work load of district courts in metropolitan areas. In criminal matters, magistrates may give judgment of conviction upon a plea of guilty to any state misdemeanor and may try state misdemeanor cases if the defendant waives his right to a district court judge. Magistrates may also hear municipal ordinance violations and state traffic infractions without the consent of the accused. In civil matters, magistrates may hear cases for recovery of money, damages or specific personal property if the amount does not exceed $5,000.

Selection of justices, judges and magistrates

Supreme court justices and judges of the court of appeals, superior court and district court are appointed by the governor from candidates submitted by the Alaska Judicial Council. All justices and judges must be citizens of the United States and have been residents of Alaska for at least five years. A justice must be licensed to practice law in Alaska at the time of appointment and have engaged in active law practice for eight years. A court of appeals judge must be a state resident for five years immediately preceding appointment, have been engaged in the active practice of law not less than eight years immediately preceding appointment and be licensed to practice law in Alaska. Qualifications of a superior court judge are the same as for supreme court justices, except that only five years of active practice are necessary. A district court judge must be 21 years of age, a resident for at least five years, and (1) be licensed to practice law in Alaska and have engaged in active practice of law for not less than three years immediately preceding appointment, or (2) have served for at least seven years as a magistrate in the state and have graduated from an accredited law school.

The chief justice of the supreme court is selected by majority vote of the justices, serves a three-year term and cannot succeed him or herself.

Each supreme court justice and each judge of the court of appeals is subject to approval or rejection by a majority of the voters of the state on a nonpartisan ballot at the first general election held more than three years after appointment. Thereafter, each justice must participate in a retention election every 10 years. A court of appeals judge must participate every eight years.

Superior court judges are subject to approval or rejection by voters of their judicial district at the first general election held more than three years after appointment. Thereafter, it is every sixth year. District court judges must run for retention in their judicial districts in the first general election held more than one year after appointment and every fourth year thereafter.

District magistrates are appointed for an indefinite period by the presiding superior court judge of the judicial district in which they will serve.

The Alaska State Supreme Court, 1959–1990: Justices and Tenure

John H. Dimond, 1959–1971
Walter H. Hodge, 1959–1960
Buell A. Nesbett, 1959–1970
  Chief Justice, 1959–1970
Harry O. Arend, 1960–1965
Jay A. Rabinowitz , 1965–
  Chief Justice, 1972–1975; 1978–1981; 1984–1987
George F. Boney, 1968–1972
  Chief Justice, 1970–1972
Roger G.Connor, 1968–1983
Robert C. Erwin, 1970–1977
Robert Boochever , 1972–1980
  Chief Justice, 1975–1978
James M. Fitzgerald, 1972–1975
Edmond W. Burke, 1975–
  Chief Justice, 1981–1984
Warren W. Mathews, 1977–
  Chief Justice, 1987–
Allen T. Compton, 1980–
Daniel A. Moore, Jr., 1983–

The Alaska State Court of Appeals, 1980–1990: Judges and Tenure

Alexander O. Bryner, 1980–
  Chief Judge, 1980–
James K. Singleton, Jr., 1980–
Robert G. Coats, 1980–

Cruises

(*See also* Ferries)

There are many opportunities for cruising Alaska waters, aboard either charter boats, scheduled boat excursions or luxury cruise ships.

Charter boats are readily available in southeastern and southcentral Alaska. Charter boat trips range from day-long fishing and sightseeing trips to overnight and longer customized trips or package tours. There is a wide range of charter boats, from simple fishing boats to sailboats, yachts and mini-class cruise ships.

In summer, scheduled boat excursions — from day trips to overnight cruises — are available at the following locations: Ketchikan (Misty Fiords); Sitka (harbor and area tours); Bartlett

Cove and Gustavus (Glacier Bay); Valdez and Whittier (Columbia Glacier, Prince William Sound); Seward (Resurrection Bay, Kenai Fjords); Homer (Kachemak Bay); and Fairbanks (Chena and Tanana rivers).

For details and additional information on charter boat operators and scheduled boat excursions, contact the Alaska Division of Tourism, P.O. Box E, Juneau 99811.

From May through September, luxury cruise ships carry visitors to Alaska via the Inside Passage. There are 25 ships to choose from and almost as many itineraries. There's also a bewildering array of travel options. Both round-trip and one-way cruises are available, or a cruise may be sold as part of a packaged tour that includes air, rail and/or motorcoach transportation.

Various shore excursions may be included in the cruise price or available for added cost. Ports of call may depend on length of cruise or time of sailing.

Because of the wide variety of cruise trip options, it is wise to work with your travel agent.

Following is a partial list of cruise ships serving Alaska in the 1990–91 season:

Alaska Sightseeing Tours, Suite 700, Fourth & Battery Bldg., Seattle, WA 98121; phone (206) 331-8687. *Sheltered Seas* (35 passengers); 4-day daylight cruise between Ketchikan and Juneau. *Spirit of Glacier Bay* (50 passengers); 3-day cruise between Juneau and Glacier Bay.

Clipper Cruise Lines, 7711 Bonhomme Ave., St. Louis, MO 63105-1965; phone 1-800-326-0010. *Yorktown Clipper* (138 passengers); 7-day cruise between Juneau and Ketchikan.

Costa Cruises, Inc., World Trade Center, 80 SW Eighth St., Miami, FL 33130; phone (305) 358-7325. MTS *Daphne* (420 passengers); 7-night round-trip cruises from Vancouver, British Columbia.

Crystal Cruises, 2121 Avenue of the Stars, Los Angeles, CA 90067. *Crystal Harmony* (960 passengers); 12-day cruise between San Francisco and Skagway.

Cunard/NAC Lines, 555 Fifth Ave., New York, NY 10017; phone (212) 880-7500. *Sagafjord* (618 passengers); 11-day cruise between Vancouver, British Columbia, and Anchorage.

Holland America Lines/Westours, 300 Elliott Ave. W., Seattle, WA 98119; phone (206) 281-3535. MS *Nieuw Amsterdam* (1,214 passengers); MS *Noordam* (1,214 passengers); SS *Rotterdam* (1,114 passengers) and the *Westerdam;* all ships offer 3-, 4- and 7-night round-trip cruises from Vancouver, British Columbia. The *Rotterdam* also offers 7- and 14-night cruises between Vancouver and Seward.

Princess Cruises, 2029 Century Park E., Los Angeles, CA 90025; phone (213) 553-1770. *Dawn Princess* (925 passengers), *Pacific Princess* (626 passengers) and *Fair Princess* (890 passengers); 7-day cruises between Vancouver, British Columbia, and Anchorage. *Star Princess* (1,470 passengers); 7-day round-trip Inside Passage cruise from Vancouver, British Columbia. *Sea Princess* (730 passengers); 10-day round-trip sailings from San Francisco.

Regency Cruises, 260 Madison Ave., New York, NY 10016; phone (212) 972-4774. MV *Regent Sea* (729 passengers); and *Regent Sun* (836 passengers); 7 days between Vancouver, British Columbia, and Whittier.

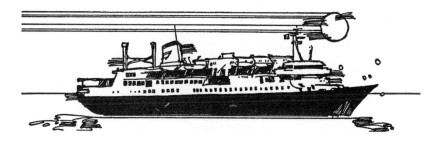

Royal Caribbean Cruise Line, 903 South America Way, Miami, FL 33132. *Viking Serenade* (980 passengers); 7 days between Vancouver and Skagway.

Royal Viking Line, 750 Battery St., San Francisco, CA 94111; phone (415) 955-4924. *Royal Viking Sea* (710 passengers); 11- and 14-day cruises from Vancouver, British Columbia.

Special Expeditions, 720 Fifth Ave., New York, NY 10019. *Sea Bird* (70 passengers) and *Sea Lion* (70 passengers); 11-day wilderness cruises between Prince Rupert, British Columbia, and Sitka.

World Explorer Cruises, 555 Montgomery St., San Francisco, CA 94111. SS *Universe* (554 passengers); 14-day round-trip cruises between Vancouver, British Columbia, and Seward.

Dalton Highway

This all-weather gravel road bridges the Yukon River, crosses the Arctic Circle, climbs the Brooks Range and passes through tundra plains before reaching the Prudhoe Bay oil fields on the coast of the Arctic Ocean.

The highway was named for James Dalton, a post–World War II explorer who played a large role in the development of North Slope oil and gas industries. It was built to provide access to the northern half of the 800-mile trans-Alaska oil pipeline during construction.

The Dalton Highway has been partially opened by the state for public use. The public may drive the road's first 215.4 miles to Disaster Creek at Dietrich. North of Dietrich, the highway is closed to the public. Permits to travel north of Disaster Creek are issued only for commercial or industrial purposes. Permits may be obtained from the Alaska Department of Transportation and Public Facilities.

Fuel, limited food services and tire repairs, as well as wrecker service at $5 per mile, are available (for cash) at the Yukon Bridge and at Coldfoot. Travelers are advised that dust clouds, large trucks traveling fast and sometimes narrow, rough road surfaces may make stopping along the roadway dangerous. Also, because safe drinking water is not available along the road, travelers should carry their own.

The 416-mile-long Dalton Highway begins at Milepost 73.1 on the Elliott Highway.

Daylight Hours

(*See also* Arctic Circle)

Maximum (At Summer Solstice, June 20 or 21)

	Sunrise	Sunset	Hours of daylight
Barrow	May 10	August 2	84 days continuous
Fairbanks	1:59 a.m.	11:48 p.m.	21:49 hours
Anchorage	3:21 a.m.	10:42 p.m.	19:21 hours
Juneau	3:51 a.m.	10:09 p.m.	18:18 hours
Ketchikan	4:04 a.m.	9:33 p.m.	17:29 hours
Adak	6:27 a.m.	11:10 p.m.	16:43 hours

Minimum (At Winter Solstice, December 21 or 22)

	Sunrise	Sunset	Hours of daylight
Barrow	*	*	0:00 hours
Fairbanks	10:59 a.m.	2:41 p.m.	3:42 hours
Anchorage	10:14 a.m.	3:42 p.m.	5:28 hours
Juneau	9:46 a.m.	4:07 p.m.	6:21 hours
Ketchikan	9:12 a.m.	4:18 p.m.	7:06 hours
Adak	10:52 a.m.	6:38 p.m.	7:46 hours

*For the period November 18 through January 24 — 67 days — there is no daylight in Barrow.

Diamond Willow

Fungi, particularly *Valsa sordida Nitschke,* are generally thought to be the cause of diamond-shaped patterns in the wood grain of some willow trees. There are 33 varieties of willow in Alaska, of which at least 5 can develop diamonds. They are found throughout the state, but are most plentiful in river valleys. Diamond willow, stripped of bark, is used to make lamps, walking sticks and novelty items.

Dog Mushing

(*See also* Iditarod Trail Sled Dog Race)

In many areas of the state where snow machines had just about replaced the working dog team, the sled dog has made a comeback, due in part to a rekindled appreciation of the reliability of nonmechanical transportation. In addition to working and racing dog teams, many people keep 2 to 10 sled dogs for recreational mushing.

Sled dog racing is Alaska's official state sport. Races ranging from local club meets to world championship class are held throughout the winter.

The sprint or championship races are usually run over two or three days, with the cumulative time for the heats deciding the winner. Distances for the heats vary from about 12 to 30 miles. The size of dog teams also varies, with mushers using anywhere from 7 to 16 dogs in their teams. Since racers are not allowed to replace dogs in the team, most finish with fewer than they started with (attrition may be caused by anything from tender feet to sore muscles).

Purses range from trophies for the club races to $50,000 (including heat money) for the championships. A purse is split between the finishers.

Statistics for two of the biggest races follow on page 38. Other major races round the state are:

Alaska State Championship Race, Kenai to Soldotna. Two heats in two days, 15.4 miles each day. Held in February.

All-Alaska Sweepstakes, Nome to Candle, round-trip. The Nome Kennel Club sponsors this 408-mile race. Held in March, not an annual event.

Clark Memorial Sled Dog Race, Soldotna to Hope, 100 miles. Held in January.

Iditarod Trail Sled Dog Race. (*See* Iditarod Trail Sled Dog Race)

Kusko 300, Bethel to Aniak. Held in January.

Tok Race of Champions, Tok. Two heats in two days, 20.5 miles a day. Held in March.

Willow Winter Carnival Race, Willow. Two heats in two days, 18 miles each day. Held in January.

Women's World Championship Race, Anchorage. Three heats in three

days, 12 miles each day. Held in February.

Yukon Quest International Sled Dog Race, Fairbanks to Whitehorse in even numbered years, with trail reversing in odd numbered years, 1,000 miles. Held in February.

WORLD CHAMPIONSHIP SLED DOG RACE, ANCHORAGE

Held in February. Best elapsed time in three heats over three days, 24 miles each day.

Elapsed Time (minutes:seconds)

	Day 1	Day 2	Day 3	Total	Purse
1974 Roland Lombard	105:32	108:34	101:36	310:10	$10,000
1975 George Attla	98:09	107:01	104:18	309:28	12,000
1976 George Attla	98:39	102:64	102:32	303:35	12,000
1977 Carl Huntington	97:42	105:29	*	201:11	12,000
1978 George Attla	102:59	108:38	107:11	318:48	15,000
1979 George Attla	99:51	97:23	99:07	296:21	15,000
1980 Dick Brunk	83:25	82:35	*	166:00	15,000
1981 George Attla	90:04	85:43	91:34	267:21	20,000
1982 George Attla	73:19	75:36	76:56	225:51	20,000
1983 Harris Dunlap	82:29	88:58	89:05	260:32	25,000
1984 Charlie Champaine	82:55	84:06	85:03	254:04	26,000
1985 Eddie Streeper	83:08	85:32	88:36	251:16	30,000
1986 — Race canceled for the first time due to lack of snow					
1987 Eddy Streeper	87:07	88:36	86:05	261:48	30,000
1988 Charlie Champaine	103:53	92:00	89:33	285:26	30,000
1989 Roxy Wright-Champaine	87:30	90:32	89:22	266.84	50,000
1990 Charlie Champaine	89:00	96:13	94:01	279:14	50,000

*Trail conditions shortened race

OPEN NORTH AMERICAN SLED DOG CHAMPIONSHIP, FAIRBANKS

Held in March. Best elapsed time in three heats over three days; 20 miles on Days 1 and 2; 30 miles on Day 3.

Elapsed Time (minutes:seconds)

	Day 1	Day 2	Day 3	Total	Purse
1974 Alfred Attla	72:00	74:25	108:29	254:54	$9,000
1975 George Attla	69:56	70:16	104:05	244:17	9,000
1976 Harvey Drake	72:00	73:43	116:00	261:43	10,000
1977 Carl Huntington	71:20	71:40	109:00	252:00	12,000
1978 George Attla	71:07	68:05	106:53	246:53	15,000
1979 George Attla	68:41	70:07	104:44	243:32	15,000
1980 Harvey Drake	63:48	66:49	94:30	225:07	15,000
1981 Peter Norberg	73:01	70:55	109:07	253:03	15,000
1982 Harris Dunlap	69:17	72:14	105:43	247:14	15,000
1983 Gareth Wright*	65:43	68:31	99:36	233:50	15,000
1984 Doug McRae	—	—	—	235:04	17,500
1985 Eddy Streeper	61:88	64:16	98:52	224:56	25,000
1986 George Attla	63:95	65:99	103:07	233:01	25,000
1987 George Attla	63:50	68:10	97:21	229:03	25,000
1988 Marvin Kokrine	63:52	66:16	95:42	225:49	30,000
1989 Roxy Wright-Champaine	62:10	62:42	92:07	216:59	44,000
1990 Charlie Champaine	62:47	67:38	95:40	226:05	45,000

*This was Gareth's second win of this race. He took his first championship in 1950.

Related reading: *Travelers of the Cold: Sled Dogs of the Far North,* by Dominique Cellura. A comprehensive text, illustrations and full-color photographs portray the strength and courage of these animals. See the ALASKA NORTHWEST LIBRARY at the back of the book.

Earthquakes

Between 1899 and early 1990, ten Alaska earthquakes occurred that equaled or exceeded a magnitude of 8 on the Richter scale. During the same period, more than 70 earthquakes took place that were of magnitude 7 or greater, the most recent occurring in the Gulf of Alaska on March 6, 1988, and registering 7.6 on the Richter scale.

According to the Alaska Tsunami Warning Center, earthquake activity in Alaska typically follows the same pattern from month to month, interspersed with sporadic swarms, or groups of small earthquakes, and punctuated every decade or so by a great earthquake and its aftershocks. Alaska is the most seismic of all the 50 states, and the most seismically active part of the state is the Aleutian Islands arc system. Seismicity related to this system extends into the Gulf of Alaska and northward into interior Alaska to a point near Mount McKinley. These earthquakes are largely the result of underthrusting of the North Pacific plate, with most seismic activity taking place along the Aleutian Island chain. Many earthquakes resulting from this underthrusting occur in Cook Inlet — particularly near Mount Illiamna and Mount Redoubt — and near Mount McKinley. North of the Alaska Range, in the central interior, most earthquakes are of shallow origin.

An earthquake created the highest seiche, or splash wave, ever recorded on the evening of July 9, 1958, when a quake with a magnitude of 7.9 on the Richter scale rocked the Yakutat area. A landslide containing approximately 40 million cubic yards of rock plunged into Gilbert Inlet at the head of Lituya Bay. The gigantic splash resulting from the slide sent a wave 1,740 feet up the opposite mountain side, denuding it of trees and soil down to bedrock. It then fell back and swept through the length of the bay and out to sea. One fishing boat anchored in Lituya Bay at the time was lost with its crew of two; another was carried over a spit of land by the wave and soon after foundered, but its crew was saved. A third boat anchored in the bay miraculously survived intact. A total of four square miles of coniferous forest was destroyed.

The most destructive earthquake to strike Alaska occurred at 5:36 P.M. on Good Friday, March 27, 1964 — a day now referred to as Black Friday. Registering between 8.4 and 8.6 on the Richter scale in use at the time, its equivalent moment magnitude has since been revised upward to 9.2, making it the strongest earthquake ever recorded in North America. With its primary epicenter deep beneath Miners Lake in northern Prince William Sound, the earthquake spread shock waves that were felt 700 miles away. The earthquake and seismic waves that followed killed 118 persons, 103 of them Alaskans. The death tally was: Chenega, 23; Kodiak 12; Point Nowell, 1; Point Whitshed, 1; Port Ashton, 1; Port Nellie Juan, 3; Seward, 11; Valdez, 31; Whittier, 12; Kalsin Bay, 6; Cape St. Elias, 1; Spruce Cape, 1.

The 1964 earthquake released 80 times the energy of the San Francisco earthquake of 1906 and moved more earth farther, both horizontally and vertically, than any other earthquake ever recorded except the 1960 Chilean earthquake. In the 69-day period after the main quake, there were 12,000 jolts of 3.5 magnitude or greater.

The highest sea wave caused by the 1964 earthquake occurred when an undersea slide near Shoup Glacier in Port Valdez triggered a wave that toppled trees 100 feet above tidewater and deposited silt and sand 220 feet above salt water.

Economy

In 1989, Alaska's economy posted 6.4 percent growth in employment. The unemployment rate of 6.7 percent shattered the previous low of 8 percent in 1976. Economic strength extended into 1990, marking the second year of employment growth. While some of this growth was attributable to the Prince William Sound oil spill cleanup effort, other gains were made in expanding oil and hard-rock mining industries, a reviving construction industry, a bottomfish boom, a successful timber industry and a new air freight operation. Trade and services remain in the forefront of employment growth.

Education

(*See also* School Districts *and* Universities and Colleges)

Alaskans are well educated. The 1980 Population Census reported 83 percent of persons older than 24 as having had 12 or more years of education. This compares to 67 percent for the rest of the country.

According to the 1989 *Alaska Education Directory,* Alaska has approximately 463 public schools and over 100 private and denominational schools. The Bureau of Indian Affairs operated schools in Alaska until 1985.

The state Board of Education has seven members appointed by the governor. (In addition, two nonvoting members are appointed by the board to represent the military and public school students.) The board is responsible for setting policy for education in Alaska schools and appoints a commissioner of education to carry out its decisions. The 463 public schools are controlled by 55 school districts and each school district elects its own school board. There are 22 Regional Education Attendance Areas that oversee education in rural areas outside the 33 city and borough school districts.

Any student in grades kindergarten through 12 (K–12) may choose to study at home through the unique state-operated Centralized Correspondence Study program, which also serves traveling students, GED students, migrant students and students living in remote areas. Summer school classes are also available through correspondence; each year, up to 2,000 students are enrolled in this program. Home study has been an option for Alaskan students since 1939.

The state Department of Education also operates the Alaska Vocational Technical Center at Seward and a number of other education programs ranging from adult basic education to literacy skills.

Alaskans 7 through 16 years old are required to attend school. According to state regulations, a student must earn a minimum of 21 high school credits to receive a high school diploma. The state Board of Education has stipulated that four credits must be earned in language arts; three in social studies; two each in math and science; and one in physical education. Local school boards set the remainder of the required credits.

Since 1976, the state has provided secondary school programs to any community in which an elementary school is operated and one or more children of high school age wish to attend high school. This mandate was the result of a suit initiated on behalf of Molly Hootch, a high-school-age student from Emmonak. Prior to the so-called Molly Hootch Decree, high school-age students in villages without a secondary school attended high school outside their village. Of the 127 villages originally eligible for high school programs under the Molly Hootch Decree, only a few remain without one.

There were approximately 7,991 teachers and administrators in the public schools and approximately 109,280 students enrolled in K–12 in public schools in 1989–90. The Anchorage School District accounted for more than 27 percent of the state's student enrollment. Private schools had over 5,500 students. The size of schools in Alaska varies greatly, from a 1,716-student high school in Anchorage to one- or two-teacher, one-room schools in remote rural areas.

Of the school district's operating fund, 73.6 percent is provided by the state, 20.6 percent by local governments and 5.8 percent by the federal government. Alaska's teachers receive the highest average salaries in the nation.

Employment

The average number of people employed in the state in 1989 was about 227,300. The annual average unemployment rate for 1989 was 6.7 percent, down significantly from the 9.5 percent unemployment rate posted in 1988.

After a two-year recession caused by an overbuilt construction market and collapsing world oil prices, Alaska's economy returned to growth. As of December 1989, the statewide growth in employment was between 1 and 2 percent on an annual basis. This rise in employment followed two years of employment losses of more than 4 percent each.

Not many of Alaska's industries were spared during the recession. Many job losses occurred in Anchorage, Alaska's largest city, and the construction and financial industries statewide were particularly hard hit. The oil and gas industry and Alaska's large government sectors were also adversely affected.

The recovery in 1989 was spurred on by a resurgence in Alaska's traditional resource-based industries of fishing and timber. This growth recovery was augmented by a growing tourist trade and an increasing military presence in the state. Higher oil prices in late 1987 and most of 1988 returned stability to the oil and gas industry as well as to government sectors dependent on revenue generated by oil. In the immediate future, hard-rock mining will be a growing employer; one major mine opened in 1989, another opened in early 1990 and several other major projects are in the works.

Although Alaska's unemployment rate is above the national average, it is best characterized by a very seasonal labor market. Increased activity of all types in the summer makes unemployment fairly low, while a lack of activity pushes up the unemployment rate in the winter months. The significant drop in the unemployment rate in Alaska in 1989 was largely due to summer employment in the massive oil spill cleanup effort in Prince William Sound.

Unemployment figures vary dramatically from winter to summer and from one region to another. High unemployment rates in Alaska's rural areas are common. In interior Alaska, for example, the unemployment rate approaches 20 percent in the winter months. On the other hand bustling seaports such as Kodiak experience unemployment rates below 3 percent during the summer. Unemployment figures for December 1989 by selected areas are as follows: statewide, 6.7 percent; Anchorage, 5 percent; Fairbanks, 8.1 percent; Juneau, 4.8 percent; Kodiak, 10.3 percent; Nome, 7.2 percent; Yukon-Koyukuk, 13.5 percent.

The presence of a high level of transient population is another characteristic of the Alaskan labor market that presumably aggravates the unemployment rate.

In the last decade, employment in Alaska grew at an average of 5 percent annually. During this period Alaska's economy experienced two surges: the construction of the trans-Alaska pipeline system in the mid-1970s and the increase in petroleum-based government revenues in the early 1980s. In early 1986, concurrent with the worldwide drop in the price of oil, the Alaskan economy began its first major contraction since World War II. More than 4 percent of total employment was lost in 1987, with a tapering off to under 1 percent for 1988.

In 1988, however, employment began a comeback, and in 1989, the state registered a 6.4 percent employment gain. While the government sector (state, local and federal) is generally a significant force in the economies of most states, historically this is particularly true in Alaska. In 1988, government employment in Alaska, excluding federal military personnel, was highest in employment numbers and total wage and salary payroll.

In 1989, service industries, transportation, the oil industry and retail sales all recorded increases in employment after several years of losing ground. Finance-insurance-real estate, construction and government industry groups stayed even and may see an upturn in employment in 1990. The smallest industry groups in Alaska, relative to the rest of the U.S., were manufacturing and wholesale trade.

Alaska law requires that for state-funded projects, 95 percent of the employees be state residents.

If you're seriously considering a move to Alaska to seek a job, first make a visit and see it for yourself. Jobs are scarce in Alaska and housing is expensive — there are now, and will be in the foreseeable future, plenty of Alaska residents out of work and anxious to find jobs. For additional information, write: Alaska Department of Labor, Alaska State Employment Service, P.O. Box 3-7000, Juneau 99802. Employment offices are located in most major communities.

End of the Trail®
1989-90

End of the Trail® reports the passing of old-timers and prominent Alaskans. See page 185 for listing.

Energy and Power

For the purposes of classifying power usage, the state of Alaska can be divided into three major regions, each having similar energy patterns, problems and resources: the Extended Railbelt region; the Southeast region; and the bush region.

The Extended Railbelt region consists of major urban areas linked by the Alaska Railroad (Seward, Anchorage and Fairbanks). The southcentral area of this region uses relatively inexpensive natural gas in Cook Inlet and small hydroelectrical power plants for electrical production and heating. The Fairbanks-Tanana Valley area uses primarily coal, and also oil, to meet its electrical needs. Future electrical demand for the Railbelt region will be met by a combination of hydropower and coal- and gas-fired generators. Currently in the planning stages are several major hydropower projects for this region. The Southeast region relies on hydropower for a large portion of its electrical generation. (Most of the existing hydroelectric power projects in Alaska are

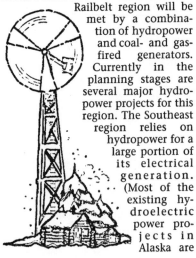

located in the Southeast region and more are planned.) In the smaller communities, diesel generators are used.

The bush region includes all communities that are remote from the major urban areas of the Extended Railbelt and Southeast regions. Electricity in bush communities is typically provided by small diesel generators. Thirty-four wind turbines are currently operating in the windy coastal areas of the bush region and more are planned. Where wind projects are feasible, such as those at Nelson Lagoon and Unalakleet, wind power can be a viable, fuel-saving alternative to diesel-powered generators. Thermal needs in the bush are currently being met almost entirely by heating oil. Wood and kerosene heaters are used to a limited extent. Natural gas is available in Barrow.

Eskimo Ice Cream

Also called *akutak* (Yup'ik Eskimo word for Eskimo ice cream), this classic Native delicacy, popular throughout Alaska, is traditionally made of whipped berries, seal oil and snow. Sometimes shortening, raisins and sugar are added. In different regions, variations are found. One uses the soopalallie berry, *Shepherdia canadensis* (also called soapberry), a bitter species that forms a frothy mass like soapsuds when beaten.

Related reading: *Discovering Wild Plants: Alaska, Western Canada, the Northwest,* by Janice J. Schofield. Profiles of more than 130 plants, including history, harvest and habitat information and recipes. *Alaska Wild Berry Guide and Cookbook,* by the Alaska Northwest Books editors. How to find, identify and prepare Alaska's wild berries. *Cooking Alaskan.* More than 1,500 recipes for cooking Alaska style. See ALASKA NORTHWEST LIBRARY in the back of the book.

Ferries

(*See also* Cruises)

The state Department of Transportation and Public Facilities, Marine

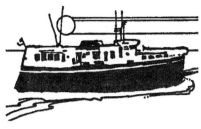

Highway System, provides year-round scheduled ferry service for passengers and vehicles to communities in southeastern and southwestern Alaska. The Southeast and Southwest Alaska ferry systems do not connect with each other.

A fleet of seven ferries on the southeastern system connects Bellingham, Washington, and Prince Rupert, British Columbia, with the southeastern Alaska ports of Hyder/Stewart, Ketchikan, Metlakatla, Hollis, Wrangell, Petersburg, Kake, Sitka, Angoon, Pelican, Hoonah, Tenakee Springs, Juneau, Haines and Skagway. These southeastern communities — with the exception of Hyder, Haines and Skagway — are accessible only by boat, ferry or airplane. The seven vessels of the southeastern system are the *Aurora*, *Columbia*, *Chilkat*, *LeConte*, *Malaspina*, *Matanuska* and *Taku*.

Southwestern Alaska is served by two ferries. The *Tustumena* serves Seward, Port Lions, Kodiak, Homer, Seldovia, Cordova and Valdez, with limited summer service to Chignik, Sand Point, King Cove, Cold Bay and Dutch Harbor. In summer, the *Bartlett* provides service between Valdez, Cordova and Whittier.

Scheduled state ferry service to southeastern Alaska began in 1963; ferry service to Kodiak Island began in 1964. The first three ferries of the Alaska ferry fleet were the *Malaspina*, *Matanuska* and *Taku*, built at an approximate cost of $4.5 million each.

Reservations should be made for all sailings. Senior Citizen and Handicapped passes are available. The address of the main office of the Alaska Marine Highway System is P.O. Box R, Juneau 99811; phone (907) 465-3941; or toll free, 1-800-642-0066.

Embarking Passenger and Vehicle Totals (in thousands) on Alaska Mainline Ferries*

Southeastern System

	Passengers	Vehicles
1988	223.9	58.9
1987	215.2	55.8
1986	214.8	56.5
1985	213.0	56.4
1984	214.9	57.8
1983	206.1	52.6
1982	220.0	51.0
1981	181.5**	44.1**
1980	189.5	44.3
1979	169.4	42.9
1978	161.9	38.6
1977	148.5	40.0
1976	181.7	46.3
1975	184.5	45.9
1974	174.7	41.4
1973	162.7	38.4
1972	162.7	39.4
1970	137.2	28.5
1965	123.7	25.8

Southwestern System

	Passengers	Vehicles
1988	50.4	16.6
1987	52.0	16.5
1986	51.8	16.0
1985	56.1	16.4
1984	55.8	15.5
1983	55.5	15.9
1982	57.0	15.5
1981	55.8	15.1
1980	49.4	14.0
1979	48.9	13.8
1978	46.6	13.2
1977	38.8	12.5
1976	44.4	11.7
1975	45.0	12.8
1974	44.6	12.4
1973	40.7	11.3
1972	35.9	9.9
1971	25.8	7.7
1970	6.9	3.2

*Mainline ports for Southeast are: Seattle (until 1989), Bellingham (since 1989), Vancouver (1970 to 1973 only), Prince Rupert, Ketchikan, Wrangell, Petersburg, Sitka, Juneau, Haines and Skagway. Mainline ports for southwestern Alaska are: Anchorage (1970 to 1973 only), Cordova, Valdez, Whittier, Homer, Seldovia, Kodiak, Seward and Port Lions.
**Does not include totals of passengers (9.5) and vehicles (2.9) on the MV *Aurora*.

Alaska State Ferry Data

Aurora: (235 feet, 14 knots), 250 passengers, 47 vehicles, no cabins.

Began service in 1977.

Bartlett: (193 feet, 14 knots), 170 passengers, 38 vehicles, no cabins. Began service in 1969.

Chilkat: (99 feet, 10 knots), 75 passengers, 15 vehicles, no cabins. Began service in 1959.

Columbia: (418 feet, 19 knots), 1,000 passengers, 170 vehicles, 96 cabins. Began service in 1973.

LeConte: (235 feet, 14 knots), 258 passengers, 47 vehicles, no cabins. Began service in 1974.

Malaspina: (408 feet, 16.5 knots), 750 passengers, 120 vehicles, 86 cabins. Began service in 1963 and was lengthened and renovated in 1972.

Matanuska: (408 feet, 16.5 knots), 750 passengers, 120 vehicles, 112 cabins. Began service in 1963.

Taku: (352 feet, 16 knots), 500 passengers, 105 vehicles, 30 cabins. Began service in 1963.

Tustumena: (296 feet, 14 knots), 220 passengers, 50 vehicles, 27 cabins. Began service in 1964.

NAUTICAL MILES BETWEEN PORTS
Southeastern System
Bellingham–Ketchikan, 600
Prince Rupert–Ketchikan, 91
Ketchikan–Metlakatla, 16
Ketchikan–Hollis, 40
Hollis–Petersburg, 122
Hollis–Wrangell, 95
Ketchikan–Wrangell, 89
Wrangell–Petersburg, 41
Petersburg–Juneau, 108
Petersburg–Kake, 59
Kake–Sitka, 110
Sitka–Angoon, 66
Angoon–Tenakee, 33
Tenakee–Hoonah, 47
Angoon–Hoonah, 60
Hoonah–Juneau (AB)*, 45
Sitka–Hoonah, 115
Hoonah–Pelican via South Pass, 58
Hoonah–Juneau, 68
Juneau–Haines, 91
Haines–Skagway, 13
Juneau (AB)–Haines, 68
Petersburg–Juneau (AB), 120
Petersburg–Sitka, 156
Juneau (AB)–Sitka, 136
*AB-Auke Bay

Southwestern System
Seward–Cordova, 146

Seward–Valdez, 143
Cordova–Valdez, 73
Valdez–Whittier, 84
Seward–Kodiak, 175
Kodiak–Port Lions, 27
Kodiak–Homer, 126
Homer–Seldovia, 16
Kodiak–Sand Point via Sitkinak Strait, 353

Fires on Wild Land

The 1989 fire season marked 50 years of fire fighting in Alaska. Back in 1939, fire guards covered only 4 percent of the area needing protection. Today, no area goes unprotected. Village crews make up the backbone of Alaska's firefighting operations.

Fire season starts in April or May, when winter's dead vegetation is vulnerable to any spark. Lightning is the leading cause of wild land fires in Alaska. In June, thunderstorms bring as many as 3,000 lightning strikes a day to the Alaska Interior. By mid-July in a normal year, rainfall in interior Alaska increases.

When wildfires threaten inhabited areas, the Bureau of Land Management's (BLM) Alaska Fire Service (in the northern half of the state) and the State of Alaska Division of Forestry (in the southern half of the state) provide fire protection to lands managed by the BLM, National Park Service, U.S. Fish and Wildlife Service, Native corporations, and the state.

All land management agencies in Alaska have placed their lands in one of four protection categories — critical, full, modified and limited. These protection levels set priorities for fire fighting.

With its 586,000 square miles of land, Alaska is more than twice the size of Texas. Most of this vast area has no roads, and transportation for fire fighters is usually by airplane. Fire camps are remote. Mosquito repellent is a necessity, but headlamps are not required since the midnight sun shines all night. Aircraft bring in all supplies, even drinking water. Radios are the only means of communication with headquarters.

Black spruce is a fire-dependent

species and burns very quickly. Fire fighters use chain saws to cut the trees and Pulaskis to cut through the underlying vegetation. It is nearly impossible to transport heavy equipment to fires in remote areas. Bulldozers are not used because they damage the delicate permafrost layer, leading to dramatic erosion.

Fire fighters no longer depend on lookout towers in the wilderness to spot wildfires. Today, computers detect the ionization from a lightning strike anywhere in the state, determine the latitude and longitude of the strike and display it on a computer screen. Detection specialists then fly to the areas of greatest risk.

When a fire is reported, computers tell the dispatcher which agency manages the land and whether the fire should be aggressively attacked.

Remote automatic weather stations report weather conditions all over Alaska, enabling weather forecasters to predict thunderstorms in any part of the state. Smokejumpers and retardant airplanes are pre-positioned close to the predicted thunderstorm activity.

The largest single fire ever reported in Alaska burned 1,161,200 acres 74 miles northwest of Galena in 1957. In 1977, the Bear Creek fire was the largest in the United States that year, consuming 361,000 acres near the Farewell airstrip. Unusually dry weather in 1990 contributed to a heavy fire season. At the end of July 1990, fire consumed more than 1.6 million acres, mostly in the Interior.

Calendar Year	No. of Fires	Acres Burned
1956	226	476,593
1957	391	5,049,661
1958	278	317,215
1959	320	596,574
1960	238	87,180
1961	117	5,100
1962	102	38,975
1963	194	16,290
1964	164	3,430
1965	148	7,093
1966	256	672,765
1967	207	109,005
1968	442	1,013,301
1969	511	4,231,820
1970	487	113,486

Calendar Year	No. of Fires	Acres Burned
1971	472	1,069,108
1972	641	963,686
1973	336	59,816
1974	782	662,960
1975	344	127,845
1976	622	69,119
1977	681	2,209,408
1978	356	7,757
1979	620	432,425
1980	417	188,778
1981	556	758,335
1982	283	70,798
1983	800	109,187*
1984	845	122,901*
1985	261	372,230
1986	396	395,169
1987	706	158,851*
1988	639	2,167,795*
1989	485	68,873*

*Combined AFS (federal) and state coverage.

Fish Wheel

The fish wheel is a machine fastened to a river shore and propelled by current, which scoops up fish heading upstream to spawn. Widely used for subsistence salmon fishing, the fish wheel provides an easy and inexpensive way of catching salmon without injuring them. Contrary to popular belief, Alaska Natives did not invent the fish wheel. Non-natives apparently first introduced the fish wheel on the Tanana River in 1904. Soon after, it appeared on the Yukon River, where it was used by both settlers and Natives. It first appeared on the Kuskokwim in 1914, when prospectors introduced it for catching salmon near Georgetown.

Today, subsistence fishing with the use of a fish wheel is allowed on the Copper River, as well as the Yukon River and its tributaries. Currently, there are 166 limited-entry permits for the use of fish wheels by commercial salmon fishermen on the Yukon River system — the only district where commercial and subsistence fishermen use the same gear. Fishing times with the wheels are regulated.

Prior to its appearance in Alaska, the fish wheel was used on the East Coast, on the Sacramento River in California and on the Columbia River in Washington and Oregon.

Fishing

Commercial

Alaska's commercial fish production is greater in value than that of any other state in the country and first in volume, according to the state Department of Fish & Game.

Value and Volume of Alaska Fish and Shellfish Landings*

Year	Value	Volume (in lbs.)
1976	$219,071,000	600,203,000
1977	333,844,000	658,754,000
1978	482,207,000	767,167,000
1979	622,284,000	854,247,000
1980	561,751,000	983,664,000
1981	639,797,000	975,245,000
1982	575,569,000	878,935,000
1983	543,941,000	963,765,000
1984	509,300,000	1,002,909,000
1985	590,751,000	1,184,807,000
1986	752,417,000	1,236,062,000
1987	941,690,000	1,697,547,000
1988	1,339,394,000	2,639,250,000
1989	1,332,000,000	5,213,100,000

*Source: National Marine Fisheries Service, U.S. Department of Commerce

Value of U.S. commercial fish landings caught off Alaska in 1988 (most current figures available) was $1.3 billion, followed by: Louisiana, second in value at $317 million; Massachusetts, $274 million; and California, $199 million.

Volume of Alaska's commercial fish landings in 1988 (a record year) of 2.6 billion pounds exceeded Louisiana, which recorded a volume of 1.4 billion pounds. In 1987, in world commercial fishery landings, Japan was first with 26.1 billion pounds; the USSR was second with 24.6 billion pounds; China was third with 20.6 billion pounds; and U.S. fourth with 12.7 billion pounds.

In 1988, out of the top 10 U.S. ports in terms of value, Alaska held six positions. Kodiak was first with $166.3 million in commercial fish landings; Dutch Harbor–Unalaska was third with $100.9 million; Kenai was fourth with $99.3 million; Petersburg was sixth

with $58.5 million; Cordova was eighth with $46.4 million; and Ketchikan was tenth with $43.5 million.

Joint-venture fisheries peaked in 1987, and though there was a decline in volume in 1988, value continued to increase. Joint ventures are catches by U.S. vessels unloaded onto foreign vessels within the U.S. Exclusive Economic Zone (EEZ). Partnerships have been formed between 18 U.S. companies and 38 foreign companies: 18 Japanese, 15 Korean, 3 Polish, 1 Chinese and 1 Russian.

Foreign Fishing

In 1987, U.S. fishermen participated in joint ventures delivering 3.5 billion pounds of fish valued at $213.8 million to foreign processors. These figures represent significant increases over 1986 landings (2.9 billion pounds worth $154.9 million).

Foreign fishing in Alaska waters, as in other U.S. waters, is governed by the Magnuson Fishery Conservation and Management Act of 1976. This act provides for the conservation and exclusive management by the U.S. of all fishery resources within the U.S. Exclusive Economic Zone (except for highly migratory species of tuna). The U.S. EEZ established by the act extends from 3 to 200 nautical miles from shore. In addition, the act provides for exclusive management authority over continental shelf fishery resources and anadromous species (those that mature in the ocean, then ascend streams to spawn in fresh water) beyond the 200-mile limit, except when they are within any recognized foreign nation's territorial sea. Foreign countries fishing within the U.S. zone do so under agreement with the U.S. and are subject to various fees.

Foreign catch within the U.S. EEZ was 328.4 million pounds in 1987, with Alaska supplying the largest share (46 percent) of the foreign catch, according to the National Marine Fisheries Service. This was a 75 percent decrease compared to 1986. Leading all other countries in the U.S. EEZ was Japan with 45 percent of the total catch. Poland was second with 33 percent of the 1987 catch. The total foreign catch of trawl fish in Alaska waters was 69,051 tons, a decrease of more than 400,000 tons over 1986. The total catch came from the Bering Sea and Aleutian Islands. In 1988, there was no foreign-directed fishery for groundfish off Alaska.

Types of Fish Caught

A dramatic strengthening of salmon runs in the mid-1970s brought new vitality to the Alaska fishing industry. Since 1977, the salmon catch more than doubled, reaching new highs in 1986. In 1989, Alaska landings of salmon were 699.2 million pounds, a new state record. The shellfish industry is suffering setbacks from the decline of all shellfish stocks except tanner crab.

In 1977, the U.S. fishing industry received priority to harvest within the 200-mile Exclusive Economic Zone, increasing future prospects of the Alaska groundfish industry, especially in the domestic U.S. market. While the price per pound of groundfish is much lower than that of salmon, the richness of the resource and the potential for value-added products, such as surimi, is beginning to capture the attention of the U.S. food industry. Surimi is a fish paste made from minced pollock and used as a base for manufactured products like imitation crab. With surimi growing in popularity, Alaska pollock landings were valued at $95 million in 1988, an increase over 1987.

Alaska's 1989 landings of salmon (699.2 million pounds) represented a 33 percent increase in volume over 1988 and were valued at $505 million. Halibut landings off Alaska in 1989 totaled 55.6 million pounds, valued at $76.1 million.

Alaska's 1989 king crab harvest increased, with a reported total catch of 26 million pounds, up from 21 million pounds in 1988. The statewide totals for other shellfish landed in 1989 included Dungeness crab, 7.5 million pounds; tanner crab, 163 million pounds; and shrimp, 1.9 million pounds.

The oil spill in Prince William Sound forced a closure of the 1989 herring roe fishery, substantially lowering the total herring harvest. In 1989, 96.7 million pounds of herring ($20.3 million value) was harvested; in 1988, there was 115 million pounds ($56 million value).

Following are Alaska Department of Fish & Game ex-vessel value figures:

Value of Alaska's Commercial Fisheries to Fishermen (in millions of dollars)

Species	1982	1983	1984*	1985	1986	1987	1988	1989
Salmon	310.3	320.6	335.0	389.0	414.0	457.9	744.9	505.0
Shellfish	213.5	147.0	102.1	106.3	186.4	213.5	235.6	274.0
Halibut	21.4	37.9	24.9	40.3	63.2	60.9	66.1	76.1
Herring	20.2	28.9	19.8	38.0	38.5	41.8	56.0	20.3
Groundfish	40.9	78.8**	108.8**	137.5**	197.9**	324.3	441.1	456.6

*Preliminary estimates.
**Includes international, joint-venture landings not previously shown in table.

1989 Preliminary Commercial Salmon Harvest (in thousands of fish)

Region	King	Red	Silver	Pink	Chum	Total
Southeast	287	2,115	2,133	59,317	1,935	65,787
Central (Prince William Sound, Cook Inlet, Kodiak, Chignik and Bristol Bay)	99	35,537	943	23,246	1,713	61,538
Arctic-Yukon-Kuskokwim	175	83	684	89	2,330	3,272
Western (Alaska Peninsula and Aleutian Islands)	21	6,840	741	13,952	1,173	22,726
Total	583	44,575	4,500	96,516	7,152	153,325

Note: Preliminary statistics are from ADF&G, 1989.

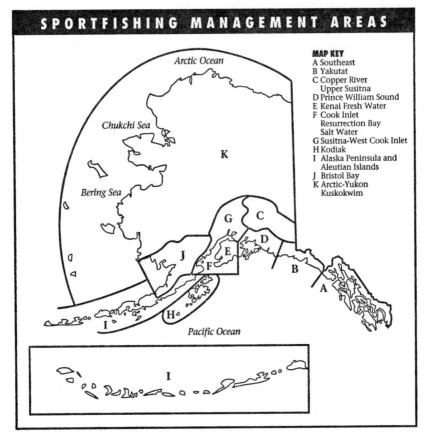

SPORTFISHING MANAGEMENT AREAS

MAP KEY
A Southeast
B Yakutat
C Copper River
   Upper Susitna
D Prince William Sound
E Kenai Fresh Water
F Cook Inlet
   Resurrection Bay
   Salt Water
G Susitna-West Cook Inlet
H Kodiak
I Alaska Peninsula and
   Aleutian Islands
J Bristol Bay
K Arctic-Yukon
   Kuskokwim

Related reading: *Alaska Blues: A Fisherman's Journal*, by Joe Upton. Award-winning saga of salmon fishing in southeastern Alaska. Illustrated with 198 black-and-white photos. *Fisheries of the North Pacific*, by Robert J. Browning. Revision of the earlier classic. *Pacific Troller: Life on the Northwest Fishing Grounds*, by Francis E. Caldwell. *The Pacific Halibut: The Resource and the Fishery*, by F. Heward Bell. Includes nearly 288 pages of history on the fishery; with more than 300 photos, maps, and illustrations. See ALASKA NORTHWEST LIBRARY in the back of the book.

Sport

There are 12 sportfishing management areas in Alaska, each with its own bag and possession limits and possible special provisions. Current copies of *Alaska Sport Fishing Regulations Summary* are available from the Department of Fish and Game, Box 3-2000, Juneau 99802. Also available from the department are the free booklets *Sport Fishing Predictions* and the *Alaska Sport Fishing Guide*.

Regulations

A sportfishing license is required for residents and nonresidents 16 years of age or older. (Alaskan residents 60 years of age or more who have been residents one year or more do not need a sportfishing license as long as they remain residents; a special identification card is issued for this exemption.)

Resident sportfishing licenses cost $10, valid for the calendar year issued (nonresident, $36; 3-day nonresident, $10; 14-day nonresident, $20). A resident is a person who has maintained a permanent place of abode within the state for 12 consecutive months and has continuously maintained a voting residence in the state. Military personnel on active duty permanently stationed in the state and their dependents can purchase a nonresident military sportfishing license ($10).

Nearly all sporting goods stores in Alaska sell fishing licenses. They are also available by mail from the Alaska Department of Revenue, Fish and Game License Section, 1111 W. Eighth St., Room 108, Juneau 99801.

The following sport fish species information includes the best bait or lure and the state record fish weight in pounds and ounces.

Arctic char: spoon, eggs, 17 lbs. 8 oz.
Arctic grayling: flies, 4 lbs. 13 oz.
Burbot: bait, 24 lbs. 12 oz.
Chum salmon: spoon, 32 lbs.
Cutthroat trout: bait, spin, flies, 8 lbs. 6 oz.
Dolly Varden: bait, spin, flies, 17 lbs. 8 oz.
Halibut: octopus, herring, 450 lbs.
King salmon: herring, 97 lbs. 4 oz.
Kokanee: spin, eggs, 2 lbs.
Lake trout: spoon, plug, 47 lbs.
Northern pike: spoon, spin, 38 lbs.
Pink salmon: small spoon, 12 lbs. 9 oz.
Rainbow trout: flies, lures, bait, 42 lbs. 3 oz.
Red salmon: flies, 16 lbs.
Sheefish: spoon, 53 lbs.
Silver salmon: herring, spoon, 26 lbs.
Steelhead trout: spoon, eggs, 42 lbs. 3 oz.
Whitefish: flies, eggs, 7 lbs. 2 oz.

Related reading: *The ALASKA WILDERNESS MILEPOST®.* Includes information on sportfishing throughout the entire state on all major river systems. *Alaska's Saltwater Fishes.* A field guide designed for quick identification of 375 species of saltwater fish. See ALASKA NORTHWEST LIBRARY in the back of the book.

Furs and Trapping

According to the state furbearer biologist, the major sources of harvested Alaska furs are the Yukon and Kuskokwim valleys. The Arctic provides limited numbers of arctic fox, wolverine and wolf, but the gulf coast areas and Southeast are more productive. Southeast Alaska is a good source of mink and otter.

Trapping is seasonal work, and most trappers work summers at fishing or other employment. (Licenses are required for trapping. See Hunting section for cost of licenses.)

State regulated furbearers are beaver, coyote, red fox (includes cross, black or silver color phases), arctic fox (includes white or blue), lynx, marmot, marten, mink, muskrat, raccoon, river (land) otter, squirrel (parka or ground, flying and red), weasel, wolf and wolverine. Very little harvest or use is made of parka squirrels and marmots.

Flying squirrels are not caught deliberately, and raccoons, introduced in a couple of coastal locations years ago, appear to have been exterminated.

Prices for raw skins are widely variable and depend on the buyer, quality, condition and size of the fur. Pelts accepted for purchase are beaver, coyote, lynx, marten, mink, muskrat, otter, red and white fox, red squirrel, weasel (ermine), wolf and wolverine. Check with a buyer for current market prices.

Related reading: *Trapline Twins,* by Julie and Miki Collins. Identical-twin sisters trap, canoe, dogsled and live off the land. *Trails of an Alaska Trapper,* by Ray Tremblay. See ALASKA NORTHWEST LIBRARY in the back of the book.

Glaciers and Ice Fields

The greatest concentrations of glaciers are in the Alaska Range, Wrangell Mountains, and the coastal ranges of the Chugach, Coast, Kenai and St. Elias mountains, where annual precipitation is high. All of Alaska's well-known glaciers fall within these areas. According to the U.S. Geological Survey, distribution of glacier ice is as follows:

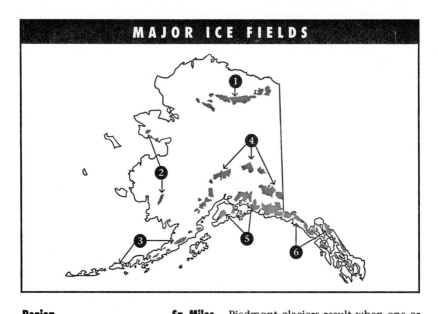

Region	Sq. Miles (approx.)
1 North: Brooks Range	279
2 West: Seward Peninsula	2
Kilbuk–Wood River mountains	89
3 Southwest: Aleutian Islands	371
Alaska Peninsula	483
4 Interior: Alaska Range	5,367
Talkeetna Mountains	309
Wrangell Mountains	3,205
5 Southcentral: Kenai Mtns	1,776
Chugach Mountains	8,340
6 Southeast: St. Elias Mtns	4,556
Coast Mountains	4,055
Total.	28,842

Glaciers cover approximately 30,000 square miles — or 3 percent — of Alaska, which is 128 times more area covered by glaciers than in the rest of the United States. There are an estimated 100,000 glaciers in Alaska, ranging from tiny cirque glaciers to huge valley glaciers.

Glaciers are formed where, over a number of years, more snow falls than melts. Alaska's glaciers fall roughly into five general categories: alpine, valley, piedmont, ice fields and ice caps. Alpine (mountain and cirque) glaciers head high on the slopes of mountains and plateaus. Valley glaciers are an overflowing accumulation of ice from mountain or plateau basins.

Piedmont glaciers result when one or more glaciers join to form a fan-shaped ice mass at the foot of a mountain range. Ice fields develop when large valley glaciers interconnect, leaving only the highest peaks and ridges to rise above the ice surface. Ice caps are smaller snow- and ice-filled basins or plateaus.

Alaska's better-known glaciers accessible by road are: Worthington and Black Rapids (Richardson Highway); Matanuska (Glenn Highway); Portage (Seward Highway) and Mendenhall (Glacier Highway). In addition, Childs and Sheridan glaciers may be reached by car from Cordova, and Valdez Glacier is only a few miles from the town of Valdez. The sediment-covered terminus of Muldrow Glacier in Denali National Park and Preserve is visible at a distance along several miles of the park road.

Many spectacular glaciers in Glacier Bay National Park and Preserve and in Prince William Sound are accessible by tour boat.

Glacier ice often appears blue because its great thickness absorbs all the colors of the spectrum except blue, which is reflected back.

Other facts about glaciers:
• About three-fourths of all the fresh

water in Alaska is stored as glacial ice. This is many times greater than the volume of water stored in all the state's lakes, ponds, rivers and reservoirs.

• Longest tidewater glacier in North America is Hubbard, 76 miles in length (heads in Canada). In 1986, Hubbard rapidly advanced and blocked Russell Fiord near Yakutat. Later in the year, the ice dam gave way.

• Longest glacier is Bering (including Bagley Icefield), over 100 miles in length.

• Southernmost active tidewater glacier in North America is LeConte.

• Greatest concentration of tidewater-calving glaciers is in Prince William Sound, with 20 active tidewater glaciers.

• Largest glacier is Malaspina, 850 square miles; the Malaspina Glacier complex (including tributary glaciers) is approximately 2,000 square miles in area. The Bering Glacier complex, which includes Bagley Icefield, is approximately 2,250 square miles.

• La Perouse Glacier in Glacier Bay National Park is the only calving glacier in North America that discharges icebergs directly into the open Pacific Ocean.

• Iceberg production in Prince William Sound is expected to increase fourfold in the next 20 years as Columbia Glacier retreats.

• There are more than 750 glacier-dammed lakes in Alaska; the largest at the present time is 28-square-mile Chakachamna Lake west of Anchorage.

Gold

The largest gold nugget ever found in Alaska was discovered near Nome. The nugget, weighing 155 troy ounces, was found Sept. 29, 1903, on Discovery Claim on Anvil Creek, Nome District. The nugget was 7 inches long, 4 inches wide and 2 inches thick.

Four other large nuggets have been found in Alaska, one of which also came from the Discovery Claim on Anvil Creek in 1899. It was the largest Alaska nugget found up to that time, weighing 82.2 troy ounces, and was 6¹/₄ inches long, 3¹/₄ inches wide, 1³/₈ inches thick at one end and ¹/₂ inch thick at the other. In 1914, the second-largest nugget mined, weighing 138.8 troy ounces, was found near Discovery Claim on Hammond River, Wiseman District. Two of the top five nuggets have been discovered this decade, with one coming from Lower Glacier Creek, Kantishna District, in 1984, weighing 91.8 troy ounces, and the other from Ganes Creek, Innoko District, in 1986, weighing 122 troy ounces.

According to *Alaska's Mineral Industry 1989*, a publication of the Alaska Division of Geological and Geophysical Surveys, major operators produced 297,900 troy ounces of gold in 1989. This was a 12 percent increase from 1988. The 1989 product was the largest recorded in Alaska in 47 years and amounted to 39 percent of the total $295 million in minerals produced in 1989. In 1988, the price of gold averaged $425 an ounce, and in 1989, the average was $382.

Following are volume (in troy ounces) and value figures for recent years of Alaska gold production.

Gold Production in Alaska, 1980–89

Year	Vol. (in troy oz.)	Value
1980	75,000	$32,000,000
1981	134,000	55,200,000
1982	174,900	69,960,000
1983	169,000	67,600,000
1984	175,000	63,000,000
1985	190,000	61,175,000
1986	160,000	60,800,000
1987	229,700	104,500,000
1988	265,500	112,837,000
1989	297,900	113,796,000

The chart following shows the fluctuation in the price of gold after the gold standard was lifted in 1967. Note that these are average annual prices and do not reflect the highest or lowest prices during the year.

Average Annual Price of Gold, per Troy Ounce

Prior to 1934 — $20.67	1978 — 193.55
1934 to 1967 — 35.00	1979 — 307.50
1968 — 39.26	1980 — 569.73
1969 — 41.51	1981 — 548.90
1970 — 36.41	1982 — 461.00
1971 — 41.25	1983 — 400.00
1972 — 58.60	1984 — 360.00
1973 — 97.81	1985 — 325.00
1974 — 159.74	1986 — 380.00
1975 — 161.49	1987 — 447.00
1976 — 125.32	1988 — 425.00
1977 — 148.31	1989 — 381.98

If you are interested in gold panning, sluicing or suction dredging in Alaska — whether for fun or profit — you'll have to know whose land you are on and familiarize yourself with current regulations.

Panning, sluicing and suction dredging on private property, established mining claims and Native lands is considered trespassing unless you have the consent of the owner. On state and federal lands, contact the agency for the area you are interested in for current restrictions on mining.

You can pan for gold for a small fee by visiting one of the commercial gold panning resorts in Alaska. These resorts rent gold pans and let you try your luck on gold-bearing creeks and streams on their property.

If you want to stake a permanent claim, the state Department of Natural Resources has a free booklet, *Regulations and Statutes Pertaining to Mining Rights of Alaska Lands,* which can be obtained by contacting the department office in Juneau, (907) 465-2400; Fairbanks, (907) 451-2790; and Anchorage, (907) 762-2518.

Gold Strikes and Rushes

1848 — First Alaska gold discovery (Russian on Kenai Peninsula)

1861 — Stikine River near Telegraph Creek, British Columbia

1872 — Cassiar district in Canada (Stikine headwaters country)

1872 — Near Sitka

1874 — Windham Bay near Juneau

1880 — Gold Creek at Juneau

1886 — Fortymile discovery

1887 — Yakutat beach areas and Lituya Bay

1893 — Mastodon Creek, starting Circle City

1895 — Sunrise district on Kenai Peninsula

1896 — Klondike strike, Bonanza Creek, Yukon, Canada

1898 — Anvil Creek near Nome; Atlin district

1898 — British Columbia

1900 — Porcupine rush out of Haines

1902 — Fairbanks (Felix Pedro, Upper Goldstream Valley)

1906 — Innoko

1907 — Ruby

1908 — Iditarod

1913 — Marshall

1913 — Chisana

1914 — Livengood

Related reading: *Chilkoot Pass: The Most Famous Trail in the North,* revised and expanded edition, by Archie Satterfield. *The Gold Hustlers,* by Lewis Green. *Nome Nuggets,* by L. H. French. See ALASKA NORTHWEST LIBRARY in the back of the book.

Government

(*See also* Courts *and* Officials)

The capital of Alaska is Juneau. In November 1976, Alaska voters chose Willow as their new capital site. In a second election six years later, voters chose to keep Juneau as the capital city.

Alaska is represented in the U.S. Congress by two senators and one representative.

A governor and lieutenant governor are elected by popular vote for four-year terms on the same ticket. The governor is given extensive powers under the constitution. He administers 15 major departments: Administration, Commerce and Economic

Development, Community and Regional Affairs, Corrections, Education, Environmental Conservation, Fish and Game, Health and Social Services, Labor, Law, Military and Veterans Affairs, Natural Resources, Public Safety, Revenue, and Transportation and Public Facilities.

The legislature is bicameral, with 20 senators elected from 14 senate districts for four-year terms, and 40 representatives from 27 election districts for two-year terms. Under the state constitution, redistricting is accomplished every 10 years, after the reporting of the decennial federal census. The latest redistricting occurred in 1981 and was carried out by the governor's office with assistance of an advisory apportionment board. The judiciary consists of a state supreme court, court of appeals, superior court, district courts and magistrates.

Local government is by a system of organized boroughs, much like counties in other states. Several areas of the state are not included in any borough because of sparse population. Boroughs generally provide a more limited number of services than cities. There are three classes. First- and second-class boroughs have three mandatory powers: education, land use planning, and tax assessment and collection. The major difference between the two classes is in how they may acquire other powers. Both classes have separately elected borough assemblies and school boards. A third-class borough has two mandatory powers: operation of public schools and taxation. All boroughs may assess, levy and collect real and personal property taxes. They may also levy sales taxes.

Incorporated cities are small units of local government, serving one community. There are two classes. First-class cities, generally urban areas, have six-member councils and a separately elected mayor. Taxing authority is somewhat broader than for second-class cities and responsibilities are broader. A first-class city that has adopted a home rule charter is called a home rule city; adoption allows the city to revise its ordinances, to the extent that the powers it assumes are those not prohibited by law or charter. Second-class cities, generally places with fewer than 400 people (but not less than 25), are governed by a seven-member council, one of whom serves as mayor. Taxing authority is limited. A borough and all cities located within it may unite in a single unit of government called a unified municipality.

There is also one community organized under federal law. Originally an Indian reservation, Metlakatla was organized so municipal services could effectively be provided to its residents.

In 1990, there were 14 organized boroughs and unified home rule municipalities: 3 unified home rule municipalities, 3 home rule boroughs, 7 second-class boroughs and 1 third-class borough.

Alaska's 149 incorporated cities include: 12 home rule cities, 22 first-class cities and 115 second-class cities. One city, Metlakatla, is organized under federal law.

BOROUGH ADDRESSES AND CONTACTS
Aleutians East Borough
P.O. Box 349, Sand Point 99661; phone (907) 383-2699
Bristol Bay Borough
Contact: Borough Clerk, P.O. Box 189, Naknek 99633; phone (907) 246-4224
City and Borough of Juneau
Contact: City-Borough Manager, 155 S. Seward St., Juneau 99801; phone (907) 586-5278
City and Borough of Sitka
Contact: Administrator, 304 Lake St., Room 104, Sitka 99835; phone (907) 747-3294
Fairbanks North Star Borough
Contact: Clerk, P.O. Box 1267, Fairbanks 99707; phone (907) 452-4761
Haines Borough
Contact: Borough Secretary, P.O. Box H, Haines 99827; phone (907) 766-2694
Kenai Peninsula Borough
Contact: Borough Clerk, 144 N. Binkley St., Soldotna 99669; phone (907) 262-4441
Ketchikan Gateway Borough
Contact: Borough Manager, 344 Front St., Ketchikan 99901; phone (907) 225-6151

Kodiak Island Borough
Contact: Borough Mayor or Borough Clerk, 710 Mill Bay Road, Kodiak 99615; phone (907) 486-5736

Lake and Peninsula Borough
c/o Lake and Peninsula School District, P.O. Box 498, King Salmon 99613; phone (907) 276-4280

Matanuska-Susitna Borough
Contact: Borough Manager, P.O. Box 1608, Palmer 99645; phone (907) 745-4801

Municipality of Anchorage
Contact: Mayor's Office or Manager's Office, P.O. Box 196650, Anchorage 99519; phone (907) 343-4431

North Slope Borough
Contact: Borough Mayor, P.O. Box 69, Barrow 99723; phone (907) 852-2611

Northwest Arctic Borough
P.O. Box 1110, Kotzebue 99752; phone (907) 442-2500

Highways

(*See also* Alaska Highway *and* Dalton Highway)

As of June 30, 1989, the state Department of Transportation and Public Facilities showed 14,418 miles of highways, including those in national parks and forests (1,963), and 2,229 miles of ferry routes. Of the roads included in the Alaska Highway System, 3,003 miles were unpaved, 2,676 miles were paved. In addition, there were 2,110 miles of local city streets, 2,030 miles of borough roads and 407 miles listed as "other." Alaska's relative sparseness of roadway is accentuated by a comparison to Austria, a country only one-eighteenth the size of Alaska but with nearly twice as many public roads.

The following chart lists each major highway in Alaska, its route number, the year the highway opened to vehicle traffic and its total length within Alaska (most of the Alaska Highway, Haines Highway and Klondike Highway 2 lie within Canada). Also indicated is whether the highway is open all year or closed in winter.

Related reading: *The MILEPOST®* All-the-North Travel Guide®. A compre-

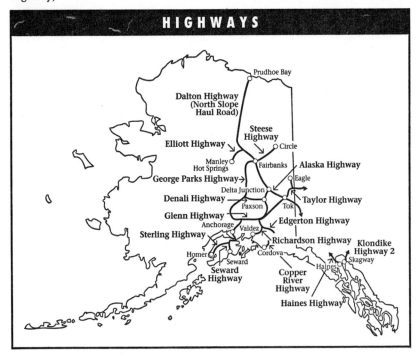

	Alaska Route	Year	Total Length (miles) Paved	Gravel	Open
Alaska	2	1942	298.2*		All year
Copper River	10	**	12.4	35.7	Apr.–Oct.
Dalton	12	1974	416		All year
Denali	8	1957	21	115	Apr.–Oct.
Edgerton	10	1923	19	14	All year
Elliott	2	1959	28	124	All year
George Parks	3	1971	322.7		All year
Glenn	1	1942	328*		All year
Haines	7	1947	40.5		All year
Klondike	98	1978	14.6		All year
Richardson	4	1923	368*		All year
Seward	1&9	1951	127		All year
Steese	6	1928	43.8	118.2	All year
Sterling	1	1950	135.8		All year
Taylor	5	1953		161	Apr.–Oct.

*The Richardson shares a common alignment with the Alaska Highway (for 98 miles) and with the Glenn (for 14 miles).

**Construction on the Copper River Highway — which was to link up with Chitina on the Edgerton — was halted by the 1964 Good Friday earthquake, which damaged the Million Dollar Bridge, and local Cordova citizens who desired semi-isolation.

hensive travel guide with mile-by-mile logs of all access highways and travel by air, rail, water. Includes accommodations, cities, villages, parks, wildlife; hints for fishermen, bicyclists, hikers. Numerous photos and maps. See ALASKA NORTHWEST LIBRARY in the back of the book.

Hiking

A variety of hiking trails for all levels of ability may be found in the state. The experienced hiker with proper topographic maps will find some of the best Alaska hiking is cross-country above tree line. Using both maps and tide tables, it is also feasible to hike along ocean shorelines at low tide.

Hikers in Alaska must plan for rapidly changing, inclement weather. Take rain gear. If staying overnight in the back country, it's wise to carry a tent if a cabin is unavailable. Above tree line, snow can be encountered at any time of year.

Sporting goods stores in Alaska feature an excellent selection of hiking equipment. In addition, back country guides often furnish equipment on escorted expeditions.

Information on hiking in Alaska's national parks and monuments is available from the Alaska Public Lands Information Centers: 605 W. Fourth Ave., Suite 105, Anchorage 99501; 250 Cushman St., Suite 1A, Fairbanks 99701; and P.O. Box 359, Tok 99780; or from park headquarters for the area you're interested in. (*See* National Parks, Preserves and Monuments.)

The Alaska Division of Parks (*see* State Park System) has information on hiking on the lands managed by that agency.

History

6,000–11,000 years ago — Human culture in southeastern, Aleutians, Interior and northwestern Arctic Alaska.

6,000 years ago — Most recent migration from Siberia across the land bridge. Earliest migration believed to have taken place 25,000 years ago.

3,000–5,000 years ago — Human culture present on the Bering Sea coast.

1725 — Vitus Bering sent by Peter the Great to explore the North Pacific.

1741 — On a later expedition, Bering in one ship and Alexei Chirikof in another ship, discover Alaska. Chirikof, according to ship logs, probably sees land on July 15, a day ahead of his leader, who was perhaps 300 miles or more to the

north. Georg Steller goes ashore on Kayak Island, becoming the first white man known to have set foot on Alaska soil.

1743 — Russians begin concentrated hunting of sea otter, continuing until the species is almost decimated; fur seal hunting begins later.

1774-94 — Explorations of Alaska waters by Juan Perez, James Cook and George Vancouver.

1784 — First Russian settlement in Alaska established at Three Saints Bay, Kodiak Island.

1794 — Vancouver sights Mount McKinley.

1799 — Alexander Baranof establishes the Russian post known today as Old Sitka. A trade charter is granted to the Russian-American Company.

1821 — Russians prohibit trading in Alaska waters by other nations, making the Russian-American Company the sole trading firm.

1824-42 — Russian exploration of the mainland leads to the discovery of the Kuskokwim, Nushagak, Yukon and Koyukuk rivers.

1847 — Fort Yukon is established by Hudson's Bay Company.

1848 — First mining begins in Alaska, on the Kenai Peninsula.

1853 — Russian explorers-trappers find the first oil seeps in Cook Inlet.

1857 — Coal mining begins at Coal Harbor, Kenai Peninsula, to supply steamers.

1859 — Baron Edoard de Stoecki, minister and chargé d'affaires of the Russian delegation to the United States, is given authority to negotiate the sale of Alaska.

1867 — United States under President Andrew Johnson buys Alaska from Russia for $7.2 million; the treaty is signed March 30 and formal transfer takes place on October 18 at Sitka. Fur seal population begins to stabilize. U.S. Army is given jurisdiction over the Department of Alaska the following year.

1872 — Gold is discovered near Sitka. Later discoveries include Windham, 1874; Juneau, 1880; Fortymile, 1886; Circle City, 1893; Sunrise District (Kenai Peninsula), 1895; Nome, 1898; Fairbanks, 1902; Innoko, 1906; Ruby, 1907; Iditarod, 1908; Marshall, 1913; Chisana, 1913; and Livengood, 1914.

1878 — First salmon canneries established at Klawock and Old Sitka.

1887 — Tsimshians, under Father William Duncan, arrive at Metlakatla from British Columbia.

1891 — First oil claims staked in Cook Inlet area.

1897-1900 — Klondike gold rush in Yukon Territory; heavy traffic through Alaska on the way to the gold fields.

1902 — First oil production, at Katalla. Telegraph from Eagle to Valdez is completed.

1906 — Peak gold production year. Alaska is granted a nonvoting delegate to Congress.

1911 — Copper production begins at Kennicott.

1912 — Territorial status for Alaska; first territorial legislature is convened the following year.

1913 — First airplane flight in Alaska, at Fairbanks; first auto trip from Fairbanks to Valdez.

1914 — President Wilson authorizes construction of the Alaska Railroad.

1916 — First bill proposing Alaska statehood is introduced in Congress; peak copper production year.

1922 — First pulp mill starts production at Speel River, near Juneau.

1923 — President Warren Harding drives spike completing the Alaska Railroad.

1930 — The first "talkie" motion picture is shown in Fairbanks, featuring the Marx Brothers in *The Cocoanuts*.

1935 — Matanuska Valley Project, which establishes farming families in Alaska, begins. First Juneau to Fairbanks flight.

1936 — All-time record salmon catch in Alaska — 126.4 million fish.

1940 — Military build-up in Alaska; Fort Richardson, Elmendorf Air Force Base are established. At this point there are only about 40,000 non-Native Alaskans and 32,458 Natives. Pan American Airways inaugurates twice-weekly service between Seattle, Ketchikan and Juneau, using Sikorsky flying boats.

1942 — Dutch Harbor is bombed and Attu and Kiska islands are occupied by Japanese forces. Alaska Highway is built — first overland connection to Lower 48.

1943 — Japanese forces are driven from Alaska.

1944 — Alaska-Juneau Mine shuts down.

1953 — Oil well is drilled near Eureka, on the Glenn Highway, marking the start of modern oil history; first plywood mill at Juneau; first big pulp mill at Ketchikan.

1957 — Kenai oil strike.

1958 — Statehood measure is passed by Congress; statehood is proclaimed officially on Jan. 3, 1959. Sitka pulp mill opens.

1964 — Good Friday earthquake, March 27, causes heavy damage throughout the gulf coast region; 131 people lose their lives.

1967 — Alaska Centennial celebration; Fairbanks flood.

1968 — Oil and gas discoveries at Prudhoe Bay on the North Slope; $900 million North Slope oil lease sale the following year; pipeline proposal follows.

1971 — Congress approves Alaska Native Land Claims Settlement Act, granting title to 40 million acres of land and providing more than $900 million in payment to Alaska Natives.

1974 — Trans-Alaska pipeline receives final approval; construction build-up begins.

1975 — Population and labor force soar with construction of pipeline; Alaska Gross Products hits $5.8 billion — double the 1973 figure.

1976 — Voters select Willow area for new capital site.

1977 — Completion of the trans-Alaska pipeline from Prudhoe Bay to Valdez; shipment of first oil by tanker from Valdez to Puget Sound.

1978 — A 200-mile off-shore fishing limit goes into effect. President Jimmy Carter withdraws 56 million acres to create 17 new national monuments as of Dec. 1, 1978.

1979 — State of Alaska files suit to halt the withdrawal of 56 million acres of Alaska land by President Carter under the Antiquities Act.

1980 — Special session of the Alaska Legislature votes to repeal the state income tax and provides for refunds of 1979 taxes. Legislature establishes a Permanent Fund as a repository for one-fourth of all royalty oil revenues for future generations. Census figures show Alaska's population grew by 32.4 percent during the 1970s. The Alaska Lands Act of 1980 puts 53.7 million Alaska acres into the national wildlife refuge system, parts of 25 rivers into the national wild and scenic rivers system, 3.3 million acres into national forest lands and 43.6 million acres into national park land.

1981 — Legislature puts on the ballot a constitutional amendment proposal to limit state spending. Secretary of the Interior James Watt initiates plans to sell oil and gas leases on 130 million acres of Alaska's nonrestricted federal land and announces a tentative schedule to open 16 offshore areas of Alaska as part of an intense national search for oil and gas on the outer continental shelf.

1982 — Oil revenues for state decrease. Vote for funds to move state capital from Juneau to Willow is defeated. First permanent fund dividend checks of $1,000 each are mailed to every six-month resident of Alaska.

1983 — Record-breaking salmon harvest in Bristol Bay. Building permits set a record at just under $1 billion.

1984 — State of Alaska celebrates its 25th birthday.

1985 — Anchorage receives the U.S. bid for the 1994 Olympics. Iditarod Sled Dog Race is won by Libby Riddles, the first woman to win in the history of the race.

1986 — World Championship Sled Dog Race held during Fur Rendezvous is canceled for the first time due to lack of snow. Iditarod Sled Dog Race is again won by a woman, Susan Butcher of Manley.

1987 — Alaska is retained as America's choice for the 1994 Olympics. The Iditarod Sled Dog Race is won by Susan Butcher for the second straight year.

1988 — The first successful solo winter ascent of Mount McKinley by Vern Tejas of Anchorage. The Iditarod Sled Dog Race is won by Susan Butcher for the third year in a row. Anchorage loses its bid to Norway for the 1994 Olympics.

1989 — Record-breaking cold hits entire state lasting for weeks. Worst oil spill in U.S. history occurs in Prince William Sound. Soviets visit Alaska, and the Bering Bridge Expedition crosses the Bering Strait by dogsled and skis. Mount Redoubt begins erupting in December.

1990 — Valdez sets a new record for snowfall. Susan Butcher wins her fourth Iditarod Sled Dog Race. (*See also* Yearly Highlights)

Related reading: Many of the books listed in the ALASKA NORTHWEST LIBRARY in the back of the book are totally or in part about Alaska history.

Holidays 1991

New Year's Day ....January 1
Martin Luther King Day .....January 21
Lincoln's Birthday.............February 12
Washington's Birthday
— holiday ....February 18
— traditional ....February 22
Seward's Day*........................March 25
Memorial Day
— holiday ....May 27
— traditional ....May 30
Independence Day ....July 4
Labor Day ....September 2
Alaska Day*........................October 18
Veterans Day ....November 11
Thanksgiving Day ....November 28
Christmas Day ....December 25

*Seward's Day commemorates the signing of the treaty by which the United States bought Alaska from Russia, signed on March 30, 1867. Alaska Day is the anniversary of the formal transfer of the territory and the raising of the U.S. flag at Sitka on Oct. 18, 1867.

Hooligan

Smelt, also known as eulachon or candlefish (because these oily little fish can be burned like candles), are known as "ooligan" in southeastern Alaska. Hooligan are caught by dip-netting as they travel upriver to spawn.

Hospitals and Health Facilities

(*See also* Pioneers' Homes)
Alaska has numerous hospitals, nursing homes and other health facilities. The only hospital in the state currently offering specialized care units is Providence Hospital in Anchorage, with its thermal unit (burn and frostbite), cancer treatment center and neonatal intensive care nursery.

A list of emergency medical services on Alaska's highways and marine highways is provided in a brochure available from the Office of Emergency Medical Services, Division of Public Health, Dept. of Health and Social Services, P.O. Box H-06C, Juneau 99811.

MUNICIPAL, PRIVATE AND STATE HOSPITALS
Anchorage
Alaska Psychiatric Institute (176 beds), 2900 Providence Drive, 99508
Alaska Treatment Center (out-patient rehabilitation facility), 3710 E. 20th Ave., 99508
Charter North Hospital (80 beds), 2530 DeBarr Road, 99514
Humana Hospital (238 beds), 2801 DeBarr Road, P.O. Box 143889, 99514
North Star Hospital (34 beds), 1650 S. Bragaw, 99508
Providence Hospital (341 beds), 3200 Providence Drive, P.O. Box 196604, 99519
Cordova
Cordova Community Hospital (23 beds), Box 160, 99574
Fairbanks
Fairbanks Memorial Hospital (177 beds), 1650 Cowles St., 99701
Glennallen
Cross Road Medical Center (6 beds), Box 5, 99588

Homer
South Peninsula Hospital (39 beds),
4300 Bartlett St., 99603
Juneau
Bartlett Memorial Hospital (51 beds),
3260 Hospital Drive, 99801
Juneau Recovery Unit (15 alcoholism
treatment beds), 3250 Hospital
Drive, 99801
Ketchikan
Ketchikan General Hospital (46 beds),
3100 Tongass Ave., 99901
Kodiak
Kodiak Island Hospital (44 beds), 1915
E. Rezanof Drive, 99615
Palmer
Valley Hospital (36 beds), P.O. Box
1687, 99645
Petersburg
Petersburg General Hospital (25 beds),
Box 589, 99833
Seward
Seward General Hospital (32 beds), Box
365, 99664
Sitka
Sitka Community Hospital (24 beds),
209 Moller Drive, 99835
Soldotna
Central Peninsula General Hospital (62
beds), 250 Hospital Place, 99669
Valdez
Harborview Developmental Center
(state-operated residential center for
the mentally handicapped; 80 beds),
Box 487, 99686
Valdez Community Hospital (15 beds),
Box 550, 99686
Wrangell
Wrangell General Hospital (14 beds),
Box 1081, 99929

U.S. PUBLIC HEALTH SERVICE HOSPITALS
Anchorage
Alaska Native Medical Center (170
beds), Box 107741, 99510
Barrow
PHS Alaska Native Hospital (14 beds),
99723
Bethel
Yukon-Kuskokwim Delta Service Unit
(51 beds), 99559
Dillingham
Bristol Bay Area Kanakanak Hospital
(15 beds), P.O. Box 10235, 99576
Kotzebue
Kotzebue Service Unit (31 beds), 99752
Nome
Norton Sound Regional Hospital (22

beds), P.O. Box 966, 99762
Sitka
SEARHC Medical Center (78 beds), 222
Tongass Drive, 99835

MILITARY HOSPITALS
Adak
Branch Hospital, NAVSTA Adak, FPO
Seattle 98791
Naval Regional Medical Center,
NAVSTA Adak, FPO Seattle 98791
Eielson Air Force Base
Eielson Air Force Base Clinic, 99702
Elmendorf AFB
Elmendorf Air Force Base Hospital,
99506
Fort Greely
Fort Greely Dispensary, Box 488, APO
Seattle 98733
Fort Richardson
U.S. Army Health Clinic, 99505
Fort Wainwright
Bassett Army Hospital, 99703
Ketchikan
Coast Guard Dispensary, 99901
Kodiak
Coast Guard Dispensary, Box 2,
99619
Mount Edgecumbe
Sitka Coast Guard Air Station, Box
6-5000, 99835

NURSING HOMES
Anchorage
Our Lady of Compassion (224 beds),
4900 Eagle, 99503
Cordova
Cordova Community Hospital Nursing
Home (10 beds), P.O. Box 160,
99574
Fairbanks
Denali Center (101 beds), 1949 Gillam
Way, 99701
Homer
South Peninsula Hospital (16 beds),
4300 Bartlett St., 99603
Juneau
Saint Ann's Nursing Home (45 beds),
415 Sixth St., 99801
Ketchikan
Island View Manor (44 beds), 3100
Tongass Ave., 99901
Petersburg
Petersburg General Hospital (14 beds),
P.O. Box 589, 99833
Seward
Wesleyan Nursing Home (66 beds),
Box 430, 99664

Soldotna
Heritage Place (45 beds), 232 Rockwell
Ave., 99669
Wrangell
Wrangell General Hospital (14 beds),
P.O. Box 80, 99929

Hostels

Alaska has 13 youth hostels, located
as follows:

Anchorage International Hostel, 700
H St., Anchorage 99501. Located on
the corner of Seventh and H streets.

Alyeska International Youth Hostel,
P.O. Box 10-4099, Anchorage 99510.
Located 40 miles south of Anchor-
age on Alpina in Girdwood.

Bear Creek Camp and Hostel, P.O. Box
334, Haines 99827. Located Mile 2
Small Tract Road.

Delta Youth Hostel, P.O. Box 971,
Delta Junction 99737. Located three
miles from Milepost 272 on Richardson Highway.

Fairbanks Youth Hostel, P.O. Box
2196, Fairbanks 99701. Located at
Tanana Valley Fairgrounds.

Juneau International Hostel, 614
Harris St., Juneau 99801. Located
four blocks northeast of the capitol
building.

Ketchikan Youth Hostel, P.O. Box
8515, Ketchikan 99901. Located in
United Methodist Church, Grant
and Main streets.

**Mentasta Mountain Wilderness
Lodge,** P.O. Box 950, Slana 99586.
Write for details.

Sheep Mountain Lodge, SRC Box
8490, Palmer 99645. Located at Mile
113.5 of the Glenn Highway.

Sitka Youth Hostel, P.O. Box 2645,
Sitka 99835. Located in United
Methodist Church, Edgecumbe and
Kimsham streets.

Snow River International Hostel,
HRC 64, Box 425, Seward 99664.
Located at Mile 16 of the Seward
Highway.

Soldotna International Youth Hostel,
P.O. Box 327, Soldotna 99669.
Located at 444 Riverview Drive.

Tok International Youth Hostel, P.O.
Box 532, Tok 99780. Located one
mile south of Mile 1322.5 of the
Alaska Highway.

The hostels in Alyeska, Anchorage,
Juneau, Seward, Slana and Soldotna are
open year-round. All others are open
only in the summer, and all of the
hostels accept reservations by mail.
Opening and closing dates, maximum
length of stay and hours vary.

Hostels are available to anyone with
a valid membership card issued by one
of the associations affiliated with the
International Youth Hostel Federation.
Membership is open to all ages. By
international agreement, each youth
hostel member joins the association of
his own country. A valid membership
card, which ranges from $10 (one night
temporary membership) to $200 (life),
entitles a member to use hostels.

Hostel memberships and a guide
to American youth hostels can be
purchased from the state office (Alaska
Council, AYH, 700 H St., Anchorage
99501; phone (907) 276-3635), national
office (American Youth Hostels, 1332 I
St. N.W., Suite 800, Washington, D.C.
20005) or from local hostels. For more
information regarding Alaska youth
hostels, write the Alaska Council,
AYH, or the Department of Natural
Resources, Division of Parks, P.O. Box
107001, Anchorage 99510.

Hot Springs

The U.S. Geological Survey identifies
79 thermal springs in Alaska. Almost
half of these hot springs occur along
the volcanic Alaska Peninsula and
Aleutian Chain. The second greatest
regional concentration of such springs
is in southeastern Alaska. Hot springs
are scattered throughout the Interior
and western Alaska, as far north as the
Brooks Range and as far west as the
Seward Peninsula.

Early miners and trappers were quick
to use the naturally occurring warm
waters for baths. Today approximately
25 percent of the recorded thermal
springs are used for bathing, irrigation
or domestic use. However, only a
handful can be considered developed
resorts.

Resorts (with swimming pools,
changing rooms and lodging) are found
at Chena Hot Springs, a 62-mile drive
east from Fairbanks; and Circle Hot

Springs, 136 miles northeast by road from Fairbanks. The less-developed Manley Hot Springs, in the small community of the same name at the end of the Elliott Highway, is privately owned, and the primitive bathhouse is used mainly by local residents. Developed, but not easily accessible, are the hot springs at Melozi Hot Springs Lodge, some 200 miles northwest of Fairbanks by air. The community of Tenakee Springs on Chichagof Island in southeastern Alaska maintains an old bathhouse near the waterfront. The state Marine Highway System provides ferry service to Tenakee Springs. Goddard Hot Springs near Sitka on Baranof Island was at one time owned by the Territory and operated as a Pioneers' Home for Alaska women. The temperature of the hot springs at Goddard Hot Springs is about 106°F/41°C. Also on Baranof Island is Baranof Hot Springs on the east shore of the island. Both Goddard and Baranof hot springs are accessible by private boat or by air; both have bathhouses.

Hunting

There are 26 game management units in Alaska with a wide variety of seasons and bag limits. Current copies of the *Alaska Game Regulations* with maps delineating game unit boundaries are available from the Alaska Department of Fish and Game (P.O. Box 3-2000, Juneau 99802) or from Fish and Game offices and sporting goods stores throughout the state.

Regulations

A hunting or trapping license is required for all residents and nonresidents with the exception of Alaska residents under 16 years and over 60 years of age. A special identification card is issued for the senior citizen exemption.

A resident hunting license (valid for the calendar year) costs $12; trapping license (valid until September 30 of the year following the year of issue), $10; hunting and trapping license, $22; hunting and sportfishing license, $22; hunting, trapping and sportfishing license, $32.

A nonresident hunting license (valid for calendar year) costs $60; hunting and sportfishing license, $96; hunting and trapping license, $200.

Military personnel stationed in Alaska may purchase a small game hunting license for $12, and a small game hunting and sportfishing license for $22. Military personnel must purchase a nonresident hunting license at full cost ($60) and pay nonresident military fees for big game tags (one-half the nonresident rate), unless they are hunting big game on military property.

Licenses may be obtained from any designated issuing agent or by mail from the Alaska Department of Fish and Game, Licensing Section, P.O. Box 3-2000, Juneau 99802. Licenses are also available at Fish and Game regional offices in Anchorage, Fairbanks, Juneau and Kodiak.

Big game tags and fees are required for residents hunting musk-ox and brown/grizzly bear and for nonresidents hunting any big game animal. These nonrefundable, nontransferable, metal locking tags (valid for calendar year) must be purchased prior to the taking of the animal. A tag may, however, be used for any species for which the tag fee is of equal or less value. Fees quoted below are for *each* animal.

All residents (regardless of age) and nonresidents intending to hunt brown/grizzly bear must purchase tags (resident, $25; nonresident, $350). Both residents and nonresidents are also required to purchase musk-ox tags (resident, $500 each bull taken on Nunivak Island, $25 each bull from Nelson Island or in Arctic National Wildlife Refuge, $25 cow; nonresident, $1,100).

Nonresident tag fees for other big game animals are as follows: deer, $135; wolf or wolverine, $150; black bear, $200; elk or goat, $250; caribou or moose, $300; bison, $350; and sheep, $400.

Nonresidents hunting brown/grizzly bear, Dall sheep or mountain goat are required to have a guide or be accompanied by an Alaska resident relative over 19 years of age within the second degree of kindship (includes parents, children, sisters or brothers). Nonresident aliens hunting big game must

have a guide. A current list of registered Alaska guides is available for $5 from the Department of Commerce, Guide Licensing and Control Board, P.O. Box D-LIC, Juneau 99811 or in *The ALASKA WILDERNESS MILEPOST®*.

Residents and nonresidents 16 years of age or older hunting waterfowl must have a signed federal migratory bird hunting stamp (duck stamp) and a state waterfowl conservation stamp. The Alaska duck stamp is available from agents who sell hunting licenses or by mail from the Alaska Department of Fish and Game, Licensing Section.

Trophy Game

Record big game in Alaska as recorded by the Boone and Crockett Club in the latest (1981) edition of *Record Big Game of North America* are as follows:

Black bear: Skull 13^7/16 inches long, 8^6/16 inches wide (1966).

Brown bear (coastal region): Skull 17^5/8 inches long, 12^{13}/16 inches wide (1952).

Grizzly bear (inland): Skull 16^5/8 inches long, 9^7/8 inches wide (1970).

Polar bear: Skull 18^1/2 inches long, 11^7/16 inches wide (1963). It is currently illegal for anyone but an Alaskan Eskimo, Aleut or Indian to hunt polar bear in Alaska.

Bison: Right horn 18^1/8 inches long, base circumference 15 inches; left horn 21 inches long, base circumference 15^1/4 inches; greatest spread 31^7/8 inches (1977).

Barren Ground caribou: Right beam 51^1/4 inches, 22 points; left beam 51^5/8 inches, 23 points (1967).

Moose: Right palm length 49^5/8 inches, width 20^3/4 inches; left palm length 49^5/8 inches, width 15^5/8 inches; right beam 18 points, left 16 points; greatest spread 77 inches (1978).

Mountain goat: Right horn 11^5/8 inches long, base circumference 5^3/4 inches; left horn 11^5/8 inches long, base circumference 5^5/8 inches (1933).

Musk-ox: Right horn 26^3/4 inches; left horn 26^1/2 inches; tip-to-tip spread 27^7/8 inches (1976).

Dall sheep: Right horn 48^5/8 inches long, base circumference 14^5/8 inches; left horn 47^7/8 inches long, base circumference 14^3/4 inches (1961).

Related reading: *Northwest Sportsman Almanac*. Writer-editor Terry Sheely has assembled the best works of writers and photographers in an informative guide to outdoor recreation. See ALASKA NORTHWEST LIBRARY in the back of the book.

Hypothermia

(*See also* Chill Factor)

Hypothermia develops when the body is exposed to cold and cannot maintain normal temperatures. In an automatic survival reaction, blood flow to the extremities is shut down in favor of preserving warmth in the vital organs. As internal temperature drops, judgment and coordination become impaired. Allowed to continue, hypothermia leads to stupor, collapse and death. Immersion hypothermia occurs in cold water.

Ice

(*See* Glaciers and Icefields *and* Icebergs)

Icebergs

Icebergs are formed in Alaska wherever glaciers reach salt water or a freshwater lake. Some accessible places to view icebergs include Glacier Bay, Icy Bay, Yakutat Bay, Taku Inlet, Endicott Arm, portions of northern Prince William Sound (College Fiord, Barry Arm, Columbia Bay), Mendenhall Lake and Portage Lake.

If icebergs contain little or no sediment, approximately 75 to 80 percent of their bulk may be underwater. The more sediment an iceberg contains, the greater its density, and an iceberg containing large amounts of sediment will float slightly beneath the surface. Glaciologists of the U.S. Geological Survey believe that some of these "black icebergs" may actually sink to the bottom of a body of water. Since salt water near the faces of glaciers may be liquid to temperatures as low as 28°F, and icebergs melt at 32°F, some of these underwater icebergs may remain unmelted indefinitely.

Alaska's icebergs are comparatively small compared to the icebergs found near Antarctica and Greenland. One of the largest icebergs ever recorded in Alaska was formed in May 1977, in Icy Bay. Glaciologists measured it at 346 feet long, 297 feet wide and 99 feet above the surface of the water.

Sea Ice

Sea water typically freezes at −1.8°C or 28.8°F. The first indication that sea water is freezing is the appearance of frazil — tiny needlelike crystals of pure ice — in shallow coastal areas of low current or areas of low salinity, such as near the mouths of rivers. Continued freezing turns the frazil into a soupy mass called grease ice and eventually into an ice crust approximately four inches thick. More freezing, wind and wave action thicken the ice and break it into ice floes ranging from a few feet to several miles across. In the Arctic Ocean, ice floes can be 10 feet thick.

Most are crisscrossed with 6- to 8-foot-high walls of ice caused by the force of winds.

Sea salt that is trapped in the ice during freezing is leached out over time, making the oldest ice the least saline. Meltwater forming in ponds on multi-year-old ice during summer months is a freshwater source for native marine life.

Refreezing of meltwater ponds and the formation of new ice in the permanent ice pack (generally north of 72° north latitude) begins in mid-September. While the ice pack expands southward, new ice freezes to the coast (shorefast ice) and spreads seaward. Where the drifting ice pack grinds against the relatively stable shorefast ice, tremendous walls or ridges of ice are formed, some observed to be 100 feet thick and grounded in 60 feet of water. They are impenetrable by all but the most powerful icebreakers. By late March the ice cover has reached its maximum extent, approximately from Port Heiden on the Alaska Peninsula in the south to the northern Pribilof Islands and northwestward to Siberia. In Cook Inlet, sea ice, usually no more than two feet thick, can extend as far south as Anchor Point and Kamishak Bay on the east and west sides of the inlet, respectively. The ice season usually lasts from mid-November to mid-March.

The Navy began observing and forecasting sea ice conditions in 1954 in support of the construction of defense sites along the Arctic coast. In 1969, the National Weather Service began a low-profile sea ice reconnaissance program, which expanded greatly during the summer of 1975, when during a year of severe ice, millions of dollars of materiel had to be shipped to Prudhoe Bay. Expanded commercial fisheries in the Bering Sea also heightened the problem of sea ice for crabbing and bottom fish trawling operations. In 1976, headquarters for a seven-day-a-week ice watch was established at Fairbanks; it was moved to Anchorage in 1981.

The National Weather Service operates a radio facsimile broadcast service that makes current ice analysis charts, special oceanographic charts and standard weather charts available to the public via standard radios equipped with "black box" receivers. Commercial fishing operators, particularly in the Bering Sea, use the radio-transmitted charts to steer clear of problem weather and troublesome ice formations. More information is available from the National Weather Service in Kodiak or Anchorage.

Related reading: *Icebound in the Siberian Arctic,* by Robert J. Gleason. Rescue of a ship by early aviators. See ALASKA NORTHWEST LIBRARY in the back of the book.

Ice Fog

Ice fog develops when air just above the ground becomes so cold, it can no longer retain water vapor and tiny, spherical ice crystals are formed. Ice fog is most common in Arctic and subarctic regions in winter when clear skies create an air inversion, trapping cold air at low elevations. It is most noticeable when man-made pollutants are also contained by the air inversion.

Iceworm

Although often regarded as a hoax, iceworms actually exist. These small, thin, segmented black worms, usually less than one inch long, thrive in temperatures just above freezing. Observers as far back as the 1880s reported that at dawn, dusk or on overcast days, the tiny worms, all belonging to the genus *Mesenchytraeus,* may literally carpet the surface of glaciers. When sunlight strikes them, they burrow back down into the ice.

The town of Cordova commemorates its own version of the iceworm each February in the Iceworm Festival, when a 150-foot-long, multilegged "iceworm" marches in a parade down Main Street.

Iditarod Trail Sled Dog Race

The first Iditarod Trail Sled Dog

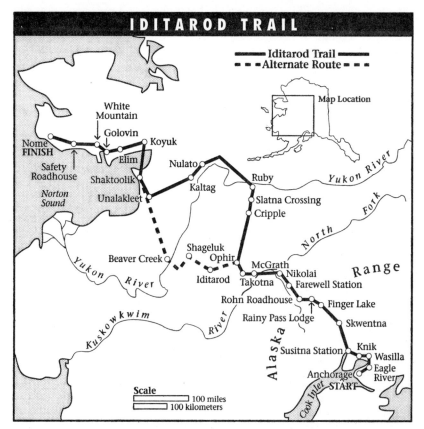

━━ Iditarod Trail ━━
■ ■ ■ Alternate Route ■ ■ ■

Map Location

White Mountain
Golovin
Koyuk
Nome FINISH
Elim
Nulato
Safety Roadhouse
Shaktoolik
Ruby
Kaltag
Norton Sound
Unalakleet
Slatna Crossing
Cripple
Yukon River
North Fork
Shageluk
Ophir
Beaver Creek
McGrath
Range
Iditarod
Nikolai
Takotna
Farewell Station
Yukon River
Rohn Roadhouse
Finger Lake
Rainy Pass Lodge
Skwentna
Kuskokwim
River
Alaska
Susitna Station
Knik
Wasilla
Anchorage
Eagle River
START
Cook Inlet

Scale
100 miles
100 kilometers

Race, conceived and organized by Joe Redington, Sr., of Knik, and historian Dorothy Page, of Wasilla, was run in 1967 and covered only 56 miles. The race was lengthened in 1973, and the first ever 1,100-mile sled dog race began in Anchorage on March 3, 1973, and ended April 3 in Nome. Of the 34 who started the race, 22 finished. The Iditarod has been run every year since its inception. In 1976, Congress designated the Iditarod as a National Historic Trail.

Following the old dog team mail route blazed in 1910 from Knik to Nome, the trail crosses two mountain ranges, follows the Yukon River for about 150 miles, runs through several bush villages and crosses the pack ice of Norton Sound.

Strictly a winter trail because the ground is mostly spongy muskeg swamps, the route attracted national attention in 1925 when sled dog mushers, including the famous Leonhard Seppala, relayed 300,000 units of life-saving diphtheria serum to epidemic-threatened Nome. However, as the airplane and snowmobile replaced the sled dog team, the trail fell into disuse. Thanks to Redington and Page, the trail has been assured a place in Alaska history.

Each year the Iditarod takes a slightly different course, following an alternate southern route in odd years (see map). While the route is traditionally described as 1,049 miles long (a figure that was selected because Alaska is the 49th state), the actual distance run each year is close to 1,100 miles. Part of it is run on frozen river ice. The official length of the Iditarod National Historic Trail System, including northern and southern routes, is 2,350 miles.

The majority of the Iditarod purse is divided among the first 20 finishers. In

1990, Lavon Barve received $3,000 in silver ingots for being the first to hit the halfway checkpoint at Cripple. Barve also received the Most Inspirational Musher award, and his lead dog Tip was given the Golden Harness award for outstanding performance.

In 1990, 70 mushers started the world's longest and richest sled dog race. Of those, 61 finished the Anchorage to Nome ordeal. Susan Butcher of Manley won the race for the fourth time and received the first-place check of $50,000 from a $291,000 purse. The 1990 race had the largest purse in the race's history and for the first time, all mushers finishing beyond position 20 received $1,000. This race also had the second-highest number of entrants, including 84-year-old Norman Vaughn, who finished the race.

Related reading: *Travelers of the Cold: Sled Dogs of the North,* by Dominique Cellura. See ALASKA NORTHWEST LIBRARY at the back of the book.

Winners and Times

Year	Musher	Days	Hrs.	Min.	Sec.	Prize
1990	Susan Butcher, Manley	11	01	53	23	$50,000
1989	Joe Runyan, Nenana	11	05	24	34	50,000
1988	Susan Butcher, Manley	11	11	41	40	30,000
1987	Susan Butcher, Manley	11	02	05	13	50,000
1986	Susan Butcher, Manley	11	15	06	00	50,000
1985	Libby Riddles, Teller	18	00	20	17	50,000
1984	Dean Osmar, Clam Gulch	12	15	07	33	24,000*
1983	Dick Mackey, Wasilla	12	14	10	44	24,000
1982	Rick Swenson, Eureka	16	04	40	10	24,000
1981	Rick Swenson, Eureka	12	08	45	02	24,000
1980	Joe May, Trapper Creek	14	07	11	51	12,000
1979	Rick Swenson, Eureka	15	10	37	47	12,000
1978	Dick Mackey, Wasilla	14	18	52	24	12,000
1977	Rick Swenson, Eureka	16	16	27	13	9,600
1976	Jerry Riley, Nenana	18	22	58	17	7,000
1975	Emmitt Peters, Ruby	14	14	43	45	15,000
1974	Carl Huntington, Galena	20	15	02	07	12,000
1973	Dick Willmarth, Red Devil	20	00	49	41	12,000

*Does not include $2,000 in silver ingots for reaching the halfway checkpoint first.

1990 Results

Place	Musher	Days	Hrs.	Min.	Sec.	Prize
1	Susan Butcher, Manley	11	01	53	23	$50,000
2	Joe Runyan, Nenana	11	04	21	12	35,000
3	Lavon Barve, Wasilla	11	07	15	04	27,000
4	Tim Osmar, Clam Gulch	11	14	40	53	20,000
5	DeeDee Jonrowe, Willow	11	14	41	31	15,000
6	Robin Jaconson, Squaw Lake, MN	11	16	32	02	12,000
7	Rick Swenson, Two Rivers	11	16	55	45	11,000
8	Linwood Fiedler, Canyon Creek, MT	12	01	19	16	10,000
9	Joe Garnie, King Salmon	12	02	05	02	9,000
10	Martin Buser, Big Lake	12	02	33	44	8,000
11	Bill Cotter, Nenana	13	03	54	28	7,500
12	Rick Mackey, Trapper Creek	13	08	19	46	7,000
13	Michael Madden, North Pole	13	08	41	06	6,500
14	Jacques Philip, By Thomery, France	13	08	42	50	6,000
15	John Barron, Big Lake	13	09	07	26	5,500
16	Sonny Russell, Kotzebue	13	09	07	41	5,000
17	Matt Desalernos, Nome	13	09	09	39	4,500
18	John Gourley, Wasilla	13	09	11	22	4,000
19	Jerry Austin, St. Michael	13	09	17	52	3,500
20	Bill Chisholm, Two Rivers	13	09	19	19	3,000

Igloo

Also known as snowhouses, these snow block structures provided temporary shelter for Arctic Alaska Eskimos. Igloos are built in a spiral with each tier leaning inward at a greater angle. The entrance is a tunnel with a cold trap in front of the sleeping platform. A vent at the top allows for ventilation, and an ice window lets in light.

Imports and Exports

Alaska's most important trading partner is Japan, to which it sent 73 percent of its exports in 1989. Other Asian nations were significant markets: Korea (6.8 percent) and Taiwan (3.9 percent). Alaska imports for 1989 were valued at $554.6 million. The largest importer to the state was Canada at $221 million, followed by Japan ($88.9 million), Singapore ($60.3 million) and the Philippines ($46.9 million).

Exports for 1989 were valued at $2.56 billion by the Alaska Center for International Business. Of this total, the state's most valuable exports were fish (43 percent), timber (25 percent) and petroleum products (16 percent).

Income

Alaska is characterized by a wide disparity in incomes. According to the September 1987 issue of *Alaska Economic Trends,* income statistics show that Alaska had one of the highest concentrations of millionaires in the nation, as well as more than one in five people living below the poverty level.

In 1988, total personal income earned by Alaskans was $10 billion. On a per capita basis, that ranked Alaska eighth in the nation at $19,079 per person. This was 16 percent above the national average. Alaska's per capita income position, the highest in the nation in 1985, has eroded in the past several years. A three-year recession dropped per capita income nearly 3 percent from 1985 to 1988.

In many sectors of the economy, Alaskans earn higher wages than their counterparts in the Lower 48. A wide disparity is apparent when comparing the average worker's earnings in different industries between the U.S. and Alaska. The disparity of Alaska to U.S. wage and salary earnings is greatest in mining and government and the least in manufacturing.

Personal income in Alaska has followed the same pattern as employment, rising during construction of the trans-Alaska pipeline and during the construction boom of the early 1980s. Since 1985, personal income has either dropped or increased at a very gradual rate. The 1985–88 recession spared few industries, adversely affecting all income averages. A slow recovery began in 1988 and continued into the 1990s.

Information Sources

Agriculture: State Division of Agriculture, P.O. Box 949, Palmer 99645; Cooperative Extension Service, University of Alaska, Fairbanks 99701.

Alaska Natives: Alaska Federation of Natives, 411 W. Fourth Ave., Anchorage 99501.

Boating, Canoeing and Kayaking: Alaska Dept. of Transportation and Public Facilities, P.O. Box Z, Juneau 99811; State of Alaska, Division of Parks and Outdoor Recreation, 3601 C St., Suite 1200, Anchorage 99503.

Business: Alaska Department of Commerce and Economic Development, P.O. Box D, Juneau 99811; State Chamber of Commerce, 217 Second St., Suite 201, Juneau 99801.

Camping and Hiking: U.S. Forest Service, P.O. Box 21628, Juneau 99802; Bureau of Land Management, 222 W. Seventh Ave., #13, Anchorage 99513; Supervisor, Chugach National Forest, 201 E. Ninth Ave., Suite 206, Anchorage 99501; National Park Service, 2525 Gambell St., Anchorage 99503; Supervisor, Tongass National Forest, P.O. Box 21628, Juneau 99802; U.S. Fish and Wildlife Service, 1011 E. Tudor Road, Anchorage 99503.

Census Data: Alaska Department of Labor, Research and Analysis, P.O. Box 107018, Anchorage 99510.

Climate: State Climatologist, University of Alaska, Arctic Environmental and

Data Center, 707 A St., Anchorage 99501.

Education: Alaska Department of Education, P.O. Box F, Juneau 99811.

Gold Panning: State Division of Geological and Geophysical Surveys, Mines Information Office, 3601 C St., Anchorage 99503; Alaska Miners Association, 501 W. Northern Lights Blvd., Suite 203, Anchorage 99503.

Health: State Department of Health and Social Services, Division of Public Health, P.O. Box H, Juneau 99811.

Housing: State Housing Authority, P.O. Box 100080, Anchorage 99510.

Hunting and Fishing Regulations: State Department of Fish and Game, P.O. Box 3-2000, Juneau 99802.

Job Opportunities: State Employment Service, P.O. Box 3-7000, Juneau 99802.

Labor: State Department of Labor, P.O. Box 25501-5501, Juneau 99802.

Land: State Division of Lands, P.O. Box 107005, Anchorage 99510; Bureau of Land Management, 222 W. Seventh Ave., #13, Anchorage 99513; Alaska Public Lands Information Centers, 605 W. Fourth Ave., Suite 105, Anchorage 99501; 250 Cushman St., Suite 1A, Fairbanks 99701; P.O. Box 359, Tok 99780.

Legislature: Legislative Information Office, 3111 C St., Anchorage 99503.

Made in Alaska Products: Alaska Association of Manufacturers, P.O. Box 142831, Anchorage 99514.

Maps (topographic): U.S. Geological Survey, 222 W. Seventh Ave., Room F-146, Anchorage 99513.

Military: Department of the Air Force, Headquarters, Alaskan Air Command, Elmendorf Air Force Base 99506; Department of the Army, Headquarters, 6th Infantry Brigade (Alaska), Fort Richardson 99505; State Department of Military Affairs, Office of the Adjutant General, 3601 C St., Anchorage 99503; Department of Transportation, U.S. Coast Guard, 17th Coast Guard District, P.O. Box 3-5000, Juneau 99802.

Mines and Petroleum: State Division of Geological and Geophysical Surveys, 3601 C St., Anchorage 99503; Petroleum Information Corp., P.O. Box 102278, Anchorage 99510; Alaska Miners Association, 501 W. Northern Lights Blvd., Suite 203, Anchorage 99503.

River Running: National Park Service, 2525 Gambell St., Anchorage 99503; U.S. Dept. of the Interior, Fish and Wildlife Service, 1011 E. Tudor Road, Anchorage 99503; Bureau of Land Management, 222 W. Seventh Ave., #13, Anchorage 99513.

Travel and Visitor Information: State Division of Tourism, P.O. Box E, Juneau 99811; Alaska Visitors Association, 501 W. Northern Lights Blvd., Anchorage 99503.

Islands

Southeastern Alaska contains about 1,000 of the state's 1,800 named islands, rocks and reefs; several thousand remain unnamed. The Aleutian Island chain, stretching southwest from the mainland, contains more than 200 islands.

Of the state's 10 largest islands, 6 are in southeastern Alaska. Of the remainder, Unimak is in the Aleutians, Nunivak and Saint Lawrence are in the Bering Sea off the west coast of Alaska, and Kodiak is in the Gulf of Alaska. The state's 10 largest islands, according to U.S. Geological Survey and Bureau of Land Management figures, are:

Kodiak, 3,588 sq. mi.
Prince of Wales, 2,731 sq. mi.*
Chichagof, 2,062 sq. mi.
Saint Lawrence, 1,780 sq. mi.
Admiralty, 1,709 sq. mi.
Baranof, 1,636 sq. mi.
Nunivak, 1,600 sq. mi.**
Unimak, 1,600 sq. mi.
Revillagigedo, 1,134 sq. mi.
Kupreanof, 1,084 sq. mi.

*The figure 2,770 square miles reported in earlier editions of THE ALASKA ALMANAC® included associated islands.
**Estimate

Related reading: *A Guide to The Queen Charlotte Islands* by Neil G. Carey. See ALASKA NORTHWEST LIBRARY in the back of the book.

Ivory

Eskimos traditionally carved ivory to make such implements as harpoon heads, dolls and ulu (fan-shaped knife) handles. For the past 80 years, however, most carvings have been made to be sold. Etching on ivory originally was done with hand tools and the scratches were filled in with soot. Today power tools supplement the hand tools and carvers may color the etching with India ink, graphite, hematite or commercial coloring.

The large islands of the Bering Sea — Saint Lawrence, Little Diomede and Nunivak — are home to the majority of Alaska's ivory carvers. Eskimos from King Island, renowned for their carving skill, now live in Nome along with talented artists from many other villages.

The bulk of the ivory used today comes from walrus tusks and teeth, seasoned for a few months. Old walrus ivory, often mistakenly called fossil ivory, is also used. This ivory has been buried in the ground or has been on beaches for years, and contact with various minerals has changed it from white to tan or any of a multitude of colors. Some highly prized old ivory exhibits rays of deep blue or areas of brown and gold that shine. Most old ivory comes from ancient sites or beaches on Saint Lawrence Island and is sold by the pound to non-Native buyers, generally for use in some kind of artwork.

Mastodon tusks are often unearthed in the summer by miners or found eroding on river cutbanks where they have been buried for thousands of years. Although these tusks are enormous and their colorations often beautiful, the material cannot be used efficiently because it dries and then separates into narrow ridges.

Various federal prohibitions govern the collection of old walrus, mammoth and mastodon ivory. Such materials may be gathered from private or reservation lands, but may not be traded or sold if found on public lands. The taking of fresh walrus ivory is prohibited to non-Natives in accordance with the Marine Mammal Protection Act of 1972.

In the 19th century, Native artists who came in contact with whalers etched realistic scenes on sperm whale teeth. Today, with the ban on the taking of sperm whales, this type of ivory is not available to Native scrimshanders.

Walrus may be taken only by Alaska Natives (Aleuts, Eskimos and Indians) who dwell on the coast of the North Pacific Ocean or the Arctic Ocean, for subsistence purposes or for the creation and sale of authentic Native articles of handicrafts or clothing.

Raw walrus ivory and other parts can be sold only by an Alaska Native to an Alaska Native within Alaska, or to a registered agent for resale or transfer to an Alaska Native within the state. Only authentic Native-processed ivory articles of handicrafts or clothing may be sold or transferred to a non-Native, or sold in interstate commerce.

Beach ivory, which is found on the beach within one-fourth mile of the ocean, may, however, be kept by anyone. This ivory must be registered by all non-Natives with the U.S. Fish and Wildlife Service (USFWS) or the National Marine Fisheries Service within 30 days of discovery. Beach-found ivory must remain in the possession of the finder even if carved or scrimshawed.

Carved or scrimshawed walrus ivory (authentic Native handicraft) or other marine mammal parts made into clothing or other authentic Native handicrafts may be exported from the United States to a foreign country, but the exporter must first obtain an export permit from the USFWS. Even visitors from the Lower 48 simply traveling through, or stopping in Canada on their way home, are required to have a USFWS export and/or transit permit. Cost is $25. Mailing the carved ivory home will avoid the need for an export/transit permit.

Importation of walrus or other marine mammal parts is illegal, except for scientific research purposes or for public display once a permit is granted.

For further information contact: Special Agent-in-Charge, U.S. Fish and Wildlife Service, 1011 E. Tudor Road, Anchorage 99503; phone (907) 786-3311; or Senior Resident, U.S. Fish and Wildlife Service, 1412 Airport Way, Fairbanks 99701; phone (907) 456-0239.

Jade

Most Alaskan jade is found near the Dall, Shungnak and Kobuk rivers, and Jade Mountain, all north of the Arctic Circle. The stones occur in various shades of green, brown, black, yellow, white and even red. The most valuable are those that are marbled black, white and green. Gem-quality jade, about one-fourth of the total mined, is used in jewelry making. Fractured jade is used for clock faces, table tops, book ends and other items. Jade is the Alaska state gem.

Kuspuk

A *kuspuk* is an Eskimo woman's parka, often made with a loosely cut back so that an infant may be carried

piggyback-style. Parkas are made from rabbit or fox skins; traditionally, the fur lining faces inward. The ruffs are usually made of wolverine or wolf fur. An outer shell, called a *qaspeg,* is worn over a fur parka to keep it clean and to prevent wearing. This outer shell is usually made of a brightly colored material, and may be trimmed with rickrack.

Labor and Employer Organizations

The Alaska State AFL-CIO *Alaska Labor Union Directory* lists the following organizations:

Anchorage
Alaska Federation of Teachers Local 8050
Alaska Metal Trades Council
Alaska Public Employees Association
Alaska State AFL-CIO
Alaska State District Council of Laborers
Alaska State Employees Association, AFSCME Local 52
American Federation of Government Employees, Anchorage Council, Local 121
Anchorage Central Labor Council
Anchorage Joint Crafts Council
Anchorage Municipal Employees Association
Anchorage Musicians Association Local 650
Anchorage Typographical Union Local 823
Asbestos Workers Local 97
Associated General Contractors of America
Boilermakers Local 502
Bricklayers and Allied Craftsmen Local 1
Brotherhood of Railroad Carmen of U.S.A. and Canada
Central and Southeastern Alaska District Council of Carpenters
Graphic Communications International Union Local 327
Hotel Employees, Restaurant Employees Union Local 878
International Alliance of Theatrical Stage Employees Local 918
International Association of Bridge, Structural and Ornamental Workers Local 751

International Association of Firefighters Local 1264
International Association of Machinists and Aerospace Workers Local 601
International Brotherhood of Electrical Workers Local 1547
International Brotherhood of Painters and Allied Trades Local 1140
International Brotherhood of Teamsters, Chauffeurs, Warehousemen and Helpers Local 959
International Union of Operating Engineers Local 302
Laborers International Union of North America Local 341
Laundry and Dry Cleaning Union Local 333
National Electrical Contractors Association
Operative Plasterers and Cement Masons Local 867
Piledrivers, Bridge, Dock Builders and Drivers Local 2520
Public Employees Local 71
Roofers and Waterproofers Local 190
Sheetmetal Workers International Association Local 23
United Association of Plumbers and Steamfitters Local 367
United Brotherhood of Carpenters and Joiners Local 1281
United Food and Commercial Workers Union Local 1496
United Transportation Union Local 1626
Western Alaska Building and Construction Trades Council

Cordova
Cordova District Fishermen United
International Longshoremen's and Warehousemen's Union Local 200

Craig
International Longshoremen's and Warehousemen's Union Local 200

Dillingham
Western Alaska Cooperative Marketing Association

Fairbanks
Alaska Public Employees Association
Fairbanks Building and Construction Trades
Fairbanks Central Labor Council
Fairbanks Firefighters Association Local 1324
Fairbanks Joint Crafts Council
Hotel Employees, Restaurant Employees Union Local 879
International Association of Bridge,

Structural and Ornamental Workers Local 751
International Brotherhood of Electrical Workers Local 1547
International Brotherhood of Painters and Allied Trades Local 1555
International Brotherhood of Teamsters, Chauffeurs, Warehousemen and Helpers Local 959
International Printing and Graphic Communications Union Local 704
International Union of Operating Engineers Local 302
Laborers International Union of North America Local 942
Operative Plasterers and Cement Masons Local 867
Public Employees Local 71
Sheetmetal Union Local 72
United Association of Journeymen and Apprentices of the Plumbing and Pipefitting Industry Local 375
United Brotherhood of Carpenters and Joiners Local 1243
United Food and Commercial Workers Union Local 1496

Haines
International Longshoremen's and Warehousemen's Union Local 200

Juneau
Alaska Public Employees Association
Alaska State District Council of Laborers
Hotel Employees, Restaurant Employees Local 878
Inland Boatmen's Union of the Pacific, Alaska Region
International Association of Machinists and Aerospace Workers Local 2263
International Brotherhood of Electrical Workers Local 1547
International Brotherhood of Teamsters, Chauffeurs, Warehousemen and Helpers Local 959
International *Longshoremen's* and Warehousemen's Union Local 200
International Longshoremen's and *Warehousemen's* Union Local 200
International Union of Operating Engineers Local 302
Juneau Building and Construction Trades Council
Juneau Central Labor Council
Laborers International Union of North America Local 942
National Education Association
National Federation of Federal Employees Local 251

Operative Plasterers and Cement
Masons Local 867
Public Employees Local 71
United Association of Journeymen and
Apprentices of the Plumbing and
Pipefitting Industry Local 262
United Brotherhood of Carpenters and
Joiners Local 2247
United Fishermen of Alaska
Kenai
Hotel Employees, Restaurant Employees
Union Local 878
International Brotherhood of Electrical
Workers Local 1547
International Brotherhood of Team-
sters, Chauffeurs, Warehousemen
and Helpers Local 959
Kenai Peninsula Central Labor Coun-
cil
Laborers International Union of North
America Local 341
Ketchikan
Alaska Loggers Association
Associated Western Pulp and Paper
Workers Local 783
Hotel Employees, Restaurant Employees
Union Local 878
Inland Boatmen's Union of the Pacific,
Alaska Region
International Brotherhood of Electrical
Workers Local 1547
International *Longshoremen's* and Ware-
housemen's Union Local 200
International Longshoremen's and
Warehousemen's Union Local 200
International Woodworkers of America
Local 3-193
Ketchikan Building and Construction
Trades Council
Ketchikan Central Labor Council
Laborers International Union of North
America Local 942
United Brotherhood of Carpenters and
Joiners Local 1501
Kodiak
Firefighters Local 3054
Hotel Employees, Restaurant Employees
Union Local 878
Inland Boatmen's Union of the Pacific,
Alaska Region
International Longshoremen's and
Warehousemen's Union Local 200
Kodiak Labor Council
Laborers International Union of North
America Local 341
Palmer
Laborers International Union of North
America Local 341

Pelican
International Longshoremen's and
Warehousemen's Union Local 200
Seward
International Longshoremen's and
Warehousemen's Union Local 200
Sitka
Hotel Employees, Restaurant Employees
Union Local 873
International Longshoremen's and
Warehousemen's Union Local 200
United Brotherhood of Carpenters and
Joiners Local 466
Unalaska
International Longshoremen's and
Warehousemen's Union Local 200
Valdez
Hotel Employees, Restaurant Employees
Union Local 878
Laborers International Union of North
America Local 341
Ward Cove
Associated Western Pulp and Paper
Workers Local 783
Wrangell
International Longshoremen's and
Warehousemen's Union Local 200
United Paperworkers Local 1341

Lakes

There are 94 lakes with surface areas
of more than 10 square miles among
Alaska's more than 3 million lakes.
According to the U.S. Geological Survey, the 10 largest (larger than 20 acres)
natural freshwater lakes in square miles
are: Iliamna, 1,000; Becharof, 458;
Teshekpuk, 315; Naknek, 242; Tustumena, 117; Clark, 110; Dall, 100; Upper
Ugashik, 75; Lower Ugashik, 72; and
Kukaklek, 72.

Land

At first glance it seems odd that such
a huge area as Alaska has not been more
heavily settled. Thousands of acres of
forest and tundra, miles and miles of
rivers and streams, hidden valleys, bays,
coves and mountains, are spread across
an area so vast that it staggers the
imagination. Yet, more than two-thirds
of the population of Alaska remains
clustered around two major centers of
commerce and survival. Compared to

the settlement of the western Lower 48, Alaska is not settled at all.

Visitors flying over the state are impressed by immense areas showing no sign of humanity. Current assessments indicate that approximately 160,000 acres of Alaska have been cleared, built on or otherwise directly altered by man, either by settlement or resource development, including mining, pipeline construction and agriculture. In comparison to the 365 million acres of land that make up the total of the state, the settled or altered area currently amounts to less than one-twentieth of 1 percent.

There are significant reasons for this lack of development in Alaska. Frozen for long periods in the dark of the Arctic, much of the land cannot support quantities of people or industry. Where the winters are "warm," the mountains, glaciers, rivers and oceans prevent easy access for commerce and trade.

The status of land is constantly changing, especially in Alaska. In most places, the free market affects patterns of land ownership, but in Alaska, all land ownership patterns until recently were the result of a century-long process of a single landowner, the United States government.

The Statehood Act signaled the beginning of a dramatic shift in land ownership patterns. It authorized the state to select a total of 104 million of the 365 million acres of land and inland waters in Alaska. (Under the Submerged Lands Act, the state has title to submerged lands under navigable inland waters.) In passing the Statehood Act, Congress cited economic independence and the need to open Alaska to economic development as the primary purposes for large Alaska land grants.

The issue of the Native claims in Alaska was cleared up with the passage of the Alaska Native Claims Settlement Act (ANCSA) on Dec. 18, 1971. This act of Congress provided for the creation of Alaska Native village and regional corporations, and gave the Alaska Eskimos, Aleuts and Indians nearly $1 billion and the right to select 44 million acres from a land "pool" of some 115 million acres.

Immediately after the settlement act passed, and before Native lands and National Interest Lands were selected, the state filed to select an additional 77 million acres of land. In September 1972, the litigation initiated by the state was resolved by a settlement affirming state selection of an additional 41 million acres.

Section 17 of the settlement act, in addition to establishing a Joint Federal–State Land Use Planning Commission, directed the secretary of the interior to withdraw from public use up to 80 million acres of land in Alaska for study as possible national parks, wildlife refuges, forests, and wild and scenic rivers. These were the National Interest Lands Congress was to decide upon, as set forth in Section 17(d)(2) of the settlement act, by Dec. 18, 1978. The U.S. House of Representatives passed a bill (HR39) that would have designated 124 million acres of national parks, forests and wildlife refuges, and designated millions of acres of these and existing parks, forests and refuges as wilderness. Although a bill was reported out of committee, it failed to pass the Senate before Congress adjourned.

In November 1978, the secretary of the interior published a draft environmental impact supplement, which listed the actions that the executive branch of the federal government could take to protect federal lands in Alaska until the 96th Congress could consider the creation of new parks, wildlife refuges, wild and scenic rivers and forests. In keeping with this objective, the secretary of the interior, under provisions of the 1976 Federal Land Policy and Management Act, withdrew about 114 million acres of land in Alaska from most public uses. On Dec. 1, 1978, the president, under the authority of the 1906 Antiquities Act, designated 56 million acres of these lands as national monuments.

In February 1980, the House of Representatives passed a modified HR39. In August 1980, the Senate passed a compromise version of the Alaska lands bill that created 106 million acres of new conservation units and affected a total of 131 million acres of land in Alaska. In November

1980, the House accepted the Senate version of the Alaska National Interest Lands Conservation Act, which President Jimmy Carter signed into law on Dec. 2, 1980. This is also known as the d-2 lands bill or the compromise HR39. (*See also* National Parks, Preserves and Monuments; National Wilderness Areas; National Wildlife Refuges; National Forests; *and* National Wild and Scenic Rivers.)

Alaska's land will continue to be a controversial and complex subject for some time. Implementation of the d-2 bill, and distribution of land to the Native village and regional corporations, the state of Alaska and private citizens in the state will require time. Much of this work is being done by the Bureau of Land Management, which also surveys federal land before a patent is issued. Numerous land issues created by large land exchanges, conflicting land use and management policies, and overlapping resources will require constant cooperation between landowners if the issues are going to be resolved successfully.

Acquiring Land for Private Use

The easiest and fastest way to acquire land for private use is by purchase from the private sector, through real estate agencies or directly from individuals. Because of speculation, land claim conflicts and delays involving Native, state and federal groups, however, private land is considered by many people to be in short supply and often is very expensive.

Private land in Alaska, excluding land held by Native corporations, is estimated to be more than 1 million acres, but less than 1 percent of the state. Much of this land passed into private hands through the federal Homestead Acts and other public land laws, as well as land disposal programs of the state, boroughs or communities. Most private land is located along Alaska's small road network. Compared to other categories of land, it is highly accessible and constitutes some of the prime settlement land.

All laws related to homesteading on federal land (as opposed to state land) in Alaska were repealed as of 1986. Federal land is not available for homesteading, or trade and manufacturing sites.

Following are programs that are in effect for the sale of state land. A one-year residency is required for all but the auction program.

Auction: The state has been selling land by public auction since statehood. The state may sell full surface rights, lease of surface or subsurface rights, or restricted title at an auction. There is a minimum bid of fair market value and the high bidder is the purchaser. Participants must be 18.

Homesite: The homesite program was passed in 1977 by the state legislature. Under its provisions, each Alaskan is eligible for up to five acres. The land is free, but the individual must pay the cost of the survey and platting. Persons enrolled in this program must live on the homesite for 35 months within seven years of entry and construct a permanent, single-family dwelling on the site within five years (this is called "proving up" on the land).

Remote Parcels: This remote parcel program replaced the old open-to-entry program. It permits entry upon designated areas to stake a parcel of up to 5, 20 or 40 acres, depending on the area, and to lease the area for five years with an option for a five-year renewal. Rental under the lease is $10 per acre per year. The lease is not transferable. During the lease period the lessee must survey the land. He may apply to purchase the land at the fair market value at the time of his initial lease application. The state will finance the sale over a period of 20 years.

Remote parcels ended July 1, 1984, when the program was replaced by the 1983 homesteading bill. Alaskans leasing remote parcels, but who have not yet purchased them, may continue under the remote parcel program or opt to obtain title by meeting homesteading requirements.

Lottery: One year of residency is required to participate in the lottery program. Successful applicants are determined by a drawing and pay the appraised market value of the land. They repay the state over a period of up to 20 years, with interest set at the current federal land loan bank rate. Lotteries require a 5 percent down payment.

The state offered 100,000 acres of land to private ownership in each fiscal year from July 1, 1979, to July 1, 1982. Disposal levels from that time forward have been based on an annual assessment of the demand for state land. Sales are scheduled for fall and spring.

On April 1, 1983, the Department of Natural Resources discontinued a program that provided Alaska residents who were registered voters a 5-percent-per-year-of-residency discount (up to $25,000) on the sale of land purchased from the state. Fifteen-year veteran residents had been eligible for up to $37,500 on this one-time program.

Homestead: Under the new state law, any resident of at least one year, who is 18 years or older and a U.S. citizen, has a chance to receive up to 40 acres of nonagricultural land or up to 160 acres of agricultural land without paying for the acreage itself. The homesteader, however, must survey, occupy and improve the land in certain ways, and within specific time frames, to receive title. This is called "proving up" on the homestead.

The state homestead act also allows homesteaders to purchase parcels at

fair market value without occupying or improving the land. This option requires only that nonagricultural land be staked, brushed and surveyed, and that parcels designated for agricultural use also meet clearing requirements.

Whether the homesteader chooses to prove up or purchase, all applicable requirements such as brushing, survey and agricultural clearing must be met. After homesteading areas have been designated, homesteaders must stake the corners and flag the boundaries of the land, pay a fee of $5 per acre and personally file a description of the land with the state. In order to acquire title to the land, homesteaders must brush the boundaries within 90 days after issuance of the entry permit, complete an approved survey of the land within two or five years (depending on purchase option), erect a habitable permanent dwelling on the homestead within three years, live on the parcel for 25 months within five years and, if the land is classified for agricultural use, clear and either put into production or prepare for cultivation 25 percent of the land within five years.

Up-to-date information and applications for state programs are available from the Alaska Division of Land and Water Management:

Northern Region, 3700 Airport Way, Fairbanks 99709
Southcentral Region, P.O. Box 107005, Anchorage 99510
Southeastern Region, 400 Willoughby Ave., Suite 400, Juneau 99801

Following is the amount of Alaska land owned by various entities as of April 1990:

Owner	Acreage (millions of acres)
U.S. Bureau of Land Management	92.4
U.S. Fish and Wildlife	75.4
State	84.7
National Park Service	50.6
Forest Service	23.2
Native	35.1
Military and other Federal	2.6
Private	1.0

(Source: U.S. Bureau of Land Management)

Languages

Besides English, Alaska's languages include Haida, Tlingit, Tsimshian, Aleut, several dialects of Eskimo and several dialects of Athabascan.

Mammals

Large Land Mammals
Black bear — Highest densities are found in Southeast, Prince William Sound, and southcentral coastal mountains and lowlands. Black bears also occur in interior and western Alaska, but are absent from Southeast islands north of Frederick Sound (primarily Admiralty, Baranof and Chichagof) and Kodiak archipelago. They are not commonly found west of about Naknek Lake on the Alaska Peninsula, in the Aleutian Islands or on the open tundra sloping into the Bering Sea and Arctic Ocean. (*See also* Bears)

Brown/grizzly bear — These large carnivores are found in most of Alaska. The grizzly is not found in the Southeast islands south of Frederick Sound and in the Aleutians (except for Unimak Island). (*See also* Bears)

Polar bear — There are two groups in Alaska's Arctic rim: an eastern group found largely in the Beaufort Sea and a western group found in the Chukchi Sea between Alaska and Siberia. The latter group are the largest polar bears in the world. Old males can exceed 1,500 pounds. (*See also* Bears)

American bison — In 1928, 23 bison were transplanted from Montana to Delta Junction to restore Alaska's bison population, which had died out some 500 years before. Today, several hundred bison graze near Delta Junction; other herds range at Farewell, Chitina and along the lower Copper River.

Barren Ground caribou — There are at least 13 distinct caribou herds, with some overlapping of ranges: Adak, Alaska Peninsula, Arctic, Beaver, Chisana, Delta, Kenai, McKinley, Mentasta, Mulchatna, Nelchina, Porcupine and Fortymile. Porcupine

and Fortymile herds range into Canada.

Sitka black-tailed deer — Sitka black-tailed deer range the coastal rain forests of southeastern Alaska. They have been successfully transplanted to the Yakutat area, Prince William Sound, and to Kodiak and Afognak islands.

Roosevelt elk — Alaska's only elk occur on Raspberry and Afognak islands and result from a 1928 transplant of Roosevelt elk from the Olympic Peninsula in Washington state. Other transplant attempts have failed.

Moose — Moose occur from the Unuk River in Southeast to the Arctic Slope, but are most abundant in second-growth birch forests, on timberline plateaus and along major rivers of Southcentral and Interior. They are not found on islands in Prince William Sound or Bering Sea, on most major islands in Southeast or on Kodiak or Aleutians groups.

Mountain goat — These white-coated animals are found in mountains throughout Southeast, and north and west along coastal mountains to Cook Inlet and Kenai Peninsula. They have been successfully transplanted to Kodiak and Baranof islands.

Musk-ox — These shaggy, long-haired mammals were eliminated from Alaska by hunters by 1865. The species was reintroduced and first transplanted to Nunivak Island, and from there to the Arctic Slope around Kavik, Seward Peninsula,

Cape Thompson and Nelson Island. (*See also* Musk-Ox)

Reindeer — Introduced from Siberia just before the 20th century, reindeer roamed much of the Bering Sea Coast region but are now confined to the Seward Peninsula and Nunivak Island.

Dall sheep — The only white, wild sheep in the world, Dall sheep are found in all major mountain ranges in Alaska except the Aleutian Range south of Iliamna Lake.

Wolf — Wolves are protected and managed as big game and valuable furbearers. Wolves are found throughout Alaska except Bering Sea islands, some Southeast and Prince William Sound islands, and the Aleutian Islands. The wolf succeeds in a variety of climates and terrains.

Wolverine — Shy, solitary creatures, wolverines are found throughout Alaska and on some Southeast islands; abundant in the Interior and on the Alaska Peninsula. They are not abundant in comparison with other furbearers.

Furbearers

Beaver — These large vegetarian rodents are found in most of mainland Alaska from Brooks Range to middle of Alaska Peninsula. Abundant in some major mainland river drainages in the Southeast and on Yakutat forelands, they have also been successfully transplanted to Kodiak area. Beaver dams are sometimes destroyed to allow salmon upstream; however, the beavers can rebuild their dams quickly and usually do so on the same site.

Coyote — The coyote is a relative newcomer to Alaska, showing up shortly after the turn of the century, according to old-timers and records. They are not abundant on a statewide basis, but are common in Tanana, Copper, Matanuska and Susitna river drainages and on Kenai Peninsula. The coyote is found as far west as Alaska Peninsula and the north side of Bristol Bay.

Fox — *Arctic* (white and blue phases): Arctic foxes are found almost entirely along the Arctic coast as far south as the northwestern shore of Bristol Bay. They have been introduced to Pribilof and Aleutian islands, where the blue color phase, most popular with fox farmers, predominates. The white color phase occurs naturally on Saint Lawrence and Nunivak islands. *Red:* Their golden fur coveted by trappers, the red fox is found throughout Alaska except for most areas of Southeast and around Prince William Sound.

Lynx — These shy night-prowlers' main food source is the snowshoe hare. The lynx is found throughout Alaska, except on Yukon-Kuskokwim Delta, southern Alaska Peninsula and along coastal tidelands. It is relatively scarce along northern gulf coast and in southeastern Alaska.

Hoary marmot — Present throughout most of the mountain regions of Alaska and along the Endicott Mountains east into Canada, the hoary marmot lives in the high country, especially the warm slopes near and above timberline.

Marten — The marten must have climax spruce forest to survive, and its habitat ranges throughout timbered Alaska, except north of the Brooks Range, on treeless sections of the Alaska Peninsula, and on the Yukon-Kuskokwim Delta. It has been successfully introduced to Prince of Wales, Baranof, Chichagof and Afognak islands in this century.

Muskrat — Muskrats are found in greatest numbers around lakes, ponds, rivers and marshes throughout all of mainland Alaska south of the Brooks Range except for the Alaska Peninsula west of the Ugashik lakes. They were introduced to Kodiak Island, Afognak and Raspberry islands.

River otter — A member of the weasel family, the river otter occurs throughout the state except on Aleutian Islands, Bering Sea islands and on the Arctic coastal plain east of Point Lay. They are most abundant in southeastern Alaska, Prince William Sound coastal areas and on the Yukon-Kuskokwim Delta.

Raccoon — The raccoon is not native to Alaska and is considered an undesirable addition because of impact on native furbearers. It is found on the west coast of Kodiak Island, on Japonski and Baranof islands, and on other islands off Prince of Wales Island in Southeast.

Squirrel — *Northern Flying:* These small nocturnal squirrels are found in interior, southcentral and southeastern Alaska where coniferous forests are sufficiently dense to provide suitable habitat. *Red:* These tree squirrels inhabit spruce forests, especially along rivers, from Southeast north to the Brooks Range. They are not found on the Seward Peninsula, Yukon-Kuskokwim Delta and Alaska Peninsula south of Naknek River.

Weasel — Least weasels and short-tailed weasels are found throughout Alaska, except for Bering Sea and Aleutian islands. Short-tailed weasels are brown with white underparts in summer, becoming snow-white in winter (designated ermine).

Other Small Mammals

Bat — There are five common bat species in Alaska.

Northern hare (arctic hare or tundra hare) — This large hare inhabits western and northern coastal Alaska, weighs 12 pounds or more and measures $2\frac{1}{2}$ feet long.

Snowshoe hare (or varying hare) — In winter, these animals become pure white; in summer, their coats are grayish to brown. The snowshoe hare occurs throughout Alaska except for lower portion of Alaska Peninsula, Arctic coast and most islands; it is scarce in southeastern Alaska. Cyclic population highs and

lows of hares occur roughly every 10 years. Their big hind feet, covered with coarse hair in winter, make for easy travel over snow.

Brown lemming — Lemmings are found throughout northern Alaska and the Alaska Peninsula; they are not present in Southeast, Southcentral or Kodiak archipelago.

Collared lemming — Resembling large meadow voles, collared lemmings are found from the Brooks Range north and from the lower Kuskokwim River drainage north.

Northern bog lemming (sometimes called lemming mice) — These tiny mammals, rarely observed, occur in meadows and bogs across most of Alaska.

Deer mouse — Inhabit timber and brush in southeastern Alaska.

House mouse — Extremely adaptive, familiar house mice are found in Alaska seaports and large communities in southcentral Alaska.

Meadow jumping mouse — These mice can jump six feet and are in the southern third of Alaska from Alaska Range to Gulf of Alaska.

Collared pika — Members of the rabbit family, pikas are found in central and southern Alaska; most common in Alaska Range.

Porcupine — These rodents are slow-moving animals that prefer forests and are found in most wooded regions of mainland Alaska.

Norway rat — The Norway rat came to Alaska on whaling ships to Pribilof Islands in mid-1800s; especially thriving in the Aleutians (the Rat Islands group is named for the Norway rats). They are now found in virtually all Alaska seaports, and in Anchorage and Fairbanks and other population centers with open garbage dumps.

Shrew — Seven species of shrew range in Alaska.

Meadow vole (or meadow mouse) — Extremely adaptive, there are seven species of meadow vole attributed to Alaska that range throughout the state.

Red-backed vole — The red-backed vole prefers cool, damp forests and is found throughout Alaska from Southeast to Norton Sound.

Woodchuck — These large, burrowing squirrels, also called groundhogs, are found in the eastern Interior between Yukon and Tanana rivers, from east of Fairbanks to Alaska-Canada border.

Bushy-tailed woodrat — Commonly called pack rats because they tend to carry off objects to their nests, woodrats are found along mainland coast of southeastern Alaska.

Marine Mammals

Marine mammals found in Alaska waters are: **dolphin** (Grampus, Pacific white-sided and Risso's); **Pacific walrus**; **porpoise** (Dall and harbor); **sea otter**; **seal** (harbor, larga, northern elephant, northern fur, Pacific bearded or *oogruk*, ribbon, ringed and spotted); **Steller sea lion**; and **whale** (Baird's beaked or giant bottlenose, beluga, narwhal, blue, bowhead, Cuvier's beaked or goosebeaked, fin or finback, gray humpback, killer, minke or little piked, northern right, pilot, sei, sperm and Stejneger's beaked or Bering Sea beaked).

The Marine Mammal Protection Act, passed by Congress on Dec. 21, 1972,

provided for a complete moratorium on the taking and importation of all marine mammals. The purpose of the act was to give protection to population stocks of marine mammals that "are, or may be, in danger of extinction or depletion as a result of man's activities." Congress further found that marine mammals have "proven themselves to be resources of great international significance, aesthetic and recreational as well as economic, and it is the sense of the Congress that they should be protected and encouraged to develop to the greatest extent feasible commensurate with sound policies of resource management and that the primary objective of their management should be to maintain the health and stability of the marine ecosystem. Whenever consistent with this primary objective, it should be the goal to obtain an optimum sustainable population keeping in mind the carrying capacity of the habitat."

At the present time, the U.S. Fish and Wildlife Service (Department of the Interior) is responsible for the management of polar bears, sea otters and walrus in Alaska. The National Marine Fisheries Service (Department of Commerce) is responsible for the

management of all other marine mammals. The state of Alaska assumed management of walrus in April 1976, and relinquished it back to the USFWS in July 1979. However, an amendment to the Marine Mammal Protection Act in 1981 makes it easier for states to assume management of marine mammals, and Alaska is currently going through the necessary steps to assume management of its marine mammals.

Masks

Masks are integral to the cultures of the Eskimos, coastal Indians and Aleuts of Alaska.

Eskimo

Eskimo masks rank among the finest tribal art in the world. Ceremonialism and the mask-making that accompanied it were highly developed and practiced widely by the time the first Russians established trading posts in southeast Alaska in the early 1800s. By the early part of the 20th century, masks were made much less frequently and were rarely made for ceremonial use.

The shaman used masks during

certain ceremonies, sometimes in conjunction with wooden puppets, in ways that frightened and entertained participants. Dancers wore religious masks in festivals that honored the spirits of animals and birds to be hunted or that needed to be appeased. Each spirit was interpreted visually in a different mask and each mask was thought to have a spirit, or *inua,* of its own. This *inua* tied the mask to the stream of spiritual beliefs present in Eskimo religion. Not all masks were benign; some were surrealistic pieces that represented angry or dangerous spirits.

Ceremonial mask-making has remained popular in some regions, notably among King Islanders, on Nunivak Island and in other areas of southwest Alaska.

Indian

Several types of masks existed among the coastal Indians of Alaska, including simple single-face masks, occasionally having an elaborately carved totemic border; a variation of the face mask with the addition of moving parts; and transformation masks, which have several faces hidden behind the first.

Masked dancers were accompanied by a chorus of tribal singers who sang songs associated with the masks and reflecting the wealth of the host. Masks were the critical element in portraying the relationship of the tribe with spirits

and projecting their power to spellbind their audiences.

Masks were always created to be worn, but not all members of the tribe held sufficient status or power to wear them. Ceremonial use of masks generally took place in the fall or winter, when the spirits of the other world were said to be nearby.

Crudely carved masks created for fun were occasionally made among the Kwakiutl.

Northwest Coast Indian maskmakers primarily used alder, though red and yellow cedar were used at times.

Aleut

Examples of masks used on various islands of the Aleutian Chain for shamanistic and ceremonial purposes are reported as early as the mid-18th century. Some of these early masks were described as bizarre representations of various animals, but many were apparently destroyed after use and none survive today. Aleut legends maintain that some masks were associated with ancient inhabitants of the region, a people apparently considered unrelated.

On the Shumagin Islands, a group of cavelike chambers yielded important examples of Aleut masks late in the 19th century. A number of wellpreserved masks, apparently associated with the burials of Aleut whalers, were found. All of them had once been painted. Some of them had attached

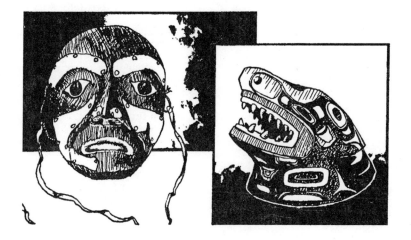

ears and pegs where tooth grips for wearing the masks would have been placed. Other pegs and holes were used for inserting feathers or carved wooden appendages similar to those of Eskimo masks of southern Alaska today. Fragments of composite masks, those decorated with feathers, appendages or movable parts, have been found on Kagamil Island with earlier remains.

Early accounts of masked Aleut dances say each dance was accompanied by special songs. Most masks were apparently hidden in caves or secret places when the ceremony ended, possibly for good luck. Bone masks worn by members of burial parties in some regions were broken and discarded at the gravesite when funeral rites were completed.

Today, no Aleut mask-makers in the old tradition survive, so further explanation of the use and significance of masks already collected depends on future archaeological investigation.

Medal of Heroism

By a law established in 1965, the Alaska governor is authorized to award, in recognition of valorous and heroic deeds, a state medal of heroism to persons who have saved a life or, at risk to their lives, have served the state or community on behalf of the health,

welfare or safety of other persons. The heroism medal may be awarded posthumously. Following are recipients of the Alaska Medal of Heroism:

Albert Rothfuss (1965), Ketchikan. Rescued a child from drowning in Ketchikan Creek.

Randy Blake Prinzing (1968), Soldotna. Saved two lives at Scout Lake.

Nancy Davis (1971), Seattle. A flight attendant who convinced an alleged hijacker to surrender to authorities.

Jeffrey Stone (1972), Fairbanks. Saved the lives of two youths from a burning apartment.

Gilbert Pelowook (1975), Savoonga. An Alaska state trooper who aided plane crash victims on Saint Lawrence Island.

Residents of Gambell (1975). Provided aid and care for plane crash victims on Saint Lawrence Island.

George Jackinsky (1978), Kasilof. Rescued two persons from a burning aircraft.

Mike Hancock (1980), Lima, Ohio. In 1977, rescued a victim of a plane crash that brought down high-voltage lines.

John Stimson (1983), Cordova. A first sergeant in the Division of Fish and Wildlife Protection who died in a helicopter accident during an attempt to rescue others.

Robert Larson (1983), Anchorage. A Department of Public Safety employee who flew through hazardous conditions to rescue survivors of the crash that took John Stimson's life.

David Graham (1983), Kenai. Rescued a person from a burning car.

Darren Olanna (1984), Nome. Died while attempting to rescue a person from a burning house.

Esther Farquhar (1984), Sitka. Tried to save other members of her family from a fire in their home; lost her life in the attempt.

Billy Westlock (1986), Emmonak. Rescued a youngster from the Emmonak River.

Lt. Comm. Whiddon, Lt. Breithaupt, ASM2 Tunks, AD1 Saylor, AT3 Milne (1987), Sitka. Rescued a man and his son from their sinking boat during high seas.

Army and Air National Guard (1988), Gambell, Savoonga, Nome and Shishmaref. Searched for seven missing walrus hunters.

Evans Geary, Johnny Sheldon, Jason Rutman, Jessee Ahkpuk Jr. and Carl Hadley (1989), Buckland. These youth rescued two friends who, while ice skating on a frozen pond, had fallen through the ice.

Metric Conversions

As in the rest of the United States, metrics are slow in coming to Alaska. These conversion formulas will help to prepare for the metric system and to understand measurements in neighboring Yukon Territory. Approximate conversions from customary to metric and vice versa:

	When you know:	You can find:	If you multiply by:
Length	inches	millimeters	25.4
	feet	centimeters	30.5
	yards	meters	0.9
	miles	kilometers	1.6
	millimeters	inches	0.04
	centimeters	inches	0.4
	meters	yards	1.1
	kilometers	miles	0.6
Area	square inches	square centimeters	6.5
	square feet	square meters	0.09
	square yards	square meters	0.8
	square miles	square kilometers	2.6
	acres	square hectometers (hectares)	0.4
	square centimeters	square inches	0.16
	square meters	square yards	1.2
	square kilometers	square miles	0.4
	square hectometers (hectares)	acres	2.5
Weight	ounces	grams	28.4
	pounds	kilograms	0.45
	short tons	megagrams (metric tons)	0.9
	grams	ounces	0.04
	kilograms	pounds	2.2
	megagrams (metric tons)	short tons	1.1
Liquid Volume	ounces	milliliters	29.6
	pints	liters	0.47
	quarts	liters	0.95
	gallons	liters	3.8
	milliliters	ounces	0.03
	liters	pints	2.1
	liters	quarts	1.06
	liters	gallons	0.26
Temperature	degrees Fahrenheit	degrees Celsius	5/9 (after subtracting 32)
	degrees Celsius	degrees Fahrenheit	9/5 (then add 32)

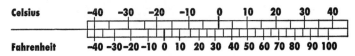

Celsius: −40 −30 −20 −10 0 10 20 30 40

Fahrenheit: −40 −30 −20 −10 0 10 20 30 40 50 60 70 80 90 100

Mileage Chart

DRIVING MILEAGES BETWEEN PRINCIPAL POINTS	Anchorage, AK	Dawson City, YT	Dawson Creek, BC	Fairbanks, AK	Haines, AK	Homer, AK	Prince Rupert, BC	Seattle, WA	Skagway, AK	Valdez, AK	Whitehorse, YT
Anchorage, AK		515	1608	358	775	226	1605	2435	832	304	724
Dawson City, YT	515		1195	393	578	741	1192	2022	435	441	327
Dawson Creek, BC	1608	1195		1486	1135	1834	706	827	992	1534	884
Fairbanks, AK	358	393	1486		653	584	1483	2313	710	284	602
Haines, AK	775	578	1135	653		1001	1132	1962	359	701	251
Homer, AK	226	741	1834	584	1001		1831	2661	1058	530	950
Prince Rupert, BC	1605	1192	706	1483	1132	1831		1033	989	1531	881
Seattle, WA	2435	2022	827	2313	1962	2661	1033		1819	2361	1711
Skagway, AK	832	435	992	710	359	1058	989	1819		758	108
Valdez, AK	304	441	1534	284	701	530	1531	2361	758		650
Whitehorse, YT	724	327	884	602	251	950	881	1711	108	650	

Military

Until the rapid escalation of war in Europe in 1940–41, Congress saw little need for a strong military presence in Alaska. Spurred by World War II, and a growing realization that Alaska could shorten the route to Asia for friend and foe, the government built and now maintains units of the Air Force, Army, Navy and Coast Guard at dozens of installations across the state and on floating units in Alaskan waters. At the state level are Air National Guard and Army National Guard units. (*See* National Guard)

The Army Corps of Engineers has three offices in Alaska: the Alaska District Office at Elmendorf Air Force Base, the Denali Area Office at Fort Richardson and the Fairbanks Resident Office at Fort Wainwright. A small number of project offices are scattered across the state at Corps construction sites. Clear, Alaska, is the site of one of three Ballistic Missile Early Warning System (BMEWS) stations (the others are in Greenland and England). Operating since 1961, the BMEWS station's three 400-foot-wide, 165-foot-high radar screens scan the skies from the North Pole to China. Designed to give the U.S. at least a 15-minute warning before the missiles hit, the BMEWS supplemented the earlier Distant Early Warning (DEW) Line, which was designed to detect bombers crossing into North American air space, but was ineffective in detecting ballistic missiles. The Alaska sector of the DEW Line System, however, is still in full operation. With facilities as shown on the accompanying map, it provides radar coverage of the North Slope and meshes with the Canadian DEW Line to provide protection from cruise-missile-carrying bombers and tactical attack at Prudhoe and all of northern Alaska. The DEW Line is operated by a civilian contractor for the Air Force Tactical Air Command.

The 6th Infantry Division (Light) is the primary Army unit in Alaska. The headquarters, located at Fort Richardson near Anchorage since the division was activated in March 1986, moved to Fort Wainwright, near Fairbanks, in the summer and fall of 1990. Besides combat and combat support forces at those two posts, the division has research facilities and extensive training land at Fort Greely, near Delta Junction. The division is under the command of a two-star general, and must be prepared to deploy rapidly in the Pacific theater and elsewhere as directed in support of contingency operations, U.S. Pacific Command objectives and United States national interests. The division is also charged with the defense of Alaska.

The primary units within the division, which carry out this mission, include: the 1st and 2nd Infantry Brigades in Alaska and the 205th Infantry Brigade, a U.S. Army Reserve unit headquartered at Fort Snelling in St. Paul, Minnesota. In the event of a national emergency, the 205th will deploy to Alaska to "round out" the division. In addition to the three infantry brigades, major units in the division include the Aviation Brigade, Division Support Command, 6th Signal Battalion, the 6th Engineer Battalion and the 106th Military Intelligence Battalion.

Primary nondivisional units and activities include the 1117th Signal Battalion, which oversees all Army communications in the state; the Northern Warfare Training Center at Fort Greely, which trains soldiers, guardsmen and representatives from other services in arctic combat and survival; and the Cold Regions Test Center, also at Fort Greely, where equipment is tested for cold weather use.

Since 1987, several emergency deployment readiness exercises have been conducted, emphasizing and improving unit movement capabilities. The 6th Infantry Division (Light) is planning for its participation in Arctic Warrior 91, the next midwinter, joint service exercise, which is scheduled for January–February 1991.

Army helicopters in the state play an important role in search and rescue, and in providing medical assistance to military and civilian personnel. In fiscal year 1989 (October 1988 through September 1989), Army aircraft were sent on 41 missions, assisting 23 soldiers and 18 civilians. Although civic involvement during the 1989 climbing season was restricted to assisting with set up of a civilian rescue and research station on Mount McKinley, the Army's High Altitude Rescue Team (HART), flying specially equipped Chinook (CH-47) helicopters, has in past years gone to the upper reaches of McKinley and other Alaska peaks to rescue injured climbers. The M.A.S.T. (Military Assistance to Safety and Traffic) helicopters based at Fort Wainwright assisted 49 military patients and 45 civilians in 1989.

The Air Force is represented in Alaska by the Alaskan Air Command, which has headquarters at Elmendorf Air Force Base and whose mission is "Top Cover for North America." This top cover is supplied by aircraft such as the F-15 Eagles of the 43rd and 54th Tactical Fighter Squadrons, the A-10A Thunderbolt IIs of the 18th Tactical Fighter Squadron, the T-33 Shooting Stars of the 5021st Tactical Operations Squadron and the OV-10 Broncos of the 25th Tactical Air Support Squadron.

The Alaskan Air Command stands ready to train and employ combat-ready, tactical air forces to preserve the national sovereignty of United States lands, waters and air space and to provide "Top Cover for North America."

The total population of the uniformed services in Alaska on Sept. 30, 1988, was approximately 76,560. Population figures include active duty personnel, Department of Defense Civil Service employees, Nonappropriated Fund and Exchange personnel, and dependents. Of the total, 25,647 were active duty uniformed personnel and 5,342 were Civil Service employees of the Department of Defense. The total makes up approximately 16 percent of Alaska's population.

On a per capita basis, Alaska's veterans population of over 71,000 is the largest of any state. In response to increasing needs, the Division of Veterans Affairs was established in 1984. It is the state's official veterans advocate and coordinator of veterans issues and programs. It is also the liaison with federal and state agencies, veterans organizations, other states' veterans affairs organizations and the state's administration. The division ensures that Alaska's veterans and their dependents are aware of every state and federal benefit available to them and assists them in taking advantage of those benefits.

The U.S. Coast Guard has been a part of Alaska since the mid-1800s, when it patrolled its extensive and unforgiving coastline with the wooden sailing and steam ships of its predecessor, the Revenue Cutter Service.

Since those early days, the service has changed names (several times, in fact) and those wooden ships have been

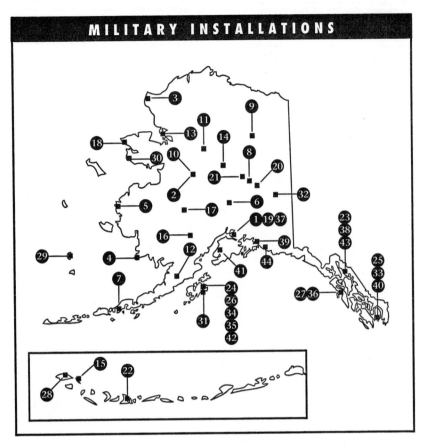

MILITARY INSTALLATIONS

Map Key/Installation/Personnel
Air Force
1 Elmendorf AFB, 6,751
2 Campion AFS*
3 Cape Lisburne AFS*
4 Cape Newenham AFS*
5 Cape Romanzof AFS*
6 Clear AFS, 122
7 Cold Bay AFS*
8 Eielson AFB, 3,282
9 Fort Yukon AFS*
10 Galena Airport, 309
11 Indian Mountain AFS*
12 King Salmon, 275
13 Kotzebue AFS*
14 Murphy Dome AFS*
15 Shemya AFB, 598
16 Sparrevohn AFS*
17 Tatalina AFS*
18 Tin City AFS*
Army
19 Fort Richardson, 4,800

20 Fort Greely, 480
21 Fort Wainwright, 5,000
Navy
22 Adak, 1,677
Coast Guard
23 17th District Office Juneau, 170
24 Kodiak Support Center, 287
25 Base/Group Ketchikan, 101
26 Air Station Kodiak, 352
27 Air Station Sitka, 124
28 LORAN Station Attu, 24
29 LORAN Station Saint Paul, 21
30 LORAN Station Port Clarence, 27
31 LORAN Station Narrow Cape, 14
32 LORAN Station Tok, 7
33 LORAN Station Shoal Cove, 15
34 Communication Station Kodiak, 94
35 LORAN Monitoring Station
   Kodiak, 17
36 Marine Safety Detachment Sitka, 1
37 Marine Safety Office Anchorage, 25
38 Marine Safety Office Juneau, 12

Map Key/Installation/Personnel

39 Marine Safety Office Valdez, 40
40 Marine Safety Detachment
   Ketchikan, 1
41 Marine Safety Detachment Kenai, 4
42 Marine Safety Detachment Kodiak, 2
43 Station Juneau, 14
44 Seasonal Air Facility Cordova*
*Now operated by civilian personnel.

U.S. Coast Guard Cutters/Personnel

Cape Carter, 14; *Cape Hatteras*, 14; *Elderberry*, 6; *Firebush*, 55; *Ironwood*, 55; *Mustang*, 16; *Naushon*, 16; *Planetree*, 55; *Sedge*, 55; *Storis*, 75; *Sweetbrier*, 56; *Woodrush*, 55; *Yocona*, 82

Total Military Expenditures in Alaska by Agency for Fiscal Year 1989 (in millions of dollars)

Service	Pay	Construction	Operations & Maintenance	Other Procurement	Total
Air Force	$359.0	$ 66.1	$259.0	$133.9	$818.0
Army	308.5	70.2	147.3	28.9	554.9
Coast Guard	43.9	20.0	51.8	2.5	118.2
Corps of Engineers	22.0	0.0	27.6	10.8	60.4
National Guard	47.2	37.3	8.0	0.3	92.8
Navy*	55.9	33.4	33.2	0.3	122.8
Total	$838.5	$227.0	$527.0	$176.7	$1,669.2

*Includes Marines

Military Expenditures in Alaska for Fiscal Years 1984-1989 (in millions of dollars)

	1984	1985	1986	1987	1988	1989
Military Payroll	$ 469.9	$ 503.1	$ 516.0	$ 567.5	$ 595.5	$605.3
Civilian Payroll	182.1	189.7	181.5	212.4	204.9	204.0
Operations & Maintenance	362.6	389.1	493.3	645.3	485.1	527.1
Construction	135.1	204.0	180.3	204.9	167.6	227.0
Subtotal Appropriated Funds	1,149.7	1,285.9	1,371.1	1,630.1	1,453.1	1,563.4
Exchange & Nonappropriated Payrolls	24.1	32.8	35.7	32.5	29.5	30.7
Other Procurement	161.0	136.9	149.5	105.4	194.5	176.7
Subtotal Other	185.1	169.7	185.2	137.9	224.0	207.4
DOD Retirement	113.1	122.3	130.4	139.5	146.4	
Total	$1,338.8	$1,568.7	$1,678.6	$1,898.4	$1,816.6	$1,917.2

replaced by today's modern fleet of ships, boats and aircraft, operated and maintained by Alaska's Coast Guard men and women.

The 17th Coast Guard District encompasses the entire state of Alaska, or 33,904 miles of coastline — more than all other states combined. As the nation's smallest military service, the U.S. Coast Guard performs its many missions in Alaska with 2,020 military and civilian employees at 38 units.

The U.S. Coast Guard's LORAN (long-range navigation) stations are a system of ground stations that transmit pulsed radio signals. The 17th Coast Guard District has six LORAN sites that collectively form an umbrella of electronic aid to navigation in the North Pacific Ocean, Bering Sea and the Gulf of Alaska. Signals are used by commercial as well as Coast Guard aircraft and ships.

Minerals and Mining

(*See also* Coal; Gold; Oil and Gas; *and* Rocks and Gems)

In 1989, there were an estimated 4,170 people employed in mineral-related mining sectors in Alaska, according to the state Division of Geological and Geophysical Surveys. The early years of the 1970s were relatively quiet in the industry, with exploration primarily limited to geological reconnaissance. Late in 1974, restrictions on gold in the United States were lifted and the price of gold soared, spurring a revival of gold mining in the state.

By 1981, several large deposits containing minerals such as copper, chromite, molybdenum, nickel and uranium were the subject of serious exploration. Estimated exploration costs were in excess of $100 million for 1981, and more than 3,000 people were employed in the industry.

In 1989, the total value of Alaska's mineral industry, as measured by the sum of exploration and development expenditures and mineral production, amounted to $472.5 million. The industry experienced positive growth during 1989, especially in the hard-rock mining and exploration sectors, but suffered declines in mineral-development expenditures and in sand-and-gravel and stone production.

Gold was the most valuable mineral commodity in 1989, accounting for 39 percent of Alaska's total mineral production revenues. Overall, metallic mineral production accounted for 65 percent of total mineral values, reversing a 25-year period dominated by the nonmetallic materials coal, sand and gravel, stone, peat and jade, which account for the remaining 35 percent of the values.

Usibelli Coal Mines near Healy continue as the state's commercial coal mine. Production of coal in 1989 was estimated at 1.45 million tons, down 6 percent from 1988. Of that total, 747,095 short tons were burned in interior Alaska power plants and 705,258 short tons were shipped to Korea.

During 1989, the Greens Creek Mine on Admiralty Island began production. This is a modern, state of the art, underground mine producing silver along with some lead, zinc and gold. This mine, near Kivalina in northwestern Alaska, employs 230 people and during 1989 produced over 6 million ounces of silver, becoming the largest silver producer in the U.S. Also in 1989, the Red Dog Mine began operation. In 1990, it became the largest zinc producer in the western world with production of 400,000 metric tons of zinc concentrate. The mine is a joint venture between Cominco Alaska and NANA Native Corporation and employs almost 300 people.

Until recently, Alaska was the only state to produce platinum, the fabled metal whose rarity exceeds that of gold. As of 1988, more than half a million ounces of platinum had been extracted by placer operations near the village of Goodnews Bay in southwestern Alaska. More recent production figures have been withheld. This information is according to the Alaska Division of Geological and Geophysical Surveys.

Miscellaneous Facts

State capital: Juneau.
State population: 537,800 in January 1988.
Land area: 586,412 square miles, or about 365,000,000 acres — largest state in the union; one-fifth the size of the Lower 48.
Area per person: There are 1.02 square miles for each person in Alaska. New York has .003 square miles per person.
Diameter: East to west, 2,400 miles; north to south, 1,420 miles.
Coastline: 6,640 miles, point to point; as measured on the most detailed maps available, including islands, Alaska has 33,904 miles of shoreline. Estimated tidal shoreline, including

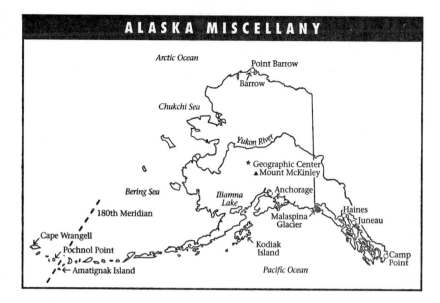

ALASKA MISCELLANY

Arctic Ocean
Point Barrow
Barrow
Chukchi Sea
Yukon River
★ Geographic Center
▲ Mount McKinley
Bering Sea
Iliamna Lake
Anchorage
180th Meridian
Malaspina Glacier
Haines
Juneau
Cape Wrangell
Pochnol Point
Kodiak Island
Camp Point
Amatignak Island
Pacific Ocean

islands, inlets and shoreline to head of tidewater, is 47,300 miles.

Adjacent salt water: North Pacific Ocean, Bering Sea, Chukchi Sea, Arctic Ocean.

Alaska/Canada border: 1,538 miles long; length of boundary between the Arctic Ocean and Mount Saint Elias, 647 miles; Southeast border with British Columbia and Yukon Territory, 710 miles; water boundary, 181 miles.

Geographic center: 63°50′ north, 152° west, about 60 miles northwest of Mount McKinley.

Northernmost point: Point Barrow, 71°23′ north.

Southernmost point: Tip of Amatignak Island, Aleutian Chain, 51°13′05" north.

Easternmost and westernmost points: It all depends on how you look at it. The 180th meridian — halfway around the world from the prime meridian at Greenwich, England, and the dividing line between east and west longitudes — passes through Alaska. According to one view, Alaska has both the easternmost and westernmost spots in the country! The westernmost is Amatignak Island, 179°10′ west; and the easternmost, Pochnoi Point, 179°46′ east. On the other hand, if you are

facing north, east is to your right and west to your left. Therefore, the westernmost point is Cape Wrangell, Attu Island, 172°27′ east; and the easternmost is near Camp Point, in southeastern Alaska, 129°59′ west.

Farthest north supermarket: In Barrow; constructed on stilts to prevent snow build-up, at a cost of $4 million.

Tallest mountain: Mount McKinley, 20,320 feet.

Largest natural freshwater lake: Iliamna, 1,150 square miles.

Longest river: Yukon, 1,400 miles in Alaska; 1,875 total.

Largest glacier: Malaspina, 850 square miles.

Largest city in population: Anchorage, population 222,950 as of July 1988.

Largest city in area: Juneau with 3,108 square miles (also largest city in square miles in North America).

Typical Alaskan: According to 1985 census figures, 27 years old and male. (About 51 percent of Alaskans are male, the highest percentage of any state.) Median age: 27.5 years, second only to Utah as the state with the youngest population.

Oldest building: Erskine House in Kodiak, built by the Russians, probably between 1793 and 1796.

World's largest and busiest seaplane

base: Lake Hood, in Anchorage, accommodating more than 800 takeoffs and landings on a peak summer day.

World's largest concentration of bald eagles: Along Chilkat River, just north of Haines. More than 3,500 bald eagles gather here in fall and winter months for late salmon runs.

Median income: $50,750, sixth highest in the nation per household income.

Per capita personal income: $19,079 in 1989, eighth highest in the nation.

Miss Alaska

The legislature has declared that the young woman selected as Miss Alaska each year will be the state's official hostess. Holders of the title are selected in Anchorage each spring in a competition sponsored by the nonprofit Miss Alaska Scholarship Pageant organization.

1990 — Holly Ann Salo, Kenai
1989 — Christine Rae McCubbins, Kenai
1988 — Launa Middaugh, Anchorage
1987 — Teresa Murton, Anchorage
1986 — Jerri Morrison, Anchorage
1985 — Kristina Christopher Taylor, Palmer
1984 — Marilin Blackburn, Anchorage
1983 — Jennifer Smith, Soldotna
1982 — Kristan Sapp, Wasilla
1981 — Laura Trollan, Juneau
1980 — Sandra Lashbrook, Chugiak–Eagle River
1979 — Lila Oberg, Matanuska Valley
1978 — Patty-Jo Gentry, Fairbanks
1977 — Lisa Granath, Kenai
1976 — Kathy Tebow, Anchorage
1975 — Cindy Suryan, Kodiak
1974 — Darby Moore, Kenai
1973 — Virginia Adams, Anchorage
1972 — Deborah Wood, Elmendorf Air Force Base
1971 — Linda Joy Smith, Elmendorf Air Force Base
1970 — Virginia Walker, Kotzebue
1969 — Gwen Gregg, Elmendorf Air Force Base
1968 — Jane Haycraft, Fairbanks
1967 — Penny Ann Thomasson, Anchorage
1966 — Nancy Lorell Wellman, Fairbanks
1965 — Mary Ruth Nidiffer, Alaska Methodist University
1964 — Karol Rae Hommon, Anchorage
1963 — Colleen Sharon Kendall, Matanuska Valley
1962 — Mary Dee Fox, Anchorage
1961 — Jean Ann Holm, Fairbanks
1960 — June Bowdish, Anchorage
1959 — Alansa Rounds Carr, Ketchikan

Mosquitoes

At least 25 species of mosquito are found in Alaska (the number may be as high as 40), the females of all species feeding on people, other mammals or birds. Males and females eat plant sugar, but only the females suck blood, which they use for egg production. The itch that follows the bite comes from an anticoagulant injected by the mosquito. No Alaska mosquitoes carry diseases. The insects are present from April through September in many areas of the state. Out in the bush they are often at their worst in June, tapering off in July. The mosquito plague usually passes by late August and September. From Cook Inlet south, they concentrate on coastal flats and forested valleys. In the Aleutian Islands, mosquitoes are absent or present only in small numbers. The most serious mosquito infestations occur in moist areas of slow-moving or standing water, of the type found in the fields, bogs and forests of interior Alaska, from Bristol Bay eastward.

Mosquitoes are most active at dusk and dawn; low temperatures and high winds decrease their activity. Mosquitoes can be controlled by draining their breeding areas or spraying with approved insecticides. When traveling in areas of heavy mosquito infestations, it is wise to wear protective clothing, carefully screen living and camping areas and use a good insect repellent.

Mountains

Of the 20 highest mountains in the United States, 17 are in Alaska, which has 19 peaks over 14,000 feet. The U.S. Geological Survey lists them as follows:

Map Key/Elevation

1 McKinley, South Peak, 20,320 feet*
1 McKinley, North Peak, 19,470 feet*
2 Saint Elias, 18,008 feet**
3 Foraker, 17,400 feet
4 Bona, 16,500 feet
5 Blackburn, 16,390 feet
6 Sanford, 16,237 feet
1 South Buttress, 15,885 feet
7 Vancouver, 15,700 feet**
8 Churchill, 15,638 feet
9 Fairweather, 15,300 feet**

Map Key/Elevation

10 Hubbard, 15,015 feet**
11 Bear, 14,831 feet
1 East Buttress, 14,730 feet
12 Hunter, 14,573 feet
13 Alverstone, 14,565 feet**
1 Browne Tower, 14,530 feet
14 Wrangell, 14,163 feet
15 Augusta, 14,070 feet**

*Note: The two peaks of Mount McKinley are known collectively as the Churchill Peaks.

**On Alaska-Canada border.

Other Well-Known Alaska Mountains/Elevation

Augustine Volcano, 4,025 feet
Deborah, 12,339 feet
Devils Paw, 8,584 feet
Devils Thumb, 9,077 feet
Doonerak, 7,610 feet
Drum, 12,010 feet
Edgecumbe, 3,201 feet
Hayes, 13,832 feet
Kates Needle, 10,002 feet
Marcus Baker, 13,176 feet
Shishaldin, 9,372 feet

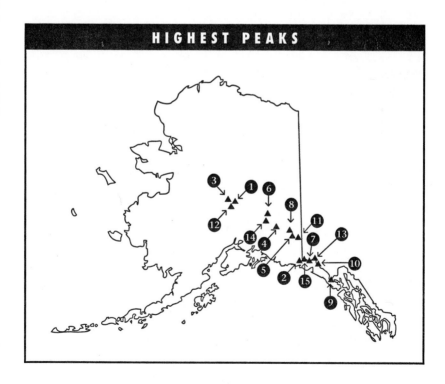

HIGHEST PEAKS

Mountain Ranges/Elevation

Ahklun Mountains, 1,000–3,000 feet
Alaska Range to 20,320 feet
Aleutian Range to 7,585 feet
Askinuk Mountains to 2,342 feet
Baird Mountains to 4,300 feet
Bendeleben Mountains to 3,730 feet
Brabazon Range to 5,515 feet
Brooks Range, 4,000–9,000 feet
Chigmit Mountains to 5,000 feet
Chugach Mountains to 13,176 feet
Coast Mountains to 18,000 feet
Darby Mountains to 3,083 feet
Davidson Mountains to 5,540 feet
De Long Mountains to 4,886 feet
Endicott Mountains to 7,000 feet
Fairweather Range to 15,300 feet
Igichuk Hills to 2,000 feet
Kaiyuh Mountains, 1,000–2,844 feet
Kenai Mountains to 6,000 feet
Kiglapak Mountains to 1,070 feet
Kigluaik Mountains to 4,714 feet
Kuskokwim Mountains to 3,973 feet
Lookout Range to 2,400 feet
Mentasta Mountains, 4,000–7,000 feet
Moore Mountains to 3,000 feet
Nutzotin Mountains, 5,000–8,000 feet
Ray Mountains, 2,500–5,500 feet
Romanzof Mountains to 8,700 feet
St. Elias Mountains to 18,000 feet
Schwatka Mountains to 8,800 feet
Shublik Mountains to 4,500 feet
Sischu Mountains to 2,422 feet
Talkeetna Mountains, 6,000–8,800 feet
Waxell Ridge, 4,000–10,000 feet
White Mountains to 5,000 feet
Wrangell Mountains to 16,421 feet
York Mountains to 2,349 feet
Zane Hills to 4,053 feet

Mount McKinley

Mount McKinley in the Alaska Range is the highest mountain on the North American continent. The South Peak is 20,320 feet high; the North Peak has an elevation of 19,470 feet. The mountain was named in 1896 for William McKinley of Ohio, who at the time was the Republican candidate for president. An earlier name had been Denali, a Tanaina Indian word meaning "the big one" or "the great one." The state of Alaska officially renamed the mountain Denali in 1975 and the state Geographic Names Board claims the proper name for the mountain is Denali. However, the federal Board of Geographic Names has not taken any action and congressional legislation has been introduced to retain the name McKinley in perpetuity.

Mount McKinley is within Denali National Park and Preserve (formerly Mount McKinley National Park). The park entrance is about 237 miles north of Anchorage and 121 miles south of Fairbanks via the George Parks Highway. (A 90-mile gravel road runs west from the highway through the park; vehicle traffic on the park road is restricted.) The park is also accessible via the Alaska Railroad and by aircraft. The mountain and its park are the top tourist attractions in Alaska. The finest times to see McKinley up close are on summer mornings. August is best, according to statistics based on 13 summers of observation by park ranger Rick McIntyre. The mountain is rarely visible the entire day. The best view is from Eielson Visitor Center, located about 66 miles from the park entrance and 33 miles northeast of the summit. The center, open from early June through the second week in September, is accessible via free shuttle bus provided by the park.

A record 1,009 climbers attempted to reach the summit of Mount McKinley by the end of the 1989 climbing season, of which 524 (52 percent) were successful. Of those 1,009 climbers, 36 percent were from outside the U.S., representing 27 foreign countries. The greatest number of foreign mountaineers came from Germany. Also in 1989, the first solo winter ascent of the West Rib route was accomplished by Anchorage climber and Mount McKinley guide Dave Stahaeli. Despite the record number of climbers, search and rescue incidents were at the lowest level since 1975. Six foreign mountaineers lost their lives in mountaineering accidents during the 1989 season.

Related reading: *To the Top of Denali,* by Bill Sherwonit. A collection of Mount McKinley climbing stories. *Grizzly Cub,* by Rick McIntyre. A bear's first five summers, recorded by a Denali National Park ranger. See ALASKA NORTHWEST LIBRARY in the back of the book.

Mukluks

Lightweight boots designed to provide warmth in extreme cold. Eskimo mukluks are traditionally made with *oogruk* (bearded seal) skin bottoms and caribou tops and trimmed with fur. (Mukluk is also another name for *oogruk.*) Athabascan mukluks are traditionally made of moose hide and trimmed with fur and beadwork.

Related reading: *Secrets of Eskimo Skin Sewing* by Edna Wilder. The complete book on the art of Eskimo skin sewing, with how-to-do-it instructions and things-to-make ideas. See ALASKA NORTHWEST LIBRARY in the back of the book.

Muktuk

This Eskimo delicacy consists of the outer skin layers of whales. The two species of whale most often used for muktuk are the bowhead whale and the beluga, or white whale. The outer skin layers consist of a corky protective layer, the true skin and the blubber. In the case of beluga muktuk, the outer layer is white, the next layer is black and the blubber is pink. It may be eaten fresh, frozen, cooked or pickled.

Museums, Cultural Centers and Repositories

Visiting any of the following museums, historic sites, or other repositories offers a look into the rich diversity of Alaskan culture and history. For information about hours of operation and features of the collections, write to the addresses given or check with the Alaska State Division of Tourism, P.O. Box E, Juneau 99811; or Museums Alaska, Inc., 3779 Bartlett St., Homer 99603.

Adak Community Museum, P.O. Box 5244, NAV/STA, FPO Seattle, WA 98791

Alaska Indian Arts, Inc., P.O. Box 271, Haines 99827 (historic site)

Alaska Resources Library, 222 W. Seventh Ave., Anchorage 99513

Alaska State Museum, 395 Whittier St., Juneau 99801

Alaskaland Air Museum, P.O. Box 437, Fairbanks 99707

Anchorage Museum of History & Art, 121 W. Seventh Ave., Anchorage 99501

George I. Ashby Memorial Museum, P.O. Box 84, Copper Center 99573

Assumption of the Virgin Mary Church, Kenai 99611 (historic site)

Baranof Museum/Erskine House, 101 Marine Way, Kodiak 99615

Bristol Bay Historical Museum, P.O. Box 43, Naknek 99633

Circle District Historical Society, P.O. Box 1893, Central 99730

Clausen Memorial Museum, P.O. Box 708, Petersburg 99833

Cordova Museum, P.O. Box 391, Cordova 99574

Damon Memorial Museum, P.O. Box 66, Soldotna 99669

Duncan Memorial Museum, P.O. Box 66, Metlakatla 99926

Eagle Historic Society, Eagle 99738

Fort Kenay Museum, P.O. Box 580, Kenai 99611

Fort Richardson Fish and Wildlife Center, Building 600, Fort Richardson 99505

Samuel K. Fox Museum, P.O. Box 3202, Dillingham 99576

Hoonah Cultural Center, P.O. Box 144, Hoonah 99829

House of Wickersham, Juneau. For information, write Alaska Division of Parks, P.O. Box M, Juneau 99811

Charlie Hubbard Museum, P.O. Box 552, Cooper Landing 99572

Iditarod Museum, P.O. Box 870800, Wasilla 99687

Juneau Mining Museum, 490 S. Franklin St., Juneau 99801

Klawock Totem Park, P.O. Box 113, Klawock 99925 (historic site)

Matanuska Valley Museum, Greater Palmer Chamber of Commerce, Palmer 99645

Carrie M. McLain Memorial Museum, P.O. Box 281, Nome 99762

Isabel Miller Museum, 330 Harbor Drive, Sitka 99835

Museum of Alaska Transportation and Industry, P.O. Box 909, Palmer 99645

NANA Museum of the Arctic, P.O. Box 46, Kotzebue 99752

National Bank of Alaska Heritage Library Museum, 303 W. Northern Lights Blvd., Anchorage 99503

Dorothy G. Page Museum, P.O. Box 870874, Wasilla 99687

Simon Paneak Memorial Museum, P.O. Box 21030, Anaktuvuk Pass 99721

Pratt Museum, 3779 Bartlett St., Homer 99603

Rasmuson Library, University of Alaska, Fairbanks 99701

Resurrection Bay Historical Society Museum, P.O. Box 871, Seward 99664

Russian Bishop's House, P.O. Box 944, Sitka 99835

Saint Herman's Theological Seminary, P.O. Box 726, Kodiak 99615 (historic site)

Saxman Totem Park and Tribal House, P.O. Box 8558, Ketchikan 99901 (historic site)

Sheldon Jackson Museum, 104 College Drive, Sitka 99835

Sheldon Museum and Cultural Center, P.O. Box 236, Haines 99827

Southeast Alaska Indian Cultural Center, P.O. Box 944, Sitka 99835

Talkeetna Historical Society Museum, P.O. Box 76, Talkeetna 99676

Tanana Valley Agricultural Museum, P.O. Box 188, Fairbanks 99707

Tok Visitor Center, P.O. Box 335, Tok 99780

Tongass Historical Museum, 629 Dock St., Ketchikan 99901

Totem Bight, Ketchikan. For information, write Alaska Division of Parks, P.O. Box M, Juneau 99811 (historic site)

Totem Heritage Center, 629 Dock St., Ketchikan 99901 (historic site)

Trail of '98 Museum, P.O. Box 415, Skagway 99840

Tribal House of the Bear, P.O. Box 868, Wrangell 99929 (historic site)

University of Alaska Museum, P.O. Box 95351, Fairbanks 99701

U.S. Historical Aircraft Preservation Museum, P.O. Box 6813, Anchorage 99502

Valdez Museum, P.O. Box 307, Valdez 99686

Jessie Wakefield Memorial Library, P.O. Box 263, Port Lions 99550

Wales Museum, Wales 99783

Whittier Historical Museum, P.O. Box 728, Whittier 99502

Wickersham House, P.O. Box 1794, Fairbanks 99707

Wildlife Museum, Elmendorf Air Force Base, Anchorage 99506

Wrangell Museum, P.O. Box 1050, Wrangell 99929

Yugtarvik Regional Museum, P.O. Box 388, Bethel 99559

Mushrooms

More than 500 species of mushroom grow in Alaska, and, while most are not common enough to be seen and collected readily by the amateur mycophile (mushroom hunter), many edible and choice species shoot up in any - available patch of earth. Alaska's "giant arc of mushrooms" extends from Southeast's panhandle through Southcentral, the Alaska Peninsula and the Aleutian Chain and is prime mushroom habitat. Interior, western and northern Alaska also support mushrooms in abundance.

Mushroom seasons vary considerably according to temperature, humidity and available nutrients, but most occur from June through September. In a particularly cold or dry season, the crop will be scant.

There are relatively few poisonous mushrooms in relation to the number of species that occur throughout Alaska. Most toxic species are not fatal to healthy adults, but may produce severe symptoms such as heart palpitations, nausea, or may act as a laxative. Even edible mushrooms may disagree with one's digestion; the only test for an inedible or poisonous mushroom is positive identification. *If you can't identify it, don't eat it.*

Musk-Ox

Musk-oxen are stocky, shaggy, long-haired mammals of the extreme northern latitudes. They remain in the open through Alaska's long winters. Their name is misleading, for they do not give musk and are more closely related to sheep and goats than to cattle. Adult males may weigh 500 to 900 pounds; females between 250 and 500 pounds. Both sexes have horns that droop down from their forehead and curve back up at the tips.

When threatened by wolves or other predators, musk-oxen form circles or lines with their young in the middle. These defensive measures did not protect them from man and his gun.

Musk-oxen were eliminated from Alaska in about 1865, when hunters shot and killed the last herd of 13. The species was reintroduced to the territory in the 1930s when 34 musk-oxen were purchased from Greenland and brought to the University of Alaska at Fairbanks. In 1935–36, the 31 remaining musk-oxen at the university were shipped to Nunivak Island in the Bering Sea, where the herd eventually thrived. Animals from the Nunivak herd have been transplanted to areas along Alaska's western and northern coasts; at least five herds — approximately 1,200 musk-oxen — now exist in the state.

Recent indications are that musk-oxen from Nelson Island are spreading to the mainland and that individuals from the eastern arctic herd have wandered west into adjacent Canada.

The soft underhair of musk-oxen is called qiviut and grows next to the skin, protected by long guard hairs. It is shed naturally every spring. Oomingmak Musk Ox Producers' Cooperative

maintains a musk-ox farm at Talkeetna, where workers gather the qiviut for cottage industry use. The hair is spun into yarn in Rhode Island and sent back to Alaska, where the cooperative arranges for knitters in villages in western Alaska, where jobs are scarce, to knit the yarn into clothing at their own pace.

Each village keeps its own distinct signature pattern for scarves knitted from qiviut. Villagers also produce stoles, tunics, hats and smoke rings, which are circular scarves that fit a person's head like a hood.

Permit hunts for musk-oxen are allowed.

Muskeg

Deep bogs where little vegetation can grow except for sphagnum moss, black spruce, dwarf birch and a few other shrubby plants. Such swampy areas cover much of Alaska.

National Forests

Alaska has two national forests, the Tongass and the Chugach. The Tongass occupies the panhandle or southeast portion of the state. The Chugach extends south and east of Anchorage along the southcentral Alaskan coast, encompassing most of the Prince William Sound area.

These two national forests are managed by the U.S. Forest Service for a variety of uses. They provide forest products for national and international markets; minerals; wilderness experiences; and superb scenery and views for Alaska residents and visitors.

Nearly 200 public recreation cabins are maintained in the Tongass and Chugach national forests. They accommodate visitors from all over the world and are a vacation bargain at $20 per night, including firewood and a boat on freshwater lakes, a boat. (*See also* Cabins)

Wildlife and fisheries are important Forest Service programs in the national forests of Alaska. The Tongass and Chugach national forests are also home to some of Alaska's most magnificent

wildlife. It is here that the United States' national bird, the bald eagle, and large brown (grizzly) bears may be encountered in large numbers. All five species of Pacific salmon spawn in the rivers and streams of the forests, and smaller mammals and waterfowl abound. The Forest Service is charged with the management of this rich habitat; the Alaska Department of Fish and Game manages the wildlife species that this habitat supports.

There are many recreational opportunities in the national forests of Alaska, including backpacking, fishing, hunting, photography, boating, nature study and camping, to list just a few. For further information concerning recreational opportunities, contact the U.S. Forest Service office nearest the area you are visiting.

The Alaska National Interest Lands Conservation Act of 1980 — also referred to as ANILCA — increased the acreage and changed the status of certain lands in Alaska's national forests. (*See also* Land; National Parks, Preserves and Monuments; *and* National Wilderness Areas)

ANILCA created approximately 5.5 million acres of wilderness (consisting of 14 units) within the 17-million-acre Tongass National Forest. It also added three new areas to the forest: the Juneau Icefield, Kates Needle and parts of the Barbazon Range, totaling more than 1 million acres.

The lands bill also provided extensive additions to the Chugach National Forest. These additions, totaling about 2 million acres, include the Nellie Juan area east of Seward, College Fiord extension, Copper/Rude rivers addition and a small extension at Controller Bay southeast of Cordova.

The following charts show the effect of the Alaska lands act on the Tongass and Chugach national forests:

	Tongass	**Chugach**
Total acreage before ANILCA	15,555,388	4,392,646
Total acreage after ANILCA	16,954,713	5,940,040*
Wilderness acreage created	5,453,366	none created
Wilderness Study	none created	2,019,999 acres
Wild and Scenic River Study	Situk River**	none created

*This lands act provides for additional transfers of national forest land to Native corporations, the state and the Fish and Wildlife Service of an estimated 296,000 acres on Afognak Island, and an estimated 242,000 acres to the Chugach Native Corporation.

**The lands act provides for a maximum of 640 acres on each side of the river, for each mile of river length.

Wilderness Units in Tongass National Forest (including acres)

Admiralty Island National Monument*, 937,396

Coronation Island Wilderness, 19,232

Endicott River Wilderness, 98,729

Maurelle Islands Wilderness, 4,937

Misty Fiords National Monument*, 2,142,243

Petersburg Creek–Duncan Salt Chuck Wilderness, 46,777

Russel Fiord Wilderness, 348,701

South Baranof Wilderness, 319,568

South Prince of Wales Wilderness, 90,996

Stikine–LeConte Wilderness, 448,841

Tebenkof Bay Wilderness, 66,839

Tracy Arm–Fords Terror Wilderness, 653,179

Warren Island Wilderness, 11,181

West Chichagof–Yakobi Wilderness, 264,747

Total Acreage, 5,453,366

*Designated monuments under ANILCA; first areas so designated in the National Forest system.

National Guard

The Department of Military Affairs administers the Alaska Army National Guard and the Air National Guard. The guard is charged with performing military reconnaissance, surveillance and patrol operations in Alaska; providing special assistance to civil authorities during natural disasters or civil disturbances; and augmenting regular Army and Air Force in times of national emergency. About 1,086 full-time employees work for the National Guard.

The Alaska Air National Guard has a headquarters unit, a composite group made up of a tactical airlift squadron, an air refueling squadron and several support squadrons and flights. The units are based at Kulis Air National Guard Base on the west side of Anchorage International Airport and at Eielson Air Force Base in Fairbanks.

Authorized staffing is 4,565 military personnel; about 35 percent are full-time technicians.

The major unit of the Alaska Army National Guard, with a muster of 2,300, is the 207th Infantry Group, consisting of five Scout Battalions and detachments in almost 100 communities across the state. In addition, it has an airborne element, an air traffic control detachment and an aviation detachment. The Scout Battalions are authorized on Twin Otter aircraft and two helicopters in their aviation sections. In all, the Alaska Army National Guard operates 48 aircraft.

The scout teams are a unique element in the Alaska Army National Guard, performing a full-time active mission of intelligence gathering. Many scouts are subsistence hunters and whalers who constantly comb the coastal zones, offshore waters and inland areas. Reports of Soviet naval and air activities are common since Alaska and the USSR are separated by less than 50 miles across the Bering Strait.

The Alaska Division of Emergency Services administers statewide disaster preparedness and response programs. The division is the primary contact for obtaining emergency assistance from state, federal, military and independent services. Its personnel also provide guidance and financial assistance to state and local agencies to help them prepare for and recover from disasters. The agency responds to threats or occurrences of disasters, and directs disaster response in unincorporated areas where local government does not have the resources to respond adequately.

National Historic Places

A "place" on the National Register of Historic Places is a district, site, building, structure or object significant to the state for its history, architecture, archaeology or culture. The national register also includes National Historic Landmarks. NHLs are properties given special status by the secretary of the Interior for the significance to the nation, as well as to the state. The register is an official list of properties recognized by the federal government as worthy of preservation. Listing on the register begins with owner's consent and entails a nomination process with reviews by the State Historic Preservation officer, the Alaska Historic Sites Advisory Committee and the keeper of the National Register. Limitations are *not* placed on a listed property: The federal government does not attach restrictive covenants to the property or seek to acquire it.

Listing on the register means that a property is accorded national recognition for its significance in American history or prehistory. Additional benefits include tax credits on income-producing properties and automatic qualification for federal matching funds for preservation, maintenance and restoration work when such funds are available. Listed properties are also guaranteed a full review process for potential adverse effects by federally funded, licensed or otherwise assisted projects. Such a review usually takes place while the project is in the planning stage: Alternatives are sought to avoid, if at all possible, damaging or destroying the particular property in question.

Southcentral

Alaska Central Railroad Tunnel #1, Seward
Alaska Nellie's Homestead, Lawing vicinity
Alex (Mike) Cabin, Eklutna
American Cemetery, Kodiak
Anchorage City Hall, Anchorage
Anderson (Oscar) House, Anchorage
Ascension of Our Lord Chapel, Karluk
Ballaine House, Seward
Beluga Point Archaeological Site, North Shore, Turnagain Arm
Bering Expedition Landing Site NHL, Kayak Island
Brown & Hawkins Store, Seward
Campus Center Site, Anchorage
Cape St. Elias Lighthouse, Kayak Island
Chilkat Oil Refinery Site, Katalla
Chisana Historic District, Chisana
Chitina Tin Shop, Chitina
Chugachik Island Archaeological Site, Kachemak Bay
Coal Village Site, Kachemak Bay
Cooper Landing Historic District, Cooper Landing
Cooper Landing Post Office, Cooper Landing
Copper River and Northwestern Railway, Chitina vicinity
Cordova Post Office and Courthouse, Cordova
Crow Creek Mine, Girdwood
Cunningham-Hall PT-6 NC692W (aircraft), Palmer
Dakah De'nin's Village Site, Chitina
David (Leopold) House, Anchorage
Diversion Tunnel, Lowell Creek, Seward
Federal Building–U.S. Courthouse (Old), Anchorage
Fourth Avenue Theatre, Anchorage
Gakona Roadhouse, Gakona
Government Cable House, Seward
Hirshey Mine, Hope vicinity
Holm (Victor) Cabin, Cohoe
Holy Assumption Russian Orthodox Church NHL, Kenai
Holy Resurrection Church, Kodiak
Holy Transfiguration of Our Lord Chapel, Ninilchik
Hope Historic District, Hope vicinity
Independence Mine Historic District, Hatcher Pass
Indian Valley Mine, Girdwood vicinity
KENI Radio Building, Anchorage
Kennecott Mines NHL, McCarthy vicinity
Kimball's Store, Anchorage
Knik Site, Knik vicinity
Kodiak Naval Operating Base (Fort Abercrombie and Fort Greely) NHL, Kodiak Island
KOD-171 Archaeological Site, Kodiak
KOD-207 Archaeological Site, Kodiak
KOD-233 Archaeological Site, Kodiak
Lauritsen Cabin, Seward Highway
McCarthy General Store, McCarthy
McCarthy Power Plant, McCarthy
Middle Bay Brick Kiln, Kodiak

Moose River Site, Naptowne, Kenai area
Nabesna Gold Mine, Nabesna area
Nativity of Holy Theotokos Church, Afognak Island
Nativity of Our Lord Chapel, Ouzinkie
Old Eklutna Power Plant, Eklutna
Old St. Nicholas Russian Orthodox Church, Eklutna
Palmer Depot, Palmer
Palugvik Archaeological District, Hawkins Island
Pioneer School House, Anchorage
Potter Section House, Anchorage
Protection of the Theotokos Chapel, Akhiok
Rebarcheck (Raymond) Colony Farm, Palmer area
Reception Building, Cordova
Red Dragon Historic District, Cordova
Russian-American Company Magazine (Erskine House) NHL, Kodiak
St. Michael the Archangel Church, Cordova
St. Nicholas Chapel, Seldovia
St. Peter's Episcopal Church, Seward
Sts. Sergius and Herman of Valaam Chapel, Ouzinkie
Sts. Sergius and Herman of Valaam Church, English Bay
Selenie Lagoon Archaeological Site, Port Graham vicinity
Seward Depot, Seward
Sourdough Lodge NHL, Gulkana area
Susitna River Bridge, Alaska Railroad, Talkeetna vicinity
Swanson River Discovery Site, Kenai
Swetman House, Seward
Tangle Lakes Archaeological District, Paxson vicinity
Teeland's Store, Wasilla
Three Saints Bay Site NHL, Kodiak Island

United Protestant Church, Palmer
Van Gilder Hotel, Seward
Wasilla Community Hall, Wasilla
Wasilla Depot, Wasilla
Wasilla Elementary School, Wasilla
Wendler Building, Anchorage
Yukon Island, Main Site NHL, Yukon Island

Southeast

Alaska Native Brotherhood Hall NHL, Sitka
Alaska Steam Laundry, Juneau
Alaska Totems, Ketchikan
Alaskan Hotel, Juneau
American Flag Raising Site NHL, Sitka
Ayson Hotel, Ketchikan
Bergmann Hotel, Juneau
Building No. 29 NHL, Sitka
Burkhart-Dibrell House, Ketchikan
Cable House and Station, Sitka
Cape Spencer Lighthouse, Cape Spencer
Chief Shakes House, Wrangell
Chilkoot Trail and Dyea NHL, Skagway
Davis (J.M.) House, Juneau
Duncan (Father William) Cottage, Metlakatla
Eldred Rock Lighthouse, Lynn Canal
Emmons House, Sitka
Etolin Canoe, Etolin Island
First Lutheran Church, Ketchikan
Fort Durham NHL, Taku Harbor, Juneau vicinity
Fort William H. Seward NHL, Haines
Frances House, Juneau
Fries Miners Cabins, Juneau
Government Indian School, Haines
Governor's Mansion, Juneau
Holy Trinity Church, Juneau
Ketchikan Ranger House, Ketchikan
Klondike Gold Rush National Historic Park, Skagway area
Mayflower School, Douglas
Mills (May) House, Sitka
Mills (W.P.) House, Sitka
New Russia Archaeological Site NHL, Yakutat
Old Sitka NHL, Sitka
Pleasant Camp, Haines Highway
Porcupine Historic District, Skagway vicinity
Russian Bishop's House NHL, Sitka
St. John the Baptist Church, Angoon
St. Michael the Archangel Cathedral NHL, Sitka
St. Nicholas Church (Russian Orthodox), Juneau
St. Peter's Church, Sitka

National Park and Preserve
Kolmakov Redoubt Site, Kuskokwim River, Aniak vicinity
Kukak Village, Katmai National Park and Preserve
McClain (Carrie) House, Nome
Norge Storage Site, Teller
Old Savonoski Site, Katmai National Park and Preserve
Onion Portage Archaeological District NHL, Noatak vicinity
Pilgrim 100B N709Y Aircraft, Dillingham
Pilgrim Hot Springs, Seward Peninsula
Port Moller Hot Springs Village Site, Alaska Peninsula
Presentation of Our Lord Chapel, Nikolai
Redoubt St. Michael Site, Unalakleet vicinity
St. George the Great Martyr Orthodox Church, St. George Island
St. Jacob's Church, Napaskiak
St. John the Baptist Chapel, Naknek
St. John the Theologian Church, Perryville
St. Nicholas Chapel, Ekuk
St. Nicholas Chapel, Igiugig
St. Nicholas Chapel, Nondalton
St. Nicholas Chapel, Pedro Bay
St. Nicholas Chapel, Sand Point
St. Nicholas Church, Nikolski
St. Nicholas Church, Pilot Point
St. Seraphim Chapel, Lower Kalskag
St. Sergius Chapel, Chuathbaluk
Sts. Constantine and Helen Chapel, Lime Village
Sts. Peter and Paul Russian Orthodox Church, St. Paul Island
Savonoski River District, Katmai National Park and Preserve
Seal Islands Historic District NHL, Pribilof Islands
Sir Alexander Nevsky Chapel, Akutan
Sitka Spruce Plantation NHL, Amaknak Island
Solomon Roadhouse, Solomon
Takli Island Archaeological District, Katmai National Park and Preserve
TEMNAC P-38G Lightning Aircraft, Aleutian Islands
Transfiguration of Our Lord Chapel, Nushagak
Wales Archaeological District NHL, Wales vicinity

Interior
Central Roadhouse, Central

Chatanika Gold Camp, Chatanika
Chena Pump House, Fairbanks
Chugwater Archaeological Site, Fairbanks
Clay Street Cemetery, Fairbanks
Creamers Dairy, Fairbanks
Davis (Mary Lee) House, Fairbanks
Dry Creek Archaeological Site NHL, Healy vicinity
Eagle Historic District NHL, Eagle
Ester Camp Historic District, Fairbanks
Fairview Inn, Talkeetna
Federal Building, U.S. Post Office, Courthouse (Old), Fairbanks
Goldstream Dredge #8, Mile 9, Old Steese Hwy.
Harding Railroad Car, Alaskaland, Fairbanks
Immaculate Conception Church, Fairbanks
Joslin (Falcon) House, Fairbanks
The Kink, Fortymile River
Ladd Field NHL (Fort Wainwright), Fairbanks
Masonic Temple, Fairbanks
Mission Church, Arctic Village
Mission House (Old), Fort Yukon

101

Mount McKinley National Park Headquarters, Denali National Park
Nenana Depot, Nenana
Oddfellows Hall (First Avenue Bathhouse), Fairbanks
Patrol Cabins, Denali National Park
Rainey's Cabin, Fairbanks
Rika's Roadhouse, Big Delta
Ruby Roadhouse, Ruby
Steele Creek Roadhouse, Fortymile
Sternwheeler *Nenana* NHL, Fairbanks
Sullivan Roadhouse, Fort Greely
Tanana Mission, Tanana
Teklanika Archaeological District, Denali National Park and Preserve
Thomas (George C.) Memorial Library NHL, Fairbanks
Tolovana Roadhouse, Tanana vicinity
Wickersham House, Fairbanks
Yukon River Lifeways District, Eagle vicinity

Far North

Aluakpak Site, Wainwright vicinity
Anaktuuk Site, Wainwright vicinity
Atanik District, Wainwright vicinity
Avalitkuk Site, Wainwright vicinity
Birnirk Site NHL, Barrow
Gallagher Flint Station Archaeological Site NHL, Sagwon
Ipiutak Archaeological District, Point Hope
Ipiutak Site NHL, Point Hope
Ivishaat Site, Wainwright vicinity
Kanitch, Wainwright vicinity
Leffingwell Camp NHL, Flaxman Island
Napanik Site, Wainwright vicinity
Negilik Site, Barrow
Point Barrow Refuge–Cape Smythe Whaling and Trading Station, Barrow vicinity
Utkeagvik Presbyterian Church Manse, Barrow
Uyagaagruk, Wainwright vicinity
Will Rogers–Wiley Post Site, Barrow vicinity

National Parks, Preserves and Monuments

The National Park Service administers approximately 50 million acres of land in Alaska, consisting of 15 units classified as national parks, national preserves and national monuments. The Alaska National Interest Lands Conservation Act of 1980 — also referred to as ANILCA (*see* Land) — created 10 new National Park Service units in Alaska and changed the size and status of the three existing Park Service units: Mount McKinley National Park, now Denali National Park and Preserve; Glacier Bay National Monument, now a national park and preserve; and Katmai National Monument, now a national park and preserve. (*See map,* pages 104-105.)

Alaska's national parks, preserves and monuments registered an increase in number of visitors in 1989. The 1,200,000 visitors in 1989 marked a 7 percent increase over 1988. Denali is still the most popular destination, with Glacier Bay the second most visited park. The most dramatic growth in tourism, however, was to newer, lesser-known parks, such as Kenai Fjords National Park, which had a record 77,500 visits in 1989, up nearly 30 percent from 1988.

National parks are traditionally managed to preserve scenic, wildlife and recreational values; mining, cutting of house logs, hunting and other resource exploitation are carefully regulated within park monument and preserve boundaries, and motorized access is restricted to automobile traffic on authorized roads. However, regulations for National Park Service units in Alaska recognize that these units contain lands traditionally occupied and used by Alaska Natives and rural residents for subsistence activities. Therefore, management of *some* parks, preserves and monuments in Alaska provides for subsistence hunting, fishing and gathering activities, and the use of such motorized vehicles as snow machines, motorboats and airplanes where such activities are customary. National preserves do permit sport hunting.

Following is a list of National Park Service parks, preserves and monuments. (The U.S. Forest Service manages another two national monuments: Admiralty Island National Monument, 937,000 acres; and Misty Fiords National Monument, 2.1 million acres. Both are in Southeast and part of the National Wilderness Preservation

System. *See also* National Wilderness Areas *and* National Wild and Scenic Rivers.)

Information on the parks, preserves and monuments is available at the Alaska Public Lands Information Centers: 605 W. Fourth Ave., Suite 105, Anchorage 99501; 250 Cushman St., Suite 1A, Fairbanks 99701; and P.O. Box 359, Tok 99780.

National Park Service Units are followed by address, acreage and major features or recreations:

Aniakchak National Monument and Preserve, Superintendent, Katmai National Park and Preserve, P.O. Box 7, King Salmon 99613 (609,500 acres). Aniakchak dry caldera.

Bering Land Bridge National Preserve, National Park Service, P.O. Box 220, Nome 99762 (2,509,360 acres). Lava fields, archaeological sites, migratory waterfowl.

Cape Krusenstern National Monument, National Park Service, P.O. Box 1029, Kotzebue 99752 (540,000 acres). Archaeological sites.

Denali National Park and Preserve, National Park Service, P.O. Box 9, Denali Park 99755 (6,000,000 acres). Mount McKinley, abundant wildlife.

Gates of the Arctic National Park and Preserve, National Park Service, P.O. Box 74680, Fairbanks 99707 (8,090,000 acres). Brooks Range, wild and scenic rivers, wildlife.

Glacier Bay National Park and Preserve, National Park Service, Bartlett Cove, Gustavus 99826 (3,283,168 acres). Glaciers, marine wildlife.

Katmai National Park and Preserve, National Park Service, P.O. Box 7, King Salmon 99613 (3,917,618 acres). Valley of Ten Thousand Smokes, brown bears.

Kenai Fjords National Park, National Park Service, P.O. Box 1727, Seward 99664 (580,000 acres). Fjords, Harding Icefield, Exit Glacier.

Klondike Gold Rush National Historical Park, National Park Service, P.O. Box 517, Skagway 99840 (2,721 acres). Chilkoot Trail.

Kobuk Valley National Park, National Park Service, P.O. Box 1029, Kotzebue 99752 (1,702,000 acres). Archaeological sites, Great Kobuk Sand Dunes, river rafting.

Lake Clark National Park and Preserve, National Park Service, 222 W. Seventh Ave., #61, Anchorage 99513 (3,661,000 acres). Backcountry recreation, fishing, scenery.

Noatak National Preserve, National Park Service, P.O. Box 1029, Kotzebue 99752 (6,550,000 acres). Abundant wildlife, river floating.

Sitka National Historical Park, National Park Service , P.O. Box 738, Sitka 99752 (106 acres). Russian Bishop's House, trails.

Wrangell–St. Elias National Park and Preserve, National Park Service, P.O. Box 29, Glennallen 99588 (12,400,000 acres). Rugged peaks, glaciers, expansive wilderness.

Yukon–Charley Rivers National Preserve, National Park Service, P.O. Box 64, Eagle 99738 (2,211,000 acres). Backcountry recreation, river floating.

National Petroleum Reserve

(*See also* Oil and Gas)

In 1923, President Warren G. Harding signed an executive order creating Naval Petroleum Reserve Number 4 (NPR-4), the last of four petroleum reserves to be placed under control of the U.S. Navy. The secretary of the Navy was charged to "explore, protect, conserve, develop, use, and operate the Naval Petroleum Reserves," including NPR-4, on Alaska's North Slope (*see map*, pages 104–105).

The U.S. Geological Survey (USGS) had begun surface exploration in the area in 1901; following creation of the 23-million-acre reserve, exploration programs were conducted by the Navy. From 1944 to 1953, extensive geological and geophysical surveys were conducted and 36 test wells were drilled. Nine oil and gas fields were discovered; the largest oil field, near Umiat, contains an estimated 70 million to 120 million barrels of recoverable oil. Active exploration was suspended in 1953.

In 1974, the Arab oil embargo, *(Continued on page 106)*

NATIONAL INTEREST LANDS

(Numbers refer to accompanying map)

NATIONAL WILDLIFE REFUGE SYSTEM
1 Alaska Maritime NWR*
    Chuckchi Sea Unit
    Bering Sea Unit
    Aleutian Island Unit
    Alaska Peninsula Unit
    Gulf of Alaska Unit
2 Alaska Peninsula
3 Arctic
4 Becharof
5 Innoko
6 Izembek
7 Kanuti
8 Kenai
9 Kodiak
10 Koyukuk
11 Nowitna
12 Selawik
13 Tetlin
14 Togiak
15 Yukon Delta
16 Yukon Flats

NATIONAL PARK SYSTEM
17 Aniakchak Nat'l. Monument and Preserve
18 Bering Land Bridge Nat'l. Preserve
19 Cape Krusenstern Nat'l. Monument

20 Denali Nat'l. Park and Preserve
21 Gates of the Arctic Nat'l. Park and Preserve
22 Glacier Bay Nat'l. Park and Preserve
23 Katmai Nat'l. Park and Preserve
24 Kenai Fjords Nat'l. Park
25 Kobuk Valley Nat'l. Park
26 Lake Clark Nat'l. Park and Preserve
27 Noatak Nat'l. Preserve
28 Wrangell-St. Elias Nat'l. Park and Preserve
29 Yukon-Charley Rivers Nat'l. Preserve
30 Klondike Gold Rush Nat'l. Historial Park
31 Sitka Nat'l. Historical Park

BUREAU OF LAND MANAGEMENT SYSTEM
32 Steese Nat'l. Conservation Areas
33 White Mountains Nat'l. Recreation Area

NATIONAL FOREST SYSTEM
34 Chugach Nat'l. Forest
35 Tongass Nat'l. Forest
36 Admiralty Island Nat'l. Monument**
37 Misty Fiords Nat'l. Monument**

NATIONAL WILD AND SCENIC RIVERS SYSTEM
There are 26 rivers designated wild and
scenic by the 1980 Alaska National Interest
Lands Conservation Act.

*The Alaska Maritime National Wildlife Refuge consists of all the public lands in the coastal
  waters and adjacent seas of Alaska including islands, islets, rocks, reefs, capes and spires.
**Admiralty Island and Misty Fiords national monuments are part of the Tongass National Forest,
  which includes 12 other wilderness areas.

Chukcl

Bering Sea

Aleutian Islands

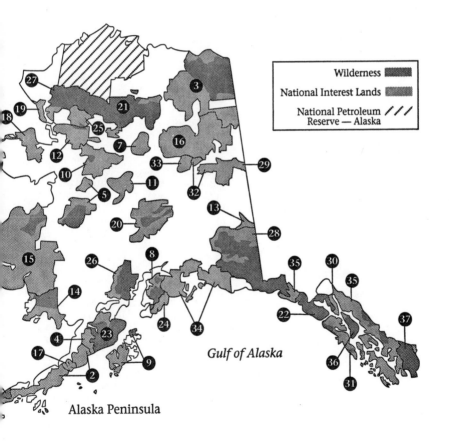

Wilderness
National Interest Lands
National Petroleum Reserve — Alaska

Gulf of Alaska

Alaska Peninsula

(Continued from page 103)
coupled with the knowledge of large petroleum reserves at nearby Prudhoe Bay, brought about renewed interest in NPR-4, and Congress directed the Navy to resume its exploration program.

In 1976, all lands within NPR-4 were redesignated the National Petroleum Reserve Alaska (NPR-A) and jurisdiction was transferred to the secretary of the interior. In 1980, Congress authorized the secretary of the interior to prescribe an expeditious program of competitive leasing of oil and gas tracts in the reserve, clearing the way for private development of the area's resources.

By mid-1983, three competitive bid lease sales, involving a total of 7.2 million acres of NPR-A, had been held. Dates of the sales and the number of acres involved were: January 1982, 1.5 million acres; May 1982, 3.5 million acres; and July 1983, 2.2 million acres. As oil prices have dropped, interest from the oil companies has lessened and leases have expired. As of mid-1989, there were 24 leases covering 558,950 acres.

The Interior Department, through USGS, continued exploration of NPR-A into the 1980s. Past naval explorations and those conducted by USGS resulted in the discovery of oil at Umiat and Cape Simpson, and several gas fields, including Walakpa, Gubic and Point Barrow. Data gathered indicates NPR-A may contain recoverable reserves of 1.85 billion barrels of crude oil and 3.74 trillion cubic feet of natural gas.

National Wild and Scenic Rivers

(See also Rivers)

The Alaska National Interest Lands Conservation Act (ANILCA) of Dec. 2, 1980, gave wild and scenic river classification to 13 streams within the National Park System, 6 in the National Wildlife Refuge System and 2 in Bureau of Land Management Conservation and Recreation areas. (See map, pages 104–105.) An additional 5 rivers are located outside designated preservation units. Twelve more rivers were designated for further study and possible wild and scenic classification.

The criteria for wild and scenic river classification cover more than just float trip possibilities. Scenic features, wilderness characteristics and recreational opportunities that would be impaired by alteration, development or impoundment are also considered.

Rivers are classified into three categories under the Wild and Scenic Rivers Act. The wild classification is most restrictive of development or incompatible uses — it stresses the wilderness aspect of the rivers. The scenic classification permits some intrusions upon the natural landscape, and recreational classification is the least restrictive category. A specified amount of land back from the river's banks is also put in protected status to ensure access, use and the preservation of aesthetic values for the public.

For those desiring to float these rivers, special consideration must be given to put-in and take-out points because most of the designated wild and scenic rivers are not accessible by road. This means that voyagers and their crafts have to be flown in and picked up by charter bush planes. Because Federal Aviation Administration regulations prohibit the lashing of canoes and kayaks to pontoons of floatplanes when carrying passengers, inflatable rafts and folding canvas or rubber kayaks are often more convenient and less expensive to transport.

Further information on rivers and river running can be obtained from the Alaska Public Lands Information Centers: 605 W. Fourth Ave., Suite 105, Anchorage 99501; 250 Cushman St., Suite 1A, Fairbanks 99701; and P.O. Box 359, Tok 99780; the U.S. Fish and Wildlife Service, 1011 E. Tudor Road, Anchorage 99503; and the Bureau of Land Management, 222 W. Seventh Ave., #13, Anchorage 99513.

Rivers within National Park Areas

Alagnak — Katmai National Preserve
Alatna — Gates of the Arctic National Park
Aniakchak — Aniakchak National Monument; Aniakchak National Preserve

Charley — Yukon–Charley Rivers National Preserve

Chilikadrotna — Lake Clark National Park and Preserve

John — Gates of the Arctic National Park and Preserve

Kobuk — Gates of the Arctic National Park and Preserve

Mulchatna — Lake Clark National Park and Preserve

Noatak — Gates of the Arctic National Park and Noatak National Preserve

North Fork Koyukuk — Gates of the Arctic National Park and Preserve

Salmon — Kobuk Valley National Park

Tinayguk — Gates of the Arctic National Park and Preserve

Tlikakila — Lake Clark National Park

Rivers within National Wildlife Refuges

Andreafsky — Yukon Delta National Wildlife Refuge

Ivishak — Arctic National Wildlife Refuge

Nowitna — Nowitna National Wildlife Refuge

Selawik — Selawik National Wildlife Refuge

Sheenjek — Arctic National Wildlife Refuge

Wind — Arctic National Wildlife Refuge

(General information on rivers not listed in refuge brochures may be obtained from respective refuge offices by addressing queries to refuge managers. Addresses for refuges are given in the brochures.)

Rivers within Bureau of Land Management Units

Beaver Creek — The segment of the main stem from confluence of Bear and Champion creeks within White Mountains National Recreation Area to the Yukon Flats National Wildlife Refuge boundary.

Birch Creek — The segment of the main stem from the south side of Steese Highway downstream to the bridge at Milepost 147.

Rivers outside of Designated Preservation Units

Alagnak — Those segments or portions of the main stem and Nonvianuk tributary lying outside and westward of Katmai National Park and Preserve.

Delta River — The segment from and including all of the Tangle Lakes to a point one-half mile north of Black Rapids.

Fortymile River — The main stem within the state of Alaska, plus tributaries.

Gulkana River — The main stem from the outlet of Paxson Lake to the confluence with Sourdough Creek; various segments of the west fork and middle fork.

Unalakleet River — Approximately 80 miles of the main stem.

Rivers Designated for Study for Inclusion in Wild and Scenic Rivers System

Colville River
Etivluk–Nigu Rivers
Kanektok River
Kisaralik River
Koyuk River
Melozitna River
Porcupine River
Sheenjek River (lower segment)
Situk River
Squirrel River
Utukok River
Yukon River (Rampart section)

National Wilderness Areas

Passage of the Alaska National Interest Lands Conservation Act (ANILCA) on Dec. 2, 1980, added millions of acres to the National Wilderness Preservation System. Administration of these wilderness areas is the responsibility of the agency under whose jurisdiction the land is situated. Agencies that administer wilderness areas in Alaska include the National Park Service, U.S. Fish and Wildlife Service and the U.S. Forest Service. Although the Bureau of Land Management has authority to manage wilderness in the public domain, no BLM wilderness areas exist in Alaska. (*See map,* pages 104–105.)

Wilderness allocations to different agencies in Alaska are: U.S. Forest Service, approximately 5,453,366 acres;

National Park Service, approximately 32,848,564 acres; and U.S. Fish and Wildlife Service, approximately 18,676,320 acres.

Wilderness, according to the Wilderness Act of 1964, is land sufficient in size to enable the operation of natural systems without undue influence from activities in surrounding areas and should be places in which people are visitors who do not remain. Alaska wilderness regulations follow the stipulations of the Wilderness Act as amended by the Alaska lands act. Specifically designed to allow for Alaska conditions, the rules are considerably more lenient about transportation access, human-made structures and use of mechanized vehicles. The primary objective of a wilderness area continues to be the maintenance of the wilderness character of the land.

In Alaska wilderness areas, the following uses and activities are permitted:

• Fishing, hunting and trapping will continue on lands within the national forests, national wildlife refuges and national park preserves. National park wilderness does not allow sport hunting, or sport or commercial trapping.

• Subsistence uses, including hunting, fishing, trapping, berry gathering and use of timber for cabins and firewood, will be permitted in wilderness areas by all agencies.

• Public recreation or safety cabins in wilderness areas in national forests, national wildlife refuges and national park preserves will continue to be maintained and may be replaced. A limited number of new public cabins may be added if needed.

• Existing special use permits and leases on all national forest wilderness lands for cabins, homesites or similar structures will continue. Use of temporary campsites, shelters and other temporary facilities and equipment related to hunting and fishing on national forest lands will continue.

• Fish habitat enhancement programs, including construction of buildings, fish weirs, fishways, spawning channels and other accepted means of maintaining, enhancing, and rehabilitating fish stocks, will be allowed in national forest

wilderness areas. Reasonable access, including use of motorized equipment, will be permitted.

• Special use permits for guides and outfitters operating within wilderness areas in the national forests and national wildlife refuges will be allowed to continue.

• Private, state and Native lands surrounded by wilderness areas will be guaranteed access through the wilderness area.

• Use of airplanes, motorboats and snow machines for *traditional* activities as a means of access into wilderness areas will be allowed to continue.

National Wildlife Refuges

There are approximately 77 million acres of National Wildlife Refuge lands in Alaska administered by the U.S. Fish and Wildlife Service. (National wildlife refuge acreage in Alaska increased nearly fourfold with the signing of the Alaska National Interest Lands Conservation Act, ANILCA, in December, 1980.) Wildlife refuges are designed to protect the habitats of representative populations of birds, fish and mammals. The 16 refuges vary widely in size. (*See map*, pages 104–105.)

Among the public recreational uses permitted within national wildlife refuges are sightseeing, nature observation and photography, sport hunting and fishing (under state law), boating, camping, hiking and picnicking. Trapping can be carried out under applicable state and federal laws. Commercial fishing and related facilities (campsites, cabins, etc.) are authorized by special use permits.

Subsistence activities within national wildlife refuges are all protected under the lands bill. Use of snowmobiles, motorboats and other means of surface transportation traditionally relied upon by local rural residents for subsistence is generally permitted. Fixed-wing aircraft access to wildlife refuges is usually allowed, though certain areas within the Kenai National Wildlife Refuge have been

closed to aircraft (a map is available from the refuge manager). A special use permit is required for all helicopter access.

National Wildlife Refuge administrative addresses are followed by acreage and major features:

Alaska Maritime National Wildlife Refuge, 202 Pioneer Ave., Homer 99603 (3,548,956 acres). Seabirds, sea lions, sea otters, harbor seals.

Alaska Peninsula National Wildlife Refuge, P.O. Box 277, King Salmon 99613 (3,500,000 acres). Brown bears, caribou, moose, sea otters, bald eagles, peregrine falcons.

Arctic National Wildlife Refuge, Box 20, Room 226, Federal Building & Courthouse, 101 12th Ave., Fairbanks 99701 (19,351,000 acres). Caribou, polar bears, grizzly bears, wolves, Dall sheep, peregrine falcons.

Becharof National Wildlife Refuge, P.O. Box 277, King Salmon 99613 (1,200,000 acres). Brown bears, bald eagles, caribou, moose, salmon.

Innoko National Wildlife Refuge, P.O. Box 69, McGrath 99627 (3,850,000 acres). Migratory birds, furbearers, moose.

Izembek National Wildlife Refuge, P.O. Box 127, Cold Bay 99571 (321,000 acres). Black brant, brown bears.

Kanuti National Wildlife Refuge, Box 11, Federal Building & Courthouse, 101 12th Ave., Fairbanks 99701 (1,430,000 acres). Migratory birds, furbearers, moose.

Kenai National Wildlife Refuge, 2139 Ski Hill Road, Soldotna 99669 (1,970,000 acres). Moose, salmon, mountain goats, Dall sheep, bears.

Kodiak National Wildlife Refuge, 1390 Buskin River Road, Kodiak 99615 (1,865,000 acres). Brown bears, black-tailed deer, bald eagles, salmon.

Koyukuk National Wildlife Refuge, P.O. Box 287, Galena 99741 (3,550,000 acres). Wolves, caribou, bear, moose.

Nowitna National Wildlife Refuge, P.O. Box 287, Galena 99741 (1,560,000 acres). Migratory waterfowl, caribou, moose, bears, furbearers.

Selawik National Wildlife Refuge, P.O. Box 270, Kotzebue 99752 (2,150,000 acres). Migratory birds, caribou.

Tetlin National Wildlife Refuge, P.O. Box 155, Tok 99780 (700,000 acres). Migratory waterfowl, Dall sheep, moose.

Togiak National Wildlife Refuge, P.O. Box 270, Dillingham 99576 (4,105,000 acres). Nearly every major wildlife species of Alaska is represented.

Yukon Delta National Wildlife Refuge, P.O. Box 346, Bethel 99559 (19,624,458 acres). Migratory birds, musk-ox are found on Nunivak Island.

Yukon Flats National Wildlife Refuge, Box 14, Federal Building & Courthouse, 101 12th Ave., Fairbanks 99701 (8,630,000 acres). Waterfowl.

Native People

Alaska's 64,000 Native people make up about 13 percent of the state's total population. Of those, roughly 34,000 are Eskimos, 22,000 are Indians and 8,000 are Aleuts. Although many live in widely scattered villages along the coastline and great rivers of Alaska, 9,000 Native persons lived in Anchorage in 1980, and Fairbanks had a Native population of nearly 3,000 that year.

At the time of European discovery in 1741, the Eskimo, Indian and Aleut people lived within well-defined regions, with little mixing of ethnic groups. But they all were hunting and gathering people who did not practice agriculture.

In southeastern Alaska, the salmon, deer and other plentiful foods permitted the Tsimshian, Haida and Tlingit Indians to settle in permanent villages and develop a culture rich in art. The Athabascan Indians of the Interior took advantage of seasonal abundance of fish, waterfowl and other game. Aleuts and coastal Eskimos subsisted primarily on the rich resources of the rivers and the sea.

The Tsimshians migrated in 1887 from their former home in British Columbia to Annette Island, under

Anglican minister Father William Duncan. About 1,000 now live in Metlakatla. As are most southeastern people, they are primarily fishermen.

Between 700 and 800 Haidas live in Alaska, about 200 of whom live in Hydaburg on the south end of Prince of Wales Island. They emigrated from Canada in the 1700s. Haidas excelled in the art of totem carving and are noted for precise and delicate working of wood, bone and shell.

About 10,000 Tlingits live throughout southeastern Alaska; another 1,000 live in other parts of the state, primarily in the Anchorage area. Tlingits, who arrived from Canada before the first European contact, commercially dominated the interior Canadian Indians, trading eulachon oil, copper pieces and Chilkat blankets for various furs. Like the Haidas, they are part of the totem culture; totems are used to provide a historic record of major events in the life of a family or clan.

Athabascan Indians, who occupied the vast area of interior Alaska, were nomadic people whose principal source of food was land animals. Hard times and famines were frequent for all Athabascans, except the Tanaina and Ahtna groups who lived along the Gulf of Alaska and could rely on salmon as their basic food.

The Aleuts have traditionally lived on the Alaska Peninsula and along the Aleutian Chain. When the Russians reached the Aleutians in the 1740s, practically every island was inhabited. Today, there are only a few Aleut settlements, including two on the Pribilof Islands, where Natives work handling seal herds for the government.

The Aleuts lived in permanent villages, taking advantage of sea life and land mammals for food. Their original dwellings were large, communal structures, housing as many as 40 families, although after Russian occupation they lived in much smaller houses, called *barabaras*. Today many Aleuts are commercial fishermen.

The Eskimos have traditionally lived in villages along the harsh Bering Sea and Arctic Ocean coastlines, and along a thin strip of the Gulf of Alaska coast, including Kodiak Island. They took salmon, waterfowl, berries, ptarmigan and a few caribou, but it was the sea and its whales, walruses and seals that provided the foundation for their existence. Houses were igloos — dwellings built partially underground and covered with sod. They did not build snow igloos.

Rapid advances in communications, transportation and other services to remote villages have altered Native life in Alaska. Economic changes, from a subsistence to a cash economy, were brought about by the passage of the Alaska Native Claims Settlement Act. The act gave Alaska Natives $962.5 million and 44 million acres of land as compensation for the loss of lands historically occupied by their people.

Native Regional Corporations

Twelve regional business corporations were formed under the 1971 Alaska Native Claims Settlement Act to manage money and land received from the government. (*See map* below.) A 13th corporation was organized for those Natives residing outside Alaska. Following is a list of corporations and the area or region each administers:

NATIVE REGIONAL CORPORATIONS

Arctic Slope Regional Corp.

Bering Straits Native Corp.

NANA Regional Corp.

Doyon Limited

Cook Inlet Region Inc.

Calista Corp.

Ahtna Inc.

Bristol Bay Native Corp.

Chugach Natives Inc.

Sealaska Corp.

The Aleut Corp.

Koniag Inc.

Ahtna Incorporated (Copper River Basin), Drawer G, Copper Center 99573 or 2701 Fairbanks St., Anchorage 99503

Aleut Corporation (Aleutian Islands), 1 Aleut Plaza, 4000 Old Seward Highway, Suite 300, Anchorage 99503

Arctic Slope Regional Corporation (Arctic Alaska), P.O. Box 129, Barrow 99723, or 313 E St., Suite 5, Anchorage 99501

Bering Straits Native Corporation (Seward Peninsula), P.O. Box 1008, Nome 99762

Bristol Bay Native Corporation (Bristol Bay area), P.O. Box 198, Dillingham 99576 or P.O. Box 100220, Anchorage 99510

Calista Corporation (Yukon-Kuskokwim Delta), P.O. Box 408, Bethel 99559 or 516 Denali St., Anchorage 99501

Chugach Alaska Corporation (Prince William Sound), 3000 A St., Suite 400, Anchorage 99503

Cook Inlet Region, Incorporated (Cook Inlet region), 2525 C St., Anchorage 99503

Doyon, Limited (interior Alaska), 201 First Ave., Suite 200, Fairbanks 99701

Koniag, Incorporated (Kodiak area), P.O. Box 746, Kodiak 99615

NANA Corporation (Kobuk region), P.O. Box 49, Kotzebue 99752 or 4706 Harding Drive, Anchorage 99503

Sealaska Corporation (southeastern Alaska), One Sealaska Plaza, Juneau 99801

Thirteenth Regional Corporation (outside Alaska), 13256 Northup Way, Suite 12, Bellevue, WA 98005

Regional Nonprofit Corporations

Aleutian-Pribilof Islands Association, Incorporated (Aleut Corporation), 1689 C St., Anchorage 99501

Association of Village Council Presidents (Calista Corporation), P.O. Box 219, Bethel 99559

Bristol Bay Native Association (Bristol Bay Native Corporation), P.O. Box 237, Dillingham 99756

Central Council of Tlingit-Haida Indian Tribes (Sealaska Corporation), One Sealaska Plaza, Suite 200, Juneau 99801

Cook Inlet Native Association (Cook Inlet Region, Incorporated), 670 W. Fireweed Lane, Anchorage 99503

Copper River Native Association (Ahtna Incorporated), Drawer H, Copper Center 99573

Inupiat Community of the Arctic Slope (Arctic Slope Regional Corporation), P.O. Box 437, Barrow 99723

Kawerak, Incorporated (Bering Straits Native Corporation), P.O. Box 948, Nome 99762

Kodiak Area Native Association (Koniag, Incorporated), P.O. Box 172, Kodiak 99615

Maniilaq (formerly Mauneluk) Association (NANA Regional Corporation), P.O. Box 256, Kotzebue 99752

North Pacific Rim Native Association (Chugach Alaska Corporation), 3000 A St., Suite 400, Anchorage 99503

Tanana Chiefs Conference (Doyon, Limited), 201 First Ave., Fairbanks 99701

Other Native Organizations

Alaska Eskimo Whaling Commission, P.O. Box 570, Barrow 99723

Alaska Federation of Natives, 411 W. Fourth Ave., Suite 1-A, Anchorage 99501

Alaska Native Brotherhood, P.O. Box 112, Juneau 99801

Alaska Native Commission on Alcoholism and Drug Abuse, P.O. Box 4-2463, Anchorage 99509

Alaska Native Foundation, 411 W. Fourth Ave., Suite 314, Anchorage 99501

Alaska Native Health Board, 1135 W. Eighth, Suite 2, Anchorage 99501

Central Council of Tlingit and Haida Indian Tribes of Alaska, One Sealaska Plaza, Suite 200, Juneau 99801

Fairbanks Native Association, Incorporated, 310 First Ave., Fairbanks 99701

Interior Village Association, 127-1/2 Minnie St., Fairbanks 99701

Inuit Circumpolar Conference, Barrow 99723

Norton Sound Health Corporation, P.O. Box 966, Nome 99762

Southeast Alaska Regional Health Corporation, P.O. Box 2800, Juneau 99803

Yukon-Kuskokwim Health Corporation, P.O. Box 528, Bethel 99559

Yupiktat Bista (a branch of the Association of Village Council Presidents), Bethel 99559

Native Village Corporations

In addition to the 12 regional corporations managing money and land received as part of the Alaska Native Claims Settlement Act, eligible Native villages were required to form corporations and to choose lands made available by the settlement act by December 1974. The 203 Native villages that formed village corporations eligible for land and money benefits are listed under their regional corporation.

Ahtna Incorporated: Cantwell, Chistochina, Chitina, Copper Center, Gakona, Gulkana, Mentasta Lake, Tazlina.

Aleut Corporation: Akutan, Atka, Belkofski, False Pass, King Cove, Nelson Lagoon, Nikolski, Saint George, Saint Paul, Sand Point, Unalaska, Unga.

Arctic Slope Regional Corporation: Anaktuvuk Pass, Atkasook, Barrow, Kaktovik, Nuiqsut, Point Hope, Point Lay, Wainwright.

Bering Straits Native Corporation: Brevig Mission, Council, Golovin, Inalik/Diomede, King Island, Koyuk, Marys Igloo, Nome, Saint Michael, Shaktoolik, Shishmaref, Stebbins, Teller, Unalakleet, Wales, White Mountain.

Bristol Bay Native Corporation: Aleknagik, Chignik, Chignik Lagoon, Chignik Lake, Clarks Point, Dillingham, Egegik, Ekuk, Ekwok, Igiugig, Iliamna, Ivanof Bay, Kokhanok, Koliganek, Levelock, Manokotak, Naknek, Newhalen, New Stuyahok, Nondalton, Pedro Bay, Perryville, Pilot Point, Portage Creek, Port Heiden, South Naknek, Togiak, Twin Hills, Ugashik.

Calista Corporation: Akiachak, Akiak, Alakanuk, Andreafsky, Aniak, Atmautluak, Bethel, Bill Moores, Chefornak, Chevak, Chuathbaluk, Chuloonwick, Crooked Creek, Eek, Emmonak, Georgetown, Goodnews Bay, Hamilton, Hooper Bay, Kasigluk, Kipnuk, Kongiganak, Kotlik, Kwethluk, Kwigillingok, Lime Village, Lower Kalskag, Marshall, Mekoryuk, Mountain Village, Napaimiute, Napakiak, Napaskiak, Newtok, Nightmute, Nunapitchuk, Ohogamiut, Oscarville, Paimiut, Pilot Station, Pitkas Point, Platinum, Quinhagak, Red Devil, Russian Mission, Saint Marys, Scammon Bay, Sheldons Point, Sleetmute, Stony River, Toksook Bay, Tuluksak, Tuntutuliak, Tununak, Umkumiut, Upper Kalskag.

Chugach Natives, Incorporated: Chenaga, English Bay, Eyak, Port Graham, Tatitlek.

Cook Inlet Region, Incorporated: Chickaloon, Knik, Eklutna, Ninilchik, Seldovia, Tyonek.

Doyon, Limited: Alatna, Allakaket, Anvik, Beaver, Bettles Field, Birch Creek, Chalkyitsik, Circle, Dot Lake, Eagle, Fort Yukon, Galena, Grayling, Healy Lake, Holy Cross, Hughes, Huslia, Kaltag, Koyukuk, Manley Hot Springs, McGrath, Minto, Nenana, Nikolai, Northway, Nulato, Rampart, Ruby, Shageluk, Stevens Village, Takotna, Tanacross, Tanana, Telida.

Koniag, Incorporated: Afognak, Akhiok, Kaguyak, Karluk, Larsen Bay, Old Harbor, Ouzinkie, Port Lions, Woody Island.

NANA Regional Corporation, Incorporated: Ambler, Buckland, Deering, Kiana, Kivalina, Kobuk, Kotzebue, Noatak, Noorvik, Selawik, Shungnak.

Sealaska Corporation: Angoon, Craig, Hoonah, Hydaburg, Kake, Kasaan, Klawock, Saxman, Yakutat.

Related reading: *Heroes and Heroines in Tlingit-Haida Legend,* by Mary L. Beck, with illustrations by Nancy DeWitt. *Roots of Ticasuk: An Eskimo Woman's Family Story,* by Emily Ivanoff Brown. See ALASKA NORTHWEST LIBRARY in the back of the book.

Nenana Ice Classic

The Ice Classic is a gigantic betting pool offering $138,000 in 1990 in cash prizes to the lucky winners who guess the time, to the nearest minute, of the ice breakup on the Tanana River at the town of Nenana. Official breakup time each spring is established when the surging ice dislodges a tripod and breaks an attached line, which stops a clock set to Yukon standard time.

Tickets for the classic are sold for $2 each, entitling the holder to one guess. Ice Classic officials estimate over $7 million has been paid to lucky guessers through the years.

The primary intention of the Ice Classic was never as a fund-raiser for the town, but as a statewide lottery, which was officially sanctioned by the first state legislature in one of its first actions back in 1959. But over the years the contest has benefited the town. Fifty percent of the gross proceeds goes to the winners. Nenana residents are paid salaries for ticket counting and compilation, and about 15 percent is earmarked for upkeep of the Nenana Civic Center and as donations to local groups such as the Dog Mushers, to the Visitors Center and to other activities or organizations.

The U.S. Internal Revenue Service also gets a large chunk of withholding taxes on the $138,000 payroll and a huge bite of each winner's share.

Another pool, the Kuskokwim Ice Classic, has been a tradition in Bethel since 1924. Initially, it was said that the winner was paid 20 fish or 20 furs, but stakes are considerably higher now, with the winner receiving 40 percent of the total ticket sales.

Breakup times for the Nenana Ice Classic from 1918 through 1990, arranged in order of date and year, are:

April	20, 1940 —	3:27	P.M.
	24, 1990 —	5:19	P.M.
	26, 1926 —	4:03	P.M.
	28, 1969 —	12:28	P.M.
	28, 1943 —	7:22	P.M.
	29, 1983 —	6:37	P.M.
	29, 1958 —	2:56	P.M.
	29, 1953 —	3:54	P.M.
	29, 1939 —	1:26	P.M.
	30, 1981 —	6:44	P.M.
	30, 1980 —	1:16	P.M.
	30, 1979 —	6:16	P.M.
	30, 1978 —	3:18	P.M.
	30, 1951 —	5:54	P.M.
	30, 1942 —	1:28	P.M.
	30, 1936 —	12:58	P.M.
	30, 1934 —	2:07	P.M.
May	1, 1956 —	11:24	A.M.
	1, 1932 —	10:15	A.M.
	1, 1989 —	8:14	P.M.
	2, 1976 —	10:51	A.M.
	2, 1960 —	7:12	P.M.
	3, 1947 —	5:53	P.M.
	3, 1941 —	1:50	A.M.
	3, 1919 —	2:33	P.M.
	4, 1973 —	11:59	A.M.
	4, 1970 —	10:37	P.M.
	4, 1967 —	11:55	A.M.
	4, 1944 —	2:08	P.M.
	5, 1963 —	6:25	P.M.
	5, 1961 —	11:31	A.M.
	5, 1957 —	9:30	A.M.
	5, 1946 —	4:40	P.M.
	5, 1929 —	3:41	P.M.
	5, 1987 —	3:11	P.M.
	6, 1977 —	12:46	P.M.
	6, 1974 —	3:44	P.M.
	6, 1954 —	6:01	P.M.
	6, 1950 —	4:14	P.M.
	6, 1938 —	8:14	P.M.
	6, 1928 —	4:25	P.M.
	7, 1965 —	7:01	P.M.
	7, 1925 —	6:32	P.M.
	8, 1971 —	10:50	P.M.
	8, 1986 —	9:31	P.M.
	8, 1968 —	9:26	P.M.

May 8, 1966 — 12:11 P.M.
     8, 1959 — 11:26 A.M.
     8, 1933 — 7:30 P.M.
     8, 1930 — 7:03 P.M.
     9, 1955 — 2:31 P.M.
     9, 1923 — 2:00 P.M.
     9, 1984 — 3:33 P.M.
    10, 1982 — 5:36 P.M.
    10, 1975 — 1:49 P.M.
    10, 1972 — 11:56 A.M.
    10, 1931 — 9:23 A.M.
    11, 1985 — 2:36 P.M.
    11, 1924 — 3:10 P.M.
    11, 1921 — 6:42 A.M.
    11, 1920 — 10:45 A.M.
    11, 1918 — 9:33 A.M.
    12, 1962 — 11:23 P.M.
    12, 1952 — 5:04 P.M.
    12, 1937 — 8:04 P.M.
    12, 1927 — 5:42 A.M.
    12, 1922 — 1:20 P.M.
    13, 1948 — 11:13 A.M.
    14, 1949 — 12:39 P.M.
    15, 1935 — 1:32 P.M.
    16, 1945 — 9:41 A.M.
    20, 1964 — 11:41 A.M.

Newspapers and Periodicals

(Rates are subject to change)

Advocate, 3933 Geneva Place, Anchorage 99508. Weekly. Annual rates: Write for information.

Air Alaska, P.O. Box 99007, Anchorage 99509. Monthly. Annual rates: $15.

Air Guardian, 600 Air Guard Road, Anchorage 99502. Monthly. Annual rates: free.

Alaska Business Monthly, P.O. Box 241288, Anchorage 99524. Monthly. Annual rates: $21.95.

Alaska Business Newsletter, 203 W. 15th Ave., Suite 102, Anchorage 99501. Weekly. Annual rates: $150.

Alaska Commercial Fisherman, 4000 Old Seward Highway, Suite 104, Anchorage 99503. Biweekly. Annual rates: $25.

Alaska Designs, P.O. Box 103115, Anchorage 99510. Monthly. Annual rates: free to members.

Alaska Directory of Attorneys, 203 W. 15th Ave., Suite 102, Anchorage 99501. Semiannually. Annual rates: $20 per issue.

Alaska Economic Report, 3037 S. Circle, Anchorage 99507. Biweekly. Annual rates: $200.

Alaska Fisherman's Journal, 1115 NW 46th St., Seattle, WA 98107. Monthly. Annual rates: $18.

The Alaska Geographic Society, P.O. Box 93370, Anchorage 99509. Quarterly. Annual rates: $39; outside the U.S., $43.

Alaska Journal of Commerce, P.O. Box 99007, Anchorage 99509. Weekly. Annual rates: $49.

Alaska Land Reporter, 801 Barnette St., Fairbanks 99701. Monthly. Annual rates: $36.

Alaska Legislative Digest, 3037 S. Circle, Anchorage 99507. Weekly during session. Annual rates: $200.

ALASKA magazine, 808 E St., Suite 200, Anchorage 99501. Monthly. Annual rates: $24; outside the U.S., $28.

Alaska Media Directory, 6200 Bubbling Brook, Anchorage 99516. Annually. Annual rates: $68.

Alaska Outdoors, P.O. Box 190324, Anchorage 99519. Monthly. Annual rates: $23.95.

Alaska Public Affairs Journal, 16831 Tidewater Drive, Suite B, Anchorage 99516. Quarterly. Annual rates: $20.

Alaska Travel News, P.O. Box 202622, Anchorage 99520. May through August. Annual rates: free.

Alaska Wilderness Milepost, P.O. Box 3007, Bothell, WA 98041-3007. Annually. Annual rates: $14.95.

AlaskaMen, 201 Danner St., Suite 100, Anchorage 99518. Bimonthly. Annual rates: $24.95.

Alaskan, 134th Public Affairs Team, 3601 C St., Suite 620, Anchorage 99503. Bimonthly. Annual rates: free.

Alaskan Viewpoint, HCR 64, Box 453, Seward 99664. Monthly. Annual rates: $8.

Aleutian Eagle, 3933 Geneva Place, Anchorage 99508. Weekly. Annual rates: $45.

The All-Alaska Weekly, P.O. Box 70970, Fairbanks 99707. Weekly. Annual rates: $24.

Anchorage Daily News, P.O. Box 149001, Anchorage 99514. Daily. Annual rates: Anchorage home delivery, $90; second-class mail, $240.

Anchorage Magazine, 733 W. Fourth Ave., Suite 310, Anchorage 99501. Monthly. Annual rates: $24.

The Anchorage Times, P.O. Box 40, Anchorage 99510. Daily. Annual rates: Anchorage home delivery, $91.26.

Anchorage Visitors Guide, 1600 A St., Suite 200, Anchorage 99501. Annually. Annual rates: free.

Arctic Soldier Magazine, Public Affairs Office, HQ, 6th Infantry Division (Light), Fort Richardson 99505. Quarterly. Annual rates: free.

Arctic Sounder, P.O. Box 290, Kotzebue 99752. Biweekly. Annual rates: $20.

Arctic Star, Public Affairs Office, HQ, 6th Infantry Division (Light), Fort Richardson 99505. Weekly. Annual rates: $24.

Barrow Sun, 3933 Geneva Place, Anchorage 99508. Biweekly. Annual rates: $30.

Boat Brokers, P.O. Box 22163, Juneau 99802. Monthly. Annual rates: free.

Borough Post, P.O. Box 456, King Salmon 99613. Weekly. Annual rates: $45.

Bristol Bay News, P.O. Box 770, Dillingham 99576. Weekly. Annual rates: $45.

Bristol BayTimes, P.O. Box 1129, Dillingham 99576. Weekly. Annual rates: $40.

Bush Buyers Guide, 3709 Spenard Road, Anchorage 99503. Monthly. Annual rates: Write for information.

Capitol City Weekly, 8365 Old Dairy Road, Juneau 99801. Weekly. Annual rates: home or mail delivery, 25¢ per week, otherwise free.

Chilkat Valley News, P.O. Box 630, Haines 99827. Weekly. Annual rates: $28.

Chugiak-Eagle River Star, 16941 North Eagle River Loop, Eagle River 99577. Weekly. Annual rates: $16.

Commercial Fisherman's Guide, P.O. Box 119, Port Ludlow, WA 98365. Annually. Annual rates: $9.95.

Community Blue Book, P.O. Box 91975, Anchorage 99509. Biannually. Annual rates: Write for information.

Copper River Country Journal, P.O. Box 336, Glennallen 99588. Bimonthly. Annual rates: $25.

Cordova Times, P.O. Box 200, Cordova 99574. Weekly. Annual rates: $50.

Daily Sitka Sentinel, P.O. Box 799, Sitka 99835. Monday through Friday. Annual rates: $60.

The Delta Paper, P.O. Box 988, Delta Junction 99737. Weekly. Annual rates: $26.

Eagle Call, Box 2 NAS Adak, FPO Seattle 98791. Weekly. Annual rates: free.

Fairbanks Daily News-Miner, P.O. Box 710, Fairbanks 99707. Daily. Annual rates: $222.

Fairbanks Magazine, 921 Woodway, Fairbanks 99709. Annually. Annual rates: $2.25.

The Frontiersman, 1261 Seward Meridian, Wasilla 99687. Semiweekly. Annual rates: $23.

Great Lander Bush Mailer, 3110 Spenard Road, Anchorage 99503. Monthly. Annual rates: free.

Greater Anchorage Tomorrow, 437 E St., Suite 300, Anchorage 99501. Monthly. Annual rates: $12.

Haines Sentinel, P.O. Box 630, Haines 99827. Annually. Annual rates: free.

Homer News, 3482 Landings St., Homer 99603. Weekly. Annual rates: Kenai Peninsula Borough, $24.

Island News, P.O. Box 19430, Thorne Bay 99919. Weekly. Annual rates: $40.

Juneau Empire, 3100 Channel Drive, Juneau 99801. Monday through Friday. Annual rates: $72.

Ketchikan Daily News, P.O. Box 7900, Ketchikan 99901. Monday through Saturday. Annual rates: $80.

Kodiak Daily Mirror, 1895 Mission, Kodiak 99615. Write for information on schedule and rates.

Marine Highway and Railroad News, P.O. Box 99007, Anchorage 99509. Monthly, April to September. Annual rates: free.

The MILEPOST®, P.O. Box 3007, Bothell, WA 98041. Annual edition, available in March. $14.95 plus $1.50 for fourth-class postage; $3.50 for first class mail.

Mukluk News, P.O. Box 90, Tok 99780. Bimonthly. Annual rates: $30.

Mushing, P.O. Box 149, Ester 99725. Bimonthly. Annual rates: $15.

New Alaskan, 8339 Snug Harbor Lane NTG, Ketchikan 99901. Monthly, except January. Annual rates: $7 outside of Ketchikan.

Nome Nugget, P.O. Box 610, Nome 99762. Weekly. Annual rates: $50.

Northern Adventures Magazine, 400 Denali, Wasilla 99687. Biannually. Annual rates: Write for information.

Northland News, P.O. Box 710, Fairbanks 99707. Monthly. Annual rates: free.

On The Market, P.O. Box 32901, Juneau 99803. Monthly. Annual rates: free in southeastern Alaska.

Peninsula Clarion, P.O. Box 4330, Kenai 99611. Monday through Friday. Annual rates: $58.

Petersburg Pilot, P.O. Box 930, Petersburg 99833. Weekly. Annual rates: $28.

The River, P.O. Box 173, Aniak 99577. Biweekly. Annual rates: $10

Senior Voice, 325 E. Third Ave., Anchorage 99501. Monthly. Annual rates: $15 seniors; $20 under 55.

Seward Phoenix Log, P.O. Box 89, Seward 99664. Weekly. Annual rates: $30.

The Skagway News, P.O. Box 1898, Skagway 99840. Biweekly, May through October; monthly, November through April. Annual rates: $30.

Sourdough Sentinel, 21st TFW, Public Affairs, Elmendorf Air Force Base 99506. Weekly. Annual rates: free.

Tundra Drums, P.O. Box 868, Bethel 99559. Weekly. Annual rates: $20.

Tundra Times, P.O. Box 104480, Anchorage 99510. Weekly. Annual rates: $20.

Valdez Pioneer, P.O. Box 367, Valdez 99686. Weekly. Annual rates: $45.

Valdez Vanguard, P.O. Box 157, Valdez 99686. Weekly. Annual rates: $90.

Valley Sun, 1261 Seward Meridian, Wasilla 99687. Weekly. Free to Matanuska-Susitna Borough boxholders.

Who's Who In Alaskan Arts & Crafts, HCR 64, Box 453, Seward 99664. Annually. Annual rates: Write for information.

Wrangell Sentinel, P.O. Box 798, Wrangell 99929. Weekly. Annual rates: $25.

No-see-ums

In its usual swarms this tiny, gray-black, silver-winged gnat is a most persistent pest and annoys all creatures. But, when alone, each insect is difficult to see. While no-see-ums don't transmit disease, their bites are irritating. Protective clothing, netting and a good repellent are recommended while in the bushes or near still-water ponds. Tents and recreational vehicles should be well screened.

Nuchalawoya

Nuchalawoya means "where the great waters meet"; it was originally a meeting of Athabascan chiefs held near the time of the summer solstice. Nuchalawoya today is a festival held in June at Tanana, a town located at the confluence of the Tanana and Yukon rivers. The festival is open to the public.

Officials

UNDER RUSSIA

Emperor Paul of Russia grants the Russian-American Company an exclusive trade charter in Alaska.

Chief Managers, Russian-American Company

Alexander Andrevich Baranof, 1799–1818

Leontil Andreanovich Hagemeister, January–October 1818

Semen Ivanovich Yanovski, 1818–1820

Matxei I. Muravief, 1820–1825

Peter Egorovich Chistiakov, 1825–1830

Baron Ferdinand P. von Wrangell, 1830–1835

Ivan Antonovich Kupreanof, 1835–1840

Adolph Karlovich Etolin, 1840–1845

Michael D. Tebenkof, 1845–1850

Nikolai Y. Rosenberg, 1850–1853

Alexander Ilich Rudakof, 1853–1854

Stephen Vasili Voevodski, 1854–1859

Ivan V. Furuhelm, 1859–1863

Prince Dmitri Maksoutoff, 1863–1867

UNDER UNITED STATES

U.S. purchases Alaska from Russia in 1867; U.S. Army given jurisdiction over Department of Alaska.

Army Commanding Officers

Bvt. Maj. Gen. Jefferson C. Davis, Oct. 18, 1867–Aug. 31, 1870

Bvt. Lt. Col. George K. Brady, Sept. 1, 1870–Sept. 22, 1870

Maj. John C. Tidball, Sept. 23, 1870–Sept. 19, 1871

Maj. Harvey A. Allen, Sept. 20, 1871–Jan. 3, 1873

Maj. Joseph Stewart, Jan. 4, 1873–April 20, 1874

Capt. George R. Rodney, April 21, 1874–August 16, 1874

Capt. Joseph B. Campbell, Aug. 17, 1874–June 14, 1876

Capt. John Mendenhall, June 15, 1876–March 4, 1877

Capt. Arthur Morris, March 5, 1877–June 14, 1877

U.S. Army troops leave Alaska; the highest ranking federal official left in Alaska is the U.S. collector of customs. Department of Alaska is put under control of the U.S. Treasury Department.

U.S. Collectors of Customs

Montgomery P. Berry, June 14, 1877–Aug. 13, 1877

H.C. DeAhna, Aug. 14, 1877–March 26, 1878

Mottrom D. Ball, March 27, 1877–June 13, 1879

U.S. Navy is given jurisdiction over the Department of Alaska.

Navy Commanding Officers

Captain L.A. Beardslee, June 14, 1879–September 12, 1880

Comdr. Henry Glass, Sept. 13, 1880–Aug. 9, 1881

Comdr. Edward Lull, Aug. 10, 1881–Oct. 18, 1881

Comdr. Henry Glass, Oct. 19, 1881–March 12, 1882

Comdr. Frederick Pearson, March 13, 1882–Oct. 3, 1882

Comdr. Edgar C. Merriman, Oct. 4, 1882–Sept. 13, 1883

Comdr. Joseph B. Coghlan, Sept. 15, 1883–Sept. 13, 1884

Lt. Comdr. Henry E. Nichols, Sept. 14, 1884–Sept. 15, 1884

Congress provides civil government for the new District of Alaska in 1884; on Aug. 24, 1912, territorial status is given to Alaska.

Presidential Appointments

John H. Kinkead (President Arthur), July 4, 1884–May 7, 1885. (He did not reach Sitka until Sept. 15, 1884.)

Alfred P. Swineford (President Cleveland), May 7, 1885–April 20, 1889

Lyman E. Knapp (President Harrison), April 20, 1889–June 18, 1893

James Sheakley (President Cleveland), June 18, 1893–June 23, 1897

John G. Brady (President McKinley), June 23, 1897–March 2, 1906

Wilford B. Hoggatt (President Roosevelt), March 2, 1906–May 20, 1909

Walter E. Clark (President Taft), May 20, 1909–April 18, 1913

John F.A. Strong (President Wilson), April 18, 1913–April 12, 1918

Thomas Riggs Jr. (President Wilson), April 12, 1918–June 16, 1921

Scott C. Bone (President Harding), June 16, 1921–Aug. 16, 1925

George A. Parks (President Coolidge), June 16, 1925–April 19, 1933

John W. Troy (President Roosevelt), April 19, 1933–Dec. 6, 1939

Ernest Gruening (President Roosevelt), Dec. 6, 1939–April 10, 1953

B. Frank Heintzleman (President Eisenhower), April 10, 1953–Jan. 3, 1957

Mike Stepovich (President Eisenhower), April 8, 1957–Aug. 9, 1958

Alaska becomes a state Jan. 3, 1959.

Elected Governors

William A. Egan, Jan. 3, 1959–Dec. 5, 1966

Walter J. Hickel,* Dec. 5, 1966–Jan. 29, 1969

Keith H. Miller,* Jan. 29, 1969–Dec. 7, 1970

William A. Egan, Dec. 7, 1970–Dec. 2, 1974

Jay S. Hammond, Dec. 2, 1974–Dec. 6, 1982

Bill Sheffield, Dec. 6, 1982–Dec. 1, 1986

Steve Cowper, Dec. 1, 1986–Dec. 3, 1990

Hickel resigned before completing his full term as governor in order to accept the position of secretary of the interior. He was succeeded by Miller.

In 1906, Congress authorized Alaska to send a voteless delegate to the House of Representatives.

Delegates to Congress

Frank H. Waskey, 1906–1907

Thomas Cale, 1907–1909
James Wickersham, 1909–1917
Charles A. Sulzer, 1917–contested election
James Wickersham, 1918, seated as delegate
Charles A. Sulzer, 1919, elected; died before taking office
George Grigsby, 1919, elected in a special election
James Wickersham, 1921, seated as delegate, having contested election of Grigsby
Dan A. Sutherland, 1921–1930
James Wickersham, 1931–1933
Anthony J. Dimond, 1933–1944
E.L. Bartlett, 1944–1958

Unofficial delegates to Congress to promote statehood, elected under a plan first devised by Tennessee. The Tennessee Plan delegates were not seated by Congress but did serve as lobbyists.
Senators:
Ernest Gruening, 1956–1958
William Egan, 1956–1958

Representative:
Ralph Rivers, 1956–1958

Alaska becomes 49th state in 1959 and sends two senators and one representative to U.S. Congress.
Senators:
E.L. Bartlett, 1958–1968
Ernest Gruening, 1958–1968
Mike Gravel, 1968–1980
Ted Stevens, 1968–
Frank Murkowski, 1980–

Representatives:
Ralph Rivers, 1958–1966
Howard Pollock, 1966–1970
Nicholas Begich, 1970–1972
Don Young, 1972–

Correspondence addresses for Alaska officials:
The Honorable Steve Cowper, Office of the Governor, P.O. Box A, Juneau 99811.
The Honorable Stephen McAlpine, Office of the Lieutenant Governor, P.O. Box AA, Juneau 99811

Alaska's Delegation in U.S. Congress:
The Honorable Ted Stevens, United States Senate, 522 Hart Bldg., Washington, D.C. 20510
The Honorable Frank H. Murkowski, United States Senate, 709 Hart Bldg., Washington, D.C. 20510
The Honorable Donald E. Young, House of Representatives, 2331 Rayburn House Office Bldg., Washington, D.C. 20515

Alaska State Legislature
Members of the Alaska Legislature as of the end of the 1990 session are listed below. During sessions, members of the legislature receive mail at P.O. Box V, Juneau 99811.

House of Representatives
District 1: Robin L. Taylor (Seat A, Republican); Cheri Davis (Seat B, Republican).
District 2: Peter Goll (Democrat).
District 3: Ben F. Grussendorf (Democrat).
District 4: Bill Hudson (Seat A, Republican); Fran Ulmer (Seat B, Democrat).
District 5: Mike Navarre (Seat A, Democrat); C.E. Swackhammer (Seat B, Democrat).
District 6: Gene Kubina (Democrat).
District 7: Jim Zawacki (Republican).
District 8: Fritz Pettyjohn (Seat A, Republican); Steven Rieger (Seat B, Republican).
District 9: Loren Leman (Seat A, Republican); Alyce A. Hanley (Seat B, Republican).
District 10: H.A."Red" Boucher (Seat A, Democrat); Virginia M. Collins (Seat B, Republican).
District 11: Dave Donley (Seat A, Democrat); Max F. Gruenberg Jr. (Seat B, Democrat).
District 12: Kay Brown (Seat A, Democrat); Johnny Ellis (Seat B, Democrat).
District 13: David Finkelstein (Seat A, Democrat); Terry Martin (Seat B, Republican).
District 14: Ramona Barnes (Seat A, Republican); Walt Furnace (Seat B, Republican).
District 15: Sam Cotten (Seat A, Democrat); Randy E. Phillips (Seat B, Republican).
District 16: Curt Menard (Seat A, Democrat); Ronald L. Larson (Seat B, Democrat).

District 17: Richard Shultz (Republican).
District 18: Mike W. Miller (Republican).
District 19: Mike Davis (Democrat).
District 20: Bert M. Sharp (Seat A, Republican); Mark Boyer (Seat B, Democrat).
District 21: Niilo Koponen (Democrat).
District 22: Eileen Panigeo MacLean (Democrat).
District 23: Richard Foster (Democrat).
District 24: Kay Wallis (Democrat).
District 25: Lyman F. Hoffman (Democrat).
District 26: George G. Jacko Jr. (Democrat).
District 27: Cliff Davidson (Democrat).

Senate

District A: Lloyd Jones (Republican).
District B: Richard I. Eliason (Republican).
District C: Jim Duncan (Democrat).
District D: Paul A. Fischer (Republican).
District E: Jalmar M. "Jay" Kerttula (Seat A, Democrat); Mike Szymanski (Seat B, Democrat).
District F: Arliss Sturgulewski (Seat A, Republican); Jan Faiks (Seat B, Republican).
District G: Drue Pearce (Seat A, Republican); Patrick M. Rodey (Seat B, Democrat).
District H: Pat Pourchot (Seat A, Democrat); Rick Uehling (Seat B, Republican).
District I: Rick Halford (Seat A, Republican); Tim Kelly (Seat B, Republican).
District J: John B. "Jack" Coghill (Republican).
District K: Steve Frank (Seat A, Republican); Bettye M. Fahrenkamp (Seat B, Democrat).
District L: Al Adams (Democrat).
District M: Johne Binkley (Republican).
District N: Fred F. Zharoff (Democrat).

Oil and Gas

Alaska's first exploratory oil well was drilled in 1898 on the Iniskin Peninsula, Cook Inlet, by Alaska Petroleum Company. According to the Alaska Oil and Gas Association, oil was encountered in this first hole at about 700 feet, but a water zone beneath the oil strata cut off the oil flow. Total depth of the well was approximately 1,000 feet.

The first commercial oil discovery was made in 1902 near Katalla, near the mouth of the Bering River east of Cordova. This field produced until 1933.

As early as 1921, oil companies surveyed land north of the Brooks Range for possible drilling sites. In 1923, the federal government created Naval Petroleum Reserve Number 4 (now known as National Petroleum Reserve-Alaska, *see* National Petroleum Reserve), a 23-million-acre area of Alaska's North Slope. Wartime needs speeded up exploration. In 1944, the Navy began drilling operations on the petroleum reserve and continued until 1953, but made no significant oil discoveries. Since 1981, the Interior Department has leased out oil and gas tracts in the reserve.

Atlantic Richfield discovered oil in 1957 on the Kenai Peninsula, at a depth of approximately 2 miles, about 20 miles northeast of Kenai at what became known as the Swanson River Oilfield. Later, Union Oil Company found a large gas field at Kalifonsky Beach (the Kenai Gas Field) and Amoco found the first gas offshore at a location known as Middle Ground Shoals in Cook Inlet in 1962. Since 1957, the oil and gas industry has invested $45 billion in Alaska. The money has gone toward exploration and development of North Shore oil fields, and construction of the trans-Alaska pipeline.

Currently, there are 15 production platforms in Cook Inlet, one of which produces only gas. Built to contend with extreme tides, siltation and ice floes, the Cook Inlet platforms are in one of three successful areas of offshore oil production in the United States. Hundreds of miles of pipeline with diameters up to 20 inches link the offshore platforms with onshore facilities at Kenai and Drift River. The deepest producing oil well in the state is in the Swanson River Oilfield on the Kenai Peninsula; total depth is 17,689 feet. Alaska had 313 active wells in 1985, including exploratory and developmental wells.

A fertilizer plant, largest of its kind

on the West Coast, is located at Nikiski, near Kenai. It uses natural gas as a feed stock to manufacture ammonia and urea. Two refineries are located at Kenai; a third is at North Pole near Fairbanks. Gasoline, diesel fuel, heavy fuel oil, propane, JP-4, Jet A and asphalt are produced for use within and outside of Alaska. Crude oil topping plants located at Prudhoe Bay and at pump stations 6, 8 and 10 provide diesel oil for oil field and pipeline use. Liquified natural gas is produced at a special Philips LNG plant and is the only LNG export facility in the U.S.

The Prudhoe Bay oil field, largest in North America, was discovered in 1968 by Atlantic Richfield Company and Exxon. Recoverable reserves were estimated to be 9.6 billion barrels of oil and 26 trillion cubic feet of natural gas. The field contains about one-quarter of the known petroleum reserves in the United States and each day produces nearly 25 percent of U.S. production and 11 percent of U.S. consumption. Peak production of 1.5 million barrels per day has begun to decline and is transported from North Slope fields via the trans-Alaska pipeline from Prudhoe Bay to Valdez (*see* Pipeline).

In spring of 1986, it was estimated that one-half of the Prudhoe Bay recoverable oil reserve had been pumped. A \$2 billion waterflood project was installed to maximize oil recovery by forcing additional oil out of the reservoir rock and into producing wells. The Central Gas Facility, recently built at Prudhoe Bay, is capable of processing 3.7 billion cubic feet of natural gas and yielding more than 54,000 barrels of natural gas liquids daily. The facility is the largest gas plant in the world with a capacity of over 4 billion cubic feet. Two new fields, Endicott and Lisburne, are in production, with Lisburne beginning production in 1986. Endicott began production in February 1985, and is owned by Standard Alaska (56.7 percent), Exxon (21 percent), Amoco (10.5 percent) and Union (10.5 percent). The remaining 1.3 percent is owned by ARCO; Cook Inlet Region, Incorporated; Doyon, Limited; and NANA Regional Corporation, and is the first offshore commercial development in the United States portion of the

Beaufort Sea. Endicott is estimated to have 350 million barrels of oil, and in early 1990 became the sixth largest field in the nation in terms of production. Milne Point, located 35 miles northwest of Prudhoe Bay, is a field operated by Conoco. Economically, this is a marginal field with estimated reserves of 100 million barrels. Conoco suspended drilling operations in February 1985, but resumed production in 1989, at the rate of 7,000 barrels per day.

The Kuparuk River Field, 40 miles west of Prudhoe Bay, is being developed by ARCO. The field went into production in mid-December 1981; approximately 303,740 barrels a day are being delivered to the trans-Alaska pipeline. In February 1989, ARCO and Exxon announced the discovery of a 300-million-barrel oil field at Point McIntyre, which is about two miles north of the Prudhoe Bay field. The reservoir for the field lies offshore beneath the Beaufort Sea, and if the estimates of the amount of recoverable reserves are correct, the field would be the largest domestic discovery since the discovery of the Endicott field in the late 1970s. If production proves economically feasible, oil could begin flowing in 1993.

In 1984, Shell Western discovered oil at Seal Island, 12 miles northwest of Prudhoe Bay. Northstar Island, five miles to the west, was the site of delineation drilling in 1985, and in the same region, Sandpiper Island reported another strike in 1985. Texaco hit a strike on the Colville River Delta of eight miles northwest of the Kuparuk River field. Exploration in Navarin Basin began when Amoco drilled five wells, Exxon drilled two wells and ARCO drilled one well. The average well took 60 days to drill and the average cost per well was \$20 to 30 million. Although none of the wells is considered commercially feasible, drilling was halted by legal action. In October 1985, the 9th Circuit Court of Appeals in San Francisco ruled that drilling must stop in Navarin Basin until a lawsuit filed by the villages of Gambell and Stebbins was fully heard. In a significant decision in early 1987, the Supreme Court overturned the 9th Circuit ruling and held that the aboriginal rights of Alaska Natives were extinguished by Section 4(b) of the Alaska Native Claims Settlement Act, and that Section 810(a) of the ANILCA, which provides protection for subsistence resources, did not extend to the outer continental shelf.

The Alaska Natural Gas Transportation System (proposed Alaska gas pipeline) was authorized by the federal government in 1977. Estimated cost was $10 billion with a completion date of 1983. A two-year delay in the northern part of the project was announced in May 1982 by Northwest Alaskan, the consortium building the project. Recent cost estimates for the gas pipeline have risen to more than $40 billion. A completion date is not set for the foreseeable future, due to problems in financing the project. Now, most industry observers feel that the proposed trans-Alaska gas system is the most viable idea for transporting North Slope gas to Valdez for shipment to market.

Alaska Oil and Natural Gas (Liquid) Production (in millions of barrels)

Year	Oil*	Natural Gas**
1972	73.6	0.608
1973	73.1	0.812
1974	72.2	0.793
1975	72.0	0.765
1976	67.0	0.770
1977	171.3	0.863
1978	444.8	0.815
1979	511.3	0.635
1980	591.6	0.735
1981	587.3	0.988
1982	618.9	0.999
1983	625.6	0.692
1984	630.4	0.678
1985	666.2	0.986
1986	681.3	1.600
1987	716.0	16.500
1988	738.1	20.300
1989	684.0	18.045

*Oil production for the years 1902–71 totaled 396,537,603 barrels; for the years 1902–82, total production amounted to 3,682,769,004 barrels.

**Natural gas (liquid) production for the years 1902–71 totaled 1,312,113 barrels; for the years 1902–83, total production was 9,218,705 barrels.
Source: *1983 Statistical Report*, Alaska Oil and Gas Conservation Commission, 3001 Porcupine Drive, Anchorage 99501.

In 1987, Alaska surpassed Texas in oil production. The top five oil-producing states, in order, were: Alaska, Texas, Louisiana, California and Oklahoma. According to the U.S. Geological Survey, Alaska provided about 20 percent of the nation's oil in 1983.

The state of Alaska receives approximately 85 percent of its general revenue from petroleum taxes and royalties, and since 1975, the state has collected more than $32 billion in oil and gas revenues. In early 1986, the price of oil dropped. Oil industry employment then declined rather than increased, and the state government was in a more tenuous fiscal situation. By early 1990, oil prices had improved, but Prudhoe Bay production had begun to decline.

While crude oil produced in the North Slope cannot be exported, there are no such restrictions on natural gas, but so far, no transportation system has been constructed for North Slope gas. In 1988, natural gas and products derived from it (ammonia and urea) made up 18.7 percent of all Alaska exports. Most natural gas produced in Alaska is either locally consumed or reinjected back into oil wells.

Natural gas provides a relatively low-cost source of energy for certain Railbelt residents and businesses of Alaska. In 1983, 60 percent of power generated by Alaska utility companies used natural gas. That year the total revenues earned by the utility companies were $264 million. There are also three refineries in Alaska, which satisfy 75 percent of gasoline, diesel and jet fuel consumption in the state.

Oil and gas leasing on state land in Alaska is managed by the Department of Natural Resources, Division of Oil and Gas. The secretary of the interior is responsible for establishing oil and gas leasing on federal lands in Alaska, including the outer continental shelf. In 1986, Chevron, in partnership with a Native corporation, left its well at Kaktovik on the coastal plain of the Arctic National Wildlife Refuge. The land was obtained in a swap with the U.S. Department of the Interior, but Congress would have to approve any development within the boundaries of the refuge. (*See also* Yearly Highlights)

Parka

Pronounced *par-kee,* this over-the-head garment worn by Eskimos was made in several versions. The work parka most often came from caribou fawn skin, while the fancy parka, reserved for special occasions, used the skin of the male ground squirrel (the male offering grayer fur than the female). The rain parka was made from *oogruk* (bearded seal) intestine. A person's wealth was judged by the quality of their best parka.

Related reading: *Secrets of Eskimo Skin Sewing,* by Edna Wilder. The complete book on the art of Eskimo skin sewing, with how-to-do-it instructions and things-to-make ideas. See ALASKA NORTHWEST LIBRARY in the back of the book.

Permafrost

Permafrost is defined as ground that remains frozen for two or more years.

In its continuous form, permafrost underlies the entire Arctic region to depths of 2,000 feet. In broad terms, continuous permafrost occurs north of the Brooks Range and in the alpine region of mountains (including those of the Lower 48).

Discontinuous permafrost occurs south of the Brooks Range and north of the Alaska Range. Much of the Interior and some of southcentral Alaska are underlain by discontinuous permafrost.

Permafrost affects many man-made structures and natural bodies. It influences construction in the Arctic because building on it may cause the ground to thaw and if the ground is ice-rich, structures will sink. Arctic and subarctic rivers typically carry 55 to 65 percent of the precipitation that falls onto their watersheds, roughly 30 to 40 percent more than rivers of more temperate climates. Consequently, northern streams are prone to flooding and have high silt loads. Permafrost is responsible for the thousands of lakes dotting the arctic tundra because groundwater is held on the surface.

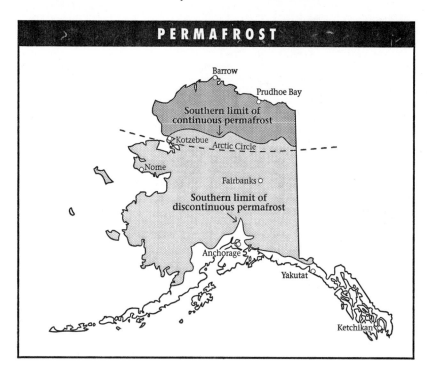

PERMAFROST

Barrow
Prudhoe Bay
Southern limit of continuous permafrost
Kotzebue   Arctic Circle
Nome
Fairbanks
Southern limit of discontinuous permafrost
Anchorage
Yakutat
Ketchikan

A tunnel excavated in permafrost near Fox, north of Fairbanks, during the early 1960s is maintained cooperatively by the University of Alaska Fairbanks, and the U.S. Army Cold Regions Research and Engineering Laboratory. It is one of the few such tunnels in the world; it offers unique research opportunities on a 40,000-year-old accumulation of sediments and ice.

The tunnel is open to the general public from June 1 through August 31 each year, by appointment only, through the CRREL office.

Permanent Fund

In 1976, state voters approved a constitutional amendment to establish the Alaska Permanent Fund. This provides that a percentage of all mineral lease rentals, royalties, royalty sales proceeds, federal mineral revenue sharing payments and bonuses shall be placed in a Permanent Fund. Essentially a trust fund for all Alaskans, money from the fund may be used in income-producing investments, but may not be used for state operating expenses (interest income from the Permanent Fund can go into the state's General Fund).

In 1980, the legislature established a Permanent Fund dividend payment program that provides for distribution of the fund's earnings (interest income and capital gains on any liquidation of assets) among the people of Alaska. Eligible residents were to receive a $50 dividend for each year of residency since 1959. The U.S. Supreme Court declared the 1980 program unconstitutional on the grounds that it discriminated against short-term residents and, in 1982, a new state program was signed into law. Under the new plan, an initial $1,000 dividend was paid to applicants who had lived in the state for at least six months prior to applying. Amounts of subsequent dividend payments are computed each fiscal year by dividing one-half of the fund's earnings by the number of applicants.

If Alaska's $10 billion Permanent Fund were a foundation trust, it would be the largest in the nation, far surpassing the J. Paul Getty Trust and the Ford Foundation, according to the fund's executive director. If it were an endowment fund, it would be the largest in the nation, also. Measured on the basis of net income, the fund would rank 24th as a "Fortune 500" company.

In 1990, the dividend from the Permanent Fund will be again over $800 per Alaska resident.

Pioneers' Homes

"The state of Alaska recognizes the invaluable contributions of its older citizens and seeks to offer a place for them in which they can live in comfort and security, while remaining active members of the Alaska community. The companionship of other pioneer Alaskans whose earlier years have been spent in the exciting days of the territory is one of the advantages of living in the Pioneers' Homes." These words were taken from a state brochure describing Pioneers' Homes. The six state-supported homes offer a comfortable, secure residence for several hundred older Alaskans. The homes provide space for 294 ambulatory residents, 60 assisted living residents and 273 nursing residents.

Applicants must be 65 years or older, have lived continuously in Alaska for 15 years immediately preceding application for admission, demonstrate a need to live in a Pioneers' Home and agree to pay the rent established by the Department of Administration. (Some exceptions are made for Alaskans who have lived in the state more than 30 years.) Race, sex, national origin and religion are not considered when determining eligibility. Some people are under the mistaken impression that to qualify for the Pioneers' Homes, one must be a member of the Pioneers of Alaska. This is not the case. Pioneers of Alaska is a private, fraternal organization and is not connected with the state-operated Pioneers' Homes.

The first Pioneers' Home was established in Sitka in 1913 for "indigent prospectors and others who have spent their years in Alaska." With the coming of statehood in 1959, the homes were officially opened to women and Alaska Natives.

For additional information about Pioneers' Homes, contact the Director of Pioneers Benefits, P.O. Box CL, Juneau 99811; phone (907) 465-4400.

Following are the locations of the six homes:

Anchorage Pioneers' Home, 923 W. 11th Ave., Anchorage 99501; phone (907) 276-3414.

Fairbanks Pioneers' Home, 2221 Eagan Ave., Fairbanks 99701; phone (907) 456-4372.

Juneau Pioneers' Home, 4675 Glacier Highway, Juneau 99801; phone (907) 780-6422.

Ketchikan Pioneers' Home, 141 Bryant, Ketchikan 99901; phone (907) 225-4111.

Palmer Pioneers' Home, 250 E. Fireweed, Palmer 99645; phone (907) 745-4241.

Sitka Pioneers' Home, 120 Katlian St., Sitka 99835; phone (907) 747-3213.

Pipeline

The trans-Alaska pipeline designer, builder and operator is the Alyeska Pipeline Service Company, a consortium of the following seven oil companies:

BP Pipeline Company, 50.01
ARCO Pipe Line Company, 21.35
Exxon Pipeline Company, 20.34
Mobil Alaska Pipeline Company, 4.08
Unocal Pipeline Company, 1.36
Phillips Alaska Pipeline Corporation, 1.36
Amerada Hess Pipeline Corporation, 1.50

Pipeline length: 800 miles, slightly less than half that length is buried, the remainder is on 78,000 aboveground supports, located 60 feet apart, built in a flexible zigzag pattern. More than 800 river and stream crossings. Normal burial of pipe was used in stable soils and rock; aboveground pipe — insulated and jacketed — was used in thaw unstable permafrost areas. Thermal devices prevent thawing around vertical supports. Has 151 stop flow valves.

Pipe: specially manufactured coated pipe with zinc anodes installed to prevent corrosion. Size is 48 inches in diameter, with thickness from 0.462 to 0.562 inch. Pipe sections before construction in lengths of 40 and 60 feet.

Cost: $8 billion, which includes terminal at Valdez, but does not include interest on money raised for construction.

Amount of oil pumped through pipeline: As of March 1990, 7.6 billion barrels of crude oil. On May 27, 1989, the 9,000th tanker sailed from the Marine Terminal at Valdez with a cargo of Alaska North Slope crude oil destined for U.S. markets. None of the North Slope oil is exported from the U.S.

Operations: Control center at Valdez terminal and 10 operating pump stations along line monitor and control pipeline.

PIPELINE ROUTE

Pipeline throughput: 1.9 million barrels a day, average.

Estimated crude oil reserves recoverable on the North Slope: approximately 7 billion barrels as of Jan. 1, 1990.

Terminal: 1,000-acre site at Port Valdez, northernmost ice-free harbor in the U.S., with 18 tanks providing storage capacity of 9,180,000 barrels of oil.

Valdez ship-loading capacity: 110,000 barrels per hour for each of three berths; 80,000 barrels per hour for one berth.

Length and cost of pipeline haul road built by Alyeska: 360 miles, from the Yukon River to Prudhoe Bay, $150 million.

Yukon River bridge: first bridge (2,290 feet long) spanning the Yukon in Alaska.

Important dates: July 1968, Prudhoe Bay oil field discovery confirmed; **1970,** suits filed to halt construction, Alyeska Pipeline Service Company formed; **Nov. 16, 1973,** presidential approval of pipeline legislation; **April 29, 1974,** construction begins on North Slope Haul Road (now the Dalton Highway) and is completed 154 days later; **March 27, 1975,** first pipe installed at Tonsina River; **June 20, 1977,** first oil leaves Prudhoe Bay, reaches Valdez terminal July 28; **Aug. 1, 1977,** first tanker load of oil shipped aboard the SS *ARCO Juneau;* **June 13, 1979,** tanker number 1,000 (SS *ARCO Heritage)* sails; **July 15, 1983,** 3 billionth barrel of oil leaves pump station. **Sept. 15, 1986,** 5 billionth barrel of oil leaves pump station. **April 19, 1987,** 7,000th tanker sails from Marine Terminal with Prudhoe Bay crude oil. **Feb. 16, 1988,** 6 billionth barrel arrives at the Marine Terminal. **May 2, 1988,** *Chevron Mississippi* is 8,000th tanker to load crude oil at Marine Terminal. **June 30, 1989,** 7 billionth barrel was loaded on the *Mobil Arctic,* and the 9,000th tanker sailed from the Marine Terminal at Valdez with a full load of crude oil.

Place Names

Alaska has a rich international heritage of place names. Throughout the state, names of British (Barrow), Spanish (Valdez), Russian (Kotzebue), French (La Perouse), American (Fairbanks) and Native Alaskan (Sitka) origin dot the map. Some Alaska place names are quite common. There are about 70 streams called Bear Creek in Alaska (not to mention Bear Bay, Bear Bluff, Bear Canyon, Bear Cove and Bear Draw) and about 50 called Moose Creek. Many place names have an unusual history. In 1910, geologist Lawrence Martin named Sherman Glacier in the Chugach Mountains after Gen. William Tecumseh Sherman, with the explanation, "He [Sherman] said 'war is hell'; so I put him on ice, near the Sheridan Glacier."

For a comprehensive listing, description and history of Alaska's usual and unusual place names, from Aaron Creek to Zwinge Valley, see Donald Orth's *Dictionary of Alaska Place Names,* U.S. Geological Survey Professional Paper 567.

Poisonous Plants

Alaska has few poisonous plants, considering the total number of plant species growing in the state. Baneberry *(Actaea rubra),* water hemlock *(Cicuta douglasii* and *C. mackenzieana)* and fly agaric mushroom *(Amanita muscaria)* are the most dangerous. Be sure you have properly identified plants before harvesting for food.

Alaska has no plants poisonous to the touch, such as poison ivy and poison oak, which are found in almost all other states.

Related reading: *Discovering Wild Plants, Alaska, Western Canada, the Northwest,* by Janice Schofield. 130 species are described; includes photographs and illustrations of each plant. *Plant Lore of an Alaskan Island,* by Frances Kelso Graham and the Ouzinkie Botanical Society. See ALASKA NORTHWEST LIBRARY in the back of the book.

Populations and Zip Codes

In the last 15 years, population in Alaska has grown at an average annual rate of 4 percent — several times higher than the national average. In 1983, the state population grew at an unprecedented rate of 10.8 percent. Such high annual growth occurred once before in the history of Alaska, in 1975 (10.3 percent). The rush of people to Alaska did slow in 1988 with more people moving from Alaska to the Lower 48 than the reverse. Today half a million people reside in the state of Alaska.

The city of Anchorage has the highest percentage of young adults — 25 to 34 years old — in the state, with 57,592 people falling in that age range. In the five-year period from mid-1980 through mid-1985, the number of Anchorage children under 5 increased by 21,369.

The populations for cities and communities in the following lists are taken from the Alaska Department of Labor Population Estimates, July 1988:

Community	Year Incorporated	Population	Zip
Akhiok (AH-key-ok)	1972	93	99615
Akiachak (ACK-ee-a-chuck)	1974	468	99551
Akiak (ACK-ee-ack)	1970	259	99552
Akutan (ACK-oo-tan)	1979	86	99553
Alakanuk (a-LACK-a-nuk)	1969	565	99554
Aleknagik (a-LECK-nuh-gik)	1973	159	99555
Allakaket (alla-KAK-it)	1975	202	99720
Ambler	1971	309	99786
Anaktuvuk Pass (an-ak-TU-vuk)	1957	253	99721
Anchor Point	—	339	99556
Anchorage (Municipality)	1920	222,950	99510
Eastchester Station	—	—	99501

Community	Year Incorporated	Population	Zip
Fort Richardson	—	—	99505
Elmendorf AFB	—	—	99506
Mountain View	—	—	99508
Spenard Station	—	—	99509
Downtown Station	—	—	99510
South Station	—	—	99511
Alyeska Pipeline Co	—	—	99512
Federal Building	—	—	99513
Anderson	1962	635	99744
Angoon	1963	624	99820
Aniak (AN-ee-ack)	1972	558	99557
Annette	—	183	99926
Anvik	1969	89	99558
Arctic Village	—	129	99722
Atka	—	83	99502
Atmautluak (an-MAUT-loo-ack)	1976	239	99559
Atqasuk	1983	221	99791
Auke Bay	—	NA	99821
Barrow	1959	3,146	99723
Beaver	—	93	99724
Belkofski (bel-KOF-ski)	—	12	99612
Bethel	1957	4,390	99559
Bettles Field	1985	45	99726
Big Delta	—	519	99737
Big Horn	—	401	NA
Big Lake	—	1,049	99652
Bodenburg Butte	—	944	99645
Border	—	NA	99780
Brevig Mission	1969	178	99785
Buckland	1966	312	99727
Cantwell	—	92	99729
Cape Yakataga	—	8	99574
Central	—	34	99730
Chalkyitsik (chawl-KIT-sik)	—	101	99788
Chatanika (chat-a-NEEK-a)	—	NA	99701
Chefornak (cha-FOR-nack)	1974	293	99561
Chevak	1967	594	99563
Chicken	—	47	99732
Chignik	1983	128	99564
Chignik Lagoon	—	87	99565
Chignik Lake	—	134	99564
Chitina (CHIT-nah)	—	60	99566
Chuathbaluk (chew-ATH-ba-luck)	1975	127	99557
Chugiak (CHOO-gee-ack)	—	NA	99567
Circle	—	64	99733
Clam Gulch	—	157	99568
Clarks Point	1971	87	99569
Clear	—	NA	99704
Clover Pass	—	537	99928
Coffman Cove	—	195	99950
Cold Bay	1982	154	99571
College	—	5,817	99709
Cooper Landing	—	279	99572
Copper Center	—	220	99573
Cordova	1909	2,048	99574
Craig	1922	1,087	99921
Crooked Creek	—	118	99575

Community	Year Incorporated	Population	Zip
Curry's Corner	—	59	99734
Deering	1970	164	99736
Delta Junction	1960	1,185	99737
Denali Park	—	59	99755
Dillingham	1963	2,232	99576
Diomede (DY-o-mede)	1970	184	99762
Dot Lake	—	83	99737
Douglas	1902	NA	99824
Dunbar	—	49	NA
Dutch Harbor	1942	1,922	99692
Eagle	1901	174	99738
Eagle River	—	NA	99577
Eek	1970	279	99578
Egegik (EEG-gah-gik)	—	142	99579
Ekwok (ECK-wok)	1974	122	99580
Elfin Cove	—	76	99825
Elim (EE-lum)	1970	293	99739
Emmonak (ee-MON-nuk)	1964	664	99581
English Bay	—	159	99695
Ester	—	148	99725
Evansville	—	41	99726
Fairbanks	1903	28,251	9970–
Main Office	—	—	99701
Eielson AFB	—	—	99702
Fort Wainwright	—	—	99703
Main Office Boxes	—	—	99706
Downtown Station	—	—	99707
College Branch	—	—	99708
Salcha	—	—	99714
False Pass	—	87	99583
Flat	—	8	99584
Fort Greely	—	1,520	99790
Fort Yukon	1959	642	99740
Fox	—	157	99712
Fritz Creek	—	482	99603
Gakona (ga-KOH-na)	—	107	99586
Galena (ga-LEE-na)	1971	928	99741
Gambell	1963	520	99742
Girdwood	—	NA	99587
Glennallen	—	595	99588
Golovin (GAWL-uh-vin)	1971	157	99762
Goodnews Bay	1970	229	99589
Grayling	1969	228	99590
Gulkana	—	87	99586
Gustavus (ga-STAY-vus)	—	219	99826
Haines	1910	1,120	99827
Halibut Cove	—	46	99603
Harding Lake	—	52	99714
Healy	—	639	99743
Herring Cove	—	118	99928
Holy Cross	1968	294	99602
Homer	1964	4,338	99603
Hoonah	1946	894	99829
Hooper Bay	1966	807	99604
Hope	—	163	99605
Houston	1966	587	99694
Hughes	1973	80	99745

Community	Year Incorporated	Population	Zip
Huslia (HOOS-lee-a)	1969	225	99746
Hydaburg	1927	457	99922
Hyder	—	91	99923
Iliamna (ill-ee-YAM-nuh)	—	131	99606
Jakolof Bay	—	25	99603
Juneau	1900	24,621	9980-
Main office	—	—	99801
Main office boxes	—	—	99802
Mendenhall Station	—	—	99803
State government offices	—	—	99811
Kachemak (CATCH-a-mack)	1961	418	99603
Kake	1952	678	99830
Kaktovik (kack-TOE-vik)	1971	224	99747
Kalifonsky	—	327	99669
Kalskag	1975	145	99607
Kaltag	1969	267	99748
Karluk	—	82	99608
Kasaan (Ka-SAN)	1976	38	99924
Kasigluk (ka-SEEG-luk)	1982	433	99609
Kasilof (ka-SEE-loff)	—	632	99610
Kenai (KEEN-eye)	1960	6,543	99611
Ketchikan	1900	7,730	99901
Kiana (Ky-AN-a)	1964	414	99749
King Cove City	1947	535	99612
King Salmon	—	708	99613
Kipnuk (KIP-nuck)	—	392	99614
Kivalina	1969	298	99750
Klawock (kla-WOCK)	1929	735	99925
Klukwan	—	160	99827
Kobuk	1973	87	99751
Kodiak	1940	6,651	99615
U.S. Coast Guard Station	—	1,709	99619
Kokhanok (KO-ghan-ock)	—	140	99606
Koliganek (ko-LIG-a-neck)	—	196	99576
Kongiganak (kon-GIG-a-nuck)	—	283	99559
Kotlik	1970	443	99620
Kotzebue (KOT-sa-bue)	1958	2,660	99752
Koyuk	1970	223	99753
Koyukuk (KOY-yuh-kuck)	1973	138	99754
Kupreanof (ku-pree-AN-off)	1975	52	99833
Kwethluk (KWEETH-luck)	1975	538	99621
Kwigillingok (kwi-GILL-in-gock)	—	264	99622
Lake Minchumina (min-CHOO-min-a)	—	22	99757
Larsen Bay	1974	149	99624
Levelock (LEH-vuh-lock)	—	132	99625
Lime Village	—	49	99627
Lower Kalskag	1969	273	99626
Manley Hot Springs	—	112	99756
Manokotak (man-a-KO-tack)	1970	370	99628
Marshall	1970	284	99585
McGrath	1975	526	99627
Medfra	—	NA	99691
Mekoryuk (ma-KOR-ee-yuk)	1969	190	99630
Mentasta Lake	—	70	99780
Metlakatla	1944	1,386	99926
Meyers Chuck	—	46	99903
Minto	—	250	99758

Community	Year Incorporated	Population	Zip
Montana	—	74	99695
Moose Creek	—	493	99705
Moose Pass	—	144	99631
Mountain Point	—	472	99928
Mountain Village	1967	742	99632
Naknek (NACK-neck)	1962	507	99633
Napakiak (NAP-uh-keey-ack)	1970	315	99634
Napaskiak (na-PASS-kee-ack)	1971	331	99559
Nelson Lagoon	—	65	99571
Nenana (nee-NA-na)	1921	555	99760
New Stuyahok (STU-ya-hock)	1972	364	99636
Newhalen	1971	122	99606
Newtok	1976	220	99559
Nightmute	1974	161	99690
Nikiski	—	1,609	99635
Nikolai	1970	113	99691
Nikolski	—	34	99638
Ninilchik	—	491	99639
Noatak	—	327	99761
Nome	1901	3,403	99762
Nondalton	1971	229	99640
Noorvik	1964	532	99763
North Pole	1953	1,610	99705
North Tongass Highway	—	2,158	99928
North Whale Pass	—	41	99950
Northway	—	138	99764
Nuiqsut (noo-IK-sut)	1975	322	99789
Nulato	1963	362	99765
Nunapitchuk (NU-nuh-pit-CHUCK)	1983	372	99641
Nyac (NY-ack)	—	NA	99642
Old Harbor	1966	322	99643
Oscarville	—	67	99695
Ouzinkie (u-ZINK-ee)	1967	204	99644
Palmer	1951	2,988	99645
Paxson	—	37	99737
Pedro Bay	—	70	99647
Pelican	1943	247	99832
Pennock Island	—	108	99928
Perryville	—	127	99648
Petersburg	1910	3,178	99833
Pilot Point	—	84	99649
Pilot Station	1969	451	99650
Pitkas Point	—	105	99658
Platinum	1975	74	99651
Point Baker	—	73	99927
Point Hope	1966	610	99766
Point Lay	—	132	99759
Port Alexander	1974	85	99836
Port Alsworth	—	40	99653
Port Graham	—	186	99603
Port Heiden	1972	121	99549
Port Lions	1966	300	99550
Prudhoe Bay	—	66	99734
Quinhagak (QUIN-a-gak)	1975	508	99655
Rampart	—	59	99767
Ruby	1973	243	99768
Russian Mission	1970	266	99657

Community	Year Incorporated	Population	Zip
Saint George	1983	156	99591
Saint Marys	1967	491	99658
Saint Michael	1969	303	99659
Saint Paul	1971	521	99660
Salamatof	—	755	99611
Salcha	—	450	99714
Sand Point	1966	615	99661
Savoonga (suh-VOON-guh)	1969	511	99769
Saxman	1930	308	99901
Saxman East	—	490	99901
Scammon Bay	1967	308	99662
Selawik (SELL-a-wick)	1977	610	99770
Seldovia	1945	535	99663
Seward	1912	2,463	99664
Shageluk (SHAG-a-look)	1970	152	99665
Shaktoolik (shack-TOO-lick)	1969	197	99771
Sheldon Point	1974	126	99666
Shishmaref (SHISH-muh-reff)	1969	430	99772
Shungnak (SHOONG-nack)	1967	237	99773
Sitka (City and Borough)	—	8,257	99835
Skagway	1900	704	99840
Skwentna	—	105	99667
Slana	—	51	99586
Sleetmute	—	119	99668
Soldotna	1967	3,733	99669
South Naknek	—	153	99670
Stebbins	1969	394	99671
Sterling	—	1,602	99472
Stevens Village	—	107	99774
Stony River	—	75	99557
Sutton	—	315	99674
Takotna (Tah-KOAT-nuh)	—	39	99675
Talkeetna (Tal-KEET-na)	—	287	99676
Tanacross	—	96	99776
Tanana (TAN-a-nah)	1961	415	99777
Tatitlek	—	101	99677
Teller	1963	237	99778
Tenakee Springs	1971	120	99841
Tetlin	—	92	99779
Thorne Bay	1982	513	99919
Togiak (TOE-gee-yack)	1969	654	99678
Tok (TOKE)	—	908	99780
Toksook Bay	1972	421	99637
Tonsina	—	149	99573
Trapper Creek	—	NA	99683
Tuluksak (tu-LOOK-sack)	1970	357	99679
Tuntutuliak (TUN-too-TOO-li-ack)	—	296	99680
Tununak	1975	335	99681
Twin Hills	—	39	99576
Two Rivers	—	477	99716
Tyonek (ty-O-neck)	—	267	99682
Unalakleet (YOU-na-la-kleet)	1974	740	99684
Unalaska (UN-a-LAS-ka)	1942	1,131	99685
Upper Kalskag	1975	149	99607
Usibelli (yoos-i-BEL-ee) Mine	—	104	99787
Valdez (val-DEEZ)	1901	3,313	99686
Venetie (VEEN-a-tie)	—	219	99781

Community	Year Incorporated	Population	Zip
Wainwright	1962	506	99782
Wales	1964	158	99783
Ward Cove	—	NA	99928
Wasilla (wah-SIL-luh)	1974	3,342	99687
White Mountain	1969	189	99784
Whittier	1969	206	99693
Willow	—	432	99688
Wrangell	1903	2,416	99929
Yakutat (YAK-a-tat)	1948	527	99689

Census Populations of Major Cities

City	1900	1920	1940	1950	1960	1970	1980
Anchorage	*	1,856	4,229	11,254	44,237	48,081	174,431
Barrow	*	*	*	*	*	2,104	2,207
Cordova	*	955	938	1,165	1,125	1,164	1,879
Fairbanks	*	1,155	3,455	5,771	13,311	14,771	22,645
Juneau	1,864	3,058	5,729	5,956	6,797	6,050	19,528
Kenai	290	332	303	321	778	3,533	4,324
Ketchikan	459	2,458	4,695	5,305	6,483	6,994	7,198
Kodiak	341	374	864	1,710	2,628	3,798	4,756
Nome	12,488	852	1,559	1,876	2,316	2,357	2,301
Petersburg	*	879	1,323	1,619	1,502	2,042	2,821
Seward	*	652	949	2,114	1,891	1,587	1,843
Sitka	1,396	1,175	1,987	1,985	3,237	3,370	7,803
Valdez	315	466	529	554	555	1,005	3,079
Wrangell	868	821	1,162	1,263	1,315	2,029	2,184

*Population figures unavailable. Source: Alaska Department of Labor

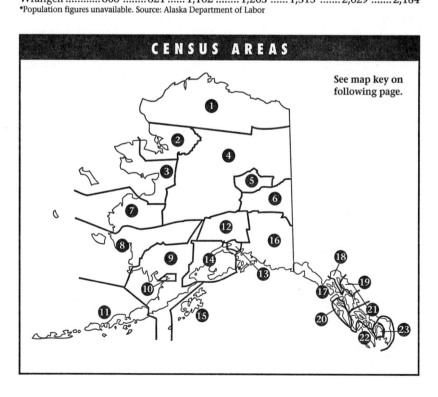

CENSUS AREAS

See map key on following page.

Population by Census Areas (see map on previous page)

Map Key	Census Area	1987	1980	1970
	Alaska	537,800	401,851	302,583
1	North Slope Borough	5,927	4,199	NA
2	Northwest Arctic Borough	5,962	4,831	4,434
3	Nome	7,774	6,537	5,749
4	Yukon-Koyukuk	9,384	7,873	NA
5	Fairbanks North Star Borough	73,164	53,983	45,864
6	Southeast Fairbanks	6,423	5,676	NA
7	Wade Hampton	5,599	4,665	3,917
8	Bethel	13,345	10,999	NA
9	Dillingham	5,836	4,616	NA
10	Bristol Bay Borough	1,402	1,094	1,147
11	Aleutian Islands	9,420	7,768	NA
12	Matanuska-Susitna Borough	37,027	17,816	6,509
13	Anchorage Borough	231,492	174,431	126,385
14	Kenai Peninsula Borough	39,170	25,282	NA
15	Kodiak Island Borough	13,658	9,939	9,409
16	Valdez-Cordova	8,831	8,348	NA
17	Skagway-Yakutat-Angoon	3,684	3,478	NA
18	Haines Borough	1,850	1,680	NA
19	Juneau City & Borough	25,369	19,528	13,556
20	Sitka City & Borough	8,416	7,803	3,370
21	Wrangell-Petersburg	6,671	6,167	NA
22	Prince of Wales-Outer Ketchikan	4,964	3,822	NA
23	Ketchikan Gateway Borough	12,432	11,316	10,041

Source: July 1, 1987, estimates, Alaska Department of Labor

Potlatch

These Native gatherings, primarily an Indian custom, are held to commemorate just about any kind of event. Traditional Native foods are served and gifts are distributed to everyone who attends. A funeral potlatch might result in the giving away of the deceased's possessions to relatives or to persons who had done favors for the deceased during his or her lifetime. Before the federal government imposed legal constraints in the 19th century, potlatches could take years of preparation. The host family might give away all its possessions in an attempt to demonstrate its wealth to the guests. Each guest in turn would feel an obligation to hold an even bigger potlatch.

Radio Stations

Alaska's radio stations broadcast a wide variety of music, talk shows, religious and educational programs. Many radio stations in Alaska also broadcast personal messages, long a popular and necessary form of communication in Alaska — especially in the bush. It was in consideration of these messages — and the importance of radio stations in providing the sole source of vital weather information to fishermen and hunters — that the United States and Canada agreed to grant some Alaska radio stations international communication status. The "clear channel" status provides protection against interference from foreign broadcasters. Personal message broadcasts are heard on:

KBRW's Tundra Drums, Barrow; KYUK's Tundra Drums, Bethel; KDLG's Bristol Bay Messenger, Dillingham; KIAK's Pipeline of the North, Fairbanks; KIYU's Yukon Wireless, Galena; KCAM's Caribou Clatter, Glennallen; KHNS's Listener Personals, Haines; KBBI's Bay Bush Lines, Homer; KGTL's Public Service Line, Homer; KRBD's Muskeg Messenger, Ketchikan; KTKN's Public Service Announcements, Ketchikan; KVOK-KJJZ-FM's Highliner

Crabbers, **Kodiak;** KSKO's KSKO Messages, **McGrath;** KICY's Ptarmigan Telegraph, **Nome;** KNOM's Hot Lines, **Nome;** KJNP's Trapline Chatter, **North Pole;** KFSK's Muskeg Messages, **Petersburg;** KRSA's Channel Chatters, **Petersburg;** KCAW-FM's Muskeg Messages, **Sitka;** KSRM's Tundra Tom Tom, **Soldotna;** and KSTK-FM's Radiograms, **Wrangell.**

A complete listing of Alaska's radio stations follows:

Anchorage
KATB-FM 89.3 MHz; P.O. Box 210389, 99521

KBYR 700 kHz; **KNIK-FM** 105.3 MHz; P.O. Box 102200, 99510

KEAG-FM 97.3 MHz; 333 W. Fourth Ave., Suite 304, 99501

KENI 550 kHz; **KBFX-FM** 100.5 MHz; 1777 Forest Park Drive, 99517

KFQD 750 kHz; **KWHL-FM** 106.5 MHz; 9200 Lake Otis Parkway, 99507

KHAR 590 kHz; **KKLV-FM** 104.1 MHz; P.O. Box 111566, 99511

KJAM-FM 94.5 MHz; 3605 Arctic Blvd., Suite 945, 99503

KKSD 1080 kHz; **KASH-FM** 107.5 MHz; 1300 E. 68th, Suite 208, 99518

KLEF-FM 98.1 MHz; 3601 C St., Suite 290, 99503

KPXR-FM 102.1 MHz; 3700 Woodland Drive, #300, 99517

KSKA-FM 91.1 MHz; 4101 University Drive, 99508

KYAK 650 kHz; **KGOT-FM** 101.3 MHz; 2800 E. Dowling Road, 99507

KYMG-FM 98.9 MHz; 500 L St., Suite 200, 99501

Barrow
KBRW 680 kHz; P.O. Box 109, 99723

Bethel
KYKD-FM 100.1 MHz; P.O. Box 905, 99559

KYUK 640 kHz; P.O. Box 468, 99559

Cordova
KCHU-FM 88.1 MHz; P.O. Box 467, Valdez 99686

KLAM 1450 kHz; P.O. Box 60, 99574

Dillingham
KDLG 670 kHz; P.O. Box 670, 99576

Eagle River
KCFA 1020 kHz; P.O. Box 773527, 99577

Fairbanks
KAYY-FM 101.1 MHz; 3504 Industrial Ave., 99701

KCBF 820 kHz; P.O. Box 950, 99707

KFAR 660 kHz; **KWLF-FM** 98.1 MHz; P.O. Box 70910, 99707

KIAK 970 kHz; P.O. Box 73410, 99707

KQRZ-FM 102.5 MHz; P.O. Box 73410, 99707

KSUA-FM 103.9 MHz; P.O. Box 83831, 99708

KUAC-FM 104.7 MHz; University of Alaska, 99775

KUWL-FM 91.5 MHz; P.O. Box 70339, 99707

Galena
KIYU 910 kHz; P.O. Box 165, 99741

Glennallen
KCAM 790 kHz; P.O. Box 249, 99588

Haines
KHNS-FM 102.3 MHz; P.O. Box 1109, 99827

Homer
KBBI 890 kHz; 215 E. Main Court, 99603

KGTL 620 kHz; **KWVV-FM,** 103.5 MHz; P.O. Box 103, 99603

Juneau
KINY 800 kHz; 1107 W. Eighth St., 99801

KJNO 630 kHz; 3161 Channel Drive, Suite 2, 99801

KSUP-FM 106.3 MHz; 1107 W. Eighth St., 99801

KTKU-FM 105.1 MHz; 3161 Channel Drive, Suite 2, 99801

KTOO-FM 104.3 MHz; 224 Fourth St., 99801

Kenai
KCZP-FM 91.9 MHz; P.O. Box 2111, 99611

KENY 980 kHz; 6672 Kenai Spur Highway, 99611

KPEN-FM 101.7 MHz; P.O. Box 103, Homer 99603

Ketchikan
KRBD-FM 105.9 MHz; 716 Totem Way, 99901

KTKN 930 kHz; **KGTW-FM** 106.7 MHz; P.O. Box 7700, 99901

Kodiak
KMXT-FM 100.1 MHz; 718 Mill Bay Road, 99615

KVOK 560 kHz; **KJJZ-FM** 101.1 MHz; P.O. Box 708, 99615

Kotzebue
KOTZ 720 kHz; P.O. Box 78, 99752

McGrath
KSKO 870 kHz; P.O. Box 70, 99627

Naknek
KAKN-FM 100.9 MHz; P.O. Box O, 99633

Nenana
KIAM 630 kHz; P.O. Box 474, 99760
Nome
KICY 850 kHz; **KICY-FM** 100.3 MHz;
P.O. Box 820, 99762
KNOM 780 kHz; P.O. Box 988, 99762
North Pole
KJNP 1170 kHz; KJNP-FM 100.3 MHz;
P.O. Box 0, 99705
Petersburg
KFSK-FM 100.9 MHz; P.O. Box 149,
99833
KRSA 580 kHz; P.O. Box 650, 99833
St. Paul
KUHB-FM 91.9 MHz; 99660
Sand Point
KSDP 840 kHz; P.O. Box 328, 99661
Seward
KRXA 950 kHz; P.O. Box 405, 99664
Sitka
KCAW-FM 104.7 MHz; 2-B Lincoln St.,
99835
KIFW 1230 kHz; P.O. Box 299, 99835
Soldotna
KCSY 1140 kHz; 374 Lovers Lane,
99669
KSRM 920 kHz; KWHQ-FM 100.1 MHz;
HC2, Box 852, 99669
Unalakleet
KNSA 930 kHz; P.O. Box 178, 99684
Unalaska
KIAL 1430 kHz; P.O. Box 181, 99685
Valdez
KCHU 770 kHz; P.O. Box 467, 99686
KVAK 1230 kHz; P.O. Box 367, 99686
Wasilla
KNBZ-FM 99.7 MHz; P.O. Box 871890,
99687
Wrangell
KSTK-FM 101.7 MHz; P.O. Box 1141,
99929
Yakutat
KJFP-FM 103.9 MHz; P.O. Box 388,
99689

In addition to the preceding commercial and public radio stations, the Detachment 1, Air Force Broadcasting Service at Elmendorf Air Force Base (Elmendorf AFB 99506) operates the Alaskan Forces Radio Network. AFRN is the oldest broadcast network in the U.S. military. It began in January 1942, on Kodiak Island with a volunteer crew that pieced together a low-power station from second-hand parts, borrowed records and local talent. Eventually, the servicemen generated enough interest

in Hollywood and Washington, D.C., to receive "official" status. Those early efforts resulted in the Armed Forces Radio and Television Service, a far-flung system of broadcast outlets serving U.S. forces around the world.

Nearly all the programming heard at AFRN locations in Alaska originates at Elmendorf AFB, although it is not broadcast in the Elmendorf vicinity. (In addition to network programming, Fort Greely originates about six hours of programming a day at their location.) Following is a list of AFRN outlets:

Fort Greely, **AFRN-FM** 90.5 MHz, 93.5 MHz

Galena Airport, **AFRN-FM** 90.5 MHz, 101.1 MHz

King Salmon Airport, **AFRN-FM** 90.5 MHz, 101.7 MHz

Shemya Air Force Base, **AFRN-FM** 90.5 MHz, 101.1 MHz

Tok Coast Guard Station, **AFRN-FM** 90.5 MHz, 101.1 MHz

Railroads

The Alaska Railroad is the northernmost railroad in North America and was for many years the only one owned by the United States government. Ownership now belongs to the state of Alaska. The ARR rolls on 470 miles of mainline track from the ports of Seward and Whittier to Anchorage, Cook Inlet and Fairbanks in the Interior.

The Alaska Railroad began in 1912 when Congress appointed a commission to study transportation problems in Alaska. In March 1914, the president authorized railroad lines in the territory of Alaska to connect open harbors on the southern coast of Alaska with the Interior. The Alaska Engineering Commission surveyed possible railroad routes in 1914 and, in April 1915, President Woodrow Wilson announced the selection of a route from Seward north 412 miles to the Tanana River (where Nenana is now located), with branch lines to Matanuska coal fields. The main line was later extended to Fairbanks. Construction of the railroad began in 1915. On July 15, 1923, President Warren G. Harding drove the golden spike, signifying completion of the railroad, at Nenana.

The railroad offers year-round passenger, freight and vehicle service. The ARR features flag-stop service along the Anchorage-to-Fairbanks corridor, as well as summer express trains to Denali National Park and Preserve. Passenger service is daily between mid-May and mid-September, and in winter, weekly service is available between Anchorage and Fairbanks. A one-day excursion to Seward is provided daily, mid-May to mid-September. Additionally, daily service to Whittier is offered from May through September and four days a week in winter. In 1989, 364,000 passengers rode the Alaska Railroad. For more information contact The Alaska Railroad, P.O. Box 107500, Anchorage 99510.

The privately owned White Pass and Yukon Route provided a narrow-gauge link between Skagway, Alaska, and Whitehorse, Yukon Territory. At the time it was built — 1898 to 1900 — it was the farthest north any railroad had operated in North America. The railway maintained one of the steepest railroad grades in North America, climbing to 2,885 feet at White Pass in only 20 miles of track. The White Pass and Yukon Route provided both passenger and freight service until 1982, when it suspended service. In May 1988, it began operating again as an excursion train only, going from Skagway to the summit of White Pass and eight miles beyond to Fraser, British Columbia. For more information contact the White Pass & Yukon Route, P.O. Box 435, Skagway 99840.

Regions of Alaska

Southeast

Southeast, Alaska's panhandle, stretches approximately 500 miles from Icy Bay, northwest of Yakutat, to Dixon Entrance at the United States–Canada border beyond the southern tip of Prince of Wales Island. Massive ice fields, glacier-scoured peaks and steep valleys, more than a thousand named islands, and numerous unnamed islets and reefs characterize this vertical world where few flat expanses break the steepness. Spruce, hemlock and cedar, the basis for the region's timber industry, cover many of the mountainsides.

Average temperatures range from 50°F to 60°F in July and from 20°F to 40°F in January. Average annual precipitation varies from 80 to more than 200 inches. The area receives from 30 to 200 inches of snow in the lowlands and more than 400 inches in the high mountains.

The region's economy revolves around fishing and fish processing, timber and tourism. Mining is taking on increasing importance with development of a world-class molybdenum mine near Ketchikan and a base metals mine on Admiralty Island.

Airplanes and boats provide the principal means of transportation. Only three communities in Southeast are connected to the road system: Haines via the Haines Highway to the Alaska Highway at Haines Junction; Skagway, via Klondike Highway 2 to the Alaska Highway; and Hyder, to the continental road system via the Cassiar Highway in British Columbia. Juneau, on the Southeast mainland, is the state capital; Sitka, on Baranof Island, was the capital of Russian America.

Southcentral/Gulf Coast

The Southcentral/Gulf Coast region curves 650 miles north and west of Southeast to Kodiak Island. About two-thirds of the state's residents live in the arc between the Gulf of Alaska on the south and the Alaska Range on the north, the region commonly called Southcentral. On the region's eastern boundary, only the Copper River valley breaches the mountainous barrier of the Chugach and St. Elias mountains. On the west rise lofty peaks of the Aleutian Range. Within this mountainous perimeter course the Susitna and Matanuska rivers.

The irregular plain of the Copper River lowland has a colder climate than the other major valley areas, with January temperatures hitting –16°F compared with average lows of 0°F in the Susitna Valley. July temperatures average 50°F to 60°F in the region.

Precipitation in the region ranges from a scant 17 inches annually in drier areas to more than 76 inches a year at Thompson Pass in the coastal mountains.

Vegetation varies from the spruce-hemlock forests of Prince William Sound to mixed spruce and birch forests in the Susitna Valley to tundra in the highlands of the Copper River–Nelchina Basin.

Alaska agriculture historically has been most thoroughly developed in the Matanuska Valley. The state's dairy industry is centered there and at a new project at Point MacKenzie across Knik Arm from Anchorage. Vegetables thrive in the area and Matanuska Valley is well known for its giant cabbages.

Hub of the state's commerce, transportation and communications is Anchorage, on a narrow plain at the foot of the Chugach Mountains, and bounded by Knik Arm and Turnagain Arm, offshoots of Cook Inlet. The population of this, Alaska's largest, city is closely tied to shifts in the state's economy.

Alaska's major banks and oil companies have their headquarters in Anchorage, as does the Alaska Railroad. The city's port handles much of the shipping in and out of the state. Anchorage International Airport saw over 4.5 million passengers pass through in 1988. Valdez, to the east of Anchorage on Prince Willam Sound, is the southern terminal of the trans-Alaska pipeline, which brings oil from Prudhoe Bay on the North Slope.

Interior

Great rivers have forged a broad lowland, known as the Interior, in the central part of the state between the Alaska Range on the south and the Brooks Range on the north. The Yukon River carves a swath across the entire state. In the Interior, the Tanana, Porcupine, Koyukuk and several other rivers join with the Yukon to create summer and winter highways. South of the Yukon, the Kuskokwim River rises in the hills of the western Interior before beginning its meandering course across the Bering Sea coast region.

Winter temperatures in the Interior commonly drop to –50°F and –60°F. Ice fog sometimes hovers over Fairbanks and other low-lying communities when the temperature falls below zero. Controlled by the extremes of a continental climate, summers usually are warmer than in any other region; high temperatures are in the 80s and 90s. The climate is semi-arid, with about 12 inches of precipitation recorded annually.

Immense forests of birch and aspen bring vibrant green and gold to the Interior's landscape. Spruce cover many of the slopes and cottonwood thrive near river lowlands. But in northern and western reaches of the Interior, the North American taiga gives way to tundra. In highlands above tree line and in marshy lowlands, grasses and shrubs replace trees.

Gold lured the first large influx of

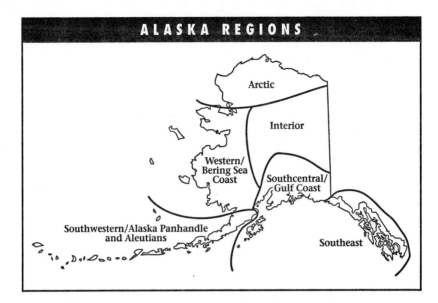

Arctic

Interior

Western/
Bering Sea
Coast

Southcentral/
Gulf Coast

Southwestern/Alaska Panhandle
and Aleutians

Southeast

non-Natives to Alaska's Interior. Fairbanks, largest community in the region, was once a booming gold-mining camp. Now the city on the banks of Chena Slough is a transportation and supply center for eastern and northern Alaska. The main campus of the University of Alaska overlooks the city.

About 100 miles east of Fairbanks, farmers at the Delta project hope to build a foundation for agriculture based on barley. With barley for feed, Alaska farmers look for development of a beef cattle industry. At Healy, southwest of Fairbanks, the state's only operating coal mine produces coal used to generate electricity for the Interior. The rest of the Interior relies primarily on a subsistence economy, sometimes combined with a cash economy where fishing or seasonable government jobs are available.

Arctic

Beyond the Brooks Range, more than 80,000 square miles of tundra interlaced with meandering rivers and countless ponds spread out along the North Slope. In far northwestern Alaska, the Arctic curves south to take in Kotzebue and other villages of the Kobuk and Noatak river drainages.

Short, cool summers with temperatures usually between 30°F and 40°F allow the permanently frozen soil to thaw only a few inches. Winter temperatures range well below zero, but the Arctic Ocean moderates temperatures in coastal areas. Severe winds sweep along the coast and through mountain passes. The combination of cold and wind often drops the chill-factor temperature far below the actual temperature. Most areas receive less than 10 inches of precipitation a year, but the terrain is wet in summer because of little evaporation and frozen ground.

Traditionally the home of Inupiat Eskimos, the Arctic was inhabited by few non-Natives until oil was discovered at Prudhoe Bay in the 1960s. Today the region's economy is focused on Prudhoe Bay and neighboring Kuparuk oil fields. Petroleum-related jobs support most of the region's residents either directly or indirectly. Subsistence hunting and fishing fill any economic holes left by the oil industry.

The largest Inupiat Eskimo community in the world, Barrow is the center of commerce and government activity for the region. Airplanes, the major means of transportation, fan out from there to the region's far-flung villages.

The 416-mile Dalton Highway, formerly the North Slope Haul Road, connects the Arctic with the Interior. The road is open to the public to

Disaster Creek near Dietrich Camp, about 200 miles north from the junction with the Elliott Highway in the Interior. Only permit holders can travel the road north of Disaster Creek.

Western/Bering Sea Coast

Western Alaska extends along the Bering Sea coast from the Arctic Circle south to where the Alaska Panhandle joins the mainland near Naknek on Bristol Bay. Home of Inupiat and Yup'ik Eskimos, the region centers around the immense Yukon-Kuskokwim river delta, the Seward Peninsula to the north and Bristol Bay to the south.

Summer temperatures range from the 30s to low 60s. Winter readings generally range from just above zero to the low 30s. Wind chill lowers temperatures considerably. Total annual precipitation is about 20 inches with northern regions drier than those to the south.

Much of the region is covered with tundra, although a band of forests covers the hills on the eastern end of the Seward Peninsula and Norton Sound. In the south near Bristol Bay, the tundra once again gives way to forests. In between, the marshy flatland of the great Yukon-Kuskokwim delta spreads out for more than 200 miles.

Gold first attracted non-Natives to the hills and creeks of the Seward Peninsula. To the south, only a few anthropologists and wildlife biologists entered the world of the Yup'ik Eskimos of the delta. At the extreme south, fish, including the world's largest sockeye salmon run, drew fishermen to the riches of Bristol Bay.

The villages of western Alaska are linked by air and water, dogsled and snow machine. Commerce on the delta radiates out from Bethel, largest community in western Alaska. To the north, Nome dominates commerce on the Seward Peninsula, while several fishing communities take their livelihood from the riches of Bristol Bay.

Southwestern/Alaska Peninsula and Aleutians

Southwestern Alaska includes the Alaska Peninsula and Aleutian Islands. From Naknek Lake, the peninsula curves southwest about 500 miles to the first of the Aleutian Islands; the Aleutians continue south and west more than 1,000 miles. Primarily a mountainous region with about 50 volcanic peaks, only on the Bering Sea side of the peninsula does the terrain flatten out.

More than 200 islands, roughly 5,500 square miles in area, form the narrow arc of the Aleutians, which separate the North Pacific from the Bering Sea. Nearly the entire chain is in the Alaska Maritime National Wildlife Refuge. Unimak Island, closest to the Alaska Peninsula mainland, is 1,000 miles from Attu, the most distant island. Five major island groups make up the Aleutians, all of which are treeless except for a few scattered stands that have been transplanted on the islands.

The Aleutian climate is cool, with

summer temperatures up to the 50s and winter readings in the 20s and lower. Winds are almost constant and fog is common. Precipitation ranges from 21 to more than 80 inches annually. The peninsula's climate is somewhat warmer than the islands' in summer and cooler in winter.

Aleuts, original inhabitants of the chain, still live at Atka, Atka Island; Nikolski, Umnak Island; Unalaska, Unalaska Island; Akutan, Akutan Island; and False Pass, Unimak Island.

The quest for furs first drew Russians to the islands and peninsula in the 1700s. The traders conquered the Aleuts and forced them to hunt marine mammals. After the United States purchased Alaska, fur traders switched their efforts to fox farming. Many foxes were turned loose on the islands, where they flourished and destroyed native wildlife. With the collapse of the fur market in the 1920s and 1930s, the islands were left to themselves. This relative isolation was broken during World War II when Japanese military forces bombed Dutch Harbor and landed on Attu and Kiska islands. The United States military retook the islands, and after the war the government resettled Aleuts living in the western Aleutians to villages in the eastern Aleutians, closer to the mainland.

Today fishing provides the main economic base for the islands and the peninsula. Many Aleuts go to Bristol Bay to fish commercially in summer.

Religion

Nearly every religion practiced in American society is found in Alaska. Following is a list of addresses for some of the major ones:

Alaska Baptist Convention, 1750 O'Malley Road, Anchorage 99516

Alaska Moravian Church, Bethel 99559

Assemblies of God, 1048 W. International Airport Road, Anchorage 99502

Baha'i Faith, 13501 Brayton Drive, Anchorage 99516

Chancery Orthodox Diocese of Alaska, P.O. Box 55, Kodiak 99615

Christian Science Church, 1347 L St., Anchorage 99501

Church of God, 1348 Bennington Drive, Anchorage 99508

Church of Jesus Christ of Latter-day Saints, 13111 Brayton Drive, Anchorage 99516

Congregation Beth Sholom, 7525 E. Northern Lights Blvd., Anchorage 99504

Episcopal Diocese of Alaska, 1205 Denali Way, Fairbanks 99701

Presbyterian Churches, 616 W. 10th Ave., Anchorage 99501

Roman Catholic Archdiocese of Anchorage, 225 Cordova, Anchorage 99501

The Salvation Army, 726 E. Ninth Ave., Anchorage 99501

United Methodist Church, 2300 Oak Drive, Anchorage 99508

Unity of Anchorage, 10821 Totem Road, Anchorage 99516

Reptiles

For all practical purposes, reptiles are not found in Alaska outside of captivity. The northern limits of North American reptilian species may be the latitude at which their embryos fail to develop during the summer. Three sightings of a species of garter snake, *Thamnophis sirtalis,* have been reported on the banks of the Taku River and Stikine River.

Rivers

(*See also* National Wild and Scenic Rivers)

There are more than 3,000 rivers in Alaska. The major navigable Alaska inland waterways are as follows:

Chilkat — Navigable by shallow-draft vessels to village of Klukwan, 25 miles above mouth.

Kobuk — Controlling channel depth is about 5 feet through Hotham Inlet, 3 feet to Ambler and 2 feet to Kobuk Village, about 210 river miles.

Koyukuk — Navigable to Allakaket by vessels drawing up to 3 feet during normally high river flow and to Bettles during occasional higher flows.

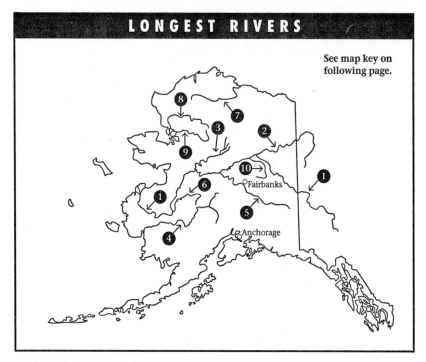

LONGEST RIVERS

See map key on following page.

Fairbanks

Anchorage

Kuskokwim — Navigable (June 1 to September 30) by 18-foot draft ocean-going vessels from mouth upriver 65 miles to Bethel. Shallow-draft (4-foot) vessels can ascend river to mile 465. McGrath is at Mile 400.

Kvichak — The river is navigable for vessels of 10-foot draft to Alaganak River, 22 miles above the mouth of Kvichak River. Remainder of this river (28 miles) navigable by craft drawing 2 to 4 feet, depending on stage of river. Drains into Lake Iliamna, which is navigable an additional 70 miles.

Naknek — Navigable for vessels of 12-foot draft for 12 miles with adequate tide. Vessels with 3-foot draft can continue an additional 7.5 miles.

Noatak — Navigable (late May to mid-June) for shallow-draft barges to a point about 18 miles below Noatak village. Shallow-draft vessels can continue on to Noatak.

Nushagak — Navigable (June 1 to August 31) by small vessels of 2^1/$_2$-foot draft to Nunachuak, about 100 miles above the mouth. Shallow-draft, ocean-going vessels can

navigate to mouth of Wood River at mile 84.

Porcupine — Navigable to Old Crow, Yukon Territory, by vessels drawing 3 feet during spring runoff and fall rain floods.

Stikine — Navigable (May 1 to October 15) from mouth 165 miles to Telegraph Creek, British Columbia, by shallow-draft, flat-bottom riverboats.

Susitna — Navigable by sternwheelers and shallow-draft, flat-bottom riverboats to confluence of Talkeetna River, 75 miles upstream, but boats cannot cross bars at mouth of river. Not navigable by ocean-going vessels.

Tanana — Navigable by shallow-draft (4-foot), flat-bottom vessels and barges from the mouth to Nenana and by smaller river craft to the Chena River 201 miles above the mouth. Craft of 4-foot draft can navigate to Chena River on high water to University Avenue Bridge in Fairbanks.

Yukon — Navigable (June 1 to September 30) by shallow-draft, flat-bottom riverboats from the mouth to near

142

the head of Lake Bennett. It cannot be entered or navigated by ocean-going vessels. Controlling depths are 7 feet to Stevens Village and 3 to 5 feet from there to Fort Yukon.

Following are the 10 longest rivers in Alaska (see accompanying map):
Map Key
1 Yukon, 1,400 miles*
2 Porcupine, 555 miles**
3 Koyukuk, 554 miles
4 Kuskokwim, 540 miles
5 Tanana, 531 miles
6 Innoko, 463 miles
7 Colville, 428 miles
8 Noatak, 396 miles
9 Kobuk, 347 miles
10 Birch Creek, 314 miles

*The Yukon flows about 1,400 miles in Alaska; the remainder is in Canada. It ranks fourth in North America in length (2,300 miles total), fifth in drainage area (327,600 square miles).

**About two-thirds of the Porcupine's length is in Canada.

Roadhouses

An important part of Alaska history, roadhouses were modest quarters that offered bed and board to travelers along early-day Alaska trails. The majority provided accommodations for sled dog teams, as most travel occurred in winter. By 1920, there were road-houses along every major transportation route in Alaska. Several road-houses are included in the National Register of Historic Places. Some of these historic roadhouses are occupied by modern businesses.

Rocks and Gems

(*See also* Gold, Jade *and* Minerals and Mining)
Gemstones are not easy to find in Alaska — you have to hunt for them and often walk quite a distance. The easiest ones to collect are float-rocks that were scattered millions of years ago by glaciers. These rocks are found on ocean beaches and railroad beds, and in creeks and rivers all over Alaska. In most rock-hunting areas, every instance of high water, wind, heavy rain and a

melting patch of snow and ice uncovers a new layer, so you can hunt in the same area over and over and make new ones.

The easiest gemstones to search out are in the crypto-crystalline group of quartz minerals. These gems have crystals not visible to the naked eye. They are the jaspers, agates, cherts and flints.

Thunder eggs, geodes and agatized wood (all in the chalcedony classification) occur in Alaska. Thunder eggs have a jasper rind enclosing an agate core; harder-to-find geodes usually have an agate rind with a hollow core filled with crystals; agatized and petrified woods come in various colors and often show the plant's growth rings. Sometimes even the bark or limb structure is visible on agatized and petrified woods.

Crystalline varieties of quartz can also be found: amethyst (purple), citrine (yellow), rose quartz (pink), rock crystal (clear) and smoky quartz (brown).

Other gems to search for in Alaska are: onyx, feldspar, porphyry, jade, serpentine, soapstone, garnet, rhodonite, sapphire, marble, amethyst, staurolite, malachite and covelite (blue copper).

School Districts

(*See also* Education)
Alaska's 55 public school districts serve approximately 109,280 pre-elementary through 12th-grade students. There are two types of school districts: city and borough school districts and Regional Educational Attendance Areas (REAA). The 33 city and borough school districts are located in municipalities, each contributing funds for the operation of its local schools. The 22 REAA are located in the unorganized boroughs and have no local government to contribute funds to their schools. The REAA are almost solely dependent upon state funds for school support. City and borough school districts are supported by about 73.6 percent state, 20.6 percent local and 5.8 percent federal funding.

The Centralized Correspondence Study program, Alaska Department of Education, P.O. Box F, Juneau 99811, provides courses by correspondence to students in grades K–12.

Following are the names and addresses of Alaska's 55 public school districts:

Adak Region Schools, Adak Naval Station, Box 34, FPO Seattle, WA 98791 (IntraAK)

Alaska Gateway Schools, Box 226, Tok 99780

Aleutian Region Schools, 1 Aleut Plaza, 4000 Old Seward Highway, Suite 301, Anchorage 99503

Anchorage Schools, 4600 DeBarr Road, Box 196614, Anchorage 99519

Annette Island Schools, Box 7, Metlakatla 99926

Bering Strait Schools, Box 225, Unalakleet 99684

Bristol Bay Borough Schools, Box 169, Naknek 99633

Chatham Schools, Box 109, Angoon 99820

Chugach Schools, 201 E. 56th Ave., Suite 210, Anchorage 99518

Copper River Schools, Box 108, Glennallen 99588

Cordova City Schools, Box 140, Cordova 99574

Craig City Schools, Box 800, Craig 99921

Delta/Greely Schools, Box 527, Delta Junction 99737

Dillingham City Schools, Box 170, Dillingham 99576

Fairbanks North Star Borough Schools, Box 1250, Fairbanks 99707

Galena City Schools, Box 299, Galena 99741

Haines Borough Schools, Box 1289, Haines 99827

Hoonah City Schools, Box 157, Hoonah 99829

Hydaburg City Schools, Box 109, Hydaburg 99922

Iditarod Area Schools, Box 90, McGrath 99627

Juneau City Schools, 10014 Crazy Horse Drive, Juneau 99801

Kake City Schools, Box 450, Kake 99830

Kashunamiut School District, 985 KSD Way, Chevak 99563

Kenai Peninsula Borough Schools, 148 N. Binkley St., Soldotna 99669

Ketchikan Gateway Borough Schools, Pouch Z, Ketchikan 99901

King Cove City Schools, Box 6, King Cove 99612

Klawock City Schools, Box 9, Klawock 99925

Kodiak Island Borough Schools, 722 Mill Bay Road, Kodiak 99615

Kuspuk Schools, Box 108, Aniak 99557

Lake & Peninsula Schools, Box 498, King Salmon 99613

Lower Kuskokwim Schools, Box 305, Bethel 99559

Lower Yukon Schools, Box 32089, Mountain Village 99632

Matanuska-Susitna Borough Schools, Box 1688, Palmer 99645

Nenana City Schools, Box 10, Nenana 99760

Nome City Schools, Box 131, Nome 99762

North Slope Borough Schools, Box 169, Barrow 99723

Northwest Arctic Borough Schools, Box 51, Kotzebue 99752

Pelican City Schools, Box 90, Pelican 99832

Petersburg City Schools, Box 289, Petersburg 99833

Pribilof Schools, Saint Paul Island 99660

Railbelt School District, Drawer 280, Healy 99743

Saint Marys School District, Box 171, Saint Marys 99658

Sand Point School District, Box 269, Sand Point 99661

Sitka Borough Schools, Box 179, Sitka 99835

Skagway City Schools, Box 497, Skagway 99840

Southeast Island Schools, Box 8340, Ketchikan 99901

Southwest Region Schools, Box 90, Dillingham 99576

Tanana Schools, Box 89, Tanana 99777

Unalaska City Schools, Pouch 260, Unalaska 99685

Valdez City Schools, Box 398, Valdez 99686

Wrangell City Schools, Box 3319, Wrangell 99929

Yakutat City Schools, Box 427, Yakutat 99689

Yukon Flats Schools, Box 359, Fort Yukon 99740

Yukon/Koyukuk Schools, Box 309, Nenana 99760

Yupiit Schools, Box 100, Akiachak 99551

Shipping

Vehicles

Persons shipping vehicles between Seattle and Anchorage are advised to shop around for the carrier that offers the services and rates most suited to the shipper's needs. Not all carriers offer year-round service and freight charges vary greatly depending upon the carrier, and the weight and height of the vehicle. Rates quoted here are only approximate. Sample fares per unit: northbound, Seattle to Anchorage, under 66 inches in height, $1,225; over 66 inches and under 84 inches, $1,785. Southbound, Anchorage to Seattle, any unit under 84 inches, $640.

Not all carriers accept rented moving trucks and trailers, and a few of those that do accept them require authorization from the rental company to carry its equipment to Alaska. Check with the carrier and your rental company before booking service.

Make your reservation at least two weeks in advance, and prepare to have the vehicle at the carrier's loading facility two days prior to sailing. Carriers differ on what items they allow to travel inside the vehicle, from nothing at all to goods packaged and addressed separately. Coast Guard regulations forbid the transport of vehicles holding more than one-quarter tank of gas and none of the carriers listed allows owners to accompany their vehicles in transit. *Remember to have fresh antifreeze installed in your car or truck prior to sailing.*

At a lesser rate, you can ship your vehicle aboard a state ferry to southeastern ports. However, you must accompany your vehicle or arrange for someone to drive it on and off the ferry at departure and arrival ports.

Carriers that will ship cars, truck campers, house trailers and motorhomes from Anchorage to Seattle/Tacoma include:

The Alaska Railroad, P.O. Box 107500, Anchorage 99510; phone (907) 265-2490.

Sea-Land Freight Service, Inc., 1717 Tidewater Ave., Anchorage 99501; phone (907) 274-2671.

Totem Ocean Trailer Express, 2511 Tidewater Ave., Anchorage 99501; phone (907) 276-5868.

In the Seattle/Tacoma area, contact:

A.A.D.A. Systems, P.O. Box 80524, Seattle, WA 98108; phone (206) 762-7840.

Sea-Land Service, Inc., 3600 Port of Tacoma Road, Tacoma, WA 98424; phone (206) 922-3100, or 1-800-426-4512 (outside Washington).

Totem Ocean Trailer Express, P.O. Box 24908, Seattle, WA 98124; phone (206) 628-9281 or 1-800-426-0074 (outside Washington, Alaska and Hawaii).

Vehicle shipment between southeastern Alaska and Seattle is provided by:

Alaska Marine Lines, 5615 W. Marginal Way SW, Seattle, WA 98106; phone (206) 763-4244 or 1-800-443-4343 (serves Ketchikan, Wrangell, Petersburg, Sitka, Juneau, Haines, Skagway, Yakutat, Excursion).

Boyer Alaska Barge Line, 7318 Fourth Ave. S., Seattle, WA 98108; phone (206) 763-8575 (serves Ketchikan and Wrangell).

Household Goods and Personal Effects

Most moving van lines have service to and from Alaska through their agency connections in most Alaska and Lower 48 cities. To initiate service, contact the van line agents nearest your starting point.

Northbound goods are shipped to Seattle and transferred through a port agent to a water-borne vessel for transportation to Alaska. Few shipments go over the road to Alaska. Southbound shipments are processed in a like manner through Alaska ports to Seattle, then on to the destination.

Haul-it-yourself companies provide service to Alaska for those who prefer to move their goods themselves. It is possible to ship a rented truck or trailer into southeastern Alaska aboard the carriers that accept privately owned vehicles (*see* Vehicles, *preceding*). A few of the carriers sailing between Seattle and Anchorage also carry rented equipment. However, shop around for this service, for it has not been common practice in the past — rates can be very high if the carrier does not yet have a specific tariff established for this type of shipment. *You will not be allowed to accompany the rented equipment.*

Sitka Slippers

Also known as Wrangell sneakers and Petersburg sneakers, Sitka slippers are heavy-duty rubber boots worn by residents of rainy southeastern Alaska.

Skiing

Both cross-country and downhill skiing are popular forms of outdoor recreation in Alaska from November through May. There are developed ski facilities in several Alaska communities, backcountry powder skiing is available by charter helicopter or ski-equipped aircraft and cross-country skiing opportunities are virtually limitless throughout the state. It is also possible to ski during the summer months by chartering a plane to reach glacier skiing spots.

Anchorage

There are two major downhill ski areas in the Anchorage area: Alyeska Resort and Arctic Valley. Alyeska Resort, 40 miles southeast of Anchorage, is the

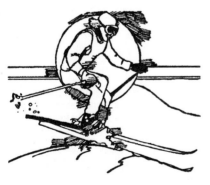

state's largest ski resort, offering four chair lifts with runs up to a mile long. Chair No. 3 is equipped for night skiing and a fifth chair lift is reserved for racer training. The resort also has two rope tows and a Poma lift. Alyeska is open year-round, with skiing from November through April. Hours of operation depend on daylight, except for chair No. 3.

Arctic Valley, a few miles from Anchorage, is owned and operated by the Anchorage Ski Club, a nonprofit corporation. Arctic Valley is open on winter weekends and holidays. Facilities include two double chair lifts, a T-bar/Poma lift combination and three rope tows on beginner slopes.

Several smaller alpine slopes maintained by the municipality of Anchorage include: Centennial Park; Russian Jack Springs Park, with rope tows; and a new area at Hilltop, south of town, featuring the closest chair lift to the Anchorage area.

There are several popular cross-country ski trails in the Anchorage area in city parks that are maintained by the municipality. These include: Russian Jack Springs, with nearly 5 miles of trails, 3 miles lighted; Kincaid Park, site of the first World Cup and U.S. National races in Alaska and the U.S. in March 1983, with 19 miles of trails, 4.5 miles lighted, and a new warm-up facility; Centennial Park, with 3 miles of trails and about 0.5 mile lighted; Hillside Park, with 5 miles of trails, 1.5 miles lighted; and Chester Creek Greenbelt, with 10 kilometers of trails, none lighted. Cross-country skiers can find trails in Chugach State Park and in the Turnagain Pass area in Chugach National Forest, about 57 miles south of Anchorage.

Palmer

Hatcher Pass, site of the Independence Mine State Park, north of Palmer, is an excellent cross-country ski area with several maintained trails. The lodge has a coffee shop and warm-up area. The ski area is open from October through May.

Fairbanks

Fairbanks has a few downhill ski areas, but none as large as Alyeska resort. Cleary Summit and Skiland, about 20 miles from town on the Steese Highway, both privately owned and operated, have rope tows, with a chair lift at Cleary Summit; Ski Boot Hill at 4.2 mile on Farmer's Loop Road has a rope tow; Birch Hill, located on Fort Wainwright, is mainly for military use; the University of Alaska has a small slope and rope tow; and Chena Hot Springs Resort at mile 57 on the Chena Hot Springs Road has a small alpine ski area that uses a tractor to transport skiers to the top of the hill.

Popular cross-country ski trails in the Fairbanks area include: Birch Hill recreation area, about 3 miles north of town on the Steese Expressway to a well-marked turnoff, then 2 miles in; the University of Alaska, Fairbanks, with 26 miles of trails that lead out to Ester Dome; Creamers Field trail near downtown; Salcha cross-country ski area, about 40 miles south of town on the Richardson Highway, with a fairly large trail system also used for ski races; Two Rivers trail area, near the elementary school at mile 10 Chena Hot Springs Road; and Chena Hot Springs Resort, offering cross-country ski trails for both novice and more experienced skiers.

Juneau

Eaglecrest Ski Area on Douglas Island, 12 miles from Juneau, has a 4,800-foot-long chair lift, a Platter Pull lift, a 3,000-foot-long chair lift and a day lodge. Cross-country ski trails are also available. Eaglecrest is open from November to May. A few smaller alpine ski areas are located at Cordova, Valdez, Ketchikan and Homer. All have rope tows.

Several cross-country ski races are held each year. The largest, the Alaska Nordic Ski Cup Series, determines contestants for the Arctic Winter Games and Junior Olympic competitions. The series of five races is held in Anchorage, Homer, Salcha and Fairbanks.

Skin Sewing

(*See also* Beadwork; Mukluks; *and* Parka)

The craft of sewing tanned hides and furs was a highly developed skill among Alaska's Natives. Although commercially made garments are now often worn by Eskimo villagers, women who are exceptional skin sewers still not only ensure the safety of family members who must face the harsh outdoors, but are regarded as a source of pride for the entire community.

Sewers place great importance on the use of specific materials, some of which are only available seasonally. For instance, winter-bleached sealskin can only be tanned during certain seasons. Blood, alder bark and red ochre are traditionally used for coloring on garments and footgear. Most sewers prefer sinew as thread, although in some areas sinew cannot be obtained and waxed thread or dental floss is substituted. Skins commonly used for making parkas and mukluks include seal, reindeer, caribou and polar bear. Wolf and wolverine are prized for ruffs.

Parka styles, materials used and ornamentation (such as pieced calfskin or beadwork trim) vary from village to village, and between Yup'ik, Inupiat and Siberian Yup'ik sewers. The cut of parkas changes from north to south.

In most regions, mukluk styles and material vary with changes in season and weather conditions. The mukluks advertise the skill of their makers and the villages where they were made.

The manufacture of children's toys, primarily clothed dolls and intricately sewn balls, still reflects the traditional ingenuity of skin sewers.

Related reading: *Secrets of Eskimo Skin Sewing* by Edna Wilder. The complete book on the art of Eskimo skin sewing, with how-to-do-it instructions and things-to-make ideas. See ALASKA NORTHWEST LIBRARY in the back of the book.

Skookum

Word meaning strong or serviceable. It originated with the Chehalis Indians of western Washington and was incorporated into the Chinook jargon, a trade language dating from the early 1800s. A skookum chuck is a narrow passage between a saltwater lagoon and the open sea. In many areas of Alaska, because of extreme tides, skookum chucks may resemble fast-flowing river rapids during changes of the tide.

Soapstone

This soft, easily worked stone is often carved into art objects by Alaskans. Most of the stone, however, is imported. Alaska soapstone is mined in the Matanuska Valley by blasting. This process creates in the stone a tendency to fracture when being worked; therefore, it is not as desirable as imported soapstone.

Sourdough

Carried by many early-day pioneers, this versatile, yeasty mixture was used to make bread and hot cakes. Sourdough cookery remains popular in Alaska today. Because the sourdough supply is replenished after each use, it can remain active and fresh indefinitely. A popular claim of sourdough cooks is that their batches trace back to pioneers at the turn of the century. The name also came to be applied to any Alaska or Yukon old-timer.

Related reading: *Alaska Sourdough: The Real Stuff by a Real Alaskan,* by Ruth Allman. *Cooking Alaskan,* hundreds of time-tested recipes, including a section on sourdough. See ALASKA NORTHWEST LIBRARY in the back of the book.

Speed Limits

The basic speed law in Alaska states the speed limit is "no speed more than is prudent and reasonable."

The maximum speeds are 15 miles per hour in an alley, 20 miles per hour in a business district or school zone, 25 miles per hour in a residential area and 55 miles per hour on any other roadway.

Locally, municipalities and the state may, and often do, reduce or alter maximums as long as no maximum exceeds 55 miles per hour.

Squaw Candy

Squaw candy is salmon that has been dried or smoked for a long time until it's very chewy. It's a staple food in winter for rural Alaskans and their dogs.

State Forest

Created in 1983, the 1.81-million-acre Tanana Valley State Forest is located almost entirely within the Tanana River basin and includes 200 miles of the Tanana River. It extends from near the Canadian border approximately 265 miles west to Manley Hot Springs, encompasses areas as far south as Tok, and is interspersed with private and other state lands throughout the basin. The Bonanza Creek Experimental Forest near Nenana is located within the state forest.

Hardwood and hardwood-spruce trees dominate almost 90 percent of the forest, and 22 percent (392,000 acres) is suitable for harvest. There are 44 rivers, streams and lakes within the forest with significant fish, wildlife, recreation and water values. Nearly all of the land will remain open for mineral development.

Approximately 85 percent of the forest is located within 20 miles of a highway, making it one of the more accessible public lands in the Interior. Rivers and trails throughout the river basin provide additional access to areas in the forest. The Eagle Trail State Recreation Site is the only developed facility in the Tanana Valley State Forest and has 40 campsites. For more information, contact the Regional Forester, Northcentral District, 3726 Airport way, Fairbanks 99701.

State Park System

The Alaska state park system began in July 1959 with the transfer of federally managed campgrounds and recreation sites from the Bureau of Land Management to the new state of Alaska. These sites were managed by the state Division of Lands until 1970 — under Forestry, Parks and Recreation until 1966; then under Parks and Recreation. The Division of Parks was created in October 1970.

The Alaska state park system consists of approximately 111 individual units divided into six park management districts. There are 58 recreation sites, 16 recreation areas, 5 historic parks, 4 historic sites, 1 state trail, 7 state parks (Chugach, Denali, Chilkat, Kachemak Bay, Point Bridget, Shuyak Island and Wood-Tikchik) and the 49,000-acre Alaska Chilkat Bald Eagle Preserve.

Campsites are available on a first-come, first-served basis for $5 per night, except Eagle River in Chugach State Park and Chena River State Recreation Site in Fairbanks, where the fee is $10 per night. A yearly pass is available. In addition to camping and picnicking, many units offer hiking trails and boat launching ramps; most developed campgrounds have picnic tables and toilets. General information on the state park system is available from the Division of Parks, P.O. Box 107001, Anchorage 99510.

State park units are listed by park management districts on the following pages. Designations for units of the Alaska state park system are abbreviated as follows: SP–State Park, SHP–State Historical Park, SHS–State Historic Site, SRA–State Recreation Area, SRS–State Recreation Site, ST-State Trail, SMP–State Marine Park, P–Preserve, WP–Wilderness Park. Park units designated "undeveloped" may have camping, hiking trails and limited facilities. Parks that indicate no developed campsites or picnic sites may offer fishing or river access, hiking and other activities. (*See* map next page.)

Map Key	Acreage	Campsites	Picnic Sites	Nearest Town
Southeast District (400 Willoughby Bldg., Juneau 99811)				
1 Totem Bight SHP	11	—	—	Ketchikan
2 Refuge Cove SRS	13	—	14	Ketchikan
3 Settlers Cove SRS	38	12	—	Ketchikan
4 Pioneer Park SRS	3	—	—	Sitka
5 Baranof Castle SHS	1	—	—	Sitka
6 Halibut Point SRS	22	—	9	Sitka
7 Old Sitka SHP	51	—	—	Sitka
8 Juneau Trail Sys. ST	15	—	—	Juneau
9 Johnson Crk SRS	65	—	—	Juneau
10 Wickersham SHS	0.5	—	—	Juneau
11 Point Bridget SP	2,800	—	—	Juneau
12 Chilkoot Lake SRS	80	32	—	Haines
13 Portage Cove SRS	7	9	3	Haines
14 Chilkat SP	6,045	15	—	Haines
15 Ak-Chilkat Bald Eagle P	49,320	—	—	Haines
16 Mosquito Lake SRS	5	10	—	Haines
17 Dall Bay SMP	585	—	—	Ketchikan
18 Thom's Place SMP	1,198	—	—	Wrangell
19 Beecher Pass SMP	660	—	—	Wrangell
20 Joe Mace Island SMP	62	—	—	Wrangell
21 Security Bay SMP	500	—	—	Petersburg
22 Taku Harbor SMP	700	—	—	Juneau
23 Oliver Inlet SMP	560	—	—	Juneau
24 Funter Bay SMP	162	—	—	Juneau

(Continued on page 152)

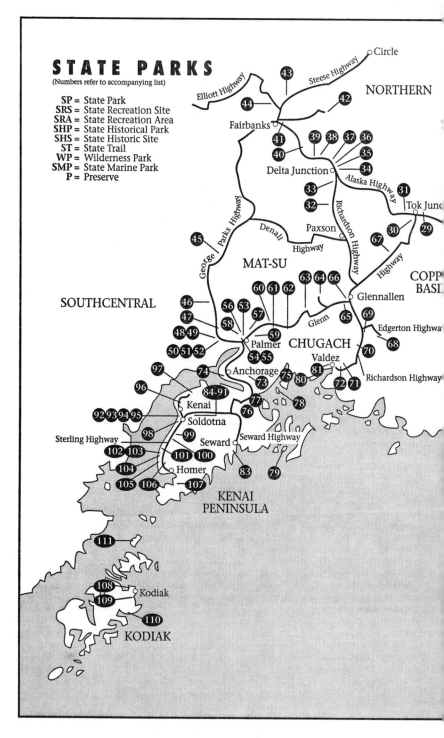

STATE PARKS
(Numbers refer to accompanying list)

SP = State Park
SRS = State Recreation Site
SRA = State Recreation Area
SHP = State Historical Park
SHS = State Historic Site
ST = State Trail
WP = Wilderness Park
SMP = State Marine Park
P = Preserve

NORTHERN

Circle

Elliott Highway

Steese Highway

43

44

42

Fairbanks

41   39 38 37 36

40   35

Delta Junction   34

Alaska Highway

33   31

32   Tok Junc

Paxson   30   29

67

45   Denali
            Highway

George Parks Highway

MAT-SU

63 64 66

60 61 62

Glennallen

COPP
BASI

SOUTHCENTRAL

46

47

48 49

50 51 52

56 53

58

57

59

Palmer

54 55

CHUGACH

65

Glenn

69

Edgerton Highwa

70   68

Valdez

68

97

74

Anchorage

73

84-91

Kenai

96

92 93 94 95

Soldotna

98

99

Sterling Highway

102 103

104

105 106

101 100

Seward

Seward Highway

83   79

107

75

80

81

78

72 71

Richardson Highway

77

76

KENAI
PENINSULA

111

108

109   Kodiak

110

KODIAK

150

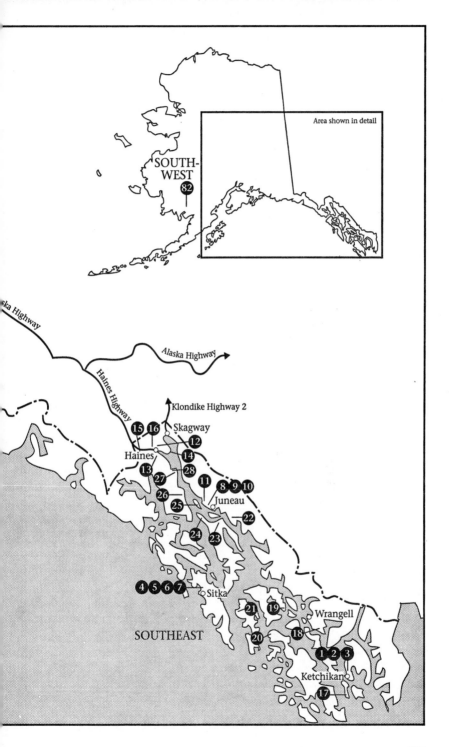

SOUTH-WEST

Area shown in detail

Alaska Highway

Haines Highway

Alaska Highway

Klondike Highway 2

Skagway

Haines

Juneau

Sitka

Wrangell

SOUTHEAST

Ketchikan

Map Key	Acreage	Campsites	Picnic Sites	Nearest Town
25 Shelter Island SMP	3,560	—	—	Juneau
26 St. James Bay SMP	10,220	—	—	Juneau
27 Sullivan Island SMP	2,163	—	—	Juneau
28 Chilkat Islands SMP	6,560	—	—	Haines

Northern District (3700 Airport Way, Fairbanks 99709)

Map Key	Acreage	Campsites	Picnic Sites	Nearest Town
29 Tok River SRS	38	50	—	Tok
30 Eagle Trail SRS	640	40	4	Tok
31 Moon Lake SRS	22	15	—	Tok
32 Fielding Lake SRS	300	7	—	Delta Junction
33 Donnelly Creek SRS	42	12	—	Delta Junction
34 Clearwater SRS	27	18	—	Delta Junction
35 Delta SRS	7	22	6	Delta Junction
36 Big Delta SHP	10	—	—	Delta Junction
37 Quartz Lake SRA	600	16	—	Delta Junction
38 Birch Lake SRS	191	10	—	Delta Junction
39 Harding Lake SRA	169	89	52	Delta Junction
40 Salcha River SRS	61	25	20	Delta Junction
41 Chena River SRS	27	59	30	Fairbanks
42 Chena River SRA	254,080	—	—	Fairbanks
43 Upper Chatanika Rvr SRS	73	25	—	Fairbanks
44 Lower Chatanika Rvr SRA	570	—	—	Fairbanks

Mat-Su/Copper Basin District (HC 32, Box 6706, Wasilla 99687)

Map Key	Acreage	Campsites	Picnic Sites	Nearest Town
45 Denali SP	324,240	—	—	Talkeetna
46 Montana Creek SRS	82	89	28	Talkeetna
47 Willow Creek SRS	240	7	—	Willow
48 Nancy Lake SRA	22,685	—	—	Willow
49 Nancy Lake SRS	36	30	30	Willow
50 Rocky Lake SRS	48	10	—	Wasilla
51 Big Lake North SRS	19	60	24	Wasilla
52 Big Lake South SRS	16	20	10	Wasilla
53 Kepler-Bradley Lakes SRA	344	—	—	Palmer
54 Finger Lake SRS	47	41	10	Palmer
55 Wolf Lake SRS	23	4	4	Palmer
56 Independence Mine SHP	761	—	—	Palmer
57 Summit Lake SRS	360	—	5	Palmer
58 Moose Creek SRS	40	12	4	Palmer
59 King Mountain SRS	20	22	2	Palmer
60 Bonnie Lake SRS	129	8	—	Palmer
61 Long Lake SRS	480	9	—	Palmer
62 Matanuska Glacier SRS	229	12	—	Palmer
63 Little Nelchina SRS	22	11	—	Glennallen
64 Lake Louise SRA	90	46	—	Glennallen
65 Tolsona Creek SRS	600	10	—	Glennallen
66 Dry Creek SRS	372	58	4	Glennallen
67 Porcupine Creek SRS	240	—	—	Tok
68 Liberty Falls SRS	10	8	—	Chitina
69 Squirrel Creek SRS	350	14	—	Copper Center
70 Little Tonsina SRS	103	8	—	Copper Center
71 Worthington Glacier SRS	113	—	—	Valdez
72 Blueberry Lake SRS	192	15	—	Valdez

Chugach/Southwest District (P.O. Box 107001, Anchorage 99510)

Map Key	Acreage	Campsites	Picnic Sites	Nearest Town
73 Chugach SP	495,204	—	—	Anchorage
74 Potter Section House SHS	0.5	—	—	Anchorage
75 Bettles Bay SMP	680	—	—	Whittier

Map Key	Acreage	Campsites	Picnic Sites	Nearest Town
76 Zeigler Cove SMP	720	—	—	Whittier
77 Surprise Cove SMP	2,280	—	—	Whittier
78 S. Esther Island SMP	3,360	—	—	Whittier
79 Horseshoe Bay SMP	970	—	—	Seward
80 Sawmill Bay SMP	2,320	—	—	Valdez
81 Shoup Bay SMP	4,560	—	—	Valdez
82 Wood-Tikchik SP	1,555,200	3	—	Dillingham

Kenai Peninsula District (P.O. Box 1247, Soldotna 99669)

Map Key	Acreage	Campsites	Picnic Sites	Nearest Town
83 Caines Head SRA	5,961	4	4	Seward
84 Kenai Keys SRA	193	—	—	Sterling
85 Bings Landing SRS	126	37	20	Sterling
86 Izaak Walton SRS	8	38	—	Sterling
87 Morgans Landing SRA	279	50	—	Sterling
88 Scout Lake SRS	195	8	—	Sterling
89 Funny River SRS	336	5	—	Sterling
90 Nilnunqa SHS	42	—	—	Sterling
91 Kenai River Islands SRS	69	—	—	Sterling
92 Slikok Creek SRS	40	—	5	Soldotna
93 Big Eddy SRS	16	—	—	Soldotna
94 Ciechanski SRS	34	—	—	Soldotna
95 Kenai River Flats SRS	832	—	—	Kenai
96 Bernice Lake SRS	152	11	1	Kenai
97 Captain Cook SRA	3,466	—	—	Kenai
98 Crooked Creek SRS	48.5	75	5	Soldotna
99 Kasilof River SRS	50	16	—	Soldotna
100 Johnson Lake SRA	324	50	—	Soldotna
101 Clam Gulch SRA	129	116	—	Soldotna
102 Ninilchik SRA	97	165	—	Homer
103 Deep Creek SRA	155	300	—	Homer
104 Stariski SRS	30	13	—	Homer
105 Anchor River SRA	213	38	—	Homer
106 Anchor River SRS	53	9	—	Homer
107 Kachemak B. SP&WP	328,290	8	1	Homer

Kodiak District (SR Box 3800, Kodiak 99615)

Map Key	Acreage	Campsites	Picnic Sites	Nearest Town
108 Fort Abercrombie SHP	183	14	—	Kodiak
109 Buskin River SRS	196	18	—	Kodiak
110 Pasagshak SRS	20	10	—	Kodiak
111 Shuyak Island SP	11,000	—	—	Kodiak

State Symbols

Flag

Alaska's state flag was designed in 1926 by Benny Benson, who entered his design in a territorial flag contest for students in grades seven through 12. The Alaska Legislature adopted his design as the official flag of the Territory of Alaska on May 2, 1927.

The flag consists of eight gold stars — the Big Dipper and the North Star — on a field of blue. In Benny Benson's words, "The blue field is for the Alaska sky and the forget-me-not,

an Alaska flower. The North Star is for the future state of Alaska, the most northerly of the Union. The Great Bear — symbolizing strength."

Benny Benson was born Oct. 12, 1913, at Chignik, Alaska. His mother was of Aleut-Russian descent and his father was a Swedish fisherman who came to Alaska in 1904. Benson's mother died of pneumonia when Benny was four and he entered the Jesse Lee Memorial Home (then located at Unalaska).

Benny, then a seventh-grade student at the Jesse Lee Home, was one of 142 students whose designs were selected for the final judging by a committee chosen by the Alaska Department of the American Legion.

Benny was awarded a $1,000 scholarship and was presented an engraved watch for winning the contest. He used the scholarship to attend the Hemphill Engineering School in Seattle in 1937.

In 1963, the Alaska Legislature awarded Benson an additional $2,500 as a way "of paying a small tribute to a fellow Alaskan." In November of the same year, Benson presented his award watch to the Alaska State Museum.

Benny's prophetic words, "The North Star is for the future state of Alaska, the most northerly of the Union," were realized on Jan. 3, 1959, when Alaska was proclaimed the 49th state of the Union. The drafters of the constitution for Alaska stipulated that the flag of the territory would be the official flag of the state of Alaska. When the flag was first flown over the capital city on July 4, 1959, Benny proudly led the parade that preceded the ceremony, carrying the flag of "eight stars on a field of blue," which he had designed 33 years before.

Benson settled in Kodiak in 1949 where he worked as a mechanic for Kodiak Airways. He was active in a movement to integrate the Elks, a whites-only national organization that now has a number of Native members in Alaska.

Benson had a leg amputated in 1969 and his health declined; he died of a heart attack on July 2, 1972, in Kodiak.

Seal

The first governor of Alaska designed a seal for the then–District of Alaska in 1884. In 1910, Gov. Walter E. Clark redesigned the original seal, which became a symbol for the new Territory of Alaska in 1912. The constitution of Alaska adopted the territorial seal as the Seal for the State of Alaska in 1959.

Represented in the state seal are icebergs, northern lights, mining, agriculture, fisheries, fur seal rookeries and a railroad. The seal is $2^1/8$ inches in diameter.

Song

Alaska's Flag

Eight stars of gold on a field of blue —
Alaska's flag.
May it mean to you the blue of the sea, the
evening sky,
The mountain lakes, and the flow'rs
nearby;
The gold of the early sourdough's dreams,
The precious gold of the hills and streams;
The brilliant stars in the northern sky,
The "Bear" — the "Dipper" — and,
shining high,
The great North Star with its steady light,
Over land and sea a beacon bright.
Alaska's flag — to Alaskans dear,
The simple flag of a last frontier.

The lyrics were written by Marie Drake as a poem that first appeared on the cover of the October 1935 *School Bulletin*, a territorial Department of Education publication that she edited while assistant commissioner of education.

The music was written by Mrs. Elinor Dusenbury, whose husband, Col. Ralph Wayne Dusenbury, was commander of Chilkoot Barracks at Haines from 1933 to 1936. Mrs.

Dusenbury wrote the music several years after leaving Alaska because, she was later quoted as saying, "I got so homesick for Alaska I couldn't stand it." She died Oct. 17, 1980, in Carlsbad, California.

The territorial legislature adopted *Alaska's Flag* as the official song in 1955.

Other Symbols

Bird: Willow ptarmigan, *Lagopus lagopus,* a small arctic grouse that lives among willows and on open tundra and muskeg. Its plumage changes from brown in summer to white in winter; feathers cover the entire lower leg and foot. Common from southwestern Alaska into the Arctic. Adopted in 1955.

Fish: King salmon, *Oncorhynchus tshawytscha,* an important part of the Native subsistence fisheries and a

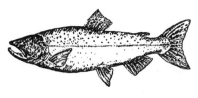

significant species to the state's commercial salmon fishery. This anadromous fish ranges from beyond the southern extremes of Alaska to as far north as Point Hope.

Flower: Forget-Me-Not.

Gem: Jade (*See* Jade).

Mineral: Gold (*See* Gold).

Motto: North to the Future, adopted in 1967.

Sport: Dog mushing (*See* Dog Mushing).

Tree: Sitka spruce, *Picea sitchensis,* the largest and one of the most valuable trees in Alaska. Sitka spruce grows to 160 feet in height and 3 to 5 feet in diameter. Its long, dark-green needles surround twigs that bear cones. It is found throughout Southeast and the Kenai Peninsula, along the gulf coast, and along the west coast of Cook Inlet. Adopted in 1962.

Subsistence

Alaska is unique among states in that it has established the subsistence use of fish and game as the highest priority consumptive use of the resource. Alaska's legislature passed subsistence priority laws in 1978 and 1986. In addition, Congress passed a priority subsistence law in 1980 for federal lands in Alaska. Studies by the Alaska Department of Fish and Game have shown that many rural communities in Alaska depend upon subsistence hunting and fishing for a large portion of their diets.

Subsistence, a controversial issue and a difficult concept to define, is defined by federal law as "the customary and traditional uses by rural Alaska residents of wild, renewable resources for direct personal or family consumption as food, shelter, fuel, clothing, tools or transportation; for the making and selling of handicraft articles out of nonedible byproducts of fish and wildlife resources taken for personal or family consumption; and for the customary trade, barter or sharing for personal or family consumption."

According to Alaska State Subsistence Statutes passed in 1986, only rural residents can be considered subsistence users. In addition to the rural requirement, subsistence uses can be identified by a variety of other criteria, such as long-term traditional use, local area use and frequent sharing of harvests. Subsistence also depends upon the biological status of fish and game resources, and is not authorized if harvesting will damage the resources.

In December 1989, the Alaska Supreme Court ruled that the state subsistence law was unconstitutional. At the close of the legislative session in May 1990, no resolutions had been made.

Subsistence fishing regulations are available as a separate pamphlet from the Alaska Department of Fish and Game, P.O. Box 3-2000, Juneau 99802. Subsistence hunting regulations are included with the annually published state hunting regulations, also available from the ADF&G.

Sundog

Sundogs are "mock suns" (parhelia) usually seen as bright spots on opposite sides of the winter sun. This optical phenomenon is created by the refraction of sunlight through tiny ice crystals suspended in the air. The ice crystals are commonly called "diamond dust."

Taiga

Taiga is a moist coniferous forest that begins where the tundra ends. Taken from a Russian word that means "land of little sticks," this name is applied to the spindly white spruce and black spruce forests found in much of southcentral and interior Alaska.

Telecommunications

History

Alaska's first telecommunications project, begun in the 1860s, was designed to serve New York, San Francisco and the capitals of Europe, not particularly the residents of Nome or Fairbanks. It was part of Western Union's ambitious plan to link California to Russian America (Alaska) with an intercontinental cable that would continue under the Bering Strait to Siberia and on to Europe. Men and material were brought together on both sides of the Bering Sea, but with the first successful Atlantic cable crossing in 1867, the trans-Siberian intercontinental line was abandoned.

The first operational telegraph link in Alaska was laid in September 1900, when 25 miles of line were stretched from military headquarters in Nome to an outpost at Port Safety. It was one part of a $450,000 plan by the Army Signal Corps to connect scattered military posts in the territory with the United States. By the end of 1903, land lines linked western Alaska, Prince William Sound, the Interior and southeastern Alaska (where underwater cable was used).

Plagued by blocks of ice that repeatedly tore loose the underwater cables laid across Norton Sound, the military developed "wireless telegraphy" to span the icy water in 1903. It was the world's first application of radio-telegraph technology and marked the completion of a fragile network connecting all military stations in Alaska with the United States and each other. Sitka, Juneau, Haines and Valdez were connected by a line to Whitehorse, Yukon Territory. Nome, Fort Saint Michael, Fort Gibbon (Tanana) and Fort Egbert (Eagle) were linked with Dawson, Yukon Territory. A line from Dawson to Whitehorse continued on to Vancouver, British Columbia, and Seattle.

In 1905, the 1,500 miles of land lines, 2,000 miles of submarine cables and the 107-mile wireless link became the Washington-Alaska Military Cable and Telegraph System. This, in turn, became the Alaska Communications System in 1935, reflecting a shift to greater civilian use and a system relying more heavily on wireless stations than land lines. The Alaska Communications System operated under the Department of Defense until RCA Corporation, through its division RCA Alascom, took control in 1971.

Alascom

Alascom, Inc., is the original long lines carrier for the state and provides a full range of modern long-distance telecommunications services to all Alaska. When Alascom purchased Alaska Communications Systems, about 5 million calls were being handled each year. Today, with more than 200 satellite communication sites in operation, Alascom handles nearly 70 million toll calls each year. To complement its satellite communications, Alascom also maintains hundreds of miles of terrestrial microwave routes.

On Oct. 27, 1982, Alascom launched its own telecommunications satellite, *Aurora,* into orbit from Cape Canaveral, Florida. The launching marked several firsts for Alaska: It was the first telecommunications satellite dedicated to a single state; it was the first completely solid-state satellite to be placed in orbit; and it was the first satellite to be named by a youngster in a contest. Sponsored by Alascom and the Alaska Chamber of Commerce, the contest drew some 5,000 entries from schoolchildren across Alaska. The winner was 8-year-old Nick Francis of Eagle River, who chose "aurora" for the name "because it's our light in the sky to tell us we are special people."

A typical long-distance telephone call from rural Alaska to points in the Lower 48 may travel more than 100,000 miles in what engineers call a "double-hop" — a signal from a village to the satellite *Aurora,* back to toll facilities in Fairbanks, Juneau or Anchorage, up again to *Aurora,* and finally to Lower 48 receiving stations. The signal is carried at speeds approaching that of light.

Improvements over the past 10 years have made long-distance telephone service available to every community of 25 persons or more in Alaska. Live or same-day television is now available to 90 percent of the state's population. In addition to message toll service and television transmissions, Alascom also provides the following services to the residents of Alaska: discounted calling plans, telex, computer data transmission and access, Wide Area Telecommunications Service (WATS), fax service, national and in-state 800 toll-free numbers, telegrams and mailgrams, dedicated line service, marine radio, foreign exchange service, and transportable satellite earth stations. Alascom is one of the largest private employers in the state.

General Communication Inc.

General Communication Inc. (GCI) provides long-distance telephone service to national and international destinations. In 1991, GCI will begin providing in-state long-distance service, as authorized by the Alaska Legislature.

GCI transmits calls via a communications satellite, tying in with the AT&T, MCI and US Sprint national phone networks.

Telephone Numbers in the Bush

Although most Alaskan bush communities now have full telephone service, a few villages still have only one telephone. For those villages, call the information number, 555-1212. The area code for all of Alaska is 907.

Television Stations

Television in Alaska's larger communities, such as Anchorage and Fairbanks, was available years before satellites were sent into orbit. The first satellite broadcast to the state was Neil Armstrong's moon walk in July 1969. Television reached the bush in the late 1970s with the construction of telephone earth stations that could receive television programming via satellite transmissions. The state funds Satellite Television Project (TVP), which supplies general programming to over 250 rural communities. For more information about TVP, contact the Department of Administration, Information Services, 5900 E. Tudor Road, Anchorage 99507.

Tapes of programming from the LearnAlaska Instructional Television Network, which is no longer on the air, are available to teachers through the state library system.

Regular network programming (ABC, CBS, NBC and PBS) from the Lower 48 reaches Alaska on a time-delayed basis. Most of the stations listed here carry a mixture of network programming, with local broadcasters specifying programming. Some stations, such as KJNP, carry locally produced programming.

Cable television is available in many communities, with the cable companies offering dozens of channels. At least one cable system offers a complete satellite earth station and 24-hour programming. Local television viewing in Bethel, for example, includes Channel 4 (KYUK), which carries ITV programming such as PBS's "NOVA" series and "Sesame Street," and local news; cable Channel 8, which carries regular network programming; and a half-dozen other cable channels carrying specialized programming such as movies, sports and specials.

The following list shows the commercial and public television stations in Alaska:

Anchorage
KAKM Channel 7 (public television); 2677 Providence Drive, 99508

KIMO Channel 13; 2700 E. Tudor Road, 99507

KTBY Channel 4; 1840 S. Bragaw, Suite 101, 99508

KTUU Channel 2; P.O. Box 102880, 99510

KTVA Channel 11; P.O. Box 102200, 99510

KYES Channel 5; 3700 Woodland Drive, #600, 99517

Bethel
KYUK Channel 4 (public television); P.O. Box 468, 99559

Fairbanks
KATN Channel 2; 516 Second Ave., 99707

KTVF Channel 11; P.O. Box 950, 99707

KUAC Channel 9 (public television); University of Alaska, 99775

Juneau
KJUD Channel 8; 1107 W. Eighth St., 99801

KTOO Channel 3 (public television); 224 Fourth St., 99801

Kenai
UHF Channel 17; P.O. Box 4665, 99611

North Pole
KJNP Channel 4; P.O. Box O, 99705

Sitka
KTNL Channel 13; 520 Lake St., 99835

Tides

In southeastern Alaska, Prince William Sound, Cook Inlet and Bristol Bay, saltwater undergoes extreme daily fluctuations, creating powerful tidal currents. Some bays may go totally dry at low tide. The second greatest tide range in North America occurs in upper Cook Inlet near Anchorage, where the maximum diurnal range during spring tides is 38.9 feet. (The greatest tide range in North America is Nova Scotia's Bay of Fundy, with spring tides to 43 feet.)

Here are diurnal ranges for some coastal communities:

Bethel, 4 feet; Cold Bay, 7.1 feet; Cordova, 12.4 feet; Haines, 16.8 feet; Herschel Island, 0.7 feet; Ketchikan, 15.4 feet; Kodiak, 8.5 feet; Naknek River entrance, 22.6 feet; Nikiski, 20.7 feet; Nome, 1.6 feet; Nushagak, 19.6 feet; Point Barrow, 0.4 feet; Port Heiden, 12.3 feet; Port Moller, 10.8 feet; Sand Point, 7.3 feet; Sitka, 9.9 feet; Valdez, 12 feet; Whittier, 12.3 feet; Wrangell, 15.7 feet; Yakutat, 10.1 feet

Timber

According to the USDA Forest Service, Anchorage Forestry Sciences Lab, 129 million acres of Alaska's 365 million acres of land surface are forested, 21 million acres of which are classified as timberland. Timberland is defined as forest land capable of producing in excess of 20 cubic feet of industrial wood per acre per year in natural stands and not withdrawn from timber utilization.

Alaska has two distinct forest ecosystems: the interior forest and the coastal rain forest. The vast interior forest covers 115 million acres, extending from the south slope of the Brooks Range to the Kenai Peninsula, and from Canada to Norton Sound. More than 13 million acres of white spruce, paper birch, quaking aspen, black cottonwood and balsam poplar stands are considered timberland, comparing favorably in size and growth with the forests of the lake states of Minnesota, Wisconsin and Michigan. However, 3.4 million acres of this timberland are unavailable for harvest because they are in designated parks or wilderness. Land management policies and remoteness from large markets have limited timber use to approximately 20 local sawmills (many cutting less than 300,000 board feet per year), with some exports of cants and chips.

The coastal rain forests extend from Cook Inlet to the Alaska-Canada border south of Ketchikan, and they continue to provide the bulk of commercial timber volume in Alaska. Of the 13.6 million acres of forested land, 7.6 million acres support timberland. About 1.9 million acres of these commercial stands are in parks and wilderness and therefore are not available for harvest. Western hemlock and Sitka spruce provide most of the timber harvest for domestic and export lumber and pulp markets. Western red cedar and Alaska cedar make up most of the balance, along with mountain hemlock and some lodgepole pine and other species. Southeastern Alaska has five major sawmills and six smaller mills, some operating intermittently.

Lands from which timber is harvested are divided into two distinct categories: privately owned by Native corporations and villages under the 1971 Native Claims Settlement Act; and publicly owned and managed federal, state and borough lands. Timber harvests from publicly owned lands are carried through short- and long-term sales offered by government agencies. Harvests on Native lands are scheduled for accelerated cutting through the early 1990s, tapering off to a lower sustained harvest in the following years.

The forest products of Alaska are also divided somewhat along the same lines as land ownership. By federal law, timber harvested from federal lands (approximately 87 percent of all timber harvested on public lands) cannot be exported without processing. Consequently, while processors dependent on federal lands produce roughly sawn lumber, pulp and chips, the Native corporations primarily produce round logs, which find more buyers in Japan. Given that the Alaska forest products industry is almost entirely dependent on the Japanese market, the processing requirement has had considerable effect on some sections of the forest industry, as it limits responsiveness to varying market conditions. Pulp mills provide a market for wood chips and for lower-quality timber from both public and private lands. A market for this so-called utility wood is critical to all operators.

In 1988, more than 400 million board feet of timber were harvested from publicly owned or managed lands in Alaska (excluding Bureau of Land Management). An estimated 300 million board feet of sawlogs, mostly for export, were harvested from private lands. The total 1988 timber harvest exceeded 800 million board feet. In 1989, timber was the second most valuable product exported, with a dollar value of over $635 million.

Time Zones

On Sept. 15, 1983, Transportation Secretary Elizabeth Dole signed a plan

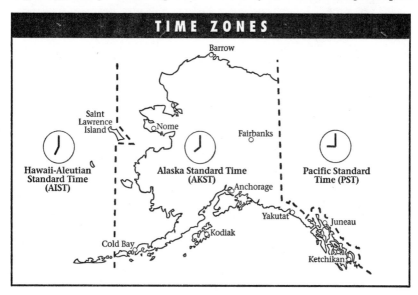

TIME ZONES

to reduce the number of time zones in Alaska from four to two. The plan, which became effective Oct. 30, 1983, when daylight saving time reverted to standard time, places 90 percent of Alaska residents on Alaska (same as Yukon) time, only one hour behind the West Coast. The far reaches of the Aleutian Islands and Saint Lawrence Island enter Hawaii-Aleutian time.

Before the change, Alaska's time zones were Pacific time (southeastern Alaska), Yukon time (Yakutat) and Alaska time (from just east of Cold Bay and west of Yakutat northward, including Nome). The shift was accomplished to facilitate doing business in Alaska, improve communications and unify residents. It had the support of the governor, the state legislature and the majority of Alaskans.

Totems

In the early days of southeastern Alaska and the Pacific Northwest coast, the Native way of life was based on the rich natural resources of the land, on respect for all living things, and on a unique and complex social structure. The totemic art of the Indians reflects this rich culture.

Totem poles, carved from the huge cedar trees of the northern coast, are a traditional art form among the Natives of the Pacific Northwest and southeastern Alaska. Although the best-known type of totem pole is tall and freestanding, totemic art also is applied to houseposts, house frontal poles and mortuary poles. Totem poles are bold statements that make public records of the lives and history of the people who had them carved and represent pride in clans and ancestors.

Animals of the region are most often represented on the poles. Commonly depicted are eagles, ravens, frogs, bears, wolves, thunderbirds and whales. Also represented are figures from Native mythology: monsters with animal features, humanlike spirits and legendary ancestors. Occasionally included are objects, devices, masks and charms, and more rarely, art illustrating plants and sky phenomena.

The poles were traditionally painted with natural mineral and vegetable pigments. Salmon eggs were chewed with cedar bark to form the binder for the ground pigment. Traditional colors are black, white and red-brown; green, blue-green, blue and yellow are also used, depending on tribal convention. The range of colors broadened when modern paints became available. Totem art grew rapidly in the late 18th century, with the introduction of steel European tools acquired from explorers and through the fur trade. Large totem poles were a thriving cultural feature by the 1830s, having become a means by which the Natives displayed their social standing.

Totem pole carving almost died out between the 1880s and 1950s during the enforcement of a law forbidding the

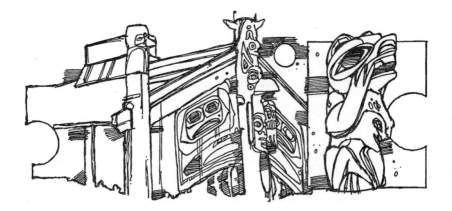

"potlatch," the core of Northwest Coast Indian culture. The potlatch is a ceremony in which major events are celebrated, such as marriages; guests are invited from near and far, dancing and feasting take place, property is given away and often poles are raised to commemorate the event. Since the anti-potlatching law was repealed in 1951, a revival of Native culture and the arts has taken place, and many tribes are actively carving and raising poles again.

Totem poles were left to stand as long as nature would permit, usually no more than 50 to 60 years. Once a pole became so rotten that it fell, it was left to decay naturally or used for firewood. Some totem poles still standing in parks today are 40 to 50 years old. Heavy precipitation and acid muskeg soils hasten decomposition, even though cedar is resistant to decay.

Collections of fine totem poles may be seen in several Alaska communities, either outdoors or in museums, including Ketchikan, Wrangell and Sitka. Carvers can be seen practicing their art at cultural centers in those towns as well as in Haines.

Tourism

Although Alaska has been attracting tourists for over 100 years, people are surprised that the visitor industry has quietly become the state's second largest primary employer. The visitor industry employs 19,000 Alaskans directly and affects 38,000 Alaskan jobs. Over 2,500 businesses in Alaska derive most of their income from visitor sales. Tourism is a renewable resource that brings dollars to all regions of Alaska. The visitor industry is expected to play a greater role in Alaska's future as the state's petroleum production decreases.

State government has long recognized the value of the visitor industry and supports this growing segment of the state's economy through the Division of Tourism. The division in 1989 received $11.7 million from the legislature, mostly for marketing Alaska as a visitor destination. The state's tourism budget is a good investment: For every dollar the state spends on tourism promotion, visitors spend $95.

While the oil spill in Prince William Sound threatened the 1989 tourism season, the negative image shown by the media was countered by a $4 million emergency marketing program developed by the Alaska Visitors Association.

The continental United States provided 82 percent of Alaska's visitors in 1989, Canadian visitors formed 12 percent and 6 percent came from overseas. Of these travelers, 60 percent had independent itineraries while the remainder came on package tour programs. The most popular mode of entry for visitors was domestic air (51 percent), cruise ships (26 percent), personal vehicles (13 percent) and the ferry system (5

Nonresident Visitor Volume and Impact

Year	Visitor Volume	In-State Sales* (in millions)	Primary Employment
1978	522,500	$ 270.3	6,970
1979	546,000	321.1	7,280
1980	570,600	360.4	7,925
1981	596,300	416.2	8,280
1982	623,100	480.7	8,900
1983	646,000	551.7	9,160
1984	691,200	620.0	9,875
1985	700,000	659.4	10,565
1986	787,000	700.0	10,888
1987	746,500	1,094.3	9,900
1988	709,664	**	**
1989	769,300	1,111.5	19,000

*Excludes transportation costs to and from Alaska
**No figures reported
Source: State of Alaska, Division of Tourism

percent). The remainder arrived by international air (3 percent) and motor coach tours (2 percent). Total arrivals for 1989 are estimated at 769,300.

Alaska's scenic beauty, abundant wildlife and colorful history remain its biggest attractions. The adventure travel market is growing rapidly in Alaska, with an increasing number of visitors participating in river rafting, back-country trekking and other wilderness experiences.

Trees and Shrubs

According to the U.S. Department of Agriculture, the number of native tree species in Alaska is less than in any other state. Species of trees and shrubs in Alaska fall under the following families: yew, pine, cypress, willow, bayberry, birch, mistletoe, gooseberry, rose, maple, elaeagnus, ginseng, dogwood, crowberry, pyrola, heath, dispensia, honeysuckle and composite.

Commercial timber species include white spruce, Sitka spruce, western hemlock, mountain hemlock, western red cedar, Alaska cedar, balsam poplar, black cottonwood, quaking aspen and paper birch.

Rare tree species include the Pacific yew, Pacific silver fir, subalpine fir, silver willow and Hooker willow.

Tundra

Characteristic of arctic and subarctic regions, tundra is a treeless plain that consists of moisture-retaining soils and permanently frozen subsoil. Tundra climates, with frequent winds and low temperatures, are harsh on plant species attempting to grow there. Soils freeze around root systems and winds wear away portions exposed above rocks and snow. Consequently, the three distinct types of Alaska tundra — wet, moist and alpine — support low-growing vegetation that includes a variety of delicate flowers, mosses and lichens.

According to a report in *Alaska Science Nuggets,* every acre of arctic tundra contains more than 2 tons of live fungi that survive by feeding on, thus decomposing, dead organic matter. Since the recession of North Slope ice age glaciers 12,000 years ago, a vegetative residue has accumulated a layer of peat 3- to 6-feet thick overlying the tundra.

Ulu

A traditional Eskimo woman's knife designed for scraping and chopping, this fan-shaped tool was originally made of stone with a bone handle. Today, an ulu is often shaped from an old saw blade and a wood handle is attached.

Umiak

An umiak is a traditional Eskimo skin-covered boat, whose design has changed little over the centuries. Although the umiak is mostly powered by outboard motors today, paddles are still used when stalking game and when ice might damage the propeller. Because umiaks must often be pulled for long distances over the ice, the boats are designed to be lightweight and easily repairable. The frames are wood, often driftwood found on the beaches, and the covering can be sewn should it be punctured. The bottom is flat and the keel is bone, which prevents the skin from wearing out as it is pulled over the ice.

Female walrus skins are the preferred covering because they are the proper thickness when split (bull hides are too thick) and because it only takes two to cover a boat. However, sometimes female walrus skins are unavailable, so the Eskimos substitute skins of the bearded seal, or *oogruk.* But *oogruk* skins are smaller and it takes six or seven skins to cover an umiak.

Once the skins are stretched over the frame and lashed into place, the outside is painted with marine paint for waterproofing. Historically, the skin would have been anointed with seal oil or other fats, but the modern waterproofing is now universally accepted because it does not have to be renewed after each trip.

Umiak is the Inupiat word for skin boat and is commonly used by the coastal Eskimos throughout Alaska. The Saint Lawrence Islanders, however, speak the Yup'ik dialect and their word for skin boat is *angyaq*.

Universities and Colleges

Higher education in Alaska is provided by the University of Alaska statewide system and private institutions. The university system includes three multicampus universities, one community college and a network of service for rural Alaska. University of Alaska institutions enroll more than 30,000 people each year.

The three regional institutions are the University of Alaska Anchorage, which includes Kenai Peninsula College, Kodiak College, Matanuska-Susitna College and Prince William Sound Community College; University of Alaska Fairbanks with campuses in Bethel, Kotzebue and Nome; and University of Alaska Southeast with campuses in Juneau, Ketchikan and Sitka. These schools offer developmental, certificate, associate, baccalaureate and graduate degree programs. Student housing is available in Anchorage, Bethel, Fairbanks and Juneau.

University of Alaska Fairbanks research facilities include the Agricultural and Forestry Experiment Station, Alaska Native Language Center, Center for Cross-Cultural Studies, Fishery Industrial Technology Center, Geophysical Institute, Juneau Center for Fisheries and Ocean Sciences, Mineral Industry Research and Petroleum Development laboratories, University of Alaska Museum, and the institutes of Arctic Biology, Marine Science, and Northern Engineering.

The University of Alaska Anchorage is the home of the Alaska Center for International Business, Institute for Social and Economic Research, Justice Center, and centers for Alcohol and Addiction Studies, High Latitude Health Research, and Economic Education.

Through the university's Cooperative Extension Service and Marine Advisory Program, research results are interpreted and transferred to people of the state.

For information on state colleges and universities, contact the following institutions:

University of Alaska Anchorage, 3211 Providence Drive, Anchorage 99508: **Kenai Peninsula College,** 34820 College Drive, Soldotna 99669; **Kodiak College,** 117 Benny Benson Drive, Kodiak 99615; **Matanuska-Susitna College,** P.O. Box 2899, Palmer 99645; **Prince William Sound Community College,** P.O. Box 97, Valdez 99686

University of Alaska Fairbanks, Fairbanks 99775: **Chukchi Campus,** P.O. Box 297, Kotzebue 99752; **Kuskokwim Campus,** P.O. Box 368, Bethel 99559; **Northwest Campus,** Pouch 400, Nome 99762

University of Alaska Southeast, 11120 Glacier Highway, Juneau 99801: **Ketchikan Campus,** Seventh and Madison, Ketchikan 99901; **Sitka Campus,** 1339 Seward Ave., Sitka 99835

For information on private institutions of higher learning, contact the following:

Alaska Bible College, P.O. Box 289, Glennallen 99588

Alaska Pacific University, 4101 University Drive, Anchorage 99508

Sheldon Jackson College, 801 Lincoln St., Sitka 99835

Many additional schools and institutes in Alaska offer religious, vocational and technical study. For a complete listing of these and other schools, write for the *Directory of Postsecondary Educational Institutions in Alaska,* Alaska Commission on Postsecondary Education, P.O. Box FP, Juneau 99811.

Volcanoes

The state's 10 tallest active volcanic peaks (those which have erupted during the last 10,000 years, based on information from the Smithsonian Institution) are as follows:

Map Key

1 Mount Wrangell, 14,163 feet
2 Mount Spurr, 11,070 feet
3 Redoubt Volcano, 10,197 feet
4 Iliamna Volcano, 10,016 feet
5 Shishaldin Volcano, 9,372 feet
6 Pavlof Volcano, 8,242 feet
7 Mount Veniaminof, 8,225 feet
8 Isanotski Peaks, 8,025 feet
9 Mount Denison, 7,600+ feet
10 Mount Griggs, 7,600+ feet

Volcanoes on the Aleutian Islands, the Alaska Peninsula and in the Wrangell Mountains are part of the "Ring of Fire" that surrounds the Pacific Ocean basin. There are more than 70 potentially active volcanoes in Alaska, the majority of which have had at least one eruption since 1760, the date of earliest recorded eruptions. Pavlof Volcano is one of the most active of Alaskan volcanoes, having had more than 41 reported eruptions. One recent spectacular eruption of Pavlof in April 1986 sent ash 10 miles high, causing black snow to fall on Cold Bay. The eruption of Augustine Volcano (elev. 4,025 feet) in lower Cook Inlet on March 27, 1986, sent ash 8 miles high and disrupted air traffic in south-central Alaska for several days. Most recently, Mount Redoubt erupted on Dec. 14, 1989, its first eruption since 1966. The biggest eruptions have sent ash throughout most of southcentral Alaska, from Homer to Talkeetna, and have disrupted air traffic. Periodic eruptions occurred throughout winter and into spring 1990, and are expected to continue. The most violent Alaskan eruption recorded and the largest volcanic eruption in the world yet this century occurred over a 60-hour period in June 1912 from Novarupta Volcano. The eruption darkened the sky over

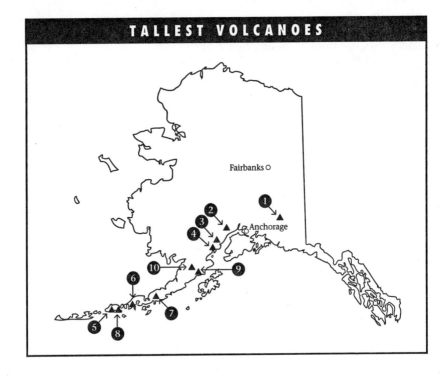

TALLEST VOLCANOES

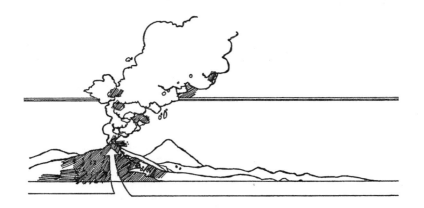

much of the Northern Hemisphere for several days, deposited almost a foot of ash on Kodiak, 100 miles away, and filled the Valley of Ten Thousand Smokes (now contained within Katmai National Park) with more than 2.5 cubic miles of ash during its brief but extremely explosive duration.

Waves

(See also Bore Tide *and* Tides)

According to the Alaska Tsunami Warning Center in Palmer, Alaska has had seven tsunamis that have caused fatalities in recorded history, although only for the last three have there been accurate counts of fatalities. These were of local origin and occurred between 1788 and 1964. Tsunamis originating in Alaska have caused all of the fatalities reported on the West Coast and in Alaska, and most of those in Hawaii. The most recent tsunami was in 1964 following the March 27, Good Friday earthquake. That wave completely destroyed three Alaskan villages before reaching Washington, Oregon and California, and continued to cause damage as far away as Hawaii, Chile and Japan. Tsunami is taken from the Japanese words "tsu" meaning harbor and "nami" meaning great wave. Although often called tidal waves, tsunamis are not caused by tides. Generated by earthquakes occurring on or below the sea floor, tsunamis can race across the Pacific Ocean at speeds up to 600 miles per hour. Tsunamis rarely cross the Atlantic. Traveling across the open ocean, the waves are only a few feet high and can be up to 100 miles from crest to crest. They cannot be seen from an airplane or felt in a ship at sea. Once they approach shore, however, shallower water causes the waves to grow taller by increasingly restricting their forward motion. Thus, a 2-foot wave traveling 500 miles per hour in deep water becomes a 100-foot killer at 30 miles per hour as it nears the shore. The wave action of a tsunami can repeat every 15 to 30 minutes and the danger for a given area is generally not considered over until the area has been free from damaging waves for two hours.

Providing information, and timely warnings, on tsunamigenic earthquakes (those quakes measuring above 7.0 on the Richter scale) is the job of the Alaska Tsunami Warning Center (ATWC), located in Palmer. Established in 1967, the ATWC now makes loss of life unnecessary for Alaska, Canada, the west coast of the United States and Hawaii, and ensures the avoidance of such a tragedy as the April 1, 1946, earthquake at Scotch Cap on Unimak Island, Alaska. Within minutes after the quake struck, waves measuring 100 feet high completely destroyed the lighthouse on the island, killing five people. In less than five hours, the first wave hit Hawaii, killing 159 people. More recently, in March 1985, after an 8.1 quake in Chile, tsunami warnings alerted coastal Alaskans in plenty of time to take precautionary measures. Normally, tsunamis from remote Pacific sources will not be destructive in Alaska.

Another type of wave action that occurs in Alaska is a seiche. A seiche is a long, rhythmic wave in a closed or partially closed body of water. Caused by earthquakes, winds, tidal currents or atmospheric pressure, the motion of a seiche resembles the back and forth movement of a tipped bowl of water. The water moves only up and down, and can remain active from a few minutes to several hours. The highest recorded wave in Alaska, 1,740 feet, was the result of a seiche that took place in Lituya Bay on July 9, 1958. This unusually high wave was due to an earthquake-induced landslide that cleared trees from the opposite side of the bay.

Whales and Whaling

(*See also* Baleen)

Fifteen species of both toothed and baleen whales are found in Alaskan waters. Baleen refers to the hundreds of strips of flexible bonelike material that hangs from the gum of the upper jaw. The strips are fringed and act as strainers that capture krill, the tiny shrimp-like organisms upon which the whales feed. Once the baleen fills with krill, whales force water back out through the sides of their mouth, swallowing the food left behind. Baleen whale cows are usually larger than bulls.

Baleen whales that inhabit Alaskan waters include blue, bowhead, northern right, fin or finback, humpback, sei, minke or little piked and gray. Toothed whales include sperm, beluga, killer, pilot, beaked (three species), dolphins (two species) and porpoises (two species). Rarely encountered in Alaskan waters is another toothed whale, the narwhal, a full-time resident of the Arctic. Saint Lawrence Islanders call narwhals *bousucktugutalik,* or "beluga with tusk," due to a tusk that grows from the left side of the upper jaw on bulls only. Spiraling in a left-hand direction, the tusk can reach lengths of 7 to 8 feet on an adult.

A few facts on three of the whales indigenous to Alaska are interesting to note. The blue whale has the distinction of being the world's largest animal, reaching lengths of 100 feet,

weighing up to 200 tons and possessing a girth up to 45 feet. It is possible for an adult elephant to stand on the floor of a blue whale's mouth without touching the whale's upper jawbone. A blue whale's tongue alone can weigh 4 tons, its heart 1,000 pounds, and its stomach can hold up to 2 tons of food. In 1948, a factory ship recorded taking an 89-foot blue with a liver weighing 1,000 pounds that produced 133 barrels of oil. While nursing, a blue whale cow provides 130 gallons of milk a day in 40 feedings. This allows the calf a weight gain of 8.5 pounds per hour.

The fin, or finback, is the second largest of the world's whale species, measuring up to 80 feet in length and weighing 70 tons. Hanging up to 3 feet from the upper jaw are 375 plates of baleen. The blow on a fin whale is 13 to 20 feet high, usually occurring once per minute between dives that vary from 2 to 28 minutes. Among the fastest swimmers of the large whales, fins can cruise at 5 or 6 knots with bursts to 20 knots when alarmed and can dive to depths of 755 feet.

The sperm whale's distinguishing feature is a huge head — one-fourth to one-third of the animal's total length depending upon sex (60 feet for males, 30 feet for females). The boxlike head can contain 3 to 4 tons of spermaceti, which is used as a heat-resistant, high-quality industrial lubricant. The deepest-diving of the whales, sperm whales have been recorded at depth of 8,200 feet and once at a depth of almost 2 miles. They can remain submerged for 30 to 60 minutes. Valued also for its 18 to 25 ivory teeth, which measure 3 to 8 inches at sexual maturity, a sperm whale grasps prey with its teeth, then swallows it whole if possible. Its favored food is squid, cuttlefish, octopus and occasionally shark. Sperm whales reach a maximum age of 77.

Whaling

Bowhead whales have been protected from commercial whaling by the Convention for the Regulation of Whaling of 1931, the International Convention for the Regulation of Whaling of 1947, the Marine Mammal
(Continued on page 168)

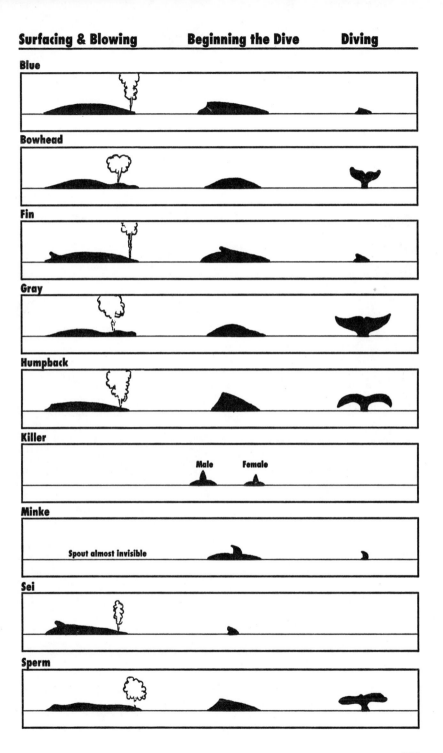

Blue

Bowhead

Fin

Gray

Humpback

Killer

Male   Female

Minke

Spout almost invisible

Sei

Sperm

(C Protection Act of 1972, the Endangered Species Act of 1973, and the Convention of International Trade in Endangered Species of Wild Fauna and Flora.

Commercial whaling for gray whales has been banned by the International Convention for the Regulation of Whaling since 1947. These conventions and acts have, however, allowed for a subsistence harvest by Alaska Indians, Aleuts and Eskimos.

Since 1978, the International Whaling Commission (IWC) has regulated the take of bowheads by establishing an annual catch limit for Alaska Eskimos. Also in 1978, the IWC reclassified the eastern stock of gray whales from a protected species to a sustained management stock with an annual catch limit of about 179 whales, based on the average known removals during the period 1968–77. The entire catch limit has been reserved for taking by Natives or by member governments on behalf of Natives. Other species of large baleen whales, such as minke and fin whales, are occasionally taken by Alaska Eskimos for food. It is not necessary to report gray and minke harvests. The only toothed whale taken by Eskimos is the beluga and its harvest is managed by the state.

According to the National Marine Mammal Laboratory and the Alaska Department of Fish and Game, harvest figures for the years 1979–1989 are as follows:

Year	Beluga	Gray	Minke
1979	138	3	2
1980	243–255*	3	1
1981	179–231*	NR	1
1982	307–354*	4	3
1983	226–236*	2	NR
1984	170*	NR	NR
1985	152–234*	1*	2*
1986	40–42*	NR	NR
1987	NA	NR	NR
1988	366**	NR	NR
1989	236**	NR	NR

*Approximate figures
**Known retrieved harvests
NR= none reported
NA=not available

Wildflowers

Wildflowers in Alaska are seldom gaudy; they are usually rather small and delicate. More than 1,500 plant species occur in the state, including trees, shrubs, ferns, grasses and sedges, as well as flowering plants.

Alpine regions are particularly rich in flora and some of the alpine species are rare. Anywhere there is tundra there is apt to be a bountiful population of flowers. The Steese Highway (Eagle Summit), Richardson Highway (Thompson Pass), Denali Highway (Maclaren Summit), Denali National Park and Preserve (Polychrome Pass), Seward Highway (Turnagain Pass), Glenn Highway just north of Anchorage (Eklutna Flats) and a locale near Wasilla (Hatcher Pass) are wonderful wildflower-viewing spots. These are all readily accessible by car. Less easily accessible floral Edens are some of the Aleutian Islands, Point Hope, Anvil Mountain and the Nome-Teller Road (both near Nome), Pribilof Islands and other remote areas.

Alaska's official flower, the forget-me-not *(Myosotis alpestris)*, is a delicate little beauty found throughout much of the state in alpine meadows and along streams. Growing to 18 inches tall, forget-me-nots are recognized by their bright blue petals surrounding a yellow "eye." A northern "cousin," the arctic forget-me-not (*Eritrichium aretioides*), grows in sandy soil on the tundra, or in the mountains, and reaches only 4 inches in height.

Related reading: *Discovering Wild Plants: Alaska, Western Canada, the Northwest,* by Janice Schofield. Descriptions, historical uses, harvest information and recipes of more than 130 plants. Full color photographs and drawings. *The Alaska-Yukon Wild Flowers Guide,* edited by Helen A. White

and Maxcine Williams; drawings by Virginia Howie. See ALASKA NORTHWEST LIBRARY in the back of the book.

Winds

Some of Alaska's windiest weather has been recorded on the western islands of the Aleutian chain. Overall, the causes are the same as elsewhere, incorporating planet rotation and the tendency of the atmosphere to equalize the difference between high and low pressure fronts (*see also* Climate). A few winds occur often and significantly enough to be given names: chinook, taku and williwaws.

Chinook

Old-timers describe chinook winds as unseasonably warm winds that can cause thaw in the middle of winter. What they also cause are power outages and property damage, especially in the Anchorage bowl, where in recent years hundreds of homes have sprung up on the Chugach Mountain hillsides over which the chinook winds howl. One such wind occurred on April Fool's Day in 1980, causing $25 million in property damage and nominating the city as a disaster area. Parts of Anchorage were without power for 60 hours.

Until recently, it was not possible to predict the coming of a chinook wind. Today, however, Anchorage meteorologists can tell if the winds are gathering, when they will arrive and their relative strength. It was discerned that such a warm wind could only originate in Prince William Sound and that its speed had to be at least 55 miles per hour or faster just to cross the 3,500-foot Chugach Mountains. Other factors that need to be present are a storm near Bethel and relatively stable air over Anchorage. Meteorologists predict the coming of chinook winds 55 percent of the time.

Taku

Taku winds are the sudden, fierce gales that sweep down from the icecap behind Juneau and Douglas, and plague residents there. Takus are shivering cold winds capable of reaching 100 miles per hour. They have been known to send a 2-by-4 timber flying through the wall of a frame house.

Williwaws

Williwaws are sudden gusts of wind that can reach 113 miles per hour after the wind "builds up" on one side of a mountain and suddenly spills over into what may appear to be a relatively protected area. Williwaws are considered the bane of Alaska mariners. The term was originally applied to a strong wind in the Strait of Magellan.

World Eskimo-Indian Olympics

An audience of thousands watches the annual spectacle of several hundred Native athletes from Alaska competing in the World Eskimo-Indian Olympics (WEIO) in Fairbanks. Held over four days during the second-to-last weekend in July, the self-supporting games draw participants from all of Alaska's Native populations (Eskimo, Aleut, Athabascan, Tlingit, Haida and Tsimshian). Canadian Eskimos are invited to participate, but funding problems have prohibited their coming since 1981.

Spectators thrill to the sight of such feats as the knuckle hop and the ear-weight competition. Other traditional Native sports and competitions include the greased pole walk, fish cutting, stick pull, Indian-Eskimo dancing, men's and women's blanket toss, and the spectacular two-foot and one-foot high kicks. Each year the judges choose a Native queen to reign over the four-day Olympics. She reigns through the year, making several appearances throughout the state, representing the WEIO. The judges also pick the most authentic Native costumes. Some of the more boisterous games include the lively white men/Native women tug of war and the muktuk eating contest.

The games will be held on Wednesday, Thursday, Friday and Saturday evenings at the Big Dipper Recreation Center in Fairbanks July 17-20, 1991. Advance tickets may be purchased from the World Eskimo-Indian Olympics Committee, P.O. Box 2433, Fairbanks 99707.

The games will be held on Wednesday, Thursday, Friday and Saturday evenings at the Big Dipper Recreation Center in Fairbanks July 17–20, 1991. Advance tickets may be purchased from the World Eskimo-Indian Olympics Committee, P.O. Box 2433, Fairbanks 99707.

Yearly Highlights, 1989 and 1990

Following is a collection of the more significant news events from mid-1989 to mid-1990 . . . the high spots for a record of the times. *FACTS ABOUT ALASKA: THE ALASKA ALMANAC®* wishes to credit the *Anchorage Daily News* and the *Anchorage Times* as the primary sources of information for Yearly Highlights.

Eleven-Year-Old Pilot
Flies Around the World

Tony Aliengena, 11, landed in Anchorage on July 20, 1989, 15,000 miles into his flight around the world. His trip, called Friendship Flight '89, began on June 5 in California, and included stops in Canada, Iceland, Norway, Sweden, Finland and 14 cities in the Soviet Union.

Tony was accompanied by his family; a Soviet pen pal; and an observer for the National Aeronautic Association, the sanctioning body for aviation world records. Also on board were reporters from the United States and Russia, and a documentary film

crew. His father, Gary Aliengena, was pilot-in-command on the trip, since aviators must be at least 16 years old before getting a license.

According to Tony, high points of the trip were the stops in Russia, and the low point was the destruction of the family's Cessna Centurion on the return to Nome following a fishing trip. But even that was overcome when Ralph Meloon of Soldotna generously loaned the family his Cessna so that they could continue the trip.

Mount McKinley 14 Feet Shorter

Mount McKinley may not be 20,320 feet high as previously thought, but Alaska won't know for sure until late 1990, when the calculations are officially reviewed. This is one finding of a June 1989 project that was originally aimed at measuring only the mountain's gravitational pull, and not checking its height, according to Ron Cothren, project coordinator.

Sponsored in part by the National Geodetic Survey and the U.S. Geological Survey, the project's goal of measuring McKinley's gravitational pull was to establish a precise "deflection of the vertical," thereby making surveying in mountainous areas more accurate. "Deflection of the vertical" is another way of saying that large masses such as mountains have their own gravitational pull in addition to the earth's, which causes plumb bobs to move off center. Since a surveying tripod and its instruments are leveled by using a plumb bob, knowing the deflection a mountainous area allows for accurate adjustment of the instruments. Getting the new, exact reading on McKinley's height is a result of measuring the mountain's gravity.

Newsweek Picks Alaskan as Hero

Kelley Weaverling, 43, was *Newsweek* magazine's hero from Alaska, an award that goes to the ultimate volunteer in each state. A Cordova resident, Weaverling was chosen for his organization of a 44-boat flotilla to rescue oil-soaked birds and otters from remote beaches of Prince William Sound following the March 24, 1989, oil spill.

Shortly after the spill, Weaverling arranged to work under contract for Exxon in the animal rescue effort. He wrote the first outline of a master rescue plan for oiled animals, and instructed his crews to pick up any soiled debris as they combed the beaches looking for animals.

After Weaverling was replaced by Exxon, the Alaska Conservation Foundation agreed to fund an observation program on Perry Island, which Weaverling had suggested. The island has a sampling of all of the sound's animals, whose movements and well-being could be recorded during the cleanup.

Weaverling says that since the spill, and because of it, he has developed a commitment to fighting for the environment. He was featured in the July 10, 1989, issue of *Newsweek*.

The Fish That Got Away

Bob Ploeger battled a king-sized king salmon for more than 37 hours only to watch it swim off — the victor of the battle.

Ploeger, a retired guard from the Minnesota state prison in Sandstone, was on his first Alaska fishing trip when he hooked into the mighty king on July 12, 1989. During the day and a half struggle, estimates of the fish's weight ranged from the high 80s to over 100 pounds; a good size, maybe even a record-breaker.

In the end, it came down to a fish-hook that slipped and a net that was too small to capture the king, who just wasn't ready to give up life in the Kenai River. Ploeger at least came away with one whale of a fish story and was ready to have another go at fishing — right after he'd had a nap.

Pilot Looks for Crash Site

Forty-two years ago, in March 1948, a chartered Northwest DC-4 plane with 30 passengers on board went down on Mount Sanford in the Wrangell Mountains. Ever since then, tales of gold and important war documents that may have been on the plane have kept a live interest in the downed aircraft.

Veteran Northwest pilot Edward Becker, 54, from Florida has been intrigued by the rumors and the crash itself for the past 10 years, and in August, the opportunity to check it out finally came. Along with Becker were noted Mount McKinley climber Vern Tejas and an expert rock climber from Copper Center, Rick Ford.

Becker didn't really care about finding riches or important historical documents as much as he wanted to find the wreck. Even then he didn't know what he'd do if he found it, since the plane is thought to be located in Wrangell-St. Elias National Park and Preserve, and would be considered not only Park Service property, but a grave-site as well. However, he didn't have to confront that problem this trip — the plane's location remained a mystery.

Water Water Everywhere

While July 1989 broke records for high temperatures and uninterrupted sunny days, August went down as the wettest month ever in Anchorage's recorded history.

It rained so hard and water was so deep that streets were closed, and cars stalled from soaked ignition systems. Creeks flooded, rivers threatened flash floods and still it kept raining. When all was said and done, Anchorage got 9.77 inches of rain in August and summer was washed away for 1989.

Bear Cub Entertains Tourists

Tourists in Ketchikan were able to go home with a story about Alaska that will be hard to top, thanks to a feisty bear cub who wandered into the airport.

The 25-pound cub tripped an electronic eye on the airport's automatic doors and found his way over to a crowded baggage carousel. Finding himself surrounded by tourists, he bolted for a stairway, but was grabbed by an airport employee, who put him in a portable dog kennel.

The little guy was held overnight by the state wildlife protection agency for observation and released the next morning in the area where his mother had last been seen.

U.S./Soviet Travel Allowed for Natives

On Aug. 4, 1989, U.S. and Soviet negotiators initialed agreements allowing visa-free travel for Natives who live along the Bering Strait. The agreement also establishes a commission composed of three Soviets and three Alaskans that will help deal with minor incidents, emergency evacuations and search and rescue operations.

Visa-free travel will be allowed for Natives living on St. Lawrence Island, the Seward Peninsula and in the Kotzebue area, and who have cultural or family ties with Soviet Natives. On the Soviet side, Yup'ik Eskimos living in the Chukotski Peninsula, which borders the east side of the Bering Strait, would be allowed visa-free travel. Trips could be for as long as 90 days. Passports are still necessary, as well as a letter of invitation from the group or individual that would act as host for the traveler.

The agreement reinstates the exchanges that were commonplace prior to 1948, when the Cold War caused suspension of travel across the Bering Strait. Now, contacts have renewed as border tensions have eased, and many cultural, academic and business exchanges take place.

Warm Water Cause of Fish Kills

In August 1989, state biologists estimated more than 25,000 salmon had died in sun-baked streams running through southeastern Alaska clear-cut forests. The salmon died before having a chance to spawn, and thousands more were at risk due to the summer dry spell.

Death of the salmon was apparently due to suffocation in warm water short of oxygen, and a link between the kills

and logging will be the basis for monitoring of Southeast streams by the Department of Fish and Game. Logging too close to temperature-sensitive spawning streams strips shade that cools the water and removes roots that slow the flow of runoff after rainfall. Most salmon deaths are occurring in streams logged-off without buffer zones, and the U.S. Forest Service now asks loggers to retain buffer strips ranging in width from 25 to 100 feet along all salmon spawning streams.

Man Mauled Twice

Don Covertson, a 32-year-old trapper and commercial fisherman, was checking out some land near Cantwell in August 1989, when he heard the crackling of brush behind him. Armed with only an ax, he turned in time to see a bear charging. Covertson was able to sink the ax into the bear's skull, but that didn't stop the grizzly. Instead, the bear knocked him down and continued attacking.

The bear eventually stopped its attack and left, but only for a short time, after which it charged a second time. It finally left for good. Covertson, with severe injuries, struggled through more than a mile of thick brush and waded the icy water of the Chulitna River to reach the Parks Highway. There, he got the attention of the first passing motorist, who drove him to a nearby lodge. From there a military helicopter flew him to Fairbanks, where he underwent more than nine hours of surgery and needed 1,500 to 2,000 stitches to repair the damage done mostly to his head and neck.

As warning, Covertson said, "Never go into the woods by yourself. . . . Never go without a large-caliber gun or a bear spray repellent." He also said he never thought this would happen to him.

New Oil Field on the North Slope

The nation's seventh-largest oil company, Arco Alaska Inc., announced on Aug. 4, 1989, the finding of a huge, new oil field on the North Slope. The new field may hold as many as 300 million barrels of crude and is one of the biggest American oil discoveries in a decade.

Called the Point McIntyre reservoir, the field is located offshore of Point McIntyre beneath the Beaufort Sea. Its location is just a couple of miles away from other major North Slope production facilities and roads, and the trans-Alaska Pipeline, which will make getting the oil out an easy proposition. Production of the new field could begin in the early 1990s.

Divers Look for War Relics

U.S. Navy divers began a successful search for World War II relics off the Aleutian island of Kiska in September 1989, and according to the National Park Service in Anchorage, they also go to Kiska and to Attu in the summer of 1990 to complete the search.

Located about 2,600 miles from Tokyo, and 1,150 miles from Anchorage, finds at Kiska and Attu are to be left where they are and nominated for National Historic Landmark status, thus receiving protection by federal law.

Kiska and Attu became strategically significant when Japanese troops occupied the islands in June of 1942 — the only U.S. soil held by foreign troops since the War of 1812. Found so far are a Japanese submarine, merchant ship and two submarine chasers; a ship that is known to have been sunk in 1942; two landing craft; one aircraft; and two areas with concentrations of debris yet to be checked. Research teams on shore are cataloging all war relics found, and the National Park Service will publish the results upon completion of the project.

Lost in the Wilderness for Three Weeks

Dennis Wilkins had never been lost before in his life, but three weeks after leaving his mine located behind Mount Susitna, he realized he was lost indeed.

It all started on Aug. 8, 1989, when he set out for Alexander Creek because he'd run out of supplies. He had hoped to hitch a ride from a passing fisherman, but when that didn't work out, Wilkins figured his only option was to hike to Alexander Creek. So without food and just the clothes he was wearing, he set off.

Friends suspected something was wrong when they flew over his mine and Wilkins didn't come out and wave — a signal that everything was OK. Nor did they see any signs of life at his cabin. Several days later, smoke was seen coming from the chimney of a cabin whose owner, Wayne Davis, was flying over to check it out.

The next morning, after hearing about Wilkins' disappearance, Davis returned and found Wilkins in his cabin, barely able to walk due to sore, blistered feet, but alive and well. At the time, Wilkins was 96 years old.

Federal Express Expands in Anchorage

Federal Express began a $10.5 million international package-sorting operation in Anchorage in October 1989, for parcels going to Europe and Asia.

Two major expansions at the Anchorage International Airport will help consolidate the increased operations that follow Federal Express's takeover of Flying Tiger. With the Flying Tiger buyout, the Memphis-based air freight company is accelerating its international expansion, doing in one year what it originally scheduled for over seven. The new complex is capable of sorting up to 1.6 million pounds of packages a day and employs more than 300 people.

Joint Search and Rescue Missions for U.S. and Soviet Union

A trip to Vladivostok, Nakhodka and Khabarovsk in the Soviet Far East by three members of the Juneau-based U.S. Coast Guard in October 1989 has moved the two countries closer to an agreement for joint search and rescue operations in the North Pacific.

The trip resulted in an exchange of information that will help in jointly responding to assistance calls, and conducting search and rescue operations in the Bering Sea. Differences between the two maritime systems were also discussed for the purpose of aiding search and rescue operations. While the Coast Guard operates as an arm of the U.S. Department of the Treasury, Soviet operations are run by a merchant fleet, as well as by the air force and navy.

Costa's Hummingbird Ends Up in Anchorage

For a bird that normally only travels as far north as Sacramento, California, a certain three-inch male Costa's hummingbird must have had a tale to tell when it got back home.

This little fellow, believed to be about a year old, spent the summer and early fall of 1989 feeding from fuchsias at a residence on the edge of Anchorage. Bird enthusiasts visited regularly, but as fall came on, the homeowners began to worry about the bird's chances of survival and called the U.S. Fish and Wildlife Service. An agent who had a seminar to attend in Washington, D.C., took the bird as far south as Seattle. From there the bird was on its own, hopefully making its way to Mexico, where it would normally winter.

How the bird got to Anchorage is anybody's guess, but a hummingbird specialist at the San Diego Zoo figures it may have been ushered north by a weather system.

Eielson Air Force Base Scores at "Gunsmoke 89"

Every two years, Air Force pilots from around the world go to Nellis Air Force Base in Nevada to test their skills and compete for the title of "Top Gun." This biennial event, called the "Gunsmoke" competition, brings together the best of the country's Air Force pilots and showcases their skills in such areas as bomb delivery, weaponry and aircraft maintenance.

Capt. Angus Simpson, from Eielson Air Force Base in Fairbanks, represented the Alaska Air Command in the 1989 competition and managed to leave with a new "Gunsmoke" record in the A-10 gunnery division. This event involves hitting a 25-foot square target that has a 4-foot bull's eye in the middle of it. Capt. Simpson set the "Gunsmoke" record with a perfect score, making 200 out of 200 possible shots in the target.

Life in the Last Frontier

Halloween took a beating in Kodiak in 1989, when a barge carrying pumpkins failed to arrive and kids ended up carving cabbages. But it wasn't just kids who got the short end of the stick.

Everyone had an unwelcome shopping reprieve because that same barge was carrying groceries to this Southwest community, and all of Kodiak was out of eggs, milk, meat and dairy products — along with pumpkins — until the barge got through.

Otter Pups Get New Home

Four sea otter pups, orphaned when their mothers died in the March 1989 oil spill, have found new homes at Shedd Aquarium in Chicago. Aged from seven to nine months, the otters will be the first of their species to live inland.

Since the otters were raised by humans, they lack the survival skills necessary to make it in the wild. Almost 1,000 otters and countless waterfowl and fish were killed when the *Exxon Valdez* tanker spilled 11 million gallons of oil into Prince William Sound.

The four pups, one male and three females, were flown to Chicago in November 1989, and will live in the new 50,000-gallon Sea Otter Habitat. The area features a pool and simulates a rocky Alaska coast.

Juneau Pair to Dine with Julia Child

Commercial fisherman Roy Smith of Juneau bid $5,500 and won the top prize in a benefit auction held in California in November 1989 for the American Institute of Food and Wine. The prize was a dinner for six prepared by world-reknowned chef Julia Child in either her California or her Massachusetts home. For Smith and his wife, both of whom have a penchant for fine food and wine, it was the thrill of a lifetime to win, and they anticipate watching Child at work and then dining with her.

Local Newspaper Sold

After 54 years as owner and publisher of the *Anchorage Times*, Bob Atwood announced the sale of the 75-year-old paper to Veco International, Inc., an Alaska-based oil service company.

The paper, under Atwood's leadership, championed the fight for Alaska statehood, and its editorial policy continually reflected its publisher's philosophy about Alaska's future. The Nov. 20, 1989, sale to Veco keeps ownership of the daily newspaper in Alaska. Anchorage remains one of fewer than a dozen communities nationwide supporting two separately owned daily papers. The *Anchorage Daily News* is owned by McClatchy Newspapers, Inc., of California.

Athabascan Fiddling Still Popular

The tradition of Athabascan fiddle playing goes back to the 1800s when Natives got their first fiddles and lessons from Canadian trappers. The trappers were followed by Irish and Scottish gold seekers who brought more fiddles and songs with them, and little by little, songs were learned or created, and passed down. Thankfully, this is one art that hasn't been lost to time, and an annual Athabascan Old-Time Fiddling Festival, with participants ranging in age from 10 years and up, is held each fall in Fairbanks to honor this longtime tradition.

Eagle and Salmon Numbers Down in Haines

Fewer bald eagles were roosting along the Chilkat River at Haines in the fall of 1989 because of a below-normal return of chum salmon. While the average number of eagles for the area is about 2,500, with as many as 4,000 wintering over, only 1,000 eagles were within view in the entire area. But despite fewer birds, there were still plenty to see and photograph, and tourism in Haines was going at its normal pace.

Alaska Gas Headed for Korea

South Korea's President Roh Tae Woo met with Gov. Steve Cowper in November 1989 to discuss exporting liquefied natural gas from the North Slope. A letter of intent to purchase 3 million tons of gas annually from Yukon-Pacific Corp. resulted from the meeting, and if the intent becomes a reality, Korea would be the major buyer of Alaska gas. Trade between Korea and Alaska now totals about $200 million a year with exports of coal, fish and timber.

Anchorage Pharmacist Honored

Anchorage pharmacist Eldon Ulmer was elected an honorary life member of the American Cancer Society's national board of directors in December 1989. He is the only Alaskan to be given this honor, and he joins the ranks of 79 doctors and celebrities who have been elected in previous years. An Anchorage resident since 1950, Ulmer has been involved with the American Cancer Society–Alaska Division and the Anchorage unit for more than 30 years.

Glasnost and Sausage Unite Soviets and Alaskan

Doug Drum, owner of Indian Valley Meats, never guessed that a visiting delegation from the Soviet Far East to his plant in September 1988 would result in a joint venture, but it did.

It all began when Soviets from the Magadan region asked to see Alaska food-processing technology and ended up thinking that a similar industry might work for them. So in May 1989, an Aeroflot cargo jet landed in Anchorage, loaded equipment and returned to Russia with Drum on board. In November, the new Soviet plant opened for inspection.

The Soviets were so impressed that they asked Drum to help them build more than a dozen other plants throughout the Soviet Far East and Siberia. Aside from the product, what also impressed the Soviets was the speed with which the plant opened and began production. Drum — the new hero of Soviet labor, who even made their national news — was told that in Russia it takes five years to do what Drum did in six months.

Reindeer Find New Homes in Ohio and Wisconsin

Eight domesticated reindeer from a ranch in Nome made their way to zoos in the Lower 48 in December 1989. The deer were purchased by the Medina County Zoological Gardens in Lodi, Ohio, and Blackhawk Ridge Zoo in Racine, Wisconsin, neither of which had reindeer. The timing was perfect, too — the reindeer arrived in time for Christmas, and according to the zoos, everybody was as excited as if Santa himself had come.

Bart Goes Big Time

One of Alaska's own has hit the

world of moviedom in a big way. "Bart," a 1,200-pound Kodiak brown bear, is the star of a $25 million movie that opened in 1989 across the country called, appropriately enough, *The Bear*.

Trained since he was a cub by Doug Seus of Utah's Wasatch Rocky Mountain Wildlife, Bart's film credentials include the television series "The Adventures of Grizzly Adams," and "White Fang," a movie based on a Jack London novel.

Weather Ups and Downs

Higher-than-usual temperatures in December 1989 didn't give residents of Anchorage a clue of what was to come in February. The springlike December warmth was due to several weather systems that moved into Alaska from the Central Pacific, and brought with them above-freezing temperatures. The warmth, rain and wind didn't break any records, and lasted about two weeks.

February 1990, on the other hand, did break the record for being the coldest February in Anchorage since 1915, and also went down as one of the snowiest. The average temperature was 3.7°F, more than 14 degrees colder than normal, and the lowest temperature of the month was –27°F on February 7, a new record. During the month, 23 inches of snow fell, making it the fifth snowiest February on record in Anchorage. The winter of 1989–90 was also the fifth snowiest on record for the city; total seasonal snowfall was 97.1 inches.

Anchorage Population on the Rise

Anchorage's population showed an increase of about 3,000 in December 1989, bringing the number of residents to 221,870, equivalent to the city's 1982 population. Since 1986, the city's population had been declining steadily from a high of 248,263 due to the statewide economic bust. The increased population, along with more jobs, is a good sign that the recession is easing up in Anchorage.

Census Costs High in Alaska

While most census questionnaires could be mailed out and mailed back, or at least mailed out and picked up, census takers in the Alaska bush were instructed to visit every house, homestead and cabin. Census takers covered their territory by plane, snowmobile and dogsled, beginning the second week of February 1990.

According to Leo Schilling, regional director for the U.S. Census Bureau in Seattle, the cost of taking the census in Alaska is higher than for any other state. Although transportation costs are high, other factors also raise the cost, such as the need for interpreters in some villages. As Schilling says, "[Alaska's] not budgeted like the rest of the country."

Power Outage Blackens State

From Kenai to Fairbanks, more than 100,000 homes and businesses were plunged into darkness when the largest electrical generating plant in Alaska shut down in late afternoon Dec. 11, 1989. Electricity was out in the area from less than one hour to more than five hours after the power plant's natural gas supply was interrupted. Because of warmer-than-usual December weather, no damage was caused by the outage. However, larger cities experienced snarled traffic as offices closed early and workers headed home without the help of traffic lights.

Alaska Salmon a Hit in Japan

Two Anchorage chefs, David Purvis and Michel Villon, traveled to Japan in December 1989 to demonstrate cooking Alaska salmon for the public. The five-day trip was sponsored by Hanakyu Oasis, a Japanese conglomerate.

Purvis, executive chef at the Sheraton Anchorage Hotel, and Villon, chairman of Chefs de Cuisine of Alaska, were invited to Japan after winning first and second place, respectively, in the Alaska Salmon Fair Seafood Cookoff, which took place in October in Anchorage. The demonstrations were such big news in Japan that one national and two local television stations covered some of the events. Besides salmon, which sells for twice the retail price in Japan that it does in Alaska, Villon and Purvis also brought along Alaska's Atakiska vodka, Chinook beer and even Alaska water.

Soviets Find Way To Use Their Rubles

Although it is illegal for Soviets to take rubles out of their country, it is not illegal for U.S. citizens to accept them. With that in mind, the Nome Chamber of Commerce is letting Soviets spend rubles they just happen to bring with them on goods and services in Nome, thus giving the nonconvertible ruble some value in the United States.

Most Soviets arrive in Alaska with $40 U.S. provided by their sponsoring organization in the U.S.S.R. While prohibited from taking rubles from home, many have done so and made black-market swaps for dollars with Nome residents planning trips to the Soviet Far East. Not all Nome businesses accept rubles, but the chamber is hoping the project will eventually lead to an official currency conversion. In the meantime, 3 rubles will buy a cab ride, and for anything else, all a Soviet visitor has to do is look for the "Rubles Accepted Here" sign.

265-Day Trek Ends in Kotzebue

Keith Nyitray, 31, left Fort McPherson in Canada's Northwest Territories in the spring of 1989 and ended up in Kotzebue in January 1990. He traveled through some of Alaska's harshest terrain without a tent or stove, and resupplied at villages often hundreds of miles apart. His only companion for the trip was Smoke, a wolf-shepherd-husky mix that packed 40 pounds of supplies while Nyitray carried up to 120 pounds.

Nyitray covered 1,450 miles on foot, 300 miles by dogsled and more than 100 miles by canoe. He crossed 30 mountain passes of more than 4,000 feet and encountered 11 grizzly bears. He lived off the land, supplementing the rice, tea and oatmeal he carried with grayling, ptarmigan, roots and berries. But the real treasure of the trip was achieving a sense of being "part of the land."

McDonald's Takes Homer to the Super Bowl

The nation got a look at Homer, Alaska, when McDonald's aired a series of ads during the 1990 Super Bowl. Filmed on location and using all local residents, the ads not only showed off Homer, but also just how much Homerites are into the game. Homer was pretty excited about doing the commercials, and the McDonald's film crew enjoyed Homer so much, they decided to stay an extra day just to see the sights.

Butcher Wins 1990 John Beargrease Sled Dog Marathon

Eight Alaskan huskies led Iditarod champ Susan Butcher of Manley to a record win in the January 1990 Beargrease race. The 475-mile round-trip course between Duluth and Grand Portage was run in 87 hours and 15 minutes, beating Alaskan Dee Dee Jonrowe's year-old record by 10 hours and 10 minutes. Second and third place finishes also went to Alaskans: Vern Halter of Trapper Creek and Jonrowe of Willow, respectively.

This Minnesota-based race, the best-known and most highly publicized long-distance event in the Lower 48, has a good-sized purse and draws big names in mushing circles. Total purse for this race was $50,000, out of which Butcher received $12,000. Butcher also came away with the distinction of holding the record for every major race she's entered.

Inupiat Tradition Revived

Inupiat Eskimos on Alaska's North Slope met in Barrow in January 1990 to revive the *Kivgig*, or Messenger Feast, a festival that has not taken place for 75 years. The *Kivgig* occurred during very productive hunting years, when the *umialik* (leader) of a North Slope village invited the *umialik* of another community to attend a festival. It was one of just a few times when far-flung northern communities came together. The revival of the *Kivgig* is seen as part of a larger cultural pride movement among Alaska Natives, and a way to preserve Inupiat values.

Soviets Honor Alaska Woman

Dixie Belcher, 49, of Juneau, was recognized by the Soviet Peace Committee for her work in opening the Bering Strait to travel between the Soviet Far East and Alaska. Also sharing in the honor were Soviet Foreign Ministry spokesman Gennadi Gerasimov, and executive director Gennadi Alferenko of the Moscow-based Foundation for Social Innovation. The ceremony took place in Moscow in January 1990.

Bears One, Biologists Zero

The garbage-raiding black bears of Juneau are one up on the Alaska Department of Fish and Game biologists in the ongoing contest of wills over garbage cans. Open garbage cans attract the bears and cause persistent problems in the community.

Seems the biologists thought they could solve the problem by spiking peanut butter with a distasteful, though harmless, chemical, then put the bait in garbage cans splashed with Pine Sol. It was hoped that this would train the bears to avoid anything that smelled of pine-scented cleaner. Not that easy, it appears. The bears ate the peanut butter and got indigestion like they were supposed to, but learned only to steer clear of peanut butter, not the smell of pine cleaner.

The biologists vow to try again, but are now wondering if it might be easier to recondition humans and their behavior, and get them to enclose their garbage. It's better than the final alternative — killing bears because they've become a nuisance.

Trapper Lost for 11 Days

Bob Allen, a 37-year-old Athabascan from Arctic Village, spent 11 days lost in the Brooks Range when he went to check a trapline about 70 miles south of his village. A trapper for three years, Allen set out on Jan. 13, 1990, on a snowmachine carrying two sleeping bags, snowshoes, a rifle, a compass and three cans of gasoline. He had food stashed at his base camp tent, and it was –30°F.

Within hours of his departure, he found himself in a whiteout and totally lost. He tried to return home, but traveled east instead of north, and seven days and 40 miles later he ran out of gasoline. With the temperature at –45°F, he melted snow for water, ate spruce pitch and lost 22 pounds. Residents of Arctic Village found him five days later. The only injury he sustained was a frostbitten finger.

Windshield Wipers Ripped Off in Kenai

Seems as though windshield wipers and car molding are the only things of interest to certain vandals in Kenai. Peculiar items to steal, unless the thief is a raven — the big, black bird that delights in pulling on stretchy or floppy things. But this thieving phase should pass. Apparently, a few years ago ravens were flying away with gas caps when people took them off to pump gas — something they don't do any longer.

Arctic Walker Nearing End of Epic Journey

Thirteen years ago, George Meegan began "Expedition Last Crossing" with the goal of being the only man to walk across the Western Hemisphere. His journey had historic as well as personal significance because it marked the end of an era of exploration: all seven continents have been crossed point to point by humans on foot. He ended his journey at Prudhoe Bay in 1983, seven years after leaving Ushuaia, Argentina.

Meegan, 37, was back in Alaska in January 1990 to work out the finishing touches on his original trip by planning a walk from Prudhoe Bay to Nuiqsut in the spring. In 1991, he plans to officially end his journey by walking from Nuiqsut to Point Barrow; each trip is over 200 miles.

Sea Lions Dwindling

A sharp decline in the number of Steller sea lions in Alaska may result in putting the animal on the federal endangered species list. The population in a core area, centered off Alaska from the Kenai Peninsula west to the eastern Aleutian Islands, declined from 150,000 sea lions during the 1950s and 1960s to 68,000 in the mid-1980s. And according to a full-scale population count done in 1989, only 25,000 of these animals are left in the area extending from California to the Aleutians and along the Soviet coastline.

Though the decline remains unexplained, the Alaska Dept. of Fish and Game suspects the cause may be connected to commercial fishing. In hopes of finding out what is killing the sea lions, a new federal program requiring trained marine mammal observers on North Pacific fishing vessels will be instigated.

Japanese Network Broadcasts from Fairbanks

Network television engineers from Japan were in Fairbanks in February 1990 to film a series of programs about the state for live broadcast back to Japan. They brought more than a ton of equipment with them to film the prime-time programs, which feature the northern lights and a Japanese man's unfinished home on Chena Ridge. Plans also call for a two-hour special to be filmed for airing on New Year's Day 1991, and a series of segments to be shown on two news magazine programs. According to Kenzo Hashimoto, news producer, the news magazine programs are a combination of straight news, "Good Morning America" and Ted Koppel's "Nightline."

Seward Chosen as Physician Training Site

Seward General Hospital has been selected as a rural physician training site by the University of Washington School of Medicine. The program offers small communities hope that by giving senior medical students exposure to a small Alaska town, some will be encouraged to return after completing their studies and ease the chronic shortage of rural doctors.

Dean Osmar Takes Montana Race

Dean Osmar of Clam Gulch won the 500-mile Montana Race to the Sky sled dog race. Osmar, 43, earned $5,500 and ended the race with 10 dogs, after starting out with 18. Total race time was 120 hours, 9 minutes, breaking the previous record by roughly 10 hours. Osmar became the first Alaska musher to win both this and the Iditarod Sled Dog Race.

Tommy Moe Wins Giant Slalom Title

Alaska athletes made the news again when Palmer's Tommy Moe, 20, won the giant slalom at the U.S. Alpine Ski Championships in Crested Butte, Colorado, on Feb. 22, 1990. Moe, no stranger to winning, has brought home gold and silver medals from competitions at the World Junior Championships, and he was the highest U.S. finisher in the men's downhill at the 1989 World Championships in Vail, Colorado. Moe specializes in the downhill, super-G and giant slalom events.

Anchorage Soccer Goes Soviet

Little did Milo Mujagic think that anything would come from his conversation with some visiting Soviets about soccer, but a formal invitation to participate in a tournament arrived in February 1990. The conversation took place the year before in Mujagic's jewelry store after the Soviet delegation spotted a soccer poster. Enthusiasts all, their talk quickly went from capitalism and free enterprise to sports, followed by the idea of a sports exchange.

According to plans made, a junior team from the Soviet Union was to play in Anchorage in June 1990, and a college-age team from Anchorage was to travel to the U.S.S.R. one month later. The only expense for the Anchorage team was to be airfare to Providenya in the Soviet Far East. From there all expenses would be paid for by the Soviet government — air fare to Moscow, housing and food. Though it wasn't brought up, Mujagic hoped to round out the exchange with an adult team from Anchorage playing the Soviets.

Third Straight Win for Linda Leonard

Linda Leonard of North Pole won her third straight Women's World Championship Sled Dog Race in February 1990. Her total time was 1 hour, 42 minutes and 51 seconds. By taking the title in 1990, she became the fourth musher to win the women's title for three consecutive years and the third musher to become a four-time winner of the race. Her winnings were $2,000 out of a $10,000 purse.

Ice Carving Competition

Anchorage held its first International Ice Carving Competition in March 1990. Eleven teams of two, using chain saws to rough-cut huge blocks of ice, participated in the event, which featured entrants from China, France, Australia, Japan and the United

States. First place and the People's Choice award went to the team of Kazu Ogino and Frank Sullivan of Los Angeles for their carving of traditional Chinese figures. Winners were selected by judges and 700 ballots turned in by spectators.

Alaska Troops Head to Middle East

A 549-troop task force left Fort Richardson, in Anchorage, for a six-month peacekeeping mission in the Middle East. The battalion, from the 6th Infantry Division (Light), is the first from Alaska to participate in the multinational peacekeeping force. Its job is to observe and report any treaty violations, but the battalion is not to engage in combat. The troops, due home in October 1990, relieved a battalion from Fort Bragg, North Carolina.

U.S./Soviet Sled Dog Race

Officially named Alaska–Chukotka Great Race, this will be one sled dog race sure to capture the attention of mushers worldwide. Scheduled for 1991, the route is from Nome to Wales, across the Bering Strait to Uelen and ending 1,000 miles away at Anadyr in the Soviet Far East. The race is invitational and will pit the best 25 to 30 mushers in the world against one another.

Two ad hoc committees, one in the Soviet Union and one in Alaska, have been formed to solve major logistical problems, such as how to get 25 to 30 dog teams and mushers over the strait. Mushing across is out of the question, as the ice is too unstable no matter what the time of year. Though mushing isn't nearly as popular in Russia as it is in Alaska, at least two Soviet mushers will enter the race, according to Victor Orlov, a Soviet promoter of the race.

Drive-in Theater
Has Snowbank Screen

If you can't beat 'em, you might as well make the best of the situation, which is exactly what Valdez did. As part of their 1990 Winter Carnival, which coincided with passing the 500-inch mark for snowfall, the movie *Back to the Beach* was shown in the parking lot of the Civic Center with a

snowbank for a screen. Seems the roof of the center had to be cleared, which left a huge pile of snow at one end of the building's parking lot. A city snowblower carved the snow into a screen 20 feet high and 18 feet wide, from which the movie was viewed. Valdez residents aren't sure if theirs was the farthest-north drive-in, but they're pretty sure it was the first movie to be shown on a snowbank.

Movie Shot in Alaska

The Scena Group, an Italian film company, was in Anchorage in April 1990 to film scenes for *The Great Hunter*, due for international release in 1992. During the month of May the company also filmed scenes in Barrow, where they built igloos and simulated the crash of a DC-3 plane. About a dozen extras from Anchorage appeared in the film, in addition to extras from Barrow.

Junior High School Wins Award

Clark Junior High School was notified in April 1990 that it had received the 1989 American Scholastic Press Association award for school newspapers. The paper, begun four years ago by teacher Dennis Stovall, is written and produced by the students, and covers not only school news and activities, but also current local and national events.

Susan Butcher and Lead Dog Granite
Go to Washington, D.C.

At the invitation of President Bush, four-time Iditarod champion Susan Butcher and her prized lead dog, Granite, went to Washington, D.C., in April 1990. Bush welcomed and congratulated Butcher on her latest win at a special commendation ceremony at the White House. While Butcher shook hands with the president, Granite went nose-to-nose with Millie, the first dog, in the Rose Garden.

20-Minute Herring Season

More than 100 fishing boats were in Tatitlek Narrows in Prince William Sound on April 12, 1990, for the 20-minute herring season. The season's total catch was estimated at 6,900 tons, with an average catch of 67 to 69 tons per boat, and an income of $50,000 or more per crew. Roe from the herring is sold principally to the Orient, where it is an expensive delicacy.

Native Food Store Sells Delicacies

Spiro George, owner of George's Meat Market and Native Foods in Anchorage, has been supplying the local Native community with the foods they love most for more than 30 years. The products run the gamut from dried fish to seal and whale oil, seal blubber, frozen tomcod, reindeer meat and Native-smoked salmon, and keep 12,000 Alaska Natives in Anchorage feeling a little closer to their villages. In talking about the logistics of a business unlike any other in town, George recommends shipping seal oil in plastic bottles. Airlines are reluctant to carry the strong-smelling oil, especially in breakable containers.

Winter Hard on Moose

As the deep snow north of Anchorage began to melt in early spring 1990, the grim tally of just how hard the winter had been on Alaska's moose became clear. Official estimates showed 4,600 moose died of starvation or from being hit by highway and railroad vehicles in the Susitna Drainage area. That's a loss of 38 percent of the total population, according to Fish and Game biologist Carl Grauvogel.

Snow depth was the primary factor behind the deaths. Annual snowfall in the winter of 1989–90 was twice what it had been in previous years. Deep snow can keep moose from reaching the willow, birch and aspen they need to survive. It also forces them to walk on trails, roads and railroad tracks where contact with humans is more likely. Fish and Game officials hope that a shortened hunting season and improvement of moose habitat will restore the population in a few years.

Martech USA To Help Soviets Clean Up

Martech USA Inc. has signed a letter of intent with the Democratic Government of Czechoslovakia to clean up evacuated Soviet bases and other environmentally sensitive areas. Martech, an Anchorage-based company specializing in environmental remediation, began work April 25, 1990, in Frenstat, Czechoslovakia. The country has more than 165 Soviet bases and other contaminated sites that need to be cleaned after the areas are evacuated and given military clearance.

Martech participated in the California oil spill cleanup off Huntington Beach and also took part in cleanup efforts in Prince William Sound after the *Exxon Valdez* spill.

Fossil Find Millions of Years Old

A large fossil skull of a vertebrate found in early May 1990 may be 60 million years old, give or take 20 million years, according to geologists. The skull has nasal passages and two rows of teeth, which strongly suggests it once belonged to a reptile at least 3 feet long. There are also several pieces of what appear to be limb bones, but it's not known if the remains are from a land- or water-dwelling creature. Located on homestead land in the foothills of the the Talkeetna Mountains near Chickaloon, the site will be methodically studied by archaeologists.

Surprise Weather in May

The Siberian Express roared through Anchorage on May 20, 1990, bringing snow, sleet and a rare thunderstorm into town. The odd weather, caused by a cold front commonly referred to as the Siberian Express, came across the Bering Strait from the Soviet Union and traveled over much of southcentral Alaska. According to the National Weather Service, 2 to 3 inches of snow fell in some areas of Anchorage. Although snow in May in Anchorage is not unusual, thunder and lightning are, and the last time Anchorage experienced either was in 1988.

Alaska Airlines May Fly to U.S.S.R.

Alaska Airlines could be flying tourists into the Soviet cities of Magadan and Khabarovsk as early as May 1991, if details can be worked out by both sides. The agreement reached by American and Soviet negotiators would allow Alaska Airlines to fly two to three round-trip flights weekly during the summer months. Also, under the terms of the tentative agreement, the Soviet airline Aeroflot would serve as a booking agent for Soviet passengers wishing to fly on the Alaska flights. This would allow the ruble to be used by some Soviet passengers to purchase tickets, and for the Soviet government to act as middleman for the two airlines. Fares for the flights have not been worked out, but Alaska expects to sell tickets mostly to tourists, with business travel becoming more frequent later.

Parrot Banned from Boat

Birdface, the parrot of Skagway, was the prime suspect in a fire investigation on board his owner's fishing boat. Birdface has a habit of moving things around the cabin of the boat, and apparently deposited some old rags on the stove, according to his owner, Rich Burroughs. Two utility employees checking an electric meter on a nearby boat at the Skagway small-boat harbor smelled the smoke and were able to put out the fire before it seriously damaged the boat. Birdface was unharmed, but his seafaring days are over. Said Burroughs, "He's not going to be allowed on the boat anymore."

Pilot To Fly Floatplane Around the World

Seaplane enthusiast Tom Casey of Everett, Washington, was in Anchorage in May 1990, on his second attempt to become the first pilot to fly around the world landing only on water. Casey, 53, expected to make 80 take-offs and landings on oceans, lakes and rivers on a route that goes from Seattle to Anchorage, across the U.S.S.R. through Moscow and Leningrad, over Scandinavia to London, northward to Iceland and Greenland, southward again to Maine, and then through the southern and midwestern U.S. If landing approval was not granted by the Soviet Union, Casey had planned a southerly route that would go from Anchorage to Japan, across Thailand, India and the Middle East, then to England. He planned to return to Seattle the day before the Goodwill Games opened on July 21.

Pioneer Explorers Make Donation to University of Alaska Fairbanks

Explorers Bradford and Barbara Washburn donated mementos from 50 years of exploring Alaska's Mount McKinley to the University of Alaska Fairbanks in May 1990. The material included 9,000 aerial photographs, thousands of photographs taken on the ground, about 100 homemade movies of Alaska adventures, and log books and diaries of climbs.

Bradford Washburn, 79, pioneered the West Buttress route on Mount McKinley, today the mountain's most popular route. He claims to be the first to have photographed the mountain from the air and the first to have landed a helicopter on its slopes. Barbara Washburn, 75, was the first woman to reach the mountain's summit. Together, the Washburns have spent 50 years mapping and exploring the world. Their most recent accomplishment, spearheading efforts to make a detailed map of Mount Everest, took eight years.

The Washburns have agreed to help the university plan a "McKinley Center" that would concentrate on mountain research and climbing in Alaska. The center may become part of the planned expansion of the University of Alaska Museum, and would highlight the rest of the mountains of the Alaska Range, the mountains of the northwest Yukon and the Wrangell–St. Elias area.

Train Derailment Causes Fuel Spill

An Alaska Railroad freight train carrying 1.3 million gallons of jet and diesel fuel derailed 39 miles south of Fairbanks on May 28, 1990. The southbound train was pulling 68 tank cars from the Mapco refinery at North Pole to Anchorage. Each car carried 20,000 gallons of fuel, and about 100,000 gallons spilled from seven cars that ruptured when the train left the tracks at a siding switch. Only the damming action of a couple of beaver ponds spared one of the richest wetlands in North America from a toxic drenching by holding back the bulk of the petroleum long enough for railroad cleanup crews to set booms across the creek.

About 250 feet of main line, 800 feet of siding and one switch were totally destroyed. The wreck shut down the line north of Nenana for two days.

Passenger trains were canceled and tourists had to be bused between Denali National Park and Fairbanks.

Four-Masted Schooner Sails Alaska Waters

Wind Spirit, a 440-foot four-masted schooner, had its maiden season as an Alaska-bound cruise ship in the summer of 1990. The 148-passenger ship carried travelers on seven-day round-trip cruises between Prince Rupert, British Columbia, and Juneau. The cruise itinerary called for the *Wind Spirit* to venture into spectacular fjords en route to Alaska. No Alaska sailings are planned for 1991, according to Windstar Sail Cruises, a subsidiary of Seattle-based Holland America Line Westours, but cruises may resume in 1992.

Weather, Weather and More Weather

Valdez had the worst of it in the winter of 1989–1990. As far as snow goes, it set an all-time record at 537.2 inches and won the honor of being the snowiest town in North America. Streets became trenches, walled in by 10-foot snowbanks so strong that kids painted graffiti on them. Drifts reached halfway up second-floor windows, a snowbank was used as a drive-in theater screen and some homeowners gave up on using their ground-floor doors, climbing out windows and walking down the walls of snow instead. But in spite of all the snow, breakup didn't have Valdez residents worried. The city has a top-notch storm drain system that empties into Port Valdez and Prince William Sound. The city is built on porous rock that acts like a sieve, allowing the water to seep through to underground water systems.

Athletes also were thwarted by the weather. First there was the Iditaski, the 210-mile cross-country ski race that never got started. With temperatures pushing 40 degrees below zero, race officials decided it was too dangerous to run the complete course, so an abbreviated race was run instead. Then there was the Iditabike, the mountain-bike version of the Iditaski. It got started, but ended only 52 miles later when the cyclists were unable to ride on the deep, soft snow. Finally, there was the Iron Dog Gold Rush Classic.

The world's longest snowmachine race that goes 1,100 miles from Nome to Big Lake suffered numerous setbacks due to deep snow, trails that wouldn't stay open and temperatures reaching –50°F.

Kotzebue had its fair share of problems, too. Record low temperatures of –40°F and below froze nearly 700 people out of their homes when weather choked off water and sewer lines. Residents resorted to using honey buckets, hotel showers (with a four-page waiting list) and rationed water. Laundry cost $2 a load.

Not one to be left out, Anchorage had a few of its own record-breakers with 50 percent more snowfall than usual by mid-January 1990, and hazardous roads to match. On Feb. 12, 1990, a whiteout caused a 56-car pileup on the Glenn Highway, injuring 25; a 32-car and two-school bus accident near Eagle River; and another 24 accidents on a 12-mile stretch of the Glenn Highway. Five other school buses managed to get stuck in traffic because of accidents around town. Police were assisted by military police from Fort Richardson in removing the injured and in providing traffic control.

Summing up the winter of '89–'90 was Jackie Hanson of Chulitna, who said, "This winter has been a real son of a gun — I've never seen it this bad."

Mount Redoubt Trembles and Blows

For the first time since 1966, Mount Redoubt erupted sending steam and ash 35,000 feet into the air on Dec. 14, 1989. Located 110 miles southwest of Anchorage, Redoubt is the second most active of the six Cook Inlet volcanoes and capable of a Mount St. Helen–size eruption, according to the Alaska Volcano Observatory.

Redoubt's activity wasn't a complete surprise. On Dec. 13, 1989, the AVO's seismology lab in Anchorage picked up serious-looking action from the five seismographs set at various places on and around the mountain. Comparing the current readings to other eruption-level readings led the lab team to send out warnings that an eruption was imminent. Just twenty hours later, Redoubt blew.

The first eruption caused no problems, but on December 15, a KLM jet flew through a volcanic ash cloud and temporarily lost power in all four engines for eight minutes. The inside of the plane filled with smoke and fumes, and dropped 28,000 feet before the pilot could restart the aircraft. The plane landed safely at Anchorage International Airport about 30 minutes later, but thereafter all flights into and out of Anchorage were canceled for the day.

It wasn't the first time flights would be canceled. Throughout the month of December, and into January, Mount Redoubt disrupted air travel and left holiday travelers stranded. Ash fell over the Kenai Peninsula, and as far north as Talkeetna, following eruptions that spewed ash 40,000 feet into the air, and caused lava flows and electrical storms around the mountain.

Anchorage residents occasionally could see Redoubt erupting, but missed out on any ash fall until Feb. 28, 1990. Then, with the wind blowing just right, the ash cloud descended, turning the morning to instant dusk. Effects from the fallout lasted several hours and left a thick gray-brown covering of dirt everywhere.

Mount Redoubt continued to erupt into June, though not with the fury or frequency of its first three months of activity. In June, higher-than-normal levels of activity were still being picked up by the Volcano Observatory. Word from the seismology lab says that Redoubt has the potential to continue erupting for quite some time, possibly years.

Denali Park Road Controversy

Denali Park officials, concerned about the adverse impact of traffic on wildlife viewing in the park, since 1972 have restricted access to the road between park headquarters and Kantishna. Private vehicle traffic on the road is limited to registered campers (only as far as their campgrounds and only one round-trip) and to landowners around Kantishna. All other public travel is by shuttle bus or by chauffeured vehicles to the lodges.

For two months during the summer of 1990, the 88-mile route was open to recreational and private vehicles. This temporary lifting of the 18-year restriction barring most cars from the road

occurred when a new campground located on private land deep inside the park opened for business. The owners demanded that their customers be allowed to travel the service road to Kantishna, and the park complied because federal regulations governing private lands within the park guarantee access for owners and their customers.

Traffic congestion in Denali's wilderness did not materialize — only about a half-dozen cars a day sought access — but a lawsuit did. A superior court judge ruled that the camp's owners violated a property settlement agreement, forcing the camp to close and ending the owner's right to keep the road open.

Alaska Teen in Macy's Parade

For East Anchorage High School senior Jay Hassler, all those years of practicing his clarinet paid off when he got to march in the famous Macy's Thanksgiving Day Parade. Hassler marched in the McDonald's All-American High School Band, one of the nation's most prestigious bands, which includes some of the best musical students from around the country.

AlaskaMen on TV

ABC television producer Aaron Spelling has purchased the movie rights to *AlaskaMen* magazine with the aim of making a TV movie. The movie could also be used as a pilot for a weekly television series or for a series of movies. The idea for a movie came about after someone at ABC saw an issue of the magazine. The movie would be filmed in Alaska, and the concept involves women coming to Alaska to meet the men they have seen in the magazine.

Skagway Vacuums Lead Out of Gardens

Skagway began a unusual spring cleanup in April 1990, to remove lead from residential soil. High levels of lead were discovered in the soil in late 1988, a result of the town being a shipping port for lead and zinc ore. State health officials say the lead is not a health threat because in its raw form it is not as easily absorbed into the body as processed lead. The cleanup was expected to take a month.

End of the Trail®

The trademark name "End of the Trail®" belongs to *ALASKA*® magazine, which reports the passing of old-timers and prominent Alaskans in its monthly "End of the Trail" column. *ALASKA*® magazine has graciously given *FACTS ABOUT ALASKA: THE ALASKA ALMANAC*® permission to use the title and pick up listings from its column. To be eligible for listing, the deceased must have achieved pioneer status by living at least thirty years in the North, or have made a significant impact upon the northern scene.

AKERS, Josephine "Josie," 63, died April 10, 1990, in Anchorage. A lifelong Alaska resident, she was born in McGrath and grew up at the Holy Cross Mission. Survived by her sons, Charles, Tim and Blackie, all of Anchorage, Bill of Chuloonawick and Mike of Bethel; six grandchildren; and one great-grandchild.

ALEXIE, Walter "Eddie" Jr., 78, died Jan. 10, 1989, in Anchorage. A lifelong resident of Togiak, he spent his life as a commercial fisherman. Survived by his wife, Anna of Togiak; five daughters; and three sons.

ALLMAN, Ruth Coffin, 84, died Sept. 22, 1989, in Juneau. She came to Alaska in the early 1900s, and was raised by her uncle, James Wickersham, Alaska's first judge and first territorial delegate to Congress. She taught music and art in Juneau, and organized the first Southeast Alaska Music Festival. She wrote *Alaska Sourdough, the Real Stuff by a Real Alaskan,* conducted tours in Juneau's House of Wickersham and founded the Wickersham Society. She was named Juneau's Woman of the Year in 1961, and was an honorary member of the Eagle Clan of the Tlingit Indians.

ANDERSON, Lester Neal, 60, died April 1, 1990, in Anchorage. An Alaska resident since 1947, he lived throughout the state working for the Alaska Railroad, the Army Corps of Engineers and the Federal Aviation Administration. Survived by his wife, Clara Jeanne of Anchorage; daughter, Leslie of Anchorage; sons, Jeffrey of Colorado, and Christopher and Michael of Anchorage.

ARGETSINGER, Louise Henderson, 85, died March 8, 1989, in Anchorage. A resident of Juneau since 1950, she was appointed by Gov. William Egan to the first Alaska State Commission on the Status of Women. Survived by her daughter, Marianne Derr of Delaware, Ohio; and sons, David and Peter of Anchorage, and Donald of Kotzebue.

ARNOLD, Winton C., 86, died Dec. 28, 1989, in Anchorage. He came to Alaska in 1927, and was U.S. commissioner and probate judge for Hyder. He was a member of the Alaska Territorial Planning Council, and later served as director of the Alaska Bar Association, director of the Anchorage Chamber of Commerce and director of the Alaska State Chamber of Commerce. Survived by his wife, Vivien of Anchorage; daughter, Alice Calvert of New York; and son, Winton of Mercer Island, WA.

AYAGALRIA, James J., 83, died June 17, 1989, in Anchorage. A lifelong Alaskan, he was a commercial fisherman and subsistence hunter in Napakiak. Survived by his wife, Elena of Napakiak; four daughters; and five sons.

BAHOVEC, Fred, 100, died Dec. 31, 1989, in Sitka. He came to Alaska in 1912, and worked in a sawmill, fished for salmon and established a mink farm. He supported the Sitka Summer Music Festival, and several political and educational organizations. Survived by his wife, Clothilde of Sitka; daughters, Cecelia Hutchinson of Arlington, VA and Louise Sauer of Calumet City, IL; and son, Larry of Wrangell.

BECK, Larry Allan, 55, died March 20, 1990, in Medford, OR. A longtime resident of Anchorage, he was an entertainer and authority on Alaska. Known as the "Bard of Alaska," his one-man shows featured songs, Robert Service poems, and stories that combined Alaska history and folklore. In the summers, he performed daily for the tourists, and in the winter, toured in the Lower 48 and abroad. In 1972, he was appointed Alaska's Ambassador of Goodwill by Gov. Keith Miller. Survived by his sons, Glenn of Scottsdale, AZ and Brian of Beaverton, OR; and two grandchildren.

BENNETT, Betty, 76, died March 29, 1989, in La Paz, Mexico. A longtime Haines resident, she came to Alaska in 1952, and lived in Fairbanks for two years before moving to Haines, where she fished commercially with her husband each summer. Survived by her husband, Arnold of Haines.

BENTLEY, The Rev. John B., 93, died June 12, 1989, in Hampton, VA. The second bishop of the Episcopal Diocese of Alaska, he came to Alaska in 1930, and served Alaskans from Ketchikan to Point Hope. Survived by three nieces.

BERNARDY, Duane George, 55, died May 27, 1990, in Clarkston, WA. An Anchorage resident since 1952, he was actively involved with Fur Rendezvous for 30 years, and employed in the hotel and restaurant industry. Survived by his daughters, Bonnie of Anchorage and

Gwen of St. Paul, MN; sons, George of Anchorage and Russell of Hilo, HA; and three grandchildren.

BETTIS, William M., 68, died Sept. 9, 1989, in Fairbanks. He came to Alaska in 1948, working for the Alaska Railroad. He was cited for bravery, and received the Award of Valor from the U.S. Secretary of Transportation and a Carnegie Hero Award for entering a burning cabin to rescue an 83-year-old occupant in 1967. Survived by his wife, Lois of Roseburg, OR; and sons, Bill of Roseburg, Gary of Anchorage and Marty of Fairbanks.

BIRD, Thelma Lucia "Butch," 75, died May 23, 1989, in Ketchikan. She came to Ketchikan in 1939, and worked as a clerk at Stenfjord's Plaza Drug store. She was a past president of the Pioneers of Alaska. Survived by her brother.

BLATCHFORD, Mary W., 71, died June 17, in Anchorage. A lifelong Alaskan, she worked as a bookkeeper and enjoyed an Alaska Native subsistence lifestyle with her husband. Survived by her husband, Percy of Anchorage; and three sisters.

BOGI, Donald T., 75, died April 21, 1989 in Puyallup, WA. He came to Alaska in 1931, worked various jobs and retired from the Federal Aviation Administration. Survived by his sister.

BOTELHO, Emmett, 89, died Oct. 22, 1989, in Sitka. He was born in Dawson City, Yukon Territory, and moved to Juneau in 1914. He began police work in the 1930s, and was Juneau's police chief and later became one of the first Alaska Highway patrolmen when the patrol was created in 1941. He served as commander for two judicial districts and as chief of the civil section. Survived by his wife, Harriet of Juneau; daughters, Julie of Florida and Catherine of Juneau; and son, Bruce of Juneau.

BRIGGS, Glenn Gillen, 87, died May 10, 1990, in Anchorage. A resident of Eagle River since 1943, he built the community's first shopping center and was a pioneer in developing residential areas. He was a borough assemblyman and was named Alaska's Outstanding Republican Leader.

BROWN, Delores C. Roulier, 70, died April 14, 1990, in Atlanta, GA. A Bureau of Indian Affairs' Realty Specialist during the Alaska Native Settlement Claims Act, she traveled extensively in Alaska to inform and provide assistance to those eligible for land during the negotiations. Survived by her husband, David of Marietta, GA; three daughters; three sons; 10 grandchildren; and one great-grandchild.

BRUCE, T.L., 85, died Nov. 12, 1988, in Shady Cove, OR. An Alaska resident for more than 40 years, he worked as a placer miner in Chicken and later homesteaded in Anchorage.

BRYANT, Arthur Craig, 87, died Feb. 13, 1989, in Encinitas, CA. Born in Ketchikan, he was associated with Tongass Trading Co. and J.R. Heckman Co., and served with the Ketchikan Volunteer Fire Department. Survived by his wife, Edith of Carlsbad, CA.

BRYSON, George W., 71, died Oct. 22, 1989, in Seattle. Born in Juneau, he was a lifelong Alaska resident, and worked for the Civil Aeronautics Administration and the Federal Aviation Administration. Survived by his wife, Isabelle of Juneau; daughter, Bonnie of Mexico; and son, Hank of Juneau.

BURCH, Marian Sullivan, 72, died April 12, 1990, in Reedsport, OR. Born in Valdez, she also lived in Anchorage and Kennicott. Survived by her daughters, Luella Dodge of Reedsport and Carol Harper of Fallon, NV; four grandchildren; and seven great-grandchildren.

CAMPBELL, Camille O. Mackay, 76, died Nov. 9, 1989, in Anchorage. She came to Alaska in 1946, and managed several Anchorage hotels. Survived by her sons, Gene of Battleground, WA and Kenneth of Anchorage.

CARROL, Joe Jr., 39, died March 13, 1989, in Fort Yukon. A professional trapper, he ran one of the longest traplines in interior Alaska. Survived by his parents.

CHANCE, Winston Cash Jr., 39, died April 6, 1990, in Anchorage. An Anchorage resident since 1959, he was a local entrepreneur with various business and real estate interests, including the firm of Winnebago Sales and Service. Survived by his wife, Emi; daughter, Yvonne Gailey; and three grandchildren, all of Anchorage.

COLE, Capt. Cecil W. "Moe," 68, died Feb. 21 1989, in Seattle. Retired captain of the USMS *North Star III*, he began sailing for the Bureau of Indian Affairs in 1937, and operated supply ships to Native villages. He also played Santa Claus each Christmas for the children of coastal Alaska. Survived by his wife, Luella; and son, Robert, both of Seattle.

COLE, Theron J., 83, died July 11, 1989, in Carington, ND. He came to Alaska in 1942, and served as superintendent of the Sitka schools. Survived by his wife, Johanna of Carrington.

DAVIE, Leroy J., 78, died Oct. 8, 1989, in Deltona, FL. He came to Alaska in 1957, and worked for the Federal Communication Commission Sand Lake station in Anchorage. He was a consultant to the governor and helped the Alaska State Troopers set up the state's emergency medical service radio link. He initiated the ham radio checkpoints for the

Iditarod Trail Sled Dog Race and also furnished radio communications for Mount McKinley climbers. Survived by his wife, LaVonne of Deltona.

DECK, Melvin L., 71, died Aug. 31, 1989, in Seward. An Alaska resident since 1946, he completed a tour of combat duty in the Aleutian Islands during World War II, and was a retired union laborer and piledriver. Survived by his wife, Margaret of Seward; a daughter; and a son.

DECKER, Doris Evelyn Sawyer, 85, died May 15, 1990, in Anchorage. A longtime resident of Anchorage, she taught school for 35 years and was assistant professor of secretarial studies at Anchorage Community College. Survived by her sons, Charles of Anchorage and Roger of Leonardtown, MD; and six grandchildren.

DELKITTIE, Thurston Ignacious, 50, died May 20, 1990, in Anchorage. Born in Nondalton, he worked most of his life as a laborer and fisherman. Survived by his wife, Amelia of Anchorage; daughters, Yolanda of Anchorage and Amelia of Wasilla; and sons, Mark, Paul and John, all of Anchorage.

DEMIENTIEFF, Margaret, 87, died Feb., 1989, in Holy Cross. A lifelong Alaskan, she was born in Anvik and raised in Holy Cross, where she was honored for her work as a medical aide and midwife. Survived by four daughters and two sons.

DEVEAU, Frederick Rodney, 79, died July 18, 1989, in Loma Linda, CA. A 50-year resident, he came to Alaska in 1930, was a World War II veteran and operated the first floating king crab cannery in Kodiak. Survived by four daughters and five sons.

DeVIAENE, Ronald John, 60, died Oct. 26, 1989, in Anchorage. He came to Alaska in 1947, and worked for the Alaska Railroad. Survived by his wife, Sofia of Anchorage; and daughters, Christine Holden, Marie Curry and Beverly, all of Anchorage.

DeVRIES, John Sr., 71, died Dec. 13, 1988, in Palmer. He came to Alaska in 1945, teaching shop and auto mechanics in the Matanuska-Susitna School District. Survived by his wife, Jesse of Palmer.

DOW, Benzie Ola "Rusty," 94, died June 18, 1989, in Palmer. She came to Palmer in 1934, worked as a truck driver and later as an artist managing the art department at the Alaska State Fair. Survived by her husband, Russ of Palmer.

DUNN, Harold Joseph, 70, died April 25, 1990, in Palmer. A resident of Alaska for 44 years, he was a World War II veteran and very active in the Elks Club. Survived by many friends and brother Elks.

ECKHART, Dorothy Patricia, 68, died April 19, 1989, in Anchorage. She came to Alaska in 1943, graduated from the University of Alaska, and worked as a real estate agent and as a schoolteacher. Survived by her husband, John of Wasilla.

EDLUND, George Eric, 82, died July 2, 1989, in Palmer. A Matanuska Valley pioneer, he came to Alaska with his family in 1915, and went on to homestead in the Fairview Loop area of Knik. After serving with the U.S. Army during WWII, he went to work for the University of Alaska's Experimental Farm in Palmer. Survived by his daughter, Alice Blythe of Keyes, CA.

EDLUND, Mary Olive Cornelius, 91, died March 2, 1989, in Palmer. She came to Alaska with her parents in 1914, and the family homesteaded in the Matanuska Valley. She worked as a nurse at the original Valley Presbyterian Hospital. Survived by her two stepdaughters and two sons.

EIDEM, Zelda Mae, 82, died March 10, 1989, in Anchorage. She came to Alaska in 1944, working as a Fairbanks public school nurse and helping to organize the public hospital. Survived by her sons, Jerald of Anchorage and Richard of Houston.

ELIEFF, Hulda, 71, died Dec. 26, 1989, in Port Angeles, WA. She received a degree in business administration from the University of Alaska Fairbanks in 1939, and later became active in several organizations. Survived by her husband, Arnold of Sequim, WA; and six grandchildren.

ENGLISH, Jack P., 84, died Aug. 15, 1989, in Homer. He came to Alaska in 1922, and worked as a trapper in Snug Harbor. He was U.S. Commissioner of the Territory, and served as city manager and mayor of Seldovia. Survived by his son, Arthur of Anchorage.

ERICKSON, Arthur F., 100, died Sept. 26, 1989, in Seattle. He came to Alaska in 1911, and in 1914, went to work for the Kennecott Copper Mine. Later he worked for the Carrington Co. and became president in 1955. Survived by his wife, Judy of Seattle.

EVANSON, C. David, 69, died Sept. 27, 1989, in Palmer. A longtime Alaskan, he was with the National Weather Service in Juneau and Anchorage. After the 1964 earthquake, he developed the Evanson subdivision and University Park area of Anchorage. Survived by his wife, Clara of Anchorage; daughter, Janie of Portland, OR; and son, Ted of Anchorage.

EVELAND, Joe A., 68, died May 17, 1989, in Portland, OR. He came to Alaska in 1956, and worked for the state of Alaska. After retirement from the state, he served as executive director of the Bristol Bay Housing Authority. Survived by his wife, Peggy of Salem, OR.

EVERN, Frederick William "Bud," 60, died April 1, 1990, in Knik. A lifelong Alaskan born in Candle, he served in the Alaska Territorial Guard, and worked for the Federal Aviation Administration, the Public Health Service and Anchorage Telephone Utility. Survived by his wife, Ida of Anchorage; daughters, Ruth of Fairbanks and Nellie of Anchorage; and sons, Bucky of Knik, and Curt, Dale and Emery, all of Anchorage.

FAIRCHILD, Clifton Louie, 80, died June 20, 1989, in Fairbanks. A longtime Alaska bush pilot, he came to Alaska in 1946, and began flying out of Fort Yukon. Survived by his wife, Margaret of Fort Yukon.

FAIRWEATHER, Hilda Eva, 94, died June 26, 1989, in Anchorage. She came to Alaska in 1922, and settled in Seward in 1929, working as an accountant. Survived by her son, Wilfred of Monterey, CA.

FARR, Orin L., 80, died Sept. 22, 1988, in Kenai. A longtime Soldotna resident, he came to Alaska in 1941, and worked for the Army Transport Command, the Alaska Railroad, in construction and for the Federal Aviation Administration. Survived by his wife, Helen of Soldotna; daughter, Pauline Bennett of Redding, CA; and sons, Terry and Thomas, both of Anchorage.

FAWCETT, Alfred J., 81, died April 12, 1989, in Ketchikan. A lifelong Ketchikan resident, he spent 40 years as a musician, playing in Ketchikan, Fairbanks and Juneau. Survived by his daughter, Sharon Maraffio of Rifle, CO.

FELTON, Thomas J., 92, died Aug. 14, 1989, in Missoula, MT. He came to Kodiak in 1928, and in 1932, began homesteading there and raising beef cattle. Survived by three nieces and nine nephews.

FERRIER, Basil "Red," 77, died Sept. 2, 1989, in Anchorage. A 48-year Alaskan, he worked in construction, mining and as a commercial fisherman. He gained recognition when he rode out the seismic wave in Valdez during the 1964 earthquake. Survived by his wife, Marion of Valdez; three daughters; and one son.

FITZPATRICK, William Lawrence "Larry," 74, died Feb. 18, 1989, in Warrenton, OR. He came to Alaska in 1938, and worked for the U.S. Army Corps of Engineers in Sitka. Survived by his wife, Ruby of Warrenton.

FORBES, Vernon D., 84, died April 17, 1990, in Vista, CA. A longtime resident of Alaska, he was a leader in setting judicial policy in Alaska while serving as the first U.S. district judge in Fairbanks, an appointment made by President Eisenhower. He served in that position until the state assumed control of the courts, and he conducted the swearing-in ceremony for delegates to the State Constitutional Covention. He changed careers after statehood and went into banking until his retirement. Survived by his wife, Ruth of Vista, CA; and daughter, Cathy Jane Parisi of Dallas, TX.

FRANKSON, David O., 85, died Jan. 29, 1989, in Anchorage. Born in Point Hope, he was a veteran of the Alaska Territorial Guard, president of the tribal council, and postmaster in Point Hope and director of the reindeer herd. Survived by his wife, Dinah, and son, Ted, both of Point Hope.

FRATIES, Gail Roy, 61, died Aug. 30, 1989, in Bethel. He came to Alaska in 1967, working as the Juneau District Attorney and an Anchorage prosecutor before being named a Bethel Superior Court judge in 1986. Survived by his wife, Bernie of Bethel; and four daughters.

FULLER, Keith A., 74, died May 18, 1989, in Anchorage. He first came to Alaska in 1943 with the U.S. Army in the Aleutians. After the war he returned to the state, making Anchorage his home. Survived by his wife, Alice of Anchorage.

GARDNER, Robert Lee, 58, died March 27, 1990, in Fairbanks. A Native Alaskan born in Aniak, he was active in Native affairs in the Interior throughout his lifetime. Survived by his daughters, Tina Gardner and Leigha Tindall, both of Fairbanks, and Roberta Tindall of Santa Ana, CA.

GEORGE, Alleine Council, 84, died Dec. 2, 1989, in Sitka. She came to Juneau in 1931 as a teacher and later became an owner of the Baranof Hotel. She was vice president of Alaska (Coastal) Airlines and was on the board of directors for Alaska Airlines. Survived by her daughter, Carol Ann Zebold of Seattle.

GIBBONS, Margaret Hansford Lightfoot, 80, died Sept. 23, 1989, in Anchorage. She came to Kodiak in 1941, worked at the Bank of Kodiak and later owned a dress shop. Survived by her husband, John of Anchorage.

GLASS, Eva Caroline "Tiny," 83, died Oct. 12, 1989, in Juneau. She came to Juneau in 1924, working for the U.S. Forest Service. Survived by her daughter, Adrienne Cooley of Juneau.

GLOVER, Lottie Ruth, 70, died Jan. 1, 1989, in Sitka. A Native Alaskan born in Sitka, she was a Tlingit Eagle of the Tae Kwa Dee Bear Clan and a lifetime member of the Alaska Native Sisterhood in Hoonah. Survived by two daughters and three sons.

GOLEM, Robert Roland, 85, died May 22, 1990, in Anchorage. A 44-year Anchorage resident, he was retired from the Air Force and from Civil Service at Elmendorf Air Force Base. Survived by his daughter, Susan E. Klamer of Anchorage; son, Harrison of Dayton, OH; five grandchildren; and five great-grandchildren.

GORSUCH, Sarah "Sally" L., 80, died May

11, 1990, in Anchorage. An Alaska resident since 1942, she managed the Anchorage office of the Alaska Steamship Lines and later ran Anchorage Business College with her husband. Survived by her daughter-in-law, Ginger Gorsuch of Anchorage; and three grandchildren.

GRACE, Volney F., 83, died Nov. 12, 1989, in Anchorage. He was born in Fairbanks, and lived in Fairbanks, Circle, Fortymile, Tanana and Anchorage. He founded V.F. Grace Inc., was an active supporter of Catholic school education in Fairbanks and Anchorage, and of Alaska Pacific University. Survived by his brother.

GREENE, Catherine I., 66, died June 26, 1989, in Anchorage. Born in Kotzebue, she lived most of her life in the Kobuk region working as a nurse's aide. She was recognized by the NANA Regional Native Corp. Elders Council for her outstanding public service. Survived by three sons, Frank, Chuck and Leo, all of Kotzebue.

HALVERSON, Margaret Mae Curtis, 72, died Sept. 9, 1989, in Eagle River. She came to Alaska in 1954, and was a voter's registrar. Survived by her daughters, Roberta Reid of Eagle River, Diana Nentwich of Oak Harbor, WA, Margaret Sinnott of Anchorage, and Kathleen Stenberg of Fairbanks; and son, Peter of Chugiak.

HANSEN, Roy Louis Sr., 62, died June 6, 1989, in Anchorage. A lifelong Alaskan, he was born in Katalla and served in the Aleutians during World War II. Survived by 11 children.

HANSON, Esther Minerva, 84, died May 9, 1990, in Palmer. A resident of Alaska since 1938, she taught school in remote areas of Alaska, and loved teaching and adventure. Survived by many nieces and nephews.

HARPER, Arthur, 75, died April 19, 1989, in Fairbanks. A lifelong Alaskan born in Rampart, he was nephew of Walter Harper, the first man to reach the summit of Mount McKinley. Survived by his wife, Angela, daughter Joyce, and son Ronald, all of Fairbanks.

HARTIGAN, Helen, 84, died Feb. 9, 1989, in Sitka. She came to Alaska in 1955, and served as Southeast Alaska nursing supervisor and later worked with the Alaska Dept. of Health. Survived by two sisters and a brother.

HARVEY, Mary M., 73, died Sept. 19, 1989, in Anchorage. Born in Chignik, she taught school in Ketchikan, Metlakatla and Seward before moving to Anchorage and working for the Alaska Railroad. Survived by her daughters, Carlene Faithful and Julie Wahl, both of Anchorage.

HILL, Eugene B., 76, died Dec. 28, 1988, in Las Vegas, NV. A longtime Alaska resident, he worked on the Alaska Highway

in the early 1940s, and later on numerous construction projects. Survived by his wife, Cleo; and daughters, DeAnna Orris, Jackie Warne-Bower and Joni, all of Fairbanks.

HOLIC, Wanda Grade, 74, died Aug. 20, 1989, in Sitka. She came to Alaska in 1941, taught at Sheldon Jackson Mission School, Sheldon Jackson High School and College, and at the public schools. Survived by her daughters, Janet Sue Gavin of Wheaton, IL and Marjorie Anne Bonney of Sitka.

HOLM, Ernest Thorwald, 71, died Sept. 7, 1989, in Anchorage. He came to Alaska in 1939, and owned and operated J. Vic Brown & Sons Jewelry store in Fairbanks. Survived by his wife, Bertha of Anchorage; daughter, Jean Patrick of Mill Creek, WA; and son, Chris of Anchorage.

HOMER, Steve, 71, died Sept. 29, 1989, in Bellingham, WA. A longtime Alaska resident and World War II veteran, he helped convert a surplus Navy landing craft into the *Chilkoot*, one of the first ferries to serve southeastern Alaska.

HOPKINS, Leonard, 93, died Dec. 13, 1988, in Santa Barbara, CA. He came to Alaska in 1924, settling in Seward and later moving to Anchorage where he established a sporting goods store. Survived by his wife, Eleanore of Santa Barbara.

HORNING, Allan E., 82, died Oct. 24, 1989, in Vancouver, WA. He grew up in Alaska, and worked as a bush pilot for Star Airways and Alaska Airlines before joining the Civil Aeronautics Administration. Survived by his wife, Louise of Vancouver; and daughter, Susan Lowe of Portland, OR.

HUBLEY, William "Billy," 64, died April 24, 1989, in Kodiak. A lifelong Alaskan born in Unga, he spent most of his life as a commercial fisherman in Kodiak. Survived by his sister and two brothers.

HUSA, Andrew M., 87, died July 13, 1989, in Palmer. A native of Norway, he came to Anchorage in 1948, building homes in the Anchorage Rabbit Creek area. Survived by a daughter, Britt Ostby of Anchorage; and sons, Mel of Wasilla and Nils of Ocean Shores, WA.

IVANOFF, Karl Misha, 76, died March 21, 1989, in Anchorage. A lifelong Alaskan born in Shaktoolik, he was career Air Force serving in World War II and the Korean conflict. Survived by his sister and brother.

JACKSON, James Andrew, 45, died May 25, 1990, in Anchorage. Born in Juneau, he was proud of his Tlingit heritage and was a member of the Central Native Council in Anchorage. Survived by his mother and two brothers.

JACQUOT, Janice Jane, 55, died Nov. 22,

1988, in Salinas, CA. A retired school-teacher, she began teaching in Alaska in 1958 at Ladd Field, and also taught at Eielson and Elmendorf Air Force Bases. Survived by her husband, Lou of Anchorage.

JERNBERG, Patricia, 80, died March 18, 1989, in Seattle. She came to Alaska in 1933, and lived in Juneau until 1937, when she moved to Washington, D.C. to work for Alaska Delegate Anthony J. Dimond. She returned to Alaska in 1940, living in Sitka and Ketchikan. Survived by her husband, Robert of Kirkland, WA.

JOHNSON, Wallace R., 71, died Feb. 9, 1989, in Ketchikan. A lifelong Alaskan born in Klawock, he was a member of the Haida Nation, the Thunderbird Clan, Veterans of Foreign Wars and a lifetime member of the Alaska Native Brotherhood. Survived by his wife, Vesta of Ketchikan.

KAIAKOKONOK, The Rev. Hariton "Father Harry" Okwan, 82, died Aug. 16, 1989, in Anchorage. Born in Katmai, he was village leader of Perryville for 20 years and ordained a Russian Orthodox pastor in Sitka in 1971. Self-educated, he spoke seven languages, and at the age of 75 earned his student pilot license. Survived by his wife, Jennie of Perryville.

KARABELNIKOFF, William, 77, died June 27, 1989, in Fairbanks. A lifelong Alaskan, he worked as a federal employee at Ladd Field and Fort Wainwright. Survived by his wife, Hazel of Fairbanks.

KARTERMAN, Jack M., 80, died Sept. 15, 1989, in Seward. He came to Alaska in 1937, and worked in mining, for the Alaska Railroad and was a member of the Anchorage Transportation Commission. In 1978, he and his wife were king and queen regents for the Anchorage Fur Rendezvous. Survived by his wife, Edith of Anchorage; and sons, Jack and Don, both of Anchorage.

KATKUS, Henry, 69, died Feb. 27, 1989, in Wasilla. Born in Lithuania, he came to Alaska in 1948, where he homesteaded in Wasilla and worked for the Alaska Railroad. A WWII veteran, he was a 40-year member of the Veterans of Foreign Wars. Survived by his wife, Joan of Wasilla; daughters, Sue Williams and Jane, both of Anchorage, and Maggie Inman of Sitka; sons, Tom of Chugiak and John of Wasilla.

KELLY, Beryl, 83, died May 16, 1989, in Poulsbo, WA. An early Alaska pioneer, he came to the state in 1930, worked various mines until 1950, then moved to Fairbanks and went into business. Survived by his wife, Catherine of Poulsbo.

KESSINGER, Arlo Walter, 77, died Aug. 12, 1989, in Anchorage. He came to Alaska in 1944, and worked as a mechanic for McGee Airways, the Territorial Road Commission, the Alaska Railroad, as a gold miner and for the Federal Aviation Administration. Survived by his wife, Ester of Anchorage; and daughters, Laine Herrmann of Sterling, VA and Arla Butcher of Anchorage.

KINDGREN, Adena Eva, 72, died June 27, 1989, in Anchorage. A lifelong Alaskan, she was born in Lower Tonsina and moved to Anchorage in 1955. She was skilled in leather and beadwork, and supplied the Alaska Native Medical Center and other shops with her crafts Survived by her daughters, Arline Moberg-Jonassen of Fairfield, TX, and Karen Jones and Julie Jacobson of Anchorage; and a son, John of Mesa, AZ.

KNIGHT, Ruth Markham, 71, died Aug. 28, 1989, in Ketchikan. She came to Ketchikan in 1952, and worked for the U.S. Forest Service. Survived by her husband, Bud of Ketchikan; daughter, July Hilbert of Wasilla; and son, Chuck of Ketchikan.

KOROPP, Rebecca Ann, 34, died March 29, 1990, in Anchorage. A lifelong resident of Alaska, she was born in Fairbanks and later lived in Anchorage doing volunteer work. Survived by her parents, grandmother, three sisters and a brother.

KRAUSE, Thomas Simon, 91, died Jan. 10, 1989, in Anchorage. A retired trapper and commercial fisherman, he came to Alaska in the 1920s. He was a member of the Pioneers of Alaska.

KRISKA, Leo E. Sr., 57, died Dec. 4, 1989, in Fairbanks. A lifelong resident of Alaska, he was a fur trader, trapper, fisherman and owner of a trading post. Survived by his wife, Mary of Koyukuk; 12 children; and 28 grandchildren.

KRIST, James G., 85, died May 1, 1989, in Sitka. A pioneer commercial fisherman, he came to Alaska in 1929, and was co-founder of Pelican, a fishing community in southeast Alaska. Survived by his wife, Aline; and two sons, Gordon and Gary, all of Sitka.

LAWRENCE, Martha "Lois," 70, died May 16, 1989, in Redland, CA. She came to Alaska in the mid-1940s, settling in Homer where she and her husband owned an air charter and repair service. Survived by her daughter, Judy Gray of Forest Grove, OR.

LEONARD, Harry, 93, died Aug. 29, 1989, in Fairbanks. He came to Alaska in 1937, settling near Wiseman where he lived for 15 years mining gold. Survived by his half-sister and half-brother.

LIEBING, Aaron "Bud," 64, died April 2, 1989, in Palmer. He came to Alaska in 1941, worked at the Gold Cord and Independence gold mines at Hatcher Pass, and later opened a cabinet shop in Palmer. Survived by his wife, June of Palmer; daughters, Ruth Marchetti of Anchorage and Patricia Ricard of Spokane; and son, Michael of Palmer.

LINCK, Lee E. "Jack," 96, died Nov. 4, 1989, in Fairbanks. He came to Alaska in 1928, and worked for the Fairbanks Exploration Co., the Fairbanks North Star Borough School District and in 1967, was appointed the first resident manager of the Fairbanks Pioneer Home by Gov. Wally Hickel. Survived by his wife, Alaska of Fairbanks.

LLOYD, Clell John "Jack" Jr., 63, died March 23, 1989, in Sitka. He came to Alaska in 1956, where he worked first as a commercial fisherman, and later as manager and owner of several businesses. Survived by his father.

LOGAN, Ronald W., 65, died June 30, 1989, in Oceanside, CA. He came to Fairbanks in 1949, and later lived in Nenana, Big Delta, Fairbanks and Anchorage working for the Federal Aviation Administration. Survived by his wife of San Luis Rey, CA.

LOVEJOY, Keith, 67, died Sept. 29, 1989, in Caldwell, ID. He came to Alaska in 1947, homesteading in Wasilla and later operated a service station. He retired to Homer, where he served as a U.S. Coast Guard auxiliary captain and led several rescue missions. Survived by his wife, Maryalice of Caldwell; daughter, Sharon Kaspere of Nuacres, ID; and son, Keith of Wasilla.

LUCAS, Isabelo H. "Benny," 77, died Aug. 25, 1989, in Ketchikan. He came to Alaska from his native Philippines in 1942, and owned a restaurant in Petersburg before moving to Ketchikan where he worked as a warehouseman and caterer.

LYNN, John Edward, 80, died July 9, 1989, in Anchorage. He came to Alaska in 1934, and was one of the Centennial Bush Pilots who flew the Fortymile mail run. Survived by his wife, Jacqueline; and sons, John Jr. and Jay, all of Anchorage.

MARSH, Clarence E. "Gramps," 85, died Aug. 7, 1989, in Bethel. He came to Alaska in 1914, and his family pioneered farming in the Matanuska Valley. He later worked at mining, at a trading post, and at one time owned Marsh Air Services and the Marsh Roadhouse. Survived by his daughter, Mary Lou Madril of Eagle River.

MARSHALL, Jack R., 74, died Sept. 29, 1989, in Fairbanks. He came to Alaska in 1946, and worked as a gold miner and dredger. Survived by three sisters and one brother.

MARTIN, Donald P., 83, died Dec. 4, 1989, in Seattle. He settled in Sitka in 1927, was an engineer and also operated a mail and freight boat. Survived by his wife, Evelyn of Seattle; daughter, Helen of San Anto-

nio; and son, Frank of Sebastopol, CA.

McCARTNEY, Charles Edward, 54, died March 26, 1990, in Anchorage. An Anchorage resident for 35 years, he worked for the Army Corps of Engineers. Survived by his daughters, Kathryn of Dobbins, CA and Anita of Anchorage; son, Edward of Anchorage; and four grandchildren.

McCARTY, Billy, 85, died Sept. 1, 1989, in Fairbanks. A lifelong Alaskan born in Chena, he spent most of his life in the Ruby area. He was one of the dog mushers who took part in the 1925 serum run from Nenana to Nome and was recognized by President Reagan in 1985 for his part in the run. He worked as a fisherman, trapper, and for the Alaska Commercial Company. Survived by his daughters, Hazel Roverts and Eleanor Captain of Fairbanks, Clara Honea of Ruby, Regina Grant of Tanana, and Margaret Nollner of Galena; and sons, William, Allen, Morris and Patrick, all of Ruby.

McCLAIN, Christine M., 74, died July 12, 1989, in Anchorage. An Anchorage author, she began her journalism career after the 1941 bombing of Pearl Harbor when she went to work as a reporter for the Alaska Communication System of the Army Signal Corps. She moved to Anchorage in 1948, and became a charter member and past president of Alaska Press Women and the Alaska Press Club. Survived by her husband, Sam of Anchorage.

McLANE, Enid, 92, died Feb. 23, 1989, in Homer. A pioneer homesteader and schoolteacher, she came to Alaska in 1920, taught school and operated a fox farm with her husband. Survived by her daughters, Joan Lahndt of Kasilof and Jettie Van Sinderen of Bellingham, WA; and son, Stan of Chinulna.

MEEHAN, Viola Mabel, 83, died April 29, 1990, in Palmer. She came to Alaska in 1945, and was a member of the Women of the Moose and the Pioneers of Alaska. Survived by her daughters, Carole Shelton of Anchorage, Betty Moore of Palmer and Gwendolyn Jensen of Fairbanks; sons, Virgil of Kenai, William of Seattle and Ronald of Fairbanks; 24 grandchildren; and 24 great-grandchildren.

MERRIL, Ralph D., 74, died May 17, 1989, in Stockton, CA. He came to Juneau in 1929, and worked in Sitka with the U.S. Army Corps of Engineers during WWII. Survived by his wife, Irene of Stockton.

MILLER, Albert Alfred, 75, died May 4, 1989, in Anchorage. A lifelong Alaskan born in Teller, he worked throughout the state as a heavy equipment operator. Survived by three daughters and a son.

MILOTTE, Alfred G. and Elma, 84 and 81 respectively, died within five days of each other in April 1989, in Seattle. The couple spent 30 years in and out of Alaska photographing and writing about wild animals. Before WWII they operated a photography studio in Ketchikan, followed by two years filming the route of the Alaska Highway. Walt Disney was inspired by their footage and the Milottes went on to win six Academy Awards for their Disney films, including *Seal Islands*, shot on St. Paul Island, and *The Alaska Eskimo*, filmed in Hooper Bay. Most recently, they were authors of the book *Toklat*, published in 1987.

MOATS, Ruth Ann, 89, died March 6, 1989, in Anchorage. She came to Alaska in 1941, where she worked in the restaurant business in Ketchikan, Cordova, Seward and Anchorage. She and her husband later operated Lake Louise Lodge. Survived by three grandsons.

MOORE, Ralph C., 75, died Jan. 18, 1990, in Chicago. Former Mayor of Palmer, he arrived in Alaska in 1935, settling in the valley and working various jobs until his retirement in 1976. He was an active member of the Loyal Order of Moose. Survived by his daughters, Mary James of Anchorage and Ruth Hodsdon of Palmer; six grandchildren; seven step-grandchildren; and 22 great-grandchildren.

MORRIS, Lawrence "Larry" W., 71, died Dec. 21, 1988, in Portland, OR. A lifelong Alaskan born in Olnes, he worked as an army engineer and for the Alaska Railroad. Survived by his wife, Irene of Portland.

MURPHY, Rika Florence, 69, died April 12, 1990, in Anchorge. Born in Kenai, she was a lifetime resident of the Kenai Peninsula and instrumental in the formation of the Alaska Federation of Natives. She was the first chief of the Kenaitze Indian Tribe and the first Chief of the Salamatof Native Association, for which she was granted honorary lifetime chief. Survived by her husband, Ray of Kenai; daughters, Virginia Hunter and Mary Ellen Israelson of Kenai; sons, Ralph Hunter of Kenai and Gene Hunter-Smagge of Anchorage; 12 grandchildren; and 16 great-grandchildren.

MURRAY, Margaret "Peggy," 75, died Dec. 31, 1989, in Douglas. A lifelong resident of Douglas, she worked for the federal government for 39 years. Survived by her husband, Don of Douglas.

NATKONG, Olive Anna, 72, died Sept. 7, 1989, in Saxman. Born in Waterfall, she spent most of her life in Ketchikan where she was a homemaker. She was a member of the Frog and Bullhead Clan under the Eagle of the Haida Nation. Survived by four daughters and eight sons.

NELSON, Pearl, 84, died July 2, 1989, in Anchorage. She came to Alaska from Finland in 1930, and worked as a hunting camp cook. She was a member of the Pioneers Auxiliary No. 4 and the Chugiak Senior Center.

NICOLIE, Katherine Suzy, 75, died May 22, 1990, in Anchorage. A lifelong Alaskan born in Talkeetna, she was a well-known Athabascan bead worker and slipper maker, and enjoyed sportfishing. Survived by her daughter, Alice Floyd; and son, Harold, both of Anchorage.

NORENE, Madeline E., 71, died June 6, 1989, in Grants Pass, OR. She came to Alaska in 1950, and with her husband, became owner and operator of 10th & M Lockers. Survived by her husband, Luther of Grants Pass.

NORENE, Vivian "Vee," 86, died Sept. 21, 1989, in Medford, OR. She came to Alaska in 1940, settling in Anchorage in 1941, where she opened Vee's Grocery in Mountain View in 1946. Survived by her daughter, Joan Anderson of Anchorage.

ODSATHER, Louis, 78, died Dec. 20, 1989, in Wasilla. He came to Alaska in 1935, and managed the Trading Post in Palmer and later owned a hotel and insurance company in Anchorage. He established the city's first self-service grocery story, and was a member of the Anchorage City Council, was on the board of the Alaska Rural Rehabilitation Corp. and on the Alaska Pioneer Home Advisory Board. Survived by his wife, Estelle of Wasilla; daughter, Kathy of Wasilla; and sons, Richard of Fairbanks and Kenneth of Anchorage.

ONEHA, Beth Marie, 81, died March 13, 1990, in Anchorage. A lifelong Alaskan, she was born in Douglas and taught school in Akiak and several other bush communities before settling in Anchorage. Survived by a niece, nephew and cousins.

O'NEIL, Dennis E., 72, died Nov. 10, 1989, in Roseburg, OR. He came to Anchorage in 1923, and worked as a locomotive engineer for the Alaska Railroad. Survived by his wife, Joy of Roseburg.

O'TOOLE, A. Dermott, 75, died Dec. 3, 1988, in Juneau. A longtime resident of Tenakee Springs, he came to Alaska in 1918, and worked on a fox farm, as a commercial fisherman, a business owner and as the Tenakee Springs postmaster. Survived by his wife, Dorothy; and daughter, Sharon, both of Juneau.

PAGE, Dorothy, 68, died Sept. 15, 1989, in Wasilla. Known as the "Mother of the Iditarod," she came to Alaska in 1961, and with Joe Redington Sr., organized a sled dog race up the historic Iditarod Trail in 1967 that laid the groundwork for the first full Iditarod Trail Sled Dog Race in 1973. She was chairman of the Wasilla-Knik Centennial Committee, a founder of the Aurora Dog Mushers Club, served on the Wasilla city council for 12 years and was the city's mayor in 1986. Survived by her husband, Von of Wasilla.

PANAMAROFF, George "Skeezix," 66, died Oct. 11, 1989, in Seattle. A lifelong Alaskan, he spent most of his life in Kodiak where he fished salmon and was a pioneer in the king crab fishery. He owned and operated a seine vessel, a cab service and worked with the city of Kodiak's public works department. Survived by his wife, Helen of Kodiak; and four children.

PARKER, Charles Harold, 79, died April 5, 1990, in Anchorage. An Alaska resident for more than 32 years, he worked as a carpenter in Dutch Harbor, Kodiak, Cold Bay, Cheniak and Anchorage. Survived by his wife, Constance of Anchorage; daughters, Beryl A. Lee of Spokane and Helen R. of Seattle; sons, Thomas F. of Seattle and Glen of Wasilla; 19 grandchildren; and 10 great-grandchildren.

PARSONS, Leroy Edward "Ed," 82, died May 5, 1989, in Fairbanks. The inventor of cable television, he came to Alaska in 1953, worked for Wien Alaska Airlines. In 1967, he brought television to Barrow when he installed the village's first closed circuit television system. Survived by two daughters and a son.

PENDER, Jane, 72, died July 21, 1989, in Fairbanks. She came to Fairbanks in 1957, and worked as a photojournalist and as an Alaska correspondent for United Press International. She also operated newspapers in Kotzebue and Delta Juncton, and wrote for some of the state's major newspapers, as well as papers in the Lower 48. Survived by her husband, Bill of Fairbanks.

PETE, Shem, 90, died July 2, 1989, in Anchorage. Born along the Susitna River, he was one of the last Tanaina Indians who still spoke the Dena'ina language. He spent much of his life in Tyonek where he helped revive the Native dance group. Survived by a son, Billy of Anchorage.

PETERSON, Mary H., 68, died March 11, 1989, in Anchorage. Born in Taku, she spent most of her life in Juneau and other Panhandle communities, commercial fishing with her husband for more than 30 years. Survived by her husband, Henry of Douglas; five daughters; and two sons.

PHILLIPS, Dr. Francis J., 84, died April 12, 1989, in Anchorage. A physician, he practiced medicine in Alaska for 38 years and

was an early leader in the nationwide battles against tuberculosis and polio. Survived by his daughters, Susan Cushing of Homer and Jane Beer of Sacramento, CA.

PIPPEL, Melva A., 89, died July 14, 1989, in Palmer. She arrived with her family in Palmer in 1935 as a member of the Matanuska Farm Colony. The family sold the farm in 1939, and later homesteaded in Eagle River, establishing the Pippel Farm. Survived by two daughters and four sons.

PLUM, C.L. "Les," 94, died April 3, 1989, in Seward. He came to Seward in 1929, and worked for the McKinley Park Tourist Co., the Alaska Railroad and the Anchorage water department. Survived by his son, Earl of Anchorage.

PLUMLEY, Lloyd Raymond "Fuzz," 60, died April 9, 1990, in Palmer. A 49-year resident of Alaska, he worked as a logger and owned Lil's Fabrics in Palmer. Survived by his father, George Henry; sons, Dale Plumley, Jack and Ron Hale, all of Wasilla, and Nick Hale of Centralia, WA; and eight grandchildren.

PONCHENE, Peter John, 60, died on July 31, 1989, in Kodiak. Born and raised in Kodiak, he worked as a commercial fisherman and laborer for the city. Survived by his wife, Susanne of Kodiak; daughters, Sandra of Kodiak and Andrea of Lacey, WA; and sons, Pete and Andrew of Kodiak.

POTTER, Charles H., 79, died April 11, 1989, in Seattle. A longtime Ketchikan resident, he arrived in 1936, and spent that winter building the Waterfall Cannery, which is now the Waterfall Resort, and later became the first full-time life insurance agent in Ketchikan. Survived by his wife, Dorothy of Ketchikan.

PRICE, Stan, 90, died Dec. 5, 1989, in Juneau. He came to Alaska in 1927, in a sailboat he'd built, and set up a mining and logging operation at Windham Bay. He later worked as a mechanic, fisherman and fox farmer. He was best known as the "Bear Man of Pack Creek" because he lived for 40 years along the shores of Pack Creek on northeast Admiralty Island in close quarters with about 25 bears. He never carried a gun, finding a smack on the nose with a stick sufficient discipline when needed. He was the subject of numerous films and televisions shows. Survived by his wife, Ester.

PUCKETT, Paul Emory, 75, died Dec. 12, 1989, in Anchorage. He came to Alaska in 1944 and homesteaded in the Kenai area. Survived by his two stepchildren.

RAMSTAD, George R., 74, died June 25, 1989, in Anchorage. He came to Alaska in 1935, worked in mining around the state and in construction in Anchorage. Survived by his four daughters.

REWOLINSKI, Ann Geibel, 73, died Feb. 15, 1989, in Anchorage. She came to Alaska in 1948 and worked for the Anchorage School District and the Alaska Railroad. Survived by her husband, John of Anchorage; and son, Chance of Nikiski.

RILEY, Carl, 70, died April 11, 1989, in Fresno, CA. An Alaska resident since 1957, he worked a number of jobs and as a welder on the trans-Alaska pipeline. Survived by his son, Carlos of Kodiak.

ROGERS, Edna, 79, died April 29, 1989, in Seattle. She came to Ketchikan in 1940 on her honeymoon and, except for a two-year absence, lived there ever since. Survived by her husband, Ralph of Ketchikan; and sons, Keith of Tacoma, R. Dale and Douglas of Ketchikan, and Bruce of Juneau.

RUSSELL, Mabel, 79, died Dec. 30, 1988, in Juneau. A longtime Juneau resident, she immigrated from Scotland to Juneau with her family in 1915. Survived by her daughter, Lorene Godkin; and son, Fred Schmitz, both of Juneau.

SCHIEWE, Warren Wesley, 68, died July 11, 1989, in Anchorage. He came to Alaska in 1952, worked for Sealand, Anchorage Cold Storage, Carr-Gottstein and as a teamster on the trans-Alaska pipeline. Survived by his daughter, Sharon Craven of Texas; and son, Howard of Huntington Beach, CA.

SCHRANTZ, Beatrice, 79, died July 2, 1989, in Anchorage. A longtime Anchorage resident, she came to Alaska in 1946 and worked for Pacific Northern Airlines and Western Airlines. Survived by two sisters.

SCHULTZ, John, 55, died May 27, 1990 in Anchorage. A lifelong Alaskan born in Valdez, he was a commercial and resident of Kodiak. Survived by two sisters and three brothers.

SEAGRAVE, Cathlia M., 75, died May 20, 1990, in Anchorage. A longtime Alaska resident, she worked as a cook in Valdez, and later with her husband, owned and operated several businesses in Kodiak and Valdez. Survived by her stepson, Gene of Valdez; and one grandchild.

SEMAKEN, Edith Mary, 62, died May 23, 1990, in Fairbanks. A lifelong resident of Alaska, she lived her entire life in Kaltag. Survived by her daughters, Victoria of Fairbanks, and Mary Dentler and Geraldine of Kaltag; sons, Harold of Galena, Anthony and George of Minto; and nine grandchildren.

SHADE, August Wilhelm, 35, died March 27, 1990, in Dillingham. A lifelong Alaskan born in Dillingham, he was a diesel mechanic, served on the board of Choggiung Ltd., and was past president of the Dillingham Dog Mushers' Club. Survived by his wife, Lynda; daughter,

Sherilyn; sons, Raymond and Wilhelm, all of Dillingham.

SHEARS, William J., 63, died Dec. 11, 1989, in Alliance, NE. A 40-year resident of Alaska, he taught at Eielson Air Force Base and in the Delta-Greely School District. He also helped develop the earliest smoke jumper units assigned in Alaska. Survived by one sister and three brothers.

SHELLABARGER, Annabelle "Belle," 91, died Nov. 21, 1989, in Anchorage. She came to Alaska in 1923, and moved to Skwentna in 1925, serving as postmistress to the village and enjoying a subsistence lifestyle. Survived by her son, Edwin of Honolulu; and four grandchildren.

SMITH, Alice A.S., 86, died May 23, 1990, in Palmer. An original Matanuska Valley colonist, she moved to Alaska in 1935, homesteading with her husband and five children. She lived in their original home until 1985. Survived by her daughter, Margaret Cabo of Palmer; sons, Charles of Homer and Jerry of Anchorage; 12 grandchildren; 30 great-grandchildren; and one great-great-grandchild.

SNEDDEN, C.W. "Bill," 76, died Aug. 6, 1989, in Fairbanks. Publisher of the *Fairbanks Daily News-Miner*, he came to Fairbanks in 1948 as a Scripps-Howard Newspapers official advisor for the failing Fairbanks newspaper. He purchased the paper two years later, and in the 1950s, was among the Alaska leaders who fought for statehood. In 1987, he was honored by the state Chamber of Commerce as Alaskan of the Year. Survived by his wife, Helen; and son, Skip, both of Fairbanks.

SOVOROFF, Sergie J., 87, died Sept. 27, 1989, in Anchorage. Born in Nikolski, he was a carver, linguist, authority for the Aleut-English Dictionary, and fluent in Russian and Japanese. In 1985, he was named Aleut of the Year by the Aleut Corp. Survived by his wife, Agnes of Nikolski.

SPECHT, Irene A., 75, died July 11, 1989, in Juneau. She came to Juneau in 1948, and worked as a shipping clerk at local food markets supplying families at lighthouse stations and logging camps throughout southeastern Alaska. Survived by her husband, Gene; and daughters Pat Costa and Barbara Lanz, all of Juneau.

STEVENS, Frances E., 78, died May 3, 1990, in Soldotna. She came to Alaska in 1946, and lived in the areas of Anchorage, Seward and Cooper Landing. Survived by her husband, Edwin F. of Cooper Landing; daughter, Donna Smith of Moose Pass; sons, Robert Onstott of Anchorage and Richard Onstott of Bothell, WA; 11 grandchildren; 18 great-grandchildren; and one great-great-grandchild.

STILES, Charles Clifton, 72, died April 21,

1990, in Oklahoma City, OK. He came to Wasilla in 1952, where he homesteaded and became a member of the Plumbers and Steamfitters Local 367. Survived by his wife, Alva of Oklahoma City; daughters, Charlotte Campbell of Oklahoma City, Melodie Starks of Alva, OK, Cheryl Snowden of Athol, ID and Marilee Quick of Anthony, KS; sons, Charles Gary of Athol, ID and Norm of Nome; 12 grandchildren; and two great-grandchildren.

STRAUB, Elmer Carl, 76, died April 30, 1989, in Anchorage. A 52-year-resident of Alaska, he spent most of that time in Nome in business and as a member of the Nome City Council. Survived by his wife, Mildred; a daughter, Claudia Doyle; and sons, Michael and Patric, all of Nome.

STUDDERT, Mary F. "Maisie," 90, died Dec. 4, 1989, in Fairbanks. A native of northern Ireland, she came to Alaska in 1934, settling in Fairbanks with her husband. Survived by her daughter, Kathleen Studdert Bronsvoort, and two grandchildren, all of Ireland.

SUNDBY, Marvene, 77, died Oct. 8, 1989, in Kenai. She came to Alaska in 1949, and lived in Seward, Soldotna and Kenai. In 1988, she received the Kenai Chamber of Commerce's Athena Award, an award honoring local businesswomen.

TAPLIN, Howard B., 70, died May 23, 1990, in Anchorage. A WWII veteran who served in Alaska, he homesteaded near Big Lake and started the Diamond-H Ranch in Anchorage. Survived by his wife, Dianna of Soldotna; daughters, Barbara Mills of Kenai and Susan Camp of Anchorage; sons, Shawn and Mark of Soldotna; and many grandchildren.

TASSELL, Harry, 78, died Oct. 5, 1989, in Anchorage. A lifelong Juneau resident, he worked in the Juneau Gold Mines during his youth, then manufactured ice cream for all of southeastern Alaska. Survived by his daughter, Mary Niesen of Juneau; and five grandchildren.

TATE, Flora A., 98, died Dec. 23, 1988, in Petersburg. A 76-year resident of Alaska, she came to the state in 1912, and ran a boarding house and cooked at the Petersburg Hospital. Survived by a daughter and two sons.

THEW, Mary Elizabeth, 64, died Nov. 24, 1989, in Anchorage. An Alaska resident since 1953, she worked as a bookkeeper at the *Anchorage Times* and at her husband's service station. She was active in local politics and in the mid-1980s, was named Alaska Republican Woman of the Year. Survived by her husband, Howard of Anchorage; and son, Kent of Fort Leavenworth, KS.

THORNTON, Florence E., 92, died Oct. 17, 1989, in Salem, OR. She moved to Alaska in 1921, and worked for 31 years in Ketchikan, Juneau and Fairbanks for the federal government. With her brother, Emery Tobin, she was cofounder of *The Alaska Sportsman* magazine, which later became *ALASKA®* magazine. She left Alaska in the mid-1950s, traveling extensively and working in 63 foreign countries. Survived by her niece, Doris Bordine of Eagle River.

TORWICK, Roy E., 81, died Feb. 25, 1989, in Petersburg. A resident of Alaska since 1907, he was a fisherman and partner in a grocery-hardware store in the 1940s, and later was a fish buyer and manager of Alaska Ice and Storage. Survived by his daughters, Camille Marifern and Lynda Fredricksen of Petersburg; and son, Roy Jr. of Sterling.

TOUT, Elias "Bud" Lavern, 76, died May 13, 1990, in Homer. He came to Alaska in 1939, and was one of the first 40 people to start construction of the Kodiak Naval Base. He later opened Anchorage Marina, designing and building boats for individuals and companies. Survived by his wife, Arneil of Homer; and son, Kenneth of Anchorage.

TOWNE, Shirley Wyman, 71, died March 24, 1990, in Palmer. A resident of Alaska since 1958, he was an auto body repairman and WWII veteran. Survived by his daughter, Donna; and grandson, Brian, both of Willow.

TROSETH, 71, died April 21, 1989, in Anchorage. An Alaska resident since 1951, he worked as a carpenter and pile driver. Survived by his wife, Rosanna of Wasilla; and sons, Roy Jr., Chris, Erik, Gordon, John and Arne, all of Wasilla; Robert Smith of Albuquerque; and Jerry Bossert and Ronnie of Seattle.

TROWER, Olive, 89, died July 17, 1989, in Sitka. She moved to Juneau in 1930, working with the Bureau of Indian Affairs. In 1966, she was presented by then-Interior Secretary Stuart Udall with the department's distinguished service award. Survived by two nieces and three cousins.

TURIAQ, Olga Mike Alvis, 36, died April 1, 1990, in St. Marys. Born in Chaneliak, she was a lifelong resident of Alaska and taught school in the village of St. Marys. Survived by her husband, John; daughter, Justina; and son Wayne.

URIE, Kathryn E., 64, died Dec. 14, 1989, in Scottsdale, AZ. Born in Anchorage, she lived most of her life in Alaska and with her husband, established Solly's Office in Kodiak. Survived by her daughter, Judy Fulp of Kodiak; and son, Tony of Seattle.

VEATCH, Harold, 84, died April 21, 1989, in Mesa, AZ. A Sitka resident since 1940, he was publisher of the *Sitka Sentinel* until

1969. Survived by his wife, Ernestine of Mesa; and a son, Harold of Peyton, CO.

VICTOR, Martin, 85, died Nov. 26, 1989, in Fairbanks. A longtime furrier he came to Alaska in 1929, and traveled around the state by dog team, and later by bush plane, buying furs. He was a third-generation furrier and owned a fur store in Fairbanks. Survived by his wife, Frances Marie of Fairbanks; daughter, Joyce Swarthout of Fairbanks; and sons, Dennis of Anchorage and Gerald of Fairbanks.

VREELAND, Willis "Bob" Robert, 84, died July 16, 1989, in Anchorage. He came to Alaska in 1923, working for the Alaska Railroad and was a bunkmate of artist Sydney Laurence. He later worked at mining, on the North Slope oil fields and as a commercial fisherman. Survived by his son, Richard Sr. of Fairbanks.

WAKEFIELD, Francoise de Ville, 86, died Oct. 25, 1989, in Winslow, WA. She came to Alaska at the age of nine months and lived in Katalla, Wrangell, Cordova and Anchorage. Survived by her daughters, Jackie Burgett of San Benito, TX and Sharon Sims of Anchorage; and sons, Bill Nettleton of Hansville, WA and Fred Handy of Anchorage.

WANSOR, Thomas B., 37, died May 20, 1990, near Sutton. A Sutton resident since 1961, he worked on the North Slope and enjoyed gardening. Survived by his daughters, Samantha and Tracy of Wasilla.

WATT, Howard H., 83, died in 1989, in Tigard, OR. A longtime Alaskan, he worked as a civil engineer for the Alaska State Highway Department. Survived by his wife, Ellen of Beaverton, OR.

WHALEN, Mary Ellen, 95, died March 2, 1989, in Valdez. She came to Valdez in 1903, and is credited with being the first woman to drive an automobile over Thompson Pass. Survived by her daughters, Frances Harris and Marie; and sons, George and John Bernard, all of Valdez.

WHITTERS, Raymond Henry, 84, died March 9, 1989, in Sequim, WA. He came to Alaska in 1940, where he worked as a gold miner in Candle, Caribou Creek, Nome Creek and Woodchopper. Survived by his wife, Geraldine of Sequim.

WILKINS, Warren M. "Red,", 82, died Sept. 11, 1989, in Sequim, WA. He came to Alaska in 1924, working around Ketchikan and Craig in fishing and construction. He was an airways station manager in Juneau and manager of the Anchorage International Airport. Survived by his wife, Doris of Sequim.

WILLIAMS, Joseph A., 93, died May 17, 1989, in Tacoma. He came to Whitehorse, Yukon Territory with his parents in 1900, then moved to Juneau in 1919, working

as an assayer and engineer for various mining companies. He was an authority on large-scale mining methods and wrote several technical articles on the subject. Survived by his wife, Nora of Tacoma; daughters, Irene Vanhala and Majorie Ross of Seattle; sons, Rodney of Tacoma and Donald of Seattle.

WILLIAMS, William Marcellis, 69, died April 18, 1990, in Anchorage. Born in Juneau, he was the grandson of Chief Billy Williams of the Taku River Tlingits, a World War II veteran and commercial fisherman. He was a member of the Alaska Native Brotherhood and the Tlingit-Haida Central Council. Survived by his wife, Marilyn of Anchorage; daughters, Anna Smith, Carmen and Gloria, all of Anchorage, and Marie of Los Angeles; son, Frank of Phoenix.

WILLMAN, Robert B., 84, died Sept. 15, 1988, in The Dalles, OR. A longtime pioneer and resident of Fairbanks, he worked for many years at Fort Wainwright. Survived by his wife, Savannah of The Dalles.

WILSON, Harry Howard, 83, died July 31, 1989, in Tidewater, OR. He came to Alaska in 1928, working on river boats out of Nenana and later with the Federal Aviation Administration. Survived by his wife, Nancy of Tidewater.

WITHEM, Elsie Myrtle, 68, died May 20, 1990, in Anchorage. An Alaska resident for 48 years, she was born in Ketchikan and enjoyed playing bingo. Survived by her daughters, Marilyn Massman, Janet Meade and Gina Aquino, all of Anchorage, and Lisa Demanttio of Colorado; sons, Leon and Eddie Ayson of Ketchikan, John Aquino of Seattle, and Frank and Robert Aquino of Portland, OR; 18 grandchildren; and three great-grandchildren.

WOODCOCK, William J., 64, died Feb. 24, 1989, in Sarasota, FL. He came to Alaska in 1955, operating several Fairbanks businesses and later was appointed to the Alcoholic Beverage Control Board. Survived by his wife, Mary of Sarasota; and daughters, Eva Boswell of New Jersey and Kathleen Brown of Fairbanks.

WRIGHT, Earl Wendell, 82, died Dec. 13, 1989, in Anchorage. A longtime resident of Anchorage, he was a civil service employee after his discharge from the Army in 1948 at Fort Richardson. Survived by his wife, Mildred; daughter, Florence; son, Harry, all of Anchorage.

YEISLEY, Claude B., 88, died Feb. 12, 1989, in Ketchikan. A longtime resident of Refuge Cove, he came to Alaska in the 1920s, and worked for the Civilian Conservation Corps. He helped build Refuge Cove State Park and Totem Bight State Park. Survived by two daughters and a son.

Alaska Northwest Library

Many North Country books are suggested as related reading throughout *FACTS ABOUT ALASKA: THE ALASKA ALMANAC®*. Following is our Alaska Northwest Library. These books are available in bookstores or direct from Alaska Northwest Books™, 22026 20th Ave. S.E., Bothell, WA 98041, or call toll free, 1-800-343-4567. Write for our free book catalog. Mail orders require a postage and handling fee of $1.50 fourth class or $3.50 first class per book.

Alaska Bear Tales, by Larry Kaniut. Encounters between bears and humans. 318 pp., $12.95 ($15.95 Canadian)

Alaska Blues: A Fisherman's Journal, by Joe Upton. True account of commercial fishing in southeastern Alaska waters with 198 black-and-white photos. 236 pp., hardbound, $14.95 ($18.95 Canadian)

The ALASKA JOURNAL®: A 1986 Collection. Limited Edition. Edited by Terrence Cole. History and arts of the North marking the 100th anniversary of the publication of Hubert How Bancroft's *History of Alaska 1730–1885.* 296 pp., hardbound, $24.95 ($31.70 Canadian)

Alaska Sourdough, by Ruth Allman. Handwritten recipes "by a real Alaskan." 190 pp., $9.95 ($12.95 Canadian)

Alaska Wild Berry Guide and Cookbook. How to find and identify edible wild berries, and how to cook them. Line drawings and color photos. 216 pp., $14.95 ($18.95 Canadian)

The ALASKA WILDERNESS MILEPOST®. Where the roads end, the real Alaska begins. A guide to 250 remote towns and villages. 480 pp., $14.95 ($18.95 Canadian)

The Alaskan Bird Sketches of Olaus Murie. With excerpts from his field notes, compiled and edited by Margaret E. Murie. 64 pp., $11.95 ($15.15 Canadian)

The Alaskan Camp Cook. Mouth-watering recipes for wild foods from the kitchens and campfires of Alaskan big game guides. 88 pp., $4.95 ($6.30 Canadian)

Alaskan Igloo Tales, by Edward L. Keithahan. Arctic oral history written down in the early 20th century, with illustrations. 139 pp., $12.95 ($15.95 Canadian)

Alaskan Mushroom Hunters Guide, by Ben Guild. Guidebook of 101 species of mushrooms found in Alaska, with illustrations and keys. 286 pp., $19.95 ($25.35 Canadian)

Alaska's Saltwater Fishes, by Doyne W. Kessler. A field guide designed for quick identification of 375 species of saltwater fishes. 358 pp., $19.95 ($25.35 Canadian)

Alaska's Wilderness Medicines, by Eleanor G. Viereck. Use of trees, flowers and shrubs for medicinal and other purposes. 111 pp., $9.95 ($12.95 Canadian)

The Alaska-Yukon Wild Flowers Guide. Large color photos and detailed drawings of 160 species. 218 pp., $16.95 ($20.95 Canadian)

Artists at Work: 25 Northwest Glassmakers, Ceramists and Jewelers, by Susan Biskeborn. Photographic portraits by Kim Zumwalt. This book examines the lives and art of these nationally recognized regional artists. Black-and-white photographs bring the reader close to the creative process by capturing the subjects in their work environments, and color photographs display the beauty of the art they produce. 220 pp., $24.95 ($29.95 Canadian)

Baidarka, by George Dyson. The history, development and redevelopment of the Aleut kayak. Illustrations and photographs. 212 pp., $19.95 ($24.95 Canadian)

Bits and Pieces of Alaskan History, Volume I, 1935–1959, 208 pp., and Volume II, 1960–1974, 216 pp. Outstanding overview of the times, including hundreds of nostalgic photographs. $14.95 each volume ($18.95 Canadian)

Building the Alaska Log Home, by Tom Walker. Comprehensive book for log home history and construction. 178 pp., $19.95 ($25.35 Canadian)

Capture of Attu. The Aleutian campaign of World War II. 80 pp., $6.95 ($8.85 Canadian)

Chilkoot Pass: The Most Famous Trail in the North, by Archie Satterfield. A guide for hikers and history buffs. 214 pp., $9.95 ($12.95 Canadian)

The Coast of British Columbia, by Rosemary Neering. Photographs by Bob Herger. Beautiful photographs reveal the scenic diversity of British Columbia's coastal region; insightful text explores its geological, natural and human history. 160 pp., $34.95 ($42.95 Canadian)

Cooking Alaskan, by Alaskans. Hundreds of time-tested recipes, including a section on sourdough. 500 pp., $16.95 ($20.95 Canadian)

Dale De Armond: A First Book Collection of Her Prints. Special color sampler featuring 63 of the Juneau artist's works. 80 pp., $14.95 ($18.95 Canadian)

Destination Washington. An insider's guide to the state of Washington. 196 pp., $4.95 ($6.30 Canadian)

Discovering Wild Plants: Alaska, Western Canada, the Northwest, by Janice Schofield. Approximately 350 pages of facts, pictures and illustrations detailing more than 130 plants. 350 pp., hardbound, $34.95 ($43.95 Canadian); softbound, $24.95 ($29.95 Canadian)

E. T. Barnette: The Strange Story of the Man Who Founded Fairbanks, by Terrence Cole. Colorful history from gold rush days. 176 pp., $7.95 ($10.10 Canadian)

An Expedition to the Copper, Tanana and Koyukuk Rivers in 1885. Adventures of Lt. Henry T. Allen as he explored and mapped thousands of miles of Alaska's Interior. 96 pp., $7.95 ($9.95 Canadian)

Eye of the Changer, by Muriel Ringstad. This excellent children's book is a Northwest Indian tale. 64 pp., $9.95 ($12.95 Canadian)

Fisheries of the North Pacific, by Robert J. Browning. Completely revised edition of the 1974 classic, with the latest on gear, processing and vessels. 432 pp., $24.95 ($31.70 Canadian)

Frank Barr, Bush Pilot, by Dermot Cole. Story of a bush pilot in Alaska and the Yukon. 116 pp., $7.95 ($10.10 Canadian)

Fruits and Berries of the Pacific Northwest, by David C. Flaherty and Sue Ellen Harvey. Colorful story of all the varieties, the growers and the industry. 101 pp., $24.95 ($31.70 Canadian)

The Gold Hustlers, By Lewis Green. Wheeling and dealing in the Klondike gold fields. 340 pp., $7.95 ($9.95 Canadian)

Golf Courses of the Pacific Northwest, by Jeff Shelley. A comprehensive guide to year-round golfing at golf courses and driving ranges in Washington, Oregon, northern Idaho, the greater Sun Valley area, and northwestern Montana. 400 pp., $19.95 ($24.95 Canadian)

Grizzly Cub: Five Years in the Life of a Bear, by Rick McIntyre. A true story of a young bear's first five summers, as recorded in words and 56 color photographs by Denali National Park ranger Rick McIntyre. 104 pp., $14.95 ($18.95 Canadian)

Guide to the Birds of Alaska, by Robert H. Armstrong. Updated and expanded; the perfect guide to species found in the 49th state. 343 pp., $19.95 ($24.95 Canadian)

A Guide to the Queen Charlotte Islands, by Neil G. Carey. This revised edition provides all the maps and information needed when visiting these rugged islands. 90 pp., $10.95 ($13.95 Canadian)

Handloggers, by W.H. Jackson with Ethel Dassow. A true story of adventure and romance. 250 pp., $9.95 ($12.65 Canadian)

Heroes and Heroines in Tlingit-Haida Legend, by Mary Beck. Nine Native legends from the Northwest Coast, with introductions that compare the characters in Tlingit and Haida tradition with classical mythology. Illustrated. 120 pp., $12.95 ($15.95 Canadian)

Hibrow Cow: Even MORE Alaskan Recipes and Stories, by Gordon R. Nelson. The former Alaska State trapper's recipes and humorous tales in his fourth cookbook. 168 pp., $9.95 ($12.65 Canadian)

How to Build An Oil Barrel Stove, by Ole Wik. Practical instructions; illustrated. 24 pp., $1.95 ($2.55 Canadian)

I Am Eskimo: Aknik My Name, by Paul Green with Abbe Abbott. Documentary of Eskimo life at the turn of the century, with illustrations. 86 pp., $9.95 ($12.95 Canadian)

I Married A Fisherman, by Dorothy Scott Rustad. Warm, human story of a successful partnership in a commercial salmon-trolling enterprise in the Southeast. 114 pp., $7.95 ($10.10 Canadian)

Icebound in the Siberian Arctic, by Robert J. Gleason. For ship, wireless and aircraft buffs. 164 pp., $4.95 ($6.30 Canadian)

Island: Our Alaskan Dream and Reality, by Joy Orth. Recounts a family's dream of settling on a remote island made a reality. 128 pp., $9.95 ($12.65 Canadian)

The Islands of Hawaii: E Komo Mai! A complete tour through the Hawaiian Islands. 152 pp., $6.95 ($8.85 Canadian)

Juneau: A Book of Woodcuts. Handsome prints by Dale De Armond; a whimsical history of Juneau. 50 pp., 8 x 10, slipcased, $12.95 ($16.45 Canadian)

Kendlers': The Story of a Pioneer Alaska Juneau Dairy, by Mathilde Kendler. A half-century of a young German girl's love affair with Alaska. 168 pp., $7.95 ($10.10 Canadian)

Kootenay Country: One Man's Life in the Canadian Rockies, by Ernest F. "Fee" Hellmen. A compelling account of the author's life fishing, hunting and guiding in the rugged Kootenays of British Columbia. With photographs and a map. 225 pp., $9.95 ($12.95 Canadian)

Land of the Fireweed, by Hope Morritt. The story of a young woman who helped build the Alaska Highway. 200 pp., $7.95 ($10.10 Canadian)

Land of the Ocean Mists, by Francis E. Caldwell. A look at the wild ocean coast west of Glacier Bay. 224 pp., $7.95 ($10.10 Canadian)

Living By Water, by Brenda Peterson. A collection of essays reflecting on the ways water shapes the lives and spirits of the inhabitants — animals and humans — near the shores of Puget Sound. 125 pp., $15.95 ($19.95 Canadian)

The Lost Patrol, by Dick North. First book to unravel the tragedy of the Mounted Police patrol that perished in the winter of 1910-11 in the Northwest Territories. 138 pp., $9.95 ($12.95 Canadian)

Lowbush Moose (And Other Alaskan Recipes), by Gordon R. Nelson. A former Alaska State trooper adds special flavor to mouthwatering family recipes by telling the stories behind them. 198 pp., $9.95 ($12.95 Canadian)

Martha Black, by Martha Black. The story of a pioneer woman from the Dawson goldfields to the halls of Parliament. 166 pp., $9.95 ($12.65 Canadian)

The MILEPOST® All-the-North Travel Guide®. 1990 edition. All travel routes in western Canada and Alaska, with photos and detailed maps. 584 pp., $14.95 ($18.95 Canadian)

More Alaska Bear Tales, by Larry Kaniut. A keen naturalist and seasoned storyteller, author Larry Kaniut in his second book recounts more true encounters between bears and humans. 295 pp., $12.95 ($15.95 Canadian)

Nome Nuggets, by L.H. French. A soldier of fortune's account of the 1900 Nome gold rush. 64 pp., $5.95 ($7.55 Canadian)

NORTHWEST MILEPOSTS®. A complete guide to Washington, Oregon, Idaho, western Montana and southwestern Canada. 328 pp., $14.95 ($18.95 Canadian)

Northwest Sportsman Almanac. Edited by Terry W. Sheely. Coffee-table beautiful, tackle-box informative guide to outdoor recreation. 291 pp., hardbound, $34.95 ($42.95 Canadian); softbound, $19.95 ($24.95 Canadian)

The Norwegian, by Harold Eide. Warm, witty and incredible story of a charming gold seeker. 128 pp., $6.95 ($8.95 Canadian)

Once Upon an Eskimo Time, by Edna Wilder. A one-year (1868) vignette in the 121-year life of an Eskimo woman. 185 pp., $9.95 ($12.65 Canadian)

101 Simple Seafood Recipes, by Pam and Bill Collins. How to select, prepare and preserve seafood, plus some general things to know about them. 156 pp., $6.95 ($8.85 Canadian)

Our Arctic Year, by Vivian and Gil Staender. A young couple's year in the wilds of the Brooks Range, color photos. 160 pp., $12.95 ($16.45 Canadian)

Pacific Halibut: The Resource and The Fishery, by F. Heward Bell. An impressive book on the history of this fish and fishery. 288 pp., softbound $19.95 ($25.35 Canadian); hardbound $24.95 ($31.70 Canadian)

Pacific Northwest Gardener's Almanac, by Mary Kenady. A master gardener tells what, where and how to grow vegetables and herbs; color photos. 162 pp., $14.95 ($18.95 Canadian)

Pacific Troller: Life on the Northwest Fishing Grounds, by Francis E. Caldwell. A close-up of the fisherman's life, the frustrations, the humor, the excitement. 143 pp., $5.95 ($7.55 Canadian)

Plant Lore of an Alaskan Island, by Frances Kelso Graham. Nutritional value, medicinal uses and recipes for eighty plants, with glimpses of Native and Russian heritage. 210 pp., $9.95 ($12.65 Canadian)

Raven: A Collection of Woodcuts. Dale De Armond woodcuts, Tlingit tales of Raven. Signed, numbered, limited edition. 132 pp., 12 x 12, $100 ($127 Canadian)

Raven. Small format edition of Dale De Armond's woodcuts. 80 pp., $13.95 ($17.75 Canadian)

Rie Munoz, Alaskan Artist. An illustrated selection of her work. A high-quality collection of limited-edition prints from one of Alaska's foremost artists. 80 pp., $19.95 ($24.95 Canadian)

River Rafting in Canada, by Richard Harrington. Presents 22 river-rafting adventures in Canada, with information on outfitters for each trip. 110 pp., $14.95 ($18.95 Canadian)

Roots of Ticasuk: An Eskimo Woman's Family Story, by Emily Ivanoff Brown. Handed down from parent to child to grandchild, this story tells of Eskimo customs and taboos and of attempts to westernize a proud culture. 108 pp., $9.95 ($12.95 Canadian)

Secrets of Eskimo Skin Sewing, by Edna Wilder. Guide to fashioning with fur and skin; patterns and color photos. 125 pp., $9.95 ($12.95 Canadian)

Sitka Man, by Al Brookman, Sr. Six decades of an adventurous life in Alaska. 172 pp., $7.95 ($10.10 Canadian)

Skagway Story, by Howard Clifford. Skagway in the late 19th century. 167 pp., $9.95 ($12.95 Canadian)

Skystruck: True Tales of an Alaska Bush Pilot, by Herman Lerdahl with Cliff Cernick. From early bush pilot to major airline captain, the remembrances of a lifetime of adventures. 175 pp., $9.95 ($12.95 Canadian)

Smokehouse Bear, by Gordon R. Nelson. Great stories and recipes from Alaska. 180 pp., $9.95 ($12.65 Canadian)

Sourdough Jim Pitcher, by James S. Pitcher. Adventures of a man who may have trekked more of Alaska than anyone else. 64 pp., $6.95 ($8.85 Canadian)

The Spirit of Massachusetts. A complete guidebook to Massachusetts. 196 pp., $4.95 ($6.30 Canadian)

Tired Wolf, by Gordon R. Nelson. More great recipes and amusing anecdotes from this popular former state trooper. 210 pp., $9.95 ($12.65 Canadian)

To the Top of Denali: Climbing Adventures on North America's Highest Peak, by Bill Sherwonit. A comprehensive collection of Mount McKinley climbing stories, written for armchair adventurers and seasoned climbers alike. 300 pp., $10.95 ($13.95 Canadian)

Toklat: The Story of an Alaskan Grizzly Bear, by Elma and Alfred Milotte. A children's book about a grizzly and her three cubs. 114 pp., $9.95 ($12.65 Canadian)

Trails of an Alaska Trapper, by Ray Tremblay. North Country adventure in a true story that reads like a novel. 170 pp., $9.95 ($12.65 Canadian)

Trapline Twins, by Miki and Julie Collins. Tales of the unique lifestyle of identical twin girls in

Interior Alaska, trapping, dogsledding, canoeing and living off the land. 215 pp., $12.95 ($15.95 Canadian)

Travelers of the Cold: Sled Dogs of the Far North, by Dominique Cellura. The author traces the history of man and sled dog beginning with Eskimo legend, to the growing interest in the sport of sled dog racing. The strength and character of these animals are captured in beautiful color photographs. 160 pp., hardbound, $32.95 ($39.95 Canadian)

Two in the Far North. Margaret Murie's classic adventure about life on the Alaska frontier. In this edition, Murie extends her story to today's Alaska wilderness and parks issues. 385 pp., $12.95 ($15.95 Canadian)

The War Canoe, by Jamie S. Bryson. A compelling novel about a young Tlingit's coming of age in an Alaska that is enriching its present by recapturing the wisdom of its Native past. 180 pp., $9.95 ($12.95 Canadian)

The Way It Was, by Jo Anne Wold. Memories of the people and happenings of pioneer Fairbanks. 170 pp., $9.95 ($12.65 Canadian)

We Live in the Alaskan Bush, by Tom Walker. True account of a young couple and their infant daughter. 135 pp., $7.95 ($10.10 Canadian)

A Whaler and Trader in the Arctic, by Arthur James Allen. True adventure at the turn of the century. 213 pp., $9.95 ($12.65 Canadian)

Wheels on Ice. Edited by Terrence Cole. The bicycle craze hit Alaska in the 1890s when "wheelmen" rode hundreds of miles across the frozen Far North. 66 pp., $6.95 ($8.85 Canadian)

Whidbey Island Sketchbook, by Dixie Rushmer. Charming watercolors and black-and-white sketches of Puget Sound's largest island, 64 pp., $9.95 ($12.65 Canadian)

Wilderness Survival Guide, by Monty Alford. Rescue techniques and build-it-yourself survival gear for the wilderness traveler. 120 pp., $9.95 ($12.95 Canadian)

Winging It!, by Jack Jefford. Pioneer Alaska aviator Jack Jefford was a "pilot's pilot," one who daily faced the dangers of bush flying, helped settle a frontier, and who now tells his own story. 320 pp., $12.95 ($15.95 Canadian)

Winter Watch, by James Ramsey. For 266 days, the author tested himself against the solitude and isolation of an Arctic winter while living in an old log cabin. 144 pp., $9.95 ($12.65 Canadian)

Wolf Trail Lodge, by Edward M. Boyd. Thirty years of adventure in Alaska. 120 pp., $5.95 ($7.55 Canadian)

Index

Many other fascinating books are available from
Alaska Northwest Books™
Ask for them at your favorite bookstore,
or write us for a complete free catalog.

A division of GTE Discovery Publications, Inc.
P.O. Box 3007
Bothell, WA 98041-3007
1-800-343-4567